Entrepreneurship Research in Europe

Entrepreneurship Research in Europe

Outcomes and Perspectives

Edited by

Alain Fayolle

Professor of Entrepreneurship, EM Lyon, INP Grenoble, CERAG, France

Paula Kyrö

Professor of Entrepreneurship Education, University of Tampere, Finland

Jan Ulijn

Professor of Innovation, Entrepreneurship and Culture, Eindhoven University of Technology, The Netherlands

Foreword by Bengt Johannisson

Edward Elgar
Cheltenham, UK • Northampton, MA, USA

Published by
Edward Elgar Publishing Limited
Glensanda House
Montpellier Parade
Cheltenham
Glos GL50 1UA
UK

Edward Elgar Publishing, Inc.
136 West Street
Suite 202
Northampton
Massachusetts 01060
USA

A catalogue record for this book
is available from the British Library

ISBN 1 84376 599 3

Typeset by Cambrian Typesetters, Frimley, Surrey
Printed and bound in Great Britain by MPG Books Ltd, Bodmin, Cornwall

Contents

Contributors

Iiris Aaltio, Lappeenranta University of Technology, Finland

Mark B. Bajramovic, McGill University, Canada

Michel Bernasconi, CERAM Sophia Antipolis, France

Ajay Bhalla, Cass Business School, City University, UK

Leo Paul Dana, University of Canterbury, New Zealand

Per Davidsson, Brisbane Graduate School of Business, QUT, Australia and Jönköping International Business School (JIBS), Sweden

Jean-Michel Degeorge, ESC Saint-Etienne, University Jean Moulin Lyon 3 and EPI, France

Frédéric Delmar, Center for Entrepreneurship and Business Creation, Stockholm School of Economics, Sweden

Alain Fayolle, EM Lyon, INP Grenoble, CERAG, France

Graham Hall, Manchester Business School, UK

Steven Henderson, Southampton Business School, UK

Tatiana Iakovleva, Bodo Graduate School of Business, Norway

Juha Kansikas, Jyväskylä University, Finland

Lars Kolvereid, Bodo Graduate School of Business, Norway

Paula Kyrö, University of Tampere, Finland

Seija Mahlamäki-Kultanen, University of Tampere, Finland

Franck Moreau, CERAM Sophia Antipolis, France

Ana Paula Silva, Manchester Business School, UK

Jan Ulijn, Eindhoven University of Technology, The Netherlands

Frans M. van Eijnatten, Eindhoven University of Technology, The Netherlands

Allen Vernier, Consultant in Management, France

David Watkins, Southampton Business School, UK

Richard W. Wright, University of Richmond, USA

Foreword

Entrepreneurship is about emergence and creative organising of resources according to opportunity and so is the making of a new discipline such as entrepreneurial studies. Over the last 15 years entrepreneurship has become recognised as an academic domain of its own. Increased institutionalisation through, for example, (endowed) chairs, research conferences and scientific journals have contributed to an enhanced legitimacy of entrepreneurship within the academic community. As entrepreneurship researchers we have an obligation to use this public recognition of our collective insights, and the self-confidence that accompanies it, whenever and wherever societal challenges call for them. Now, in 2004, when the European context is radically changing, is the right time to offer such contributions. Therefore the publication of this book, its variety of entrepreneurial phenomena and how they may be researched, is very timely. Its different contributions do not just provide a state of the art, a historical image of European entrepreneurship research. In addition, and perhaps more importantly, this volume offers a point of departure for further inquiries into entrepreneurship that recognise its embeddedness in unique social and cultural settings.

European entrepreneurship research originally very much replicated North American theories, methods and empirical representations of the phenomenon. Over the years, European researchers, however, have not only refined originally American frameworks and methodologies. We have also made significant independent contributions to the field, such as constructionist thinking and narrative methodology. Our greater concern for the interface between business and society, historically well founded in the European context, has generated new interesting research approaches that demonstrate how entrepreneurial phenomena bridge between different societal sectors. The European setting obviously invites comparative research, empirically illustrating the importance of the socio-cultural context. In this volume the significance of such cultural contingencies and associated institutional settings is well demonstrated by its many contributions. Thereby their authors collectively contribute to the creation of a genuine dialogue between European and North American researchers, offering mutual learning on equal terms. The recognised need for joint academic venturing into entrepreneurship is also reflected in an increasing number of journals including both authors and editorial board members from both sides of the Atlantic. Research conferences on entrepreneurship, independent of where they are held, today attract researchers from countries all over the world. The entrepreneurship research community has become truly global.

Offering a broad variety of approaches this book contributes significantly to the making of entrepreneurship into an academic discipline of its own. Still in its infancy, entrepreneurship research must adopt an eclectic view and establish a broad interface with other disciplines. As much as management (once) co-opted economics, systems and operations analysis as well as sociology with their well-established models and concern for regularities, entrepreneurship benefits more from anthropology, ethnography and social psychology with their interest in everyday life and sensemaking. The entrepreneurial phenomenon lends itself to multidisciplinary approaches considering its concern for process as well as for structure, for economic rules of the game as well as for social embedding. In contrast to management studies, entrepreneurship research and education thus cannot be reduced to an activity that to a considerable extent is possible to discipline as a professional field where formal training and codified knowledge go hand in hand with universal models and normative statements. Entrepreneurship is as much associated with identity making as with profit making, as much with creativity and spontaneity as with the enactment of visions. These generic features must be reflected in the ways we research and teach entrepreneurship.

In my mind the variety in terms of what issues are addressed and how, as well as the diversity with respect to national origin, that this volume offers thus is much needed. Its contributors jointly signal that many challenges remain for scholars in entrepreneurship all over the world. We in Europe are privileged, though, since the changing European scene makes several of these potential research issues visible. The new member states, still with an underdeveloped infrastructure, make obvious the need for appropriate institutions so taken for granted in mature welfare states. Entrepreneurship for job and wealth creation remains an important issue, whether as a generic strategy for the reconstruction of old-new economies in former Eastern Europe, for marginal regions in any mature economies or for developing countries. The emergence of the strong Asian economies carried by their own constructions of entrepreneurship tells us to be more humble as regards our European understanding of the phenomenon and its reach. It is obviously important that multifaceted approaches to entrepreneurship are carefully tried out before conclusive recommendations as regards knowledge for use at universities and by practitioners are made. As researchers we are driven by the ambition to produce universal knowledge, whether as theoretical models, appropriate vocabularies or generic approaches. Aiming for those ideals we, though, have to realise that it is still far too early to make ourselves comfortable as explorers in entrepreneurship. The research must go on!

Bengt Johannisson
Växjö University

Acknowledgements

Two years ago, in September 2002, the First European Summer University was organised by one of us in Valence (the South of France). This research conference addressed some key issues in entrepreneurship research, highlighting some European specificities. Around sixty scholars attended the conference and shared ideas and recent results of research in entrepreneurship. The idea of our book started during the conference, from which we could draw numerous chapters.

First of all we would like to thank the organisers of the Valence conference at ESISAR, one of the engineering schools of a French university of technology, INP Grenoble. We hope to continue this tradition of special European research conferences on entrepreneurship bringing together PhD students and their supervisors in the Netherlands (Twente, September 2004) and in Finland (Tampere, September 2006), apart from the traditional entrepreneurship conferences also devoted to teaching and policy-making in this field.

Moreover, we would like to warmly thank the reviewers of our chapters who helped us to improve the quality of the book a great deal. Some of them are colleagues from the Netherlands. We thank for his mediation Dr Aard Groen, director of NIKOS, University of Twente and his colleagues: Professor Wim During, Paula Harveston (also Berry college, US) and Padmakumar Nair (also Texas University at Dallas, US). Let us also express our thanks to the Eindhoven University of Technology colleagues: Hanns Menzel and Bert Sadowksi, and Irene Lammers (Free University of Amsterdam, formerly at Eindhoven University of Technology). We would like to thank Professor Antti Haahti, University of Lapland and Professor Pekka Ruohotie, director of the Research Centre for Vocational Education, University of Tampere, both from Finland. Finally, our warm thanks go to Christian Bruyat and Jean-Michel Degeorge, research fellows at Entrepreneurship and Process Innovation (EPI) research laboratory located at Valence, France.

Without any doubt, this edited book is a very good example of a collaborative work in which more than thirty scholars working in at least ten European countries have made a strong contribution by writing or reviewing a chapter. Europe is becoming more and more a reality at the academic level in the field of entrepreneurship.

1. The entrepreneurship debate in Europe: a matter of history and culture?

Alain Fayolle, Paula Kyrö and Jan Ulijn

In this introductory chapter, we would like to talk about the richness and the specificities of the European research in entrepreneurship. First we will approach entrepreneurship research from a historical perspective thus positioning and identifying the European cultural roots and re-emergence for entrepreneurship debates. This positioning also addresses attention to the specificities that characterise the current European research. In the second section we will explore these specificities aiming to advance the debate of the future European approach to entrepreneurship research. Finally, in the last section we will present how this book participates in these debates by introducing our authors and their studies. As a result we wish to provide some new insights into the landscape of entrepreneurship research in Europe and thus advance the European-specific debate on entrepreneurship research.

THE EUROPEAN ROOTS OF ENTREPRENEURSHIP AND ENTREPRENEURSHIP RESEARCH

The multidisciplinary character of the field of entrepreneurship is a fact which immediately appears to all persons who have some knowledge of this scholarly domain. Entrepreneurship is still in a theory-building stage (Wiseman and Skilton, 1999) and for some researchers is a 'multidisciplinary jigsaw' with a high level of research fragmentation (Harrison and Leitch, 1994). Hence, it would seem difficult to give a complete and detailed representation of the scientific scope of entrepreneurship and all related disciplines. However, it is possible to identify the current state of entrepreneurship research in Europe by delineating the historical changes in its development. By posing such questions as what, how and why provides us with a view that outlines the essential changes in the approaches, targets of the study and methodological aspects.

1

These together generate some exciting opportunities for a European view of entrepreneurship research.

The historical and cultural approaches to the development of entrepreneurship research suggest that its emergence and importance in Europe relate to two transitions. The first, modern transition, took place at the beginning of industrialization from the 18th to the beginning of the 20th century, when the traditional era finished (Dillard 1967; Beck et al., 1995; Harvey, 1990; Turner, 1990). The descriptions of entrepreneurship followed the industrialization and liberalization processes from country to country. Since these processes are country-specific, this transition as a whole was relatively long. Out of the modern transition developed the modern era, which, for its part, started to draw to its close in the 1970s, when the post-modern transition occurred. These transitions are culturally constructed, complex processes closely relating to freedom and welfare at the individual, micro- as well as at the macro-level. The characteristics of these transitions are change and complexity, which affects social life, businesses and economies. In fact, the role of entrepreneurship relates to change in its broad sense from two perspectives: on one hand it creates new practices, while on the other it breaks down old systems and institutions (Kyrö, 1997; 2000a; 2001).

Each phase, transition or era produced its own modifications of entrepreneurship according to its specific needs. In the transition from traditional to modern the focus was, on the one hand, the economic process at the macro-level, and on the other hand, the extraordinary individual producing this process. The firm was not at that time the target of these descriptions, since the guild system tried to prevent the accumulation of capital, through legislation that prevented founding a company in Europe. The situation in the USA was easier in this respect. Thus in the modern era, when development was more stable and predictable and the conceptions of welfare and economic progress changed, the target of entrepreneurship changed as well. The dominating explanations of the economy were based on rational equilibrium and the human being as an essential actor in the economy was lost from the macro- as well as the micro-perspective. (Barreto, 1989; Bell, 1981). The need for growth as well as institutional, collective and externally-organized rules and norms started to replace and subordinate human choices and small-scale practices (Etzioni, 1968; Zuboff, 1988). As Etzioni (1968) expressed it, 'society produced individuals suitable for organisation'. Schumpeter (1996) identified this declining economic importance of the entrepreneur as one of the major forces in the economy, and he titled his last work *The March into Socialism*. Innovations would no longer be connected with the efforts and the brilliance of a single person. They were increasingly to become the fruits of the organized effort of large teams. This would be done most effectively within the framework of large corporations. When these ideals gained dominance, entrepreneurship was subordinated too and lost its role as a main creator of economic progress, starting to refer to small business management, while ownership and innovations were connected to large organizations.

When the Western world met a decline in growth rates in the 1970s, followed by the notions of complexity and unpredictability, a new stream of discussions emerged (Piore and Sabell, 1984). The discovery was made that actually large organizations did not create new work, but it was rather small firms and organizations that stimulated this discussion (Drucker, 1986). In this post-modern transition, entrepreneurship has penetrated organizational and learning theories with its original features, aiming to renew practices and to break up old systems. (Gibb, 1993; Fiet, 1999; Petrin, 1991; Pinchot and Pinchot, 1996). Thus in the transition from modern to post-modern, entrepreneurship again found a new object, now a product of the modern era, the organization. Consequently we have three different forms or targets of present-day entrepreneurship: 1) Individual, self-oriented entrepreneurship, meaning an individual's self-oriented behaviour; 2) The small enterprise, meaning the individual entrepreneur/s and her/his/their business; and 3) Intrapreneurship, meaning an organisation's collective behaviour.

The qualities of entrepreneurship have remained the same during this development. First, entrepreneurship referred to extraordinary human beings who, with freedom and responsibility for their own life, through their own efforts and thinking, and by recognizing opportunities and exploiting them, created something new, which in turn generated economic progress (Barreto, 1989; Casson, 1982; Wilken, 1979). Later these qualities, or some of them with different combinations, were attached to small businesses and finally to organizations.

Not only has the focus of research on entrepreneurship changed according to each phase, but also the contribution of different countries and geographical areas has changed. The scientific descriptions of entrepreneurship were born in France during the Enlightenment and at the beginning of the modern transition the European contribution on theory-building was dominant. However, quite soon the USA's contribution to entrepreneurship research grew, and today most leading scientific journals have editors and/or editorial boards from the United States (Kyrö and Kansikas, 2004). But in the current transition the re-emergence of the European contribution has also started to stand out, looking for a European-specific approach and questions for entrepreneurship research. The geographical orientation has also expanded towards a more global view of the phenomenon. The current transition has attracted contributors from all over the world. In the future we expect that this development will continue and the European contribution will again occupy a more established position as an equal and unique partner in entrepreneurship debates.

We have delineated these phases in our Table 1.1, which presents how the

Table 1.1   Outline of research in entrepreneurship

	Modern transition	Modern era	Post-modern transition	Expectations for the future
Time scale	18th–20th centuries: toward industrial-isation	At the end of 19th century till 1970: industrialization	1970–	21st century
Europe's position	Entrepreneurship was born in Europe	The impact of Europe declined	Re-emergence of a European view	Europe as an equal partner with expanding partners in different geographical areas
Geographical/cultural dominance	Western Europe	USA	USA, but with European and global flavour	North America and Europe with a global view
Principal scientific field	Economics	(Social) psychology, Sociology, Management and Organization Science Anthropology	Besides previous Management Marketing Education	Management, Marketing Education, Methodological related fields of science Philosophy and Economics?

WHY STUDY ENTREPRENEURSHIP?

The motive for research	To create new kinds of welfare and work for and by free individuals	To identify personal traits of entrepreneurs and demographic background of an entrepreneur understanding different functions of small businesses	From understanding different functions of small businesses towards creating new work, increase the efficiency of organizations and their renewal in order to stimulate growth	To support and understand human individual and collective processes of creating new activities and welfare in different cultural contexts
Basic hypotheses/ assumptions	The entrepreneur plays/does not play an important role in the economy	Entrepreneurs are different from non-entrepreneurs Small firms and businesses are reductions from large firms.	Entrepreneurial processes are different and needed for renewal. Men and women are or are not different as entrepreneurs	The role of entrepreneurs is essential for the renewal of economy In order to understand how to create new entrepreneurial activities, we need to understand the dynamics of the complex, individual and collective human processes in the local, regional and national contexts

Table 1.1 continued

	Modern transition	Modern era	Post-modern transition	Expectations for the future
WHAT TO STUDY				
The target of the research	Study of the relationship between individual and the economy. The role of an entrepreneur in the economy. The process of generating new economic welfare	Individual and small businesses	The dynamics and processes of creating new economic activities in different contexts: individual, small businesses, organizations and networks	Processes and dynamics of creating new value and economic activities between individual, small businesses organizations and networks with more rigour and comprehensive theories and culture-bound approaches
Theories	Process theories challenged by equilibrium theories	Trait theories Functional theories of business activities	Culture and grounded theories Strategic management Social network theory Life-cycle theories of the businesses	Additionally new action-bound theories and complex, non-linear modelling

6

The basic question	Identifying entre-preneurship as a special kind of ownership and management in the economy. Creating process models for economic progress	Identifying an entre-preneur as different from a non-entrepreneur	Developing approaches for studying the action and processes	Developing methods for studying complex reality and the inter-action between individual and collective human processes
The nature of reasoning	Subjectivity as a contradiction to abductive and deductive reasoning as a contradiction to historical, empirical research	Deductive reasoning with empirical studies and statistical analyses	Inductive and deductive reasoning with on one hand more sophisticated statistical methods, on the other hand through qualitative methods	The combination of abductive, inductive and deductive reason-ing with a variety of new action-bound methods
Dominant paradigm	Non-dualistic, but not defined	Dualistic	Non-dualistic	Non-dualistic with more comprehensive bases

questions of why, what and how to study entrepreneurship and their relationship to the theories and assumptions underlining them have changed in each phase. It should be noticed that this table is partly propositional, since a major part of European research on entrepreneurship has been and still is embedded in different languages not open to our reflection.

CHANGES IN WHY, WHAT AND HOW TO STUDY ENTREPRENEURSHIP

Using Table 1.1 to support our reflection, we will next make an effort to examine how the questions of why, what and how to study have changed through time.

Changes in the Scientific Field of Entrepreneurship Research

The historical foundations of entrepreneurship belong to economics (Barreto, 1989; Casson, 1982; Hebert and Link, 1988). Towards the end of the modern era the scientific base expanded to psychology (cognitive, behavioural, social, clinical), sociology, social psychology as well as to anthropology (Landstrom, 1998; Filion, 1997; Tornikoski, 1999). During the post-modern transition these approaches were joined by management, marketing and finally by education (Alberti, 1999; Gorman and Hanlon, 1997; Grant, 1998; Scott, Rosa and Klandt, 1998). The expectations for the future concern not only a more comprehensive involvement from management (strategic and innovation), organization science, marketing and education but also contributions from philosophy, methodological fields of science and perhaps again from economics (Buchanan 1982; Choi 1993; Henrekson and Jakobsson, 2001). This development does not reflect only the changes in the interest of entrepreneurship researchers, but also how different disciplines evolved their own identities during this quarter of a century (Kuhn, 1962; Popper, 1992; Rorty, 1986).

Why Study Entrepreneurship – Changes in Motives and Assumptions

The questions of 'why study entrepreneurship' and the basic hypotheses and/or assumptions underlying these motives closely relate to each other. These motives, for their part, correspond to the role and value of entrepreneurial practices in society and the economy, which concerns the need to provide new work and wealth for the citizens in a complex and changing world. In the modern transition this was also characterized by the freedom and equality and in the post-modern transition by the gender issues studying the differences between men and women entrepreneurs (Bowen, 1981; 1985; Brush, 1992; Lindeqvist, 1905). During the modern era, when industrialization, large firms and organizations brought wealth and growth to Western countries, the interest of entrepreneurship was attached to individual entrepreneurs and small-scale business practices. The questions of economy were best understood by classical and neo-classical theories (Kenwood and Lougheed, 1983; Smith, 1937).

During that time psychology in particular was used as a tool when identifying the characteristics and personal traits and motivations of an entrepreneur. It also involved efforts to define an entrepreneurial profile by identifying one main characteristic or a group of characteristics for an entrepreneur (McClelland, 1961; Hornaday, 1982; Timmons, 1978; Kets de Vries, 1977). One of the first questions concerning the individual was (and still is) based on the innate character of the entrepreneur. Are entrepreneurs born with a sixth sense or some sort of an entrepreneurial instinct? Some people are ready to believe this is true.[1] However, many others, both researchers and practitioners, reject this theory. Human behaviourists have subsequently expanded their research to analyse and to understand the traits and behaviours of the entrepreneur (Filion, 1997). Eventually discussion about the entrepreneur as an individual has left behind the biological interpretations and through behavioural theories has started to inquire into education as a basis for supporting entrepreneurial behaviour (Gibb, 1993). This has developed together with more collective network and cultural approaches assuming that individuals are living in, are influenced by and affect the culture and other individuals. In this respect a more individualistic-oriented approach dominating the modern discussion has extended to include collective, culture-bound views (Bond and Hofstede, 1989; Hofstede et al., 2004; Kim et al., 2003; Van Luxemburg et al., 2002; Ulijn and Fayolle, 2004; Ulijn et al., forthcoming).

Accordingly Table 1.1 no longer stresses an individualistic view on entrepreneurship, but a growing combination with collective and networking activities and processes.

The other direction towards the end of the modern era related to different business functions in small firms. The underlying assumption was that small firms and businesses are reductions from large firms. Thus in the post-modern transition, the main debates have consisted of the relationship between firms and innovations and on the other hand the individual-oriented approach. The former discussion focuses on new venture creation, new economic activities and innovativeness (Timmons, 1994). Growth is also an important topic and it is often combined with the debate on newness or is taken as a measure of it (Davidsson et al., 2002; Venkataraman, 1997).

The focus, however, has changed from a functional approach to the process approach (Kirzner, 1982; Gartner, 1985; 1988; 1993; Stevenson and Jarillo, 1990; Bygrave and Hofer, 1991; Van de Ven, 1992). The problem is how to combine individual actors, firms and the nation, or the macro-level in general, in order to understand entrepreneurial processes, since this is what is needed in the cultural approach, assuming that innovative processes are different and need to be understood as a complex interaction between technology, environment and social practices.

To sum up the why question, we have moved from the question of the entrepreneur's role in the economy through identifying the assumptions of specificities of an individual entrepreneur and the basic functions of the small firm, towards the idea of the importance of entrepreneurial practices and processes first for growth, but in the future also for a more extended cultural and networking view of its contribution to renewing society.

What to Study in Entrepreneurship – Changes in Targets and Theories

These basic assumptions and motives emerge in theory development in this field. From process theories of economic development, we have proceeded to trait theories and later to behavioural theories of entrepreneurial traits, further to the theories of cultural development, strategic management and social networks. We address our expectations for the future to the development of action-bound theories and to the theories for understanding and modelling holistic, complex and non-linear reality and practices. Also the cultural diversity and strategic changes in international networking will probably lead to the consideration of different cultural entities like local, regional, national, crossnational and professional or sectorial alliances. All of these changes relate directly to the target of research. The focus of research has changed accordingly, from the relationship between the entrepreneur and the economy, to the relationship between the individual and the small business, and still further to the dynamics and processes of creating new economic activities in different contexts: individual, small businesses, organizations and networks. We expect this development to expand its scope and to become even more rigorous and comprehensive in the future.

How to Study Entrepreneurship – Methodological Changes

Methodology affects, but is also dependent on the questions of why and what to study. Actually methodological development gives access to the required knowledge, but it also might limit the possibilities to expand our knowledge base. In this respect it is affected by larger paradigm changes in scientific inquiry.

The question of how to study also has its roots in Europe. It is as old as entrepreneurship discussion itself and relates to two debates. The first one took place within the historical research, and the second concerns the large 19th century methodological debate between the German Historical School and Classical School (Böhm-Bawerk, 1890–91). Up until the Enlightenment the aim of historical writing was very practical. It was not science but a form of practical, life-oriented activity consisting of narratives of single and separate facts. In this, content played a leading role (Topolsky, 1976). During the Enlightenment, however, this changed, and more systematic empirical findings were required for truth statements. These requirements conflicted with the German Historical School and the Classical School. The Classical School offered an abstract-deductive method as a solution. Actually, the abstract-deductive method refers to abductive-deductive reasoning. Indeed, the Classical School practically invented the idea of equilibrium and thought, so that it might describe the relationship between demand and supply in practice. Entrepreneurship research, however, parted from this methodologically and focused on subjectivity. We can regard Ludwig von Mises as one of its early contributors (1981). Mises called his approach a praxeology, the science of human intentional action (Böhm-Bawerk, 1890–91; Buchanan, 1982; Rizzo, 1982).

When entrepreneurship lost its importance as an economic explanation, the methodologically dualistic ideas of reality also gained dominance, especially in the form of empiricism. This ideal of dualism stimulated both the methodological debate in the modern era and also sustained its position as the main discussion in the post-modern transition. However, in recent studies nondualism and qualitative methods have also joined this discussion providing opportunities for finding new approaches for understanding the complexity (Choi, 1993; Hill and Wright, 2001; MacMillan and Katz, 1992; Stevenson and Harmeling, 1990). Expectations for the future involve developing methods for studying complex reality and the interaction between individual and collective human processes, which requires the combination of an abductive, inductive and deductive reasoning with a variety of new action-bound methods. Also there is a need to follow the non-dualistic view of reality, but with more comprehensive bases.

This cultural, transitional approach to the history of entrepreneurship research identifies the European contribution in both transitions – modern and post-modern. It also indicates that the European approach has, probably more than others, defended the holistic and complex, non-dualistic view with a philosophical flavour throughout history. In transitions this emerges as a growing tendency to participate in the entrepreneurship debate. This is evident in more recent studies on entrepreneurship conceptualizing efforts and studies on the dynamics of entrepreneurial processes (Venkataraman, 1997; Shane and Venkataraman, 2000; Bruyat and Julien, 2001; Shane, 2003).

Since the authors of this book have inspired us to examine the questions of why, what and how to study and also encouraged us to provide some insights into the future expectations for European entrepreneurship research, next we would like to share their contributions to the current European debate with the readers.

AN OVERVIEW OF THE BOOK

As of April 2004, the EU consists of 25 countries, and this still does not complete the European context which includes Iceland, Norway, Switzerland, Romania, Bulgaria and other Balkan countries, the Russian federation and other members of the Commonwealth of Independent States, with even Turkey and Israel trying to become EU members. So it is not possible to include all this geographical diversity in this book. Instead we have carefully chosen, as representatives of the European view, 15 examples which study some new essential angles of entrepreneurship. Each of these 15 refereed chapters not only theoretically, but also empirically, describes some of the specificities in European entrepreneurship research.

Thus, as often in the global scientific community, this book offers a nice assortment of countries and individuals, providing a good snapshot of European countries represented in the EU member list: Finland, the UK, Germany, Portugal, Sweden, the Netherlands, Norway and France. As an example, Chapter 1, the introduction itself, comes from an international team including Kyrö (Finland), Fayolle (France) and Ulijn (The Netherlands). To present and comment on, each of our chapters, we will follow the structure of the book according to its three parts.

Part I: Entrepreneurship Research in Europe: Some Key Issues

Chapters in this part are written by scholars from different countries. Sweden is represented by two chapters (Chapters 2 and 3), one written by Davidsson and one written by Delmar, who has dual nationality (Swedish and French). The fourth chapter is written by Kolvereid (Norway) and Iakovleva, a Russian researcher working in Norway. The last chapter of this first part is written by the Canadian/English/New Zealand combination of Dana, Bajramovic and Wright.

Chapter 2 (Davidsson): 'Method issues in the study of venture start-up processes'. In this chapter, Davidsson first recalls his attempt to merge some key ideas proposed by Gartner and Venkataraman which has led him to suggest a new domain delineation for entrepreneurship research:

Starting from assumptions of uncertainty and heterogeneity, the scholarly domain of entrepreneurship encompasses the processes of (real or induced, and completed as well as terminated) emergence of new business ventures, across organizational contexts. This entails the study of the origin and characteristics of venture ideas as well as their contextual fit; of behaviors in the interrelated processes of discovery and exploitation of such ideas, and how the ideas and behaviors link to different types of direct and indirect antecedents and outcomes on different levels of analysis (Davidsson, 2003).

Taking this departure point, Davidsson then examines the consequences of specifically studying the start-up process. These implications concern major research challenges in conducting this type of study related to sampling, data collection, variable operationalization and measurement or data analysis. In this chapter, Davidsson discusses more specifically the first two topic issues.

Davidsson's chapter is for us an excellent one to introduce the set of contributions and we think that it should be studied by everyone who is working (or expecting to work) on a dissertation in the field of entrepreneurship. Davidsson discusses some key issues related to the methodological aspects, which should be carefully examined in studying the start-up process. In this work we can find useful examples and practical research ideas which are of prime importance in understanding the essence of entrepreneurship research. No doubt these insights will be useful for anybody who is expecting to make good progress in doing research in entrepreneurship. For Davidsson, sampling is a difficult task where the necessary intellectual rigour leads to high costs. This implies that in the future one condition for carrying out high quality research in the field will be the creation of consistent research teams having a collective ability to develop research programmes where each researcher will deal with a specific aspect or dimension in relation to the research object.

We think that perhaps a new era is opening for research in entrepreneurship. It could be seen as the transition from an individual position to a collective and structured one for doing research in this field.

Chapter 3 (Delmar): 'The entrepreneurial process: emergence and evolution of new firms in the knowledge-intensive economy'. Delmar presents an interesting research project in this chapter. He is also working on the entrepreneurial process, defining entrepreneurship as 'the process of how, by whom, and with what consequences opportunities to discover future products and services are discovered, evaluated and exploited' (Venkataraman, 1997). Delmar is expecting to investigate the entrepreneurial process in the context of the research-intensive sector due to its importance for economic development.

In the chapter, Delmar discusses the project's theoretical framework and presents the methods and data to be used. At the theoretical level, he argues for using an evolutionary theory perspective to understand the dynamic entrepreneurial process, after having clearly demonstrated that this process depends on both the existence of opportunities and of enterprising individuals. Another aspect of Delmar's research work is the discussion about methods which could be used. He argues for longitudinal studies, asking relevant questions in so doing and bringing consistent solutions, as this book also does in other chapters (Bernasconi and Moreau (Chapter 8), Vernier (Chapter 11), and Aaltio (Chapter 12)). Data to be used will come from a combination of Swedish database and specific studies. Data origin and data collection are then presented and discussed.

This chapter is a good example of a very active research stream in the field of entrepreneurship, centred on the notion of opportunity and on the entrepreneurial process. As we have seen above in this introductory chapter, Delmar's research project is very much in line with Venkataraman's school of thought. The chapter is of interest for several reasons. Firstly, it offers an argument in trying to explain the notion of opportunity. Secondly, it defines the entrepreneurial process, taking as a departure point Venkataraman's initial definition and using examples to illustrate the dynamic character of the concept. Thirdly, the chapter gives us an opportunity to see how it is possible to use an evolutionary theory perspective in studying the entrepreneurial process. Here, Delmar presents the advantage of the evolutionary perspective and he is convincing. Finally, the chapter raises methodological issues, as does Davidsson's chapter, and at this level, it is a good thing to have the opportunity to compare and contrast these two research papers coming from well known and rigorous scholars in the field of entrepreneurship.

Chapter 4 (Iakovleva and Kolvereid): 'New firm performance: conceptual perspectives'. The purpose of the chapter is to provide a conceptual framework to explain performance differences among young businesses. In this line, Iakovleva and Kolvereid review four theoretical perspectives in relation to the notion of performance. The first perspective is the population ecology framework which is best suited for a macro-level interpretation of organizational performance. Strategic adaptation is the second perspective. In this case, managers have some degree of freedom in selecting the best strategy among a set of strategic orientations, and so have a direct influence on the level of firm performance. The third perspective is the resource-based view (RBV). RBV suggests that differences in performance among firms may be explained through differences in firm resource accumulation and exploitation. The last perspective is the behavioural/psychological approach. Here, firm performance comes from the personality and the characteristics of entrepreneurs themselves. Using variables from these four perspectives, Iakovleva and Kolvereid provide a research model and a framework for explaining new venture performance.

New firm performance is a very important topic in entrepreneurship and also a major issue. The first chapter provides us with an impressive literature review, focusing successively on four perspectives from the macroeconomic level to the individual one. The authors argue that just one perspective is not sufficient to provide a relevant explanation of such a complex reality and the best way, for them, is to combine all the useful perspectives within a unique global framework. We have now to wait for the results from the empirical testing of the suggested model.

Chapter 5 (Dana, Bajramovic and Wright): 'The new paradigm of multi-polar competition and its implications for entrepreneurship research in Europe'. This chapter suggests that the environment for business in Europe is changing radically. Two major trends affecting the 'New Europe' are developed in this work. On the one hand, the importance of the nation-state in proposing the rules of the economic game and in controlling them in declining. On the other, the stand-alone firm is experiencing more and more difficulties in obtaining competitive and sustainable positions.

For the authors, these changes in Europe lead to the emergence of a new paradigm of multi-polar competition, highlighting the role and the importance of networks of firms, collaborating interdependently.

Dana and his colleagues provide an interesting chapter based on a fresh, new, and also a rather provocative approach. Their work is more related to dealing with small business in general and less with entrepreneurship as defined, for instance, by Davidsson and Delmar in this book. It suggests that changes in power distribution at different levels influence the small firm's strategic alternatives and argues further that future research should reflect the new realities. By doing so, the authors emphasise the notions of networks and value chains which seem, in their opinion, under-used and under-studied in the context of small and medium enterprises.

Part II: European Research Methodologies in Entrepreneurship: Is There Some Place for Newness and Innovation?

Part II adds one chapter from Finland (Kyrö and Kansikas), one from the UK (Bhalla, Henderson and Watkins), one from France (Bernasconi and Moreau) and finally one from The Netherlands (Van Eijnatten). This part focuses on 'how questions' with four chapters. It thus participates in the debate about developing methods for studying complex reality and the interaction between innovative individual and collective human processes. It gives some ideas about how to approach a non-dualistic reality and complexity in entrepreneurship research. It also presents examples of how methodological considerations affect and interact with the questions of why and what to study, thus continuing and advancing the future needs and the process discourse of the first part of this book.

Chapter 6 (Kyrö and Kansikas): 'Current state of methodology in entrepreneurship research and some expectations for the future' discusses the paradigm's role as a mediator between onto- and epistemological bases and both the methods and theories. By employing only a recently developed interpretative descriptive concept method it further suggests that the conceptual confusion of paradigm and methodology, and their relationship, leads to dualistic rather than non-dualistic reasoning and ideas of reality. By generating a structural view of these concepts and their relationship, the study finally explores the methodological choices of 337 articles published in leading entrepreneurship journals in 1999 and 2000.

The results indicated that the contemporary profile of leading journals focused on the current problems of businesses and firms by employing traditional, sophisticated statistical methods.

Thus even though the need to advance methodology in entrepreneurship research has been on the agenda since its early phases, little has actually happened. There were hardly any signs of creating an entrepreneurship-specific methodology and defining ontological and epistemological commitments. This obvious paradox seemed like a hidden agenda – a paradigm itself as Kuhn defined it as universally recognised scientific achievements that for a time provide model problems and solutions to a community of practitioners.

The study also leaves us to wonder where the history and future of entrepreneurship are and what is the role and impact of entrepreneurship to the surrounding society and environment. Are our model problems and solutions focused mainly on contemporary problems and are we able or interested in studying only what seems to be immediate and obvious in the surrounding reality? The authors suggest that this challenges us also to include in the future the axiological problems in the entrepreneurship debate.

On the other hand the structural view of the concept of a paradigm reopened the discussion of the nature and position of a paradigm as a concept in a scientific inquiry suggesting that we might benefit from viewing concepts as developing entities of different elements and their relationships rather than demarcating the definitions into strictly defined sentences.

Chapter 7 (Bhalla, Henderson and Watkins): 'The origins, lessons and definition of entrepreneurial achievement: a multi-paradigm perspective via the case method' continues this discussion by suggesting that cases could be used as narratives, which create reality rather than describe it. Thus it is possible to view cases as becoming 'a contributory part of truth – or principle – creation, rather than dissemination or clarification of an external, objective, understood reality'.

By applying Whittington's and Burrell and Morgan's paradigmatic frameworks to an award-winning case study, ChocExpress Ltd, the authors challenge us to expand our horizons of those opportunities that cases offer us for learning and research. Step by step they guide us to understand how different paradigms allow us to pose different questions and judgements about factors that might normally be invisible in mainstream thinking about entrepreneurship.

Consequently they explicate how theoretical and methodological choices are indeed interrelated and how we should be aware of our own interpretations in order to provide internally consistent research designs. Their excellent contribution to entrepreneurship debate focuses on helping us to identify hidden agendas in our teaching and research and thus to reflect and explicate our own implicit ideas and research designs.

Chapter 8 (Bernasconi and Moreau): 'From forecast to realisation – a systemic approach to understanding the evolution of high-tech start-ups' deepens our understanding of the evolution of high-tech enterprises, comparing the conception of the initial project with the strategy actually implemented. In this longitudinal case study the authors show us through three different high-tech enterprises in their early phases of development, how defining the enterprise as an evolving project facilitates a systemic representation which favours the creation of practitioner-oriented knowledge. They point out that the systemic approach complements the process approach by allowing us to take into consideration the complexity of the start-up, since it focuses on the evolution of the relationships between the components rather than on the components themselves.

This chapter in practice verifies the results of the previous chapter. It shows how identifying our paradigmatic assumptions allows us both to pose different questions and to develop methodological solutions for studying these questions.

Chapter 9 (van Eijnatten): 'A chaordic lens for understanding entrepreneurship and intrapreneurship' leads us directly to the world of complexity. By introducing a Chaordic Systems Thinking lens based on population-ecology the author opens up a new approach to understanding the dynamics of entrepreneurship/intrapreneurship. It views the entre-/intrapreneur as a holon: an entity that is both dependent and autonomous at the same time. This approach also generates a framework for understanding and studying the dynamics between individual and collective processes. The author argues for chaordic thinking by carefully introducing its essential elements, concepts and properties and along with this, using as an example the life cycle of a high-tech start-up.

The chapter expands our knowledge of systemic approaches in entrepreneurship research in a quite new direction. Thus it continues the suggestions made in the previous chapter and challenges us to apply and also further develop its exciting suggestions.

These four chapters all share the vision of the need to extend our horizons towards more complex reality and the human actor as a creator of this reality. Together they open new doors for studying the dynamics of individual and collective processes and systems as well as their interaction. Besides this they can also be considered to represent the European-specific contribution to the entrepreneurship debate.

Part 3: Entrepreneurship, Innovation and Culture as a Set of Interrelated Fields: Why the European Context is of Importance

The third part of the book comprises six chapters reflecting on entrepreneurship, innovation and culture issues. Two chapters (Aaltio and Mahlamäki-Kultanen) focus on Finland, the economy of which was the most competitive in the world after the US (World Economic Forum, 2003), Germany, The Netherlands and France, with one comparative chapter (Fayolle, Ulijn and Degeorge). France has another chapter (Vernier) and we end with two comparative chapters on entrepreneurship in the UK and Portugal (Hall and Silva, and Silva and Hall).

Culturally speaking, Part III is comprised of one Nordic (Finland), two Latin (France and Portugal), and three Anglo-Germanic countries (the UK, Germany and the Netherlands). Applying the Hofstedian approach (Hofstede, 2001), we notice: France and Portugal scoring the highest on Power Distance (68 and 63) and Uncertainty Avoidance (86 and 104), both supposed to be harmful for entrepreneurship and innovation. The UK would score the highest on individualism (89), whereas Portugal would score the lowest (27), which would probably be very beneficial for developing collective entrepreneurship. Elsewhere we argue (Ulijn, forthcoming), however, that not so much National Culture (NIS), but rather Regional Culture (RIS) or Sectorial (SIS) and Technological Culture (TIS) in their relation with Professional Culture (PC) might predict entrepreneurial success. In sum, the sample has some representativeness from an economical and national culture point of view, but the case studies presented serve rather as illustrations than as proof.

Chapter 10 (Fayolle, Ulijn and Degeorge): 'The entrepreneurial and innovative orientation of French, German and Dutch engineers: the proposal of a European context based upon some empirical evidence from two studies'. The aim of this exploratory study is to analyse possible intercultural differences between French, Dutch and German engineers in their behaviour towards innovation and entrepreneurship. It is obvious that the transition from a technological to a market orientation would take place differently for entrepreneurial engineers in both start-ups, Small-Medium Enterprises (SMEs) and Multinational Corporations (MNCs) in this part of Europe. The authors try to compare two separate approaches towards studying the entrepreneurial and innovative orientation of the European engineer: one based upon French engineers and another one based upon a comparison of their German and Dutch colleagues (12 in each country). The purpose of this study is to outline what those two approaches can learn from each other: how should one act to replicate the French study for comparable samples of German and Dutch entrepreneurial and innovative engineers? And the opposite with the German–Dutch study: how could an assessment of their technology versus market orientation (MO), being major aspects of entrepreneurship, be applied to a comparable set of French firms? The ultimate aim would be the creation of more European high-tech start-ups and more cooperation within the European Union (EU) across member-state borders and cultures.

The comparison of three European countries shows a truly European context: it focuses on entrepreneurial engineers and their education, and links it up to their innovative capacity, including changing their culture, spirit and mindset to create a realistic technology entrepreneurship. It brings Entrepreneurship, Innovation and Culture (EIC) as an interrelated set of fields and uses the sociological survey method to some extent, but has its methodological shortcomings since the two research projects compared were conducted with different objectives, in different time periods and using different concepts and operationalization. In a mutual replication (the French study in the Netherlands and Germany, and the Dutch–German study in France) methodologies might complement each other and in doing so might contribute to the development of an entrepreneurial and innovative culture of engineers. Moreover, the chapter does not yet clearly address cooperation and networking processes, so important for the European context of entrepreneurship. An overall conclusion might be that, whereas Ulijn and Brown (2004) suggested an Innovation, Entrepreneurship, Culture order (IEC), this book and this chapter in particular, offer another order: EIC, in a close interaction and cooperation, to make entrepreneurial engineers stimulate their innovative fellows to create their own business proactively rather than waiting until technological innovation eventually produces more technology entrepreneurship in a reactive way. The next chapter will serve, however, as an example of an IEC process that would not react, but would be proactive through strategic spin-off. IEC can complement EIC.

Chapter 11 (Vernier): 'The strategic spin-off project: an opportunity for organizational learning and change'. This chapter defines strategic spin-off (in French: essaimage) in its multiple links with spin-off practice, change and organizational learning and with an impact on organizational culture by mobilizing effective entrepreneurship and strategic management. This strategic spin-off process is illustrated by a complete corporate case in the Telecom sector in France, examining seven detailed cases of spinning-off using 21 interviews (with three stakeholders/spin-off team members for each case). The spin-off practice proved to be a relevant experiment to overcome cultural resistances in a team from 1998–2002, hence in a shorter period than Aaltio's study (see Chapter 12). The following changes were witnessed:

- The spin-off teams radically changed their point of view about small firms and entrepreneurship. Indeed, the team learned to do business and to create interesting collaborations with small firms. Some of them belonged to the network of spin-offs, others had no links. But, without the spin-off policy, the team would not have changed their old MNC traditions. This similarly happened with regard to intrapreneurship: the spin-off practice attracted new manager profiles, opened the door to other experimentation, such as entrepreneurship, or extrapreneurship and created new skills like valuation, business development and training.
- The spin-off experiment led to R&D being exploited and highlighted in a better way. Indeed, before adopting a spin-off policy, the R&D department was considered as a cocoon in which engineers and scientists were working on unusable technologies. Now R&D is fully integrated in the business activities, since it demonstrated its abilities to industrialize processes through the spin-offs. Its business credibility increased.
- The spin-off teams experienced a new way to manage their innovation. With the deregulation of the Telecom sector, they had to stop their fundamental research and concentrate on core business. The spin-off practice enabled them to manage this transition at a low human cost. Moreover, the spin-off process created new opportunities of technology exploration. If a research project led to a technology which seemed not to be usable in the firm, it could be spun off.

Since the deregulation of the telecommunication sector is a recent European phenomenon, the European context is very relevant here. The strategic spin-off process has clear consequences for extra-, intra- and entrepreneurship. In five out of the seven cases studied, technology transfer has been realized as a way of dissemination of an innovation. The R&D culture changed from inward to outward looking and strengthened corporate culture change in a positive sense. In the above five transfers of technology cases co-development of products and services was fostered with a contract signed in three cases; only in two was there no intention to co-develop. Although the general conclusion is that R&D skills were fostered in what used to be Public Research Organisations (PROs) including now entre-, intra- or extrapreneurship skills through this strategic spin-off process, we should caution against overgeneralisation. There are some methodological shortcomings in this study, such as the spin-off typology used which may be overcome in follow-up studies.

The study by Bekkers and Van der Steen (2003) on Innovation Policy-based spin-offs of public research organisations in the Dutch life sciences and ICT sectors might give some suggestions for extending this typology to Innovation Policy (IP), which is used by regional, national and EU governments as a tool to get more patents and licences through a spin-off process of Public Research Organisations. One way is to turn around a slogan uttered by Dr Plooij, a Member of the European Parliament (see Ulijn et al. (forthcoming): 'R&D returns euros to EU sponsors by more patents and licenses through a strategic spin-off process'. Bekkers and Van der Steen summarize research highlighting the importance of this process for regional and technological cooperation with private SMEs (RIS and TIS), although they do not mention the important results of more high-tech start-ups. The Vernier study can also be relevant for the spin-off process through patents for universities. Bekkers and Van der Steen list for the Eindhoven area, which is very important for a technological focus in the Netherlands, a lower number of patents than for Delft (17 vs. 90), whereas the number of spin-offs of the three Dutch technical universities were comparable (around 50). Although there is no systematic comparison of the spin-off process in different European firms and countries, turning science into business needs intra-, extra- and entrepreneurship as a new culture for R&D employees of both public and private organisations.

Chapter 12 (Aaltio): 'Cultural change from entrepreneurship to intrapreneurship'. This ethnographic longitudinal study compares three stages of a small innovative firm (growing to about 600 workers and then going back to about 300 in 34 years) in sports goods, under the fictitious name of FENIX. Its entrepreneurial and intrapreneurial development is investigated from a start-up founded in 1966 to a merger with a stateowned company in 1987, which was one of the biggest in this sector at that time in Finland (about 2000 employees). This implied a dramatic change in the organization culture of FENIX, now faced with the organizational practices of a big company. It reflects the lifephases of the entrepreneur going from an owner–manager dependent working style, which is often peculiar to new enterprises with rapid growth and good teamwork, to the moment when the entrepreneur leaves the firm. What kind of management and organizing solutions should be found to remain entrepreneurial and successful over time in the merger with a privatised partner? The subsistence of the new organizational culture is evaluated in two later stages of reaching higher quality and more innovative products in 1993 and in 2000 with a decreasing number of employees from 600 in 1987 to 300 in 2000. The methodology is based on ethnographic data by interviews, minutes of meetings, organizational charts, advertisement material and visible artefacts in the company, such as buildings and architecture. In 1987, 52 persons were interviewed from FENIX (from a total of 600 employees) and the acquiring firm, in addition to a questionnaire collecting stories and anecdotes; in 1993

25 people were interviewed and in 2000, 38 (out of 300 employees), focusing both on old timers and the newcomers.

Intrapreneurship and entrepreneurship appeared to be very much related concepts in this analysis: the entrepreneurship of the owner–manager creates intrapreneurship within the organization. When the founder leaves the firm a cultural gap widens and with the different work practices a new culture begins to evolve. An entrepreneurship highly dependent on the founder's personality transforms gradually into an intrapreneurial culture with shared entrepreneurship and teamwork ideals. Entrepreneurship in a small firm is saved over time through intrapreneurship, based on a new insightful management style.

Overall, longitudinal studies of entre- or intrapreneurial firms are extremely rare because of the difficulty of gathering data over time (see Davidsson et al.'s view on the need for longitudinal research on firm development, Davidsson et al., 2002, pp. 27–8 and Delmar's chapter in this book). This study, spanning 15 years of development of the organizational culture of a firm, is a welcome exception (see also Bernasconi and Moreau, this book).

The firm expands from a European context to global markets with broader supply of export products, for instance in addition to ski poles, walking poles become a new innovative product. The strong aspect of this chapter is the longitudinal nature of an entrepreneurship study, with some change from a technology driven to a human driven innovation culture. This involves cooperation within the firm as well as with external partners.

There are still many aspects to study using this longitudinal data basis. As often, more questions remain than can be answered through one single firm case study:

- How does this diachronic study compare to other ones?
- The interface between an entrepreneurial and an intrapreneurial culture seems to be crucial here, with questions such as: Does the existence of an entrepreneur exclude the existence of intrapreneurs? Is an entrepreneur able to 'educate'/'form' intrapreneurs that will survive in a merged culture of two organizations? Who influences the corporate performance more: one entrepreneur or several intrapreneurs?

These are basic questions that relate to any change the firm goes through, when the owner–manager with entrepreneurial orientation leaves the firm, and when it develops to an intrapreneurial organization culture.

Chapter 13 (Mahlamäki-Kultanen): 'Gender and sector effects on Finnish rural entrepreneurs' culture: some educational implications'. What is the rural entrepreneurial culture like in Finland and how is entrepreneurship promoted in such regions where young people leave in large numbers? In sharp contrast with the country's position as the second most attractive economy in the world in which to invest (see above) there is a presumed handicap to starting new businesses. Entrepreneurial effort is accepted, but success is NOT, and according to the last Global Entrepreneurship Monitor, Finns have the least motivation to become entrepreneurs. Why is this? There might be an effect from a high Uncertainty Avoidance (60) and a low Masculinity index (26), a lack of personal confidence and some impact of the Jante law. *Jantelagen* is based upon the Viking ritual and underlying value of *lagom* (lag is a team, om is a circle: make sure that everybody gets an equal share in a drink around the table). This Jante law was proposed by Aksel Sandemoses, who was born in 1989 in Denmark, moved to Norway in 1929 and as part of the resistance against the Nazis fled to Sweden in WW2 and died in Copenhagen in 1965. His 1933 book *A Fugitive Crosses his Track*, which includes a chapter on *Jantelagen*, is very much cited in Nordic schools, including in Finland through the compulsory Swedish language teaching. This chapter examines the entrepreneurial culture in rural Finland with some retrospective as far back as the 16th century (based upon literature, books, poems and journals) and the opportunities this provides for students with a vocational education to become entrepreneurs themselves.

The methodology and analysis used are rather unique. One hundred and forty-six middle-aged business owners (83 men and 63 women) from ten promising business sectors were interviewed in cooperation with six rural vocational institutes by ten teachers from these institutes, causing a varied sample size. By interpretation post hoc it appeared that those ten sectors represent certain sectorial subcultures: agriculture, service, breeding pet animal care, arts and handicraft, timber, construction, electronics, car repair, transport and telephone answering and selling services. A verbatim description of one to two hours' interviews was interpreted by two independent researchers and led to many unelicited metaphorical expressions with which the ten subcultures could be typified using an estimate of the four Hofstedian dimensions for each of them on the basis of those interpretations. The implications of this theory for education are presented: narratives can be discussed in class. Young people are attracted to rural areas in Finland by some idealistic image. The reality is that rural entrepreneurs want to have successors motivated to work, rather than innovators demonstrating their theoretical knowledge. By asking the pupils themselves, in both rural and urban areas, future research might increase the exploitation of the innovative capacity which Finland demonstrates through its attractive economy. Since the present rural entrepreneurs appeared to see Finnish youth more as future employees, they do not seem to be the ideal role models for entrepreneurs who get credit for succeeding in exploiting innovation in their country.

This study tackles rural entrepreneurship, which is very much relevant to the whole of Europe. To what extent are these results valuable for the

European context in general? Is there any link between those ten small business sectors and the outside world, and what impact does it have? Finland is still a big exporter of lumber and has a large paper mill industry. The link between entrepreneurship and innovation is not very clear here, whereas the coverage of the rural sector with ten subsectors might have a high potential for a Finnish SIS congruent with RIS, sectorial innovation based upon well defined regional areas. Although there are some reliability and validity problems with distilling a subculture from two interviewers' findings, the overall results for the whole rural area on the basis of Hofstede calls for further research, particularly when compared with the national culture results of Finland. Vocational students seem to have a much higher power distance (average 60 vs. 35) than in general, similarly for the masculinity index (59 vs. 26). The researchers interpret this as a good sign for the development of even female entrepreneurship (there were 63 female business owners), but one might argue also that the female affiliation attitude would strengthen cooperation within family and rural neighbourhoods. Is this different in Finland from other parts of the world? Although this sample includes much more than some technology related entrepreneurship, one can say that overall this study proves through the use of a unique metaphor and narrative analysis that the ethnographic approach contributes to the interdisciplinary set of interrelated fields. Replication of such studies in other parts of Europe and elsewhere would be very welcome.

Chapter 14 (Hall and Silva): 'Factors associated with the performance of UK SMEs: are they country specific?' and Chapter 15 (Silva and Hall): 'Influences on the growth of Portuguese SMEs'. The last two chapters of this part are presented and discussed together, because they are to some extent comparable as country studies for the UK and Portugal in a European context, using the same step-wise logit regression analysis. The UK study covers 285 SMEs, of which 121 are start-ups and 164 are established firms both in England and in Scotland in mostly the manufacturing and distribution/services sectors, in which Europe's largest venture capitalist 3i made investments during the 1990s. The Portuguese sample consisted of 29 face-to-face interviews of firm owners from the Braga district (in the North) in different sectors, textiles (31 per cent), clothing (14 per cent), construction (14 per cent), and so on. The variables chosen and tested also partly overlapped, since the original 51 in the UK study lead to 63 in the Portuguese setting. The variables remained mostly unexplored and/or controversial with regard to their impact on growth. In the UK setting the following factors appeared to be significant for the survival and growth of start-ups: adopting a focus strategy (which seems to be counterproductive in Portugal) and a strong commitment from owners to accept losses, in particular in the beginning of a start-up. Counterintuitively human capital and export overseas were not significant for the growth of UK start-ups. The growth of Portuguese SMEs in this sample, however, depended significantly on performance indicators such as size (the bigger, the better), age of firms and owners (the younger, the better in both cases), time commitment of owners (the more, the better), training of work-force and educational level of managers (the more, the better in Portugal, but rather the opposite in the UK). Finally working with accurate internal data is beneficial to growth in Portugal.

It is striking that in those two European countries the growth of the sample of SMEs examined seems to be only loosely related to the opportunities of the European internal market. This might be due to a measurement bias, or are those start-ups in different stages of development 'just' serving in the internal market? In general there is no export orientation. Both studies have in common that they focus on the entrepreneurship of established firms, whereas the UK sample also includes start-ups. The most striking difference in the UK between start-ups and survivors is that in the latter, creditor bills were more quickly paid than in failures (Portuguese firms seems to be more relaxed towards late payments). The UK firms had higher overdraft facilities as well and more product differentiation. This last factor was the only sign of innova-tion being a success factor in the start-up and survival stages of the samples that was common to both countries, which is again striking. Is it due to the focus of those studies on growth rather than on risk or innovation? However, it is difficult to know how to disentangle those factors. Or, are all those firms rather followers or smart implementers, serving only local markets? If the answer is yes than this might explain also why education and training is less important as a success factor for growth in the UK, but on the other hand Portuguese firms had a strong need for both and also for external advice. Wisdom of age appeared not to be important in either of the two countries, but financial assessment was more so in Portugal than in the UK which is in line with the above-mentioned UK factor of better financial management. In sum, not very many variables survived as success factors. Out of the 51 UK vari-ables, only two appeared to be success factors for start-ups and 11 for estab-lished firms and out of the 63 Portuguese variables only ten could explain start-up survival and growth. So, as has been shown in the past by Germany and Japan and lately by the new Asian dragons and tigers, smart following-up and implementation or exploiting existing innovation possibilities seems more likely to lead to entrepreneurial success, than to keep exploring or conceptu-alising new ideas without developing them into new products or services.

Can some of the differences between the two be explained by national culture factors? The biggest difference is uncertainty avoidance (35 for the UK and 104 for Portugal), but this might affect risk-taking more than growth. The second one is individualism (89 vs. 27), showing that Portugal has a compar-atively high collectivism which might predict a high need for cooperation, networking, wisdom of the experienced owner, help from families, which is not the case: again, is this a measurement bias? We agree with the authors that the value of stereotyping countries according to national culture differences should not be exaggerated. Moreover, regional and sector cultures might be of more importance: the UK sample is more a cross-regional one, whereas the Portuguese sample related to one region and one predominant sector (textile and clothing in the Braga district) which makes the two samples hard to compare from both a national and a regional/sectoral point of view. Looking at European entrepreneurship as an interrelated set of fields, those two chapters are unique in this part of the book in stressing the importance of financial assessment as a success factor in particular for the survival stage of start-ups.

CONCLUDING REMARKS

Our efforts to identify and explain the emergence of a European position in the entrepreneurship debate turned out to be an inspiring journey to its history and in some respect to the future as well. Europe shows itself to be a subcontinent of a new entrepreneurial and innovative culture, based upon a rich diversity of former national cultures growing now into one region and strongly supported by an ever-expanding European Union. We expect that the European voice will be listened to more in the future, and why not in conjunction with the one from Asia which becomes louder and louder, as one Eurasian continent? Therefore we sincerely hope that the reader finds this book to be as rewarding a reading experience as it was for us, its editors. Advancing a European approach requires a contribution from all of us, both Europeans and non-Europeans, to develop innovative entrepreneurship towards the social welfare of everybody on this earth. As French structuralists express it, all of us are part of the process of becoming.

NOTE

1. See the authors quoted by Cunningham and Lischeron (1991) in the paragraph devoted to 'the Great Person School of Entrepreneurship'.

REFERENCES

Alberti, F. (1999), 'Entrepreneurship education: scope and theory', in C. Salvato, P. Davidsson and A. Persson (eds), *Entrepreneurial Knowledge and Learning, Conceptual Advances and Directions for Future Research*, JIBS Research Reports No. 1999–6, pp. 64–84, Jönköping: Jönköping International Business School.
Barreto, H. (1989), *The Entrepreneur in Microeconomic Theory. Disappearence and Explanation*, London and New York: Routledge.

Beck, U., A. Giddens and S. Lash (1995), *Nykyajan jäljillä*, Tampere: Vastapaino.

Bekkers, R. and M. van der Steen (2003), 'IP-based spin-offs of public research organisations in the Dutch life sciences and ICT sectors', in *Turning Science into Business: Patenting and Licensing at Public Research Organisations*, Paris: OECD, pp. 263–90.

Bell, D. (1981) 'Models and reality in economic discourse', in D. Bell and I. Kristol (eds) *The Crisis in Economic Theory*, USA: Basic Books, pp. 46–80.

Böhm-Bawerk E. (1890–91), *The Historical vs. the Deductive Method in Political Economy*, translated by Henrietta Leonard, Annals of the American Academy, Volume 1, (1890–91), Lähde: http://socserv2.mcmaster.ca/econ/ugcm/3113/pawerk/pohm001.html.

Bond, M. and G. Hofstede (1989), 'The cash value of Confucian values', *Human System Management*, **8**, 195–200.

Bowen, J. (1981 and 1985), *A History of Western Education. Vol. 3. The Modern West, Europe and the New World*, London: Methuen & Co Ltd.

Brown, I.E. and J. Ulijn (eds) (2004), *Entrepreneurship, Innovation and Culture*, Cheltenham, UK and Northampton, MA: Edward Elgar.

Brush, C.G. (1992), 'Research on women business owners: past trends, a new perspective and future directions'. *Entrepreneurship Theory and Practice*, **16**(4), 5–30.

Bruyat, C. and P.A. Julien (2001), 'Defining the field of research in entrepreneurship', *Journal of Business Venturing*, **16**(2), 165–80.

Buchanan J.M. (1982), 'The domain of subjective economics: between predictive science and moral philosophy', in I. E. Kirzner (ed.), *Method, Process and Austrian Economics. Essays in Honour of Ludwig von Mises*, Toronto: Lexington Books, pp. 7–20.

Bygrave, W.D. and C.W. Hofer (1991), 'Theorizing about entrepreneurship', *Entrepreneurship Theory and Practice*, Winter, pp. 13–22.

Casson, M. (1982), *The Entrepreneur. An Economic Theory*, Totowa, NJ: Barnes and Noble Book.

Choi, Young Back (1993), *Paradigms and Conventions – Uncertainty, Decision Making and Entrepreneurship*, The University of Michigan Press.

Cunningham, J.B. and J. Lischeron (1991), 'Defining entrepreneurship', *Journal of Small Business Management*, **29**(1), 45–61.

Davidsson, P. (2003) 'The domain of entrepreneurship research: some suggestions', in J. Katz and D. Shepherd (eds), *Advances in Entrepreneurship, Firm Emergence and Growth*, **6**, Greenwich CT: JAI Press.

Davidsson, P., F. Delmar, and J. Wiklund (2002), 'Conceptual and empirical challenges in the study of firm growth', in: Donald, L. Sexton and Hans Landström (eds), *Handbook of Entrepreneurship*, Blackwell Publishing Ltd, UK, pp. 26–44.

Dillard, D. (1967), *Economic Development of the North Atlantic Community: Historical Introduction to Modern Economics*, Englewood Cliffs, New Jersey: Prentice-Hall. Inc.

Drucker, P.F. (1986), *Innovation and Entrepreneurship*, London: Heinemann.

Etzioni A. (1968), *Nykyajan organisaatiot (Modern Organizations)*, Helsinki: Tammi Publishers.

Farris, G.F., C.A. Hartz, K. Krishnamurphy, B. Mcilvaine, S.R. Postle, R.P. Taylor and G.E. Whitwell (2003), 'Web-enabled innovation in new product development', *Research-Technology Management*, **46**(6), 24–35.

Fiet, J.O. (1999), 'The pedagogical side of entrepreneurship theory', *Journal of Business Venturing*, **16**(2), 101–17.

Filion, L.J. (1997), 'Le champ de l'entrepreneuriat: historique, évolution, tendances', Cahier de recherche no. 97.01, HEC Montréal, 36 pp.

Gartner, W.B. (1985), 'A framework for describing the phenomenon of new venture creation', *Academy of Management Review*, **10**, pp. 696–706.

Gartner, W.B. (1988), ' "Who is an entrepreneur?" Is the wrong question', *American Journal of Small Business*, **12**(4), Spring 1988, 11–31.

Gartner, W.B. (1993), 'Words lead to deeds: towards an organizational emergence vocabulary', *Journal of Business Venturing*, **8**(3), 231–9.

Gibb, A. (1993), 'The enterprise culture and education. Understanding enterprise education and its links with small business, entrepreneurship and wider educational goals', *International Small Business Journal*, **11**(3), 11–24.

Gorman, G. and D. Hanlon (1997), 'Some research perspectives on entrepreneurship education, enterprise education and education for small business management: a ten-year literature review', *International Small Business Journal*, **15**(3), 56–77.

Grant, Alan (1998), 'Entrepreneurship – the major academic discipline for the business education curriculum for the 21st century', in M.G. Scott, P. Rosa and H. Klandt (eds), *Educating Entrepreneurs for Wealth Creation*, USA: Ashgate, pp. 16–28.

Harrison, R.T. and C.M. Leitch (1994), 'Entrepreneurship and leadership: the implications for education and development', *Entrepreneurship and Regional Development*, **6**, pp. 111–25.

Harvey, D. (1990), *The Condition of Postmodernity*, Oxford: Basil Blackwell.

Hebert, R.F. and A.N. Link (1988), *The Entrepreneur. Mainstream Views and Radical Critiques* (2nd edn), New York: Praeger.

Henrekson, Magnus and Ulf Jakobsson (2001), 'Where Schumpeter was nearly right – the Swedish model and capitalism, socialism and democracy', *Journal of Evolutionary Economics*, **11**, pp. 331–58.

Hill, J. and L.T. Wright (2001), 'A qualitative research agenda for small to medium-sized enterprises', *Marketing Intelligence & Planning*, **19**(6), 432–43.

Hofstede, G. (1991), *Culture and Organizations: Software of the Mind*, London: McGraw Hill.

Hofstede, G. (2001), *Culture's Consequences: Comparing Values, Behaviors, Institutions, and Organizations across Nations*, 2nd edn, London: Sage.

Hofstede, G., N. Noorderhaven, R. Thurik, A. Wennekers and L. Uhlaner (2004), 'Culture's role in entrepreneurship: self-employment out of dissatisfaction', in T. Brown and J. Ulijn (eds), *Entrepreneurship, Innovation and Culture: The Interaction between Technology, Progress and Economic Growth*, Cheltenham, UK and Northampton, MA, USA: Edward Elgar, pp. 162–203.

Hornaday, J.A. (1982), 'Research about living entrepreneurs', in C.A. Kent et al. (eds), *Encyclopedia of Entrepreneurship*, Englewood Cliffs, N.J.: Prentice Hall, pp. 20–34.

Kenwood A.G. and A.L. Lougheed (1983), *The Growth of the International Economy 1820–1980*, London: Allen & Unwin.

Kets de Vries, M.F.R. (1977), 'The entrepreneurial personality', *Journal of Management Studies*, **14**, pp. 34–57.

Kim, U., H. Triandis, C. Kagitcibasi, S.C. Choi and G. Yoon (eds) (2003), *Individualism and Collectivism: Theory, Method, and Applications*, Thousand Oaks: Sage.

Kirzner, I.E. (ed.) (1982), *Method, Process and Austrian Economics, Essays in Honour of Ludwig von Mises*, Toronto: Lexington Books.

Kuhn, T. (1962), *The Structure of Scientific Revolutions*, Chicago: University of Chicago Press.

Kyrö, P. (1997), *Yrittäjyyden muodot ja tehtävät ajan murroksessa* (The forms and roles of entrepreneurship in the transitions), dissertation, Jyväskylä: University of Jyväskylä. Jyväskylä Studies in Computer Science, Economics and Statistics, 269 pp.

Kyrö, Paula (2000a), *Entrepreneurship in the Postmodern Society*, Wirtschafts Politische Blätter 2000/47 Jahrgang (ed.) Vienna: Wirtschaftskammer Österreich, 2000, pp. 37–45.

Kyrö, P. (2000b), 'Entrepreneurship paradigm building – towards a discipline?', in Jarna Heinonen (ed.), *Emerging Aspects on Entrepreneurship and SME in Finland*, Turku School of Economics and Business Administration, Business Research and Development Center, Series A, Economic and Business Studies A1, pp. 17–40.

Kyrö, P. (2001), 'To grow or not to grow? Entrepreneurship and sustainable development', *International Journal of Sustainable Development and World Ecology*, **8**, pp. 15–28.

Kyrö, P. and J. Kansikas (2004, this volume) 'Current state of methodology in entrepreneurship research and some expectations for the future'.

Landstrom, H. (1998), 'The roots of entrepreneurship research: the intellectual development of a research field', paper presented at the RENT XII (Research in Entrepreneurship and Small Business) Conference, Lyon, 26–27 November, 18 pp.

Lindeqvist, K.O. (1905), *Yleinen historia (The General History)*, Uusi Aika. WSOY. Porvoo.

MacMillan, I.C. and J.A. Katz (1992), 'Idiosyncratic milieus of entrepreneurial research: the need for comprehensive theories', *Journal of Business Venturing*, **7**(1), 1–8.

Mises, Ludvig von (1981), *Epistemological Problems of Economics* (translated by George Reisman), New York: New York University Press (originally published in German in 1933).

McClelland, D.C. (1961), *The Achieving Society*, Princeton, N.J.: Van Nostrand.

Petrin, T. (1991), 'Entrepreneurship and its development in public enterprises', in J. Prokopenko and I. Pavlin (eds), *International Labour Office Geneva*, Management and Development Series, No. 29, International Center for Public Enterprises in Developing Countries, Ljubljana, pp. 15–20.

Pinchot, G. and E. Pinchot (1996), *Älykäs organisaatio (Intelligent Organization)* Maarianhamina: Mermerus.

Piore and Sabell, (1984), *The Second Industrial Divide. Possibilities for Prosperity*, New York: Basic Books.

Popper, K. R. (1992), *The Logic of Scientific Discovery*, USA and Canada: Routledge, (First published in English 1959 by Hutchinson Education).

Rizzo, M.J. (1982), 'Mises and Lakatos: A reformulation of Austrian methodology', in I.E. Kirzner (ed.), *Method, Process and Austrian Economics*, Toronto: Lexington Books, pp. 53–74.

Rorty, R. (1986), *Consequences of Pragmatism* (Essays: 1972–80), 3rd edn, Minneapolis, USA: University of Minnesota Press.

Schumpeter, J. (1996), 'The march into socialism', in J. Schumpeter, *Capitalism, Socialism and Democracy*, Introduction by Richard Swedberg, pp. 421–31, first published in 1943, London: Routledge.

Scott. M.G., P. Rosa and H. Klandt (1998), 'Educating entrepreneurs for wealth creation', in Michale G. Scott, Peter Rosa and Heinz Klandt (eds), *Educating Entrepreneurs for Wealth Creation*, Ashgate: USA, pp. 11–15.

Shane, S. (2003), *A General Theory of Entrepreneurship: The Individual–Opportunity Nexus*, Cheltenham, UK and Northampton, MA, USA: Edward Elgar.

Shane, S. and S. Venkataraman (2000), 'The promise of entrepreneurship as a field of research', *Academy of Management Review*, **25**(1), 217–26.

Smith, A. (1937), *An Inquiry into the Nature and Causes of the Wealth of Nations*, ed. by Edwin Cannan, New York, first published in 1776.

Stevenson, H. and S. Harmeling (1990), 'Entrepreneurial management's need for a more "chaotic" theory', *Journal of Business Venturing*, **5**, 1–14.

Stevenson, H. and J.C. Jarillo (1990), 'A paradigm of entrepreneurship: entrepreneurial management' in J. Kao and H. Stevenson (eds), *Entrepreneurship: What it is and how to Teach it*, Cambridge MA: Harvard Business School, pp. 11–27.

Timmons, J.A. (1978), 'Characteristics and role demands of entrepreneurship', *American Journal of Small Business*, **3**(1), 5–17.

Timmons, J. (1994), *New Venture Creation. Entrepreneurship for the 21st century*, 4th edn, Illinois: Irwin-McGraw Hill.

Topolsky, J. (1976), *Methodology of History*, Poland: D. Reidel.

Tornikoski, E. (1999), 'Entrepreneurship through constructivist lenses: visionary entrepreneurship process – a conceptual development', Licentiate thesis in *Management and Organization*, University of Vaasa, 167 pp.

Turner, B.S. (ed.) (1990), *Theories of Modernity and Postmodernity. Theory, Culture and Society*, London: SAGE Publications.

Ulijn, J.M. and A. Fayolle (2004), 'Comparing entrepreneurial and innovation cultures: The European perspective of French, German, and Dutch engineers, some empirical evidence about their technology vs. market orientation', in T. Brown and J. Ulijn (eds), *Innovation, Entrepreneurship and Culture: The Interaction between Technology, Progress and Economic Growth*, Cheltenham, UK and Northampton, MA, USA: Edward Elgar, pp. 204–32.

Ulijn, J., G. Guerra, S. Chiolo, R. Masiello and M. Pozzi (forthcoming), 'Cooperating in technology start ups, a local or a European entrepreneurship challenge? An Italian study compared with Dutch, British and German findings', *International Journal of Entrepreneurship and Small Business*, **1**(1).

Usunier, J.C. (1999), *International and Cross-cultural Management Research*, London: Sage.

Van De Ven, A.H. (1992), 'Longitudinal methods for studying the process of entrepreneurship', in D.L. Sexton and J.D. Kasarda, (eds), *State of the Art of Entrepreneurship*, Boston: PWS-Kent Publishing Company, pp. 214–42.

Van Luxemburg, A.P.D., J. Ulijn and N. Amare (2002), 'Interactive design process including the customer in 6 Dutch SME cases: traditional and ICT-media compared', special issue of the *IEEE Journal of Professional Communication* on 'The Future of ICT-studies and their Implications for Human Interaction and Culture in the Innovation Management Process', edited by J. Ulijn, D. Vogel and T. Bemelmans, **45**(4), 250–64 (won the IEEE PCS best article award).

Venkataraman, S. (1997), 'The distinctive domain of entrepreneurship research: an editor's perspective', in J. Katz and R. Brockhaus (eds), *Advances in Entrepreneurship, Firm, Emergence, and Growth*, vol. 3, Greenwich, CT: JAI Press, pp. 119–38.

Wilken, P.H. (1979), *Entrepreneurship. A Comparative and Historical Study*, USA: Ablex Publishing Corporation.

Wiseman, R.M. and P. Skilton (1999), 'Divisions and differences: exploring publication preferences and productivity across management sub-fields', *Journal of Management Inquiry*, **8**, 299–320.

World Economic Forum (2003), http://www.weforum.org.

Zuboff, S. (1988), *In The Age of The Smart Machine. The Future of Work and Power*, New York: Basic Books.

PART I

Enterpreneurship Research in Europe:
Some Key Issues

2. Method issues in the study of venture start-up processes

Per Davidsson

INTRODUCTION

It is increasingly agreed that the centre of gravity for entrepreneurship research should rest with the *process of emergence*. It is in particular three partly related strands, associated with three influential scholars who have led this development. First, Bill Gartner argued that entrepreneurship research ought to redirect interest from who the entrepreneur *is* to what he or she *does* in the process of firm emergence (Gartner, 1988; 1993; 2001). By so doing, entrepreneurship research would fill an important gap in organization theory, where the question of how organizations come into being has been a neglected issue. This perspective – that entrepreneurship is about the emergence of new organizations – has also been adopted by prominent sociologists (Aldrich, 1999; Thornton, 1999).

Second, inspired by Austrian economics and by empirical work at the intersection of innovation and entrepreneurship, Sankaran Venkataraman (1997, cf. Shane and Venkataraman, 2000; Van de Ven et al., 1989; van de Ven et al., 1999) has suggested that entrepreneurship is about the processes of *discovery and exploitation of opportunities to create future goods and services*. This perspective shares with Gartner the view that entrepreneurship is about emergence, and that entrepreneurship research can make a distinct contribution to social science by applying this focus, because other fields have not done a particularly good job with it. However, Venkataraman's interest is more directed at the new activity rather than the new organization (Shane and Venkataraman, 2000).

Third, in parallel with these conceptual developments Paul Reynolds – originally with colleagues Nancy Carter and Timothy Stearns when they were all at Marquette University – has initiated large empirical research programmes such as The Panel Study of Entrepreneurial Dynamics (PSED) and the Global Entrepreneurship Monitor (GEM), which are aimed at capturing emerging new ventures and (in the case of PSED) following their development over time (Carter et al., 1996; Reynolds, 1997; Reynolds, 2000;

Reynolds et al., 2001; Reynolds and Miller, 1992). The relatedness of the three lines of development is demonstrated by Gartner's and Shane's work on data from PSED or its sister projects (Delmar and Shane, 2002; Gartner and Carter, 2003).

In an attempt to merge the ideas advocated by Gartner and Venkataraman, and reconcile the apparent differences between them, I have suggested the following domain delineation for entrepreneurship research.

> Starting from assumptions of uncertainty and heterogeneity, the scholarly domain of entrepreneurship encompasses the processes of (real or induced, and completed as well as terminated) emergence of new business ventures, across organizational contexts. This entails the study of the origin and characteristics of venture ideas as well as their contextual fit; of behaviors in the interrelated processes of discovery and exploitation of such ideas, and of how the ideas and behaviors link to different types of direct and indirect antecedents and outcomes on different levels of analysis (Davidsson, 2003).

This domain delineation implies that in order for research to belong in the entrepreneurship domain there has to be an explicit consideration of emergence of new ventures (independent or within/from existing organizations), preferably from a process perspective and paying attention to antecedents and/or effects as well. As long as the requirement of explicit consideration of emergence of new ventures is fulfilled, the research can be conducted on any level of analysis – individual, firm, industry, region, nation, or something else (cf. Davidsson and Wiklund, 2001). That is, the research design should at least include the middle box in Figure 2.1.

However, one type of study is pointed out as particularly central to entrepreneurship research. That is when 'entity X' – the unit of analysis – is the venture idea itself, and (eventually) the activities and organization that evolve around it. Such a study would capture the venture idea (that is, the emerging new business activity) at the earliest possible point in time, and follow it through whatever changes that might occur as regards human champions and organizational affiliations, until it is either abandoned or has become an established business activity. In short, the unit studied would be neither 'the firm' nor 'the entrepreneur', but specifically the *start-up process*.

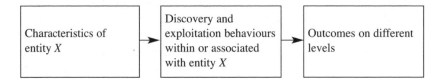

Figure 2.1   Entrepreneurship research design possibilities

Based on experiences from personal involvement with PSED and related studies, the purpose of this chapter is to point out and discuss some of the design and method challenges that one encounters when conducting this type of study. I will also attempt to suggest satisfactory solutions to some of the problems that are identified. Before turning to method issues I will briefly discuss what the chosen perspective and level of analysis imply for the use of theory. The main part of the chapter will be devoted to sampling and data collection issues, although operationalization and measurement will not be dealt with here in an elaborative manner. Towards the end, I will also discuss briefly the data analysis implications.

THE THEORY CHALLENGE

Whether entrepreneurship research should develop its own theoretical base or not is a hotly debated issue (Gartner, 2001; Low, 2001; Shane and Venkataraman, 2000). Despite Shane and Venkataraman's (2000) alleged emphasis on explaining and predicting phenomena not explained or predicted in other fields, I would argue that there are few contingencies of interest to entrepreneurship scholars – according to the domain delineation I have suggested above – that are completely void of consideration in theories in *any* discipline in the social sciences (cf. Acs and Audretsch, 2003; Delmar, 2000; Kirzner, 1983; Thornton, 1999). Not making full use of the tools available within the disciplines would be a wasteful practice. In addition, adherence to the quality standards that prevail in the disciplines contributes both to legitimacy and quality of entrepreneurship research.

It is not so easy, however, to see that all the theory entrepreneurship researchers need already exists in the disciplines. No matter how sophisticated the tools, they may not always be adequate for the task at hand (cf. Davidsson and Wiklund, 2000). In particular as regards studies applying the venture start-up process as the unit of analysis, some of the questions one should ask before applying existing theory 'as is' are the following:

1. Does the theory acknowledge uncertainty and heterogeneity?
2. Can it be applied to the problem of emergence, or does it presuppose the existence of markets, products or organizations in a way that clashes with the research questions?
3. Does the theory allow a process perspective?
4. Does it apply to the preferred unit of analysis?
5. Is it compatible with an interest in the types of outcomes that are most relevant from an entrepreneurship point of view?

I advocate that whenever possible, entrepreneurship researchers should use theory from psychology, sociology and economics as well as from various branches of business research. Possibly, theories from other disciplines or fields are also relevant. However, while theories allowing heterogeneity and uncertainty exist and are often partially applicable, the problem is that few existing theories would stand the test of all five questions above. In particular, while certain concepts may be highly useful, few score well on process and unit of analysis. Therefore, the entrepreneurship researcher must also be prepared to fill gaps and ask new questions through inductive, theory-building approaches. Importantly, however, the non-use of theory out of ignorance remains inexcusable, and when theories are not applicable 'as is' there may still be elements of them that are of great value for making progress with the research questions entrepreneurship research asks.

THE METHOD ISSUES

Sampling and Data Collection

The need to study on-going processes

In many countries it is possible to identify and sample established firms or business owner-managers from existing registers of reasonable quality in terms or coverage and accuracy. This may explain why the firm and the individual are by far the most frequently applied levels of analysis in published entrepreneurship research (Davidsson and Wiklund, 2001). But analysing data that is readily available rather than data that is relevant will not lead to credible answers to central questions in entrepreneurship research (cf. Cooper, 1995). In order to study *start-up processes* one has to face much bigger sampling challenges than usual.

The very realization that start-up is not *one* decision or behaviour, but indeed a *process* – a whole array of actions that are spread out over time – indicates the problem to be faced (Gartner and Carter, 2003). How can we identify start-up processes? All existing business activities are eligible for retrospective studies, but such studies would be subject to severe selection and hindsight biases. Regarding the latter, it is well known in cognitive psychology that memory is constructive in nature (Anderson, 1990). This means that no matter how honest and careful a respondent is, he or she will still distort the image of what happened during the start-up process. Dead ends are likely to be forgotten, and certain actions will be ascribed a rationale that only fell into place afterwards. Such problems can to some extent be remedied through triangulation (second informant; written documentation), but serious distortions are likely to remain regardless of such efforts. The problem of selection bias is potentially even more serious. In order to illustrate this, consider the following example. Imagine that we wanted to study 'factors that lead to success at betting on horses'. We design the study so that we include only those gamblers who actually won (net gain) from their betting on horses (cf. only those founders who actually got their venture up and running). Analysing our data, we would arrive at the following conclusions:

a.   Betting on horses is profitable
b.   The more you bet, the more you will win
c.   The more unlikely winners you bet on (higher odds) the more you will win

While true for *winners,* these conclusions are, of course, blatantly false inferences for the *entire population of gamblers.* On average, gamblers do not win – the organizer of the gambling does. Likewise, *ceteris paribus* the expected loss increases linearly with the size of the bet, and not the other way around. And, of course, the proportion of gamblers who lose is larger among those who bet on long shots. But since we study only winners, the above are the results we will get. The scary fact is that by studying only those start-up processes that led to a successful start-up we make ourselves guilty of the same kind of error, and open up for the potential of arriving at equally biased results.

Identifying an eligible sample of on-going processes
So how can we identify *on-going* start-up processes? What are the options? Some of the not-so-good ones are the following:

1.   Use informants at support agencies and the like. Again, selection bias would severely hamper representativeness. For sure, few internal ventures can be identified that way, and also among independent start-ups a large proportion – 61 per cent according to unpublished analyses of the Swedish version of PSED, for example – have not been in contact with a support agency. Moreover, experienced business founders are less likely to take such contacts, so the self-selection is likely to really cause a bias.
2.   Use the first visible trace that the new venture leaves in some type of regis-ter, for example registration of a new firm. While this could be a satisfac-tory solution in some countries and for some purposes, it would be unsatisfactory in most cases. In many countries, the smallest firms *never* enter any registers (Aldrich et al., 1989). If they do, they often do so at a later stage, when they are already an established entity rather than an emerging one. Thus, they would not be eligible for a study of on-going start-up processes. Using registration as identification remains problematic even when registration is a prerequisite during the process of emergence.

This is so because start-up processes follow many different sequences (Bhave, 1994; Carter et al., 1996; Delmar and Shane, 2002; Sarasvathy, 2001), and while registration may in some cases be a very early step in the start-up process it may in other cases be a very late one. Thus, even though the same indicator is used to approximate the initiation of the process, the cases will all the same be at different stages of development when they are sampled. This may make the researcher confuse 'caught at late stage' with 'quick to finish'. For start-up processes within established organizations (that is, internal ventures) registration is even less useful as a means of identifying eligible cases.

3. Snowball sampling (Douglas and Craig, 1983). The logic of snowball sampling is that members of small, expert populations are likely to know (about) one another. That is, the sampling strategy would be to find some on-going start-up processes through whatever means, and have those involved report on others who are also in the process of starting new ventures. Again, this would lead to a known and specific selection bias. Start-up processes led by better networked champions would be more likely to be caught, and this would have a serious biasing effect as networking or social capital is known to have an important influence on making progress in the start-up process (Davidsson and Honig, 2003).

The simple fact is that there is no fully satisfactory solution to the challenge of obtaining a representative sample of on-going start-up processes. There is no way we will ever be able to sample strictly randomly (or probabilistically) from the universe of venture ideas. This is not a problem only for deductive, theory-testing work but also for exploratory, case-study designs. Although valuable ideas for theory development can be obtained from *any* empirical case, there is the risk that the resulting theory will have limited applicability. Indeed, the most important conclusion from Samuelsson's (2001) work is that existing theories do a reasonable job at explaining the start-up process for innovative ventures, but not so for reproducing ventures – which happens to be the majority of new ventures. Theorizing based on non-representative cases or samples may be the reason for this.

The fact that obtaining the ideal sample is impossible does not mean that trying to approach that ideal is a futile effort. Realizing the limitations of the above approaches, the PSED and related research has adopted a two-step procedure. The first step is to approximate as closely as possible a very large random sample of *adult individuals*. In the US case this was done through a random digit dialling procedure, whereas the Swedish sister study benefited from the availability of a complete register of resident individuals. The sample thus obtained is the *screening sample*. The focal screening questions posed to these individuals were:

1. Are you, alone or with others, now trying to start a new business? (indication of being a *nascent entrepreneur*; NE)
2. Are you, alone or with others, now starting a new business or new venture for your employer? An effort that is part of your job assignment? (indication of being a *nascent intrapreneur*; NI)

Those who identified themselves as NEs or NIs were (along with a randomly selected comparison group) directed to a longer interview, and eligible cases were then followed up longitudinally. I consider this approach to capturing emerging ventures a giant leap forward, and I feel confident that it will in some form remain a standard tool in entrepreneurship research in the future. Nevertheless, the approach has shortcomings that have to be considered and eliminated, to the extent possible.

The first problem is that the procedure is costly. Hit rates of 1–10 per cent should be expected (Davidsson and Henreksson, 2002; Reynolds et al., 2001), which means that very large samples have to be screened in order to obtain a sizeable valid sample in the end. Attempts to employ techniques for more efficient, yet probabilistic sampling (see Reynolds and Miller, 1992) have not proven very successful in this context (Reynolds, personal communication). The second problem has to do with relying on the respondents' *subjective interpretations* of what should and should not be counted as 'now trying to start a business'. People differ in what they mean by 'now' as well as by 'trying' and 'business'. This problem may be different in different countries, and therefore the specific wording of the screening questions is crucial when conducting international comparative work. For example, work related to PSED and GEM have indicated that in Germany and Ireland, a substantial number of 'no' or 'don't know' answers may occur when the researcher would have wanted a 'yes'. This could be due to an uncertainty among independent professionals and founders of 'craft' businesses as to whether what they start is really a 'business'. I also feel personally that the subjectivity of what is being reported is greater for NIs than for NEs. For that reason I favour a different methodology for capturing internal ventures (see below).

Also within countries or cultures, and with respect to being a nascent *entrepreneur*, people differ in their perceptions of what qualifies. As a remedy to this, the PSED research has applied more objective supplementary criteria for eligibility. Here the PSED questions about 'gestation activities' are useful. Respondents were asked whether they had initiated or completed each of more than twenty activities (such as writing a business plan, talking to the bank, registering the business, talking to would-be customers, and the like, cf. Davidsson and Honig, 2003; Gartner and Carter, 2003). In addition, each such activity was time stamped by year and month. A common minimum criterion employed by PSED researchers is that at least one 'gestation activity' has been undertaken (Delmar and Davidsson, 2000). Sometimes stricter criteria are employed. In the Swedish PSED, it turns out that some self-appointed 'nascent entrepreneurs' initiated the start-up process many, many years ago – and still have not completed it. Based on the assumption that such respondents probably are not very serious about the reported start-up, one might consider eliminating such cases entirely (cf. Delmar and Shane, 2002). Likewise, a criterion that at least x activities have been undertaken during the last y months may be considered, so as to ensure that it is really an active start-up effort (Shaver, Gartner et al., 2001).

A maximum criterion is also needed, in order to establish that the case is an on-going start-up and not an already established business. Because of the multitude of gestation activities and the many different sequences in which they are undertaken – as well as the fact that not all activities apply to all start-ups – there is no simple criterion that is fully satisfactory. PSED researchers have sometimes employed a single criterion, namely that the venture had achieved sufficient cash flow for three months to pay expenses and the owner-manager's salary (Shaver, Gartner et al., 2001). Other PSED researchers have preferred a combination of criteria. For example, Delmar and Davidsson (2000), who included NEs only, considered the venture as already started if a) money had been invested, b) a legal entity had been formed, and c) the venture had generated some income. See also (Shaver, Carter et al., 2001) on the problem of operationalizing 'nascent entrepreneur'.

Sampling bias
Having solved the eligibility problem, and assuming that the sampling frame of adult individuals is relatively complete as well as that there is no devastating non-response bias, the above procedure leads (approximately) to a random sample of 'nascent entrepreneurs'. While this is for many purposes far better than having a non-random sample, it is not the random (or probability) sample of *start-up processes* that we were after. This is so for two reasons, the first one relatively obvious and the other less so. First, the above procedure over-samples team start-ups, because the more team members that consider themselves NEs, the more chances the venture has to be sampled. If information on the number of team members is available – as is the case with PSED, albeit truncated at five – this should be relatively easy to correct for, if deemed important. As will be explained below, I do for most purposes not find this type of statistical non-representativeness to be much of a problem at all.

A much more problematic and intriguing source of bias is that start-up processes have different durations. Assuming that the team vs. solo effect has been accounted for, the resulting sample is, in a sense, representative for the population of business start-ups at the time of the empirical investigation. It is *not*, however, a representative sample of all start-up efforts that were undertaken during that *year*. In order to see this, consider the following example. Assume that the entire population of start-up processes in a given year is 40. They consist of ten 'slow' start-ups, which are initiated on 1 January and completed on 31 December. The other 30 are 'quick' start-ups, which take four months from initiation to completion. Ten each are initiated on 1 January, 1 May and 1 September, and consequently ten 'quick' start-ups are completed on 30 April, 31 August and 31 December.

Now, although the proportion of 'quick' to 'slow' start-ups is three to one on a yearly basis, we will sample from a population with a 50/50 distribution no matter what date we select for our sampling. That is, the procedure over-samples 'slow' start-up processes. This is a serious bias by the logic of statistical inference theory, because it is likely to distort results. On the one hand, there is the risk that the over-sampling represents less serious and/or less successful start-up efforts. On the other hand, technology-based, high-potential start-ups are also likely to require longer time. Rather than hoping that these effects cancel out, the analyst should be aware of this problem, and try different strategies for solving it. This might include elimination of cases that appear to be 'eternal start-ups'; weighing; sub-sample analysis by length of process, and the use of process length as control variable.

Yet another source of bias makes it uncertain whether even 'snapshot' representativeness for 'nascent entrepreneurs' is fully achieved with the suggested procedure. Bhave (1994) identified two main processes leading to independent start-ups. The first, which he labels 'externally stimulated', starts with a wish to strike out on one's own, followed by search, screening and selection of business ideas ('opportunities'). The second, labelled 'internally stimulated', starts with identification of a personal need; continues with need fulfilment, and only then does the individual realize that this problem is general and the solution have commercial potential. In this latter case, the individuals involved may get much further into the process before they start to consider – and report – themselves as 'nascent entrepreneurs'. If so, the researcher should be aware that this type of start-up process will be under-sampled, and try to find a remedy as fit for the research problem at hand. As will be explained below, I do not think deviations from proportionate representation of the empirical population are necessarily a huge problem, as long as theoretically important categories have satisfactory representation in the sample. A much worse problem may result not from under-sampling of 'internally stimulated' processes but from the fact that they are further into the process when first caught. If this is not carefully controlled for in the analysis there is a risk that differences in performance be attributed to process type when differences in starting point are the real cause.

Sampling on-going internal venture start-ups

As briefly mentioned above, I am less convinced that starting from a sample of individuals, and the PSED screening questions, are the ideal tools for sampling of internal ventures. We have therefore employed a slightly different strategy in our study of on-going new internal venture start-ups (Chandler et al., 2003). Instead of screening individuals, we choose to screen firms for new initiatives. One advantage of this is that it eliminates the over-sampling of team efforts. Arguably, it should also reduce the problems of over- and under-reporting relative to the NI item in the PSED research (cf. above). We were fortunate enough to have an on-going study of a very large sample of firms from the 1994 cohort of 'genuine start-ups' (Dahlqvist and Davidsson, 2000a; 2000b), so we used the surviving firms (in year 2000) in this study as the sampling frame. Because these firms had previously been approached with mail questionnaires (where the first few question were mandatory data collection for a government agency, thus yielding high response rates) we chose a mail questionnaire directed at the CEO for the screening. Under other circumstances phone interviewing would probably yield a higher response rate. The focal screening questions were the following:

1. Have you after the start of this company in 1994, started any new venture within the company, which during some period has provided income to the company? We are interested in new business initiatives in your company, which have lead or could lead to new income-generating activities. NB! Not mergers or acquisitions.
2. Do you have a business initiative in progress now, which you yourself or others in the company have devoted time and possibly other resources to develop, but where the new activity does not yet yield a steady income?

Additional questions asked when the new initiative in (2) was initiated, and whether the respondent had started any additional *firms* (separate from the sampled one) since 1994. The first question above is intended to define 'new initiative' and to separate up-and-running initiatives from on-going ones. The critical screening question is (2). Those who answered this question affirmatively were later contacted for a phone interview. In the phone interview the eligibility of the initiative was double-checked. It was also classified in terms of what type of novelty it represented (cf. Bhave, 1994; Schumpter, 1934). If the firm had several eligible, on-going initiatives to choose from, the one deemed by the respondent to be 'most important for the company right now' was chosen.

So far, this strategy for sampling on-going internal ventures seems to be working satisfactorily. However, it shares some of the problems with the PSED approach. First, the screening is costly. In our case, 4950 firms were contacted for a yield of only 250 eligible cases, a sample size which is further reduced through attrition in the longitudinal follow-ups (Chandler et al., 2003). The yield would almost certainly be much higher if somewhat older and (in particular) larger firms were sampled – the firms in our sample were predominantly micro-businesses – but increasing firm size also introduces new complications, to which we shall return below. The eligibility problem is similar to the PSED and soluble through criteria for being over- or under-qualified. The problem of sampling bias because of variations in process length remains the same. There is also a parallel to the concern discussed above that externally and internally stimulated independent start-ups may be caught, on average, at different stages in the process. Chandler et al. (2003) discuss three search processes behind ideas for new internal ventures: proactive search, reactive search, and fortuitous discovery. It may be suspected that the latter category is less likely to be reported as a new initiative at very early stages of the process. This would lead to the same problem with under-sampling and possible confounding of effects as discussed above for internally stimulated processes in the context of independent start-ups.

Letting the respondent choose 'the most important' initiative when several eligible initiatives existed is, of course, a threat to representativeness. From a statistical point of view a more defensible procedure would be to check the number of eligible processes in a firm, pick one randomly, and adjust in the analysis for the resulting under-sampling of new ventures within multi-initiative firms. However, in our study this problem was of little practical importance, as very few firms had more than one new initiative under way. With larger firms in the sampling frame it would be more of a problem. Indeed, above a certain firm size almost every sampled firm would be likely to have more than one new internal venture under way. This calls for a more sophisticated procedure for choosing among them and – if several ventures per firm are included in the sample – techniques for adjusting for statistical dependence between cases with the same origin.

Before selecting what ventures to include, however, one should ascertain that all relevant new ventures have been identified. In our cohort of young and mostly very small firms, it was reasonable to assume that the CEO/respondent be aware of all new initiatives going on in the firm. A study starting from a sample of large firms would either have to give up ambitions towards statistical representativeness, or develop a procedure for first locating a sufficient number of relevant informants representing different roles in the company. All of these informants would then have to be screened for information on the existence and nature of on-going internal venture initiatives.

What is probably more of an issue with small (and independently owned) firms than with large ones is whether the new venture is going to form part of the original firm, or become a legally separate business. These two possibilities should be acknowledged in the design of the study and considered in the analysis. I personally see no reason to decide *a priori* to include only one type or only the other. On the contrary, this choice of 'mode of exploitation' (Shane and Venkataraman, 2000) can be an interesting research question in itself. Moreover, it would be impractical to introduce such a limitation, as the respondent has not necessarily taken this decision when the start-up process is first captured.

Heterogeneity and Representativeness

In my discussions of representativeness above I have implicitly referred to *statistical* representativeness. That is, the sample should reflect the composition of the underlying population in a probabilistically known manner. This is required for statistical inference theory (significance testing; estimation of confidence intervals) to be applicable – at least in the strict sense. Representative sampling and significance testing are important safeguards against ignoring important parts of empirical populations; giving undue weight to atypical cases, and ascribing substantive meaning to results that can easily have been generated by chance factors.

The problem is that statistical inference theory is a tool that is tailor made for opinion polls and industrial quality control rather than for social science research (cf. Cohen, 1994; Oakes, 1986). Consider opinion polls. Here we have a clearly defined population, which in most countries is also reasonably reachable: all eligible voters. What we want to know is their political preferences on the day of investigation. Hence we can draw a random sample and ask them about their preferences. Applying statistical inference theory, we can with high accuracy estimate with what uncertainty our sample results are associated, and determine whether the difference between two political parties, or the change for one party over time, deserves a substantial interpretation. Alternatively, we may conclude that these differences are likely to be the result of random sampling error. Clearly, probability sampling and significance testing are useful tools in this situation – we can say much more on the basis of this probability sample than on the basis of just any equally sized voter sample of unknown origin.

Social science research, however, is not the same as opinion polls, and theories are not built by democratic vote. That is, it is not a given that every empirical case should be deemed equally important for our theory building and theory testing. What we are really after in social science research is *theoretical representativeness* – that the studied cases are relevant for the theory we try to test or develop. There is no way we can draw a random sample from the theoretically relevant empirical population, because that population does not exist in one place at one time. This problem is aggravated by the fact that start-up processes are very heterogeneous. Some are solo efforts while others are team based. Some are championed by experienced, habitual entrepreneurs (Ucbasaran et al., 2001). Some are actively searched for whereas others are stumbled over (Bhave, 1994; Chandler et al., 2003). Many are part-time endeavours at least initially while others may involve full-time efforts by several individuals. They also differ in terms of industrial affiliations, start-up motives, growth potential, and a range of other dimensions. The questions are: what is the theory about and hence, what should be represented in the sample?

An empirical population of independent start-up processes is at the present time likely to be dominated by efforts that are necessity-based and non-innovative (Reynolds et al., 2001; Samuelsson, 2001), and championed by first-time, male founders with limited growth aspirations (Davidsson and Honig, 2003; Delmar and Davidsson, 1999). Does this make these categories theoretically more interesting or important, so that we should let them dominate in our efforts to develop and test theory? I would emphatically say *no*. First, those who are smaller in numbers may still be more important to the economy from which the sample is drawn. Second, that particular country in that particular year is but one of an endless pool of empirical settings for which the theory should have some relevance.

To illustrate the limitations of simple random sampling, consider first a firm-level example. If a simple random sample of small firms, here meaning firms with fewer than 50 employees, were drawn in Sweden it would have the following composition of firm sizes: 62 per cent self-employed without employees; just short of 35 per cent micro-firms with 1–9 employees, and a remainder of less than 4 per cent firms with 10–49 employees (NUTEK, 2002). I dare ask, are the solo self-employed economically and theoretically 16 times more important just because there are 16 times as many of them as the 'large' small firms? I dare answer no, for most conceivable research questions they are not! The same goes for start-up processes. Such processes are a heterogeneous mix of different 'types' (Bhave, 1994; Carter et al., 1996; Samuelsson, 2001; Sarasvathy, 2001), some of which may be larger in numbers whereas others may be economically more significant on a *per capita* basis. Mixing them all in one sample and giving little weight to those that are small in numbers in the specific empirical population from which the sample was drawn is likely to lead us to forgo important findings about significant economic phenomena.

We have noted that the population of 'start-up processes' is not well defined; that the theoretically valid population is not existent in one place at one point in time, and that start-up processes are heterogeneous along several dimension. There are several implications emanating from these lines of reasoning. The first is that simple random sampling is not necessarily the ideal.

Stratified and deliberately 'narrow' statistical samples, and even judgement samples, may be preferable. However, it should be noted that the possibility of pre-stratification is much more restricted for emerging ventures than for firms or individuals, which are often classified by age, size, industry, location, legal form and possibly other characteristics in the sampling frame already. Some homogenization of emerging ventures can be achieved through pre-stratification of the firms or individuals in the screening sample (for example, by education level or industry).

This first implication relates to the second, that the more important issue about sampling is not statistical but *theoretical* representativeness. That is, it should be carefully ascertained – and communicated – that the elements in the sample represent the type of phenomenon that the theory makes statements about. This is equally relevant for case study research. The third implication, again related to the previous ones, is that *replication* – not statistical significance testing – is the crucial theory test. The development and testing of sound theory requires replication in several sub-groups of analysable size within the same study, as well as across several studies that investigate theoretically relevant samples from different empirical populations. Achieving theoretical relevance involves, for example, the above-mentioned criteria for ascertaining that cases are neither under- nor over-qualified, and that those 'types' of processes that are deemed theoretically relevant have adequate representation in the sample. It is when findings hold up for several theoretically valid samples across time and space – that is when findings are proven replicable – that we can make strong inferences to the theoretical population.

Response Rates and Attrition

Another problem with the application of statistical inference is that typical response rates are way below 50 per cent (Chandler and Lyon, 2001), which makes inference dubious also with respect to the empirical population actually used for sampling. When the research is longitudinal the problem is aggravated by attrition over time. Because some start-up efforts are given up and in other cases the respondent refuses to continue to participate in the study, the worst-case scenario of ending up with a sample too small for statistical analysis may be realized.

In these matters it is a blessing to conduct research in Sweden, where we for some peculiar cultural reason have been able to reach close to 85 per cent response rate in telephone screening for 'nascent entrepreneurs', and figures in the 90s (of the still eligible sample) for continued participation over time (Davidsson and Honig, 2003; Delmar and Shane, 2002). Mail surveys rarely achieve much more than 50 per cent in Sweden, but this is already a figure researchers in other countries can only dream about. Regardless of the maximum attainable level in a specific country, however, there is little doubt that proper attention to and application of the 'craft' of survey research – cover letter, timing, layout, reminders, call-back schemes, and so on – will help the situation (Fink, 1995). Likewise, there are well-developed ways to deal with partially missing data (Hair et al., 1998; Little and Rubin, 1987) – a problem that is more pronounced with multi-wave as opposed to cross-sectional data. These are general issues that are relevant to any longitudinal survey research. A valid generalization specifically for new venture start-up research seems to be that initial non-response actually is a worse problem than is non-coopera-tion in subsequent waves of data collection. Just like in Sweden, the experi-ence with the American PSED is that once captured, those involved in venture start-ups often enjoy talking to interviewers about their efforts (Reynolds, personal communication).

The occurrence of substantial non-response is an additional reason to give statistical testing a somewhat lesser role than it is often given. I would suggest that the defensible use of statistical testing is not to answer questions about non-investigated populations, but to answer the following question: '*within a sample* of this size, could the effect or difference we have esti-mated have been generated by *some* kind or stochastic process, or can we with little risk ascribe it substantive meaning'? That is, the function of statis-tical testing is limited, but it is still valuable for within-sample safeguarding against unwarranted interpretations. Statisticians debate whether such within-sample interpretation of the test is permissible (Oakes, 1986). If this is not a valid use one might justifiably question whether there exists any valid use at all of statistical testing for most research questions in the social sciences.

Data Analysis

In our reasoning above we have already drifted into several issues of data analysis. For example, we have noted that the heterogeneity of venture start-up processes call for sub-sample analysis. We have observed that because of non-response and the impossibility of drawing a representative sample directly from the theoretically relevant population, statistical significance should be given a somewhat smaller role, and replication a bigger role, than what is conventional in social science practice. We have also noted that unless care-fully considered in the analysis there is risk of confounding 'caught late in the process' with 'fast completion of the process', and that the problem of catch-ing cases at different stages of the process is particularly problematic when time of catching is correlated with a potential explanatory variable, such as type of process. In short, when moving from existing to emerging phenomena and from cross-sectional to longitudinal data, the analyst has to be aware that familiar problems may be even more pronounced in this context, and also that a new set of challenges must be dealt with in a satisfactory manner.

As regards analysis techniques it is possible to attain new insights from the process data based on application of the usual collection of analysis techniques (Carter et al., 1996; Davidsson and Honig, 2003). However, in order to deal better with the specific data challenges, and to make full use of the longitudinal aspects of the data, other techniques may have to be learned and applied. This is a development that has only just begun. I will here just mention briefly a few examples that probably point out the right direction. First, we have Gimeno et al.'s (1997) careful adaptation of analysis tools to the analysis problem. In particular, this study is exceptional in its attention to heterogeneity regarding what is deemed an acceptable level of success. This mirrors Venkataraman's (1997) argument that performance relative to other ventures may not be the most relevant outcome variable for entrepreneurship research (cf. Davidsson, 2003).

As regards making use of the longitudinal aspects of the data there are two (sets of) techniques that appear especially promising, namely *Event History Analysis* (Blossfeld and Rohwer, 2002) and *Longitudinal Growth Modelling* (Muthén, 1997). In event history analysis the problem that cases are caught at different stages of the process can be dealt with. This is achieved through converting the data set to monthly (or weekly, bi-monthly, and so on) spells, using the time stamped first or nth gestation behaviour, or a specific event like registration, as marker for the initiation of the process. This way, the initiation of the process is synchronized despite the calendar time differences among the studied cases. The technique further makes use of the longitudinal aspect of the dependent as well as independent variables. Independent variables can be entered as time invariant or time variant. In the latter case the value of the independent variable is allowed to change over time. The dependent variable changes its value in the month when the event to be predicted has occurred. Cases where the event has still not occurred when the last data collection is made are treated as right censored – a problem the technique is designed to deal with. The logic of the technique makes it especially suited for predicting abandonment (vs. continuation) of the start-up processes, but can also be applied for analysing, for example, 'up and running' vs. 'still trying'. See Delmar and Shane (2002; forthcoming) for relevant applications.

Although independent variables in event history analysis can be either quantitative or qualitative (dichotomous), the dependent variable is always qualitative. Thus, the technique is a longitudinal equivalent to logistic regression. Although other, regression techniques for longitudinal analysis with a quantitative dependent variable also exist, latent growth modelling (LGM) is a particularly interesting alternative for this situation. In the context of new venture emergence the dependent variable might be, for example, the accumulation of gestation activities in PSED (cf. Davidsson and Honig, 2003; Gartner and Carter, 2003); the gradual attainment of the cornerstones of Klofsten's Business Platform Model (cf. Davidsson, and Klofsten, 2003), or any other variable that is analogous to growth. Being a longitudinal cousin to structural equation modelling techniques like LISREL, LGM has the advantages of being applicable to models with latent variables and indirect as well as direct relationships. The problem of different starting points is at least partly solved by simultaneously predicting the initial situation and development over time. A shortcoming of LGM is that cases that dissolve during the studied period cannot be included in the analysis. In order to avoid erroneous conclusions based on success bias the LGM analysis should therefore be supplemented with other types of analyses of the discontinued cases, so as to make sure that these do not share the characteristics that appear as success factors in LGM. For a relevant application see Samuelsson (2001).

CONCLUSION

In this chapter I have promoted longitudinal study of on-going venture start-up processes, using the evolving venture itself as the unit of analysis. I argue that this type of study holds great promise of yielding new insights for entrepreneurship both as a field of research and as business practice. However, it is clearly the case that conducting this type of research is not easy. On the contrary, it involves an array of tricky challenges like assessing the applicability of existing theory (and making necessary adaptations of the same); identifying a relevant sample; balancing the acknowledgement of heterogeneity as a fundamental characteristic of economic agents and entities with the wish to delimit heterogeneity in order to achieve clear results, as well as the need to identify, learn and apply analysis techniques that make full use of the longitudinal data. The problems may seem plentiful, but the reason for this is not so much that the situation is much worse for this type of study than for more conventional research; it is just that we have developed a habit of neglecting some of the fundamental problems inherent in the type of studies we are more familiar with. For every type of research an equally long list of inherent method issues could be discussed, and many of the challenges I have discussed here, such as the problems of theoretical relevance and non-applicability of statistical inference theory, are in fact much more general than the specific type of research discussed in this manuscript.

It is my hope that fellow researchers will view the method issues discussed in this chapter as interesting and inspiring challenges. If the challenges feel like just a little bit too much I offer as consolation that for those who take them on, the potential reward is great. Here we have a virgin field where there is a real chance to make important scholarly contributions regarding issues that are of utmost societal importance. A researcher can be worse off than that.

REFERENCES

Acs, Z.J. and D.B. Audretsch (eds) (2003), *Handbook of Entrepreneurship Reseach: An Interdisciplinary Survey and Introduction*, Dordrecht, NL: Kluwer.

Aldrich, H. (1999), *Organizations Evolving*, Newbury Park, CA: Sage Publications.

Aldrich, H., A.L. Kalleberg, P.V. Marsden and J. Cassell (1989), 'In pursuit of evidence: strategies for locating new businesses', *Journal of Business Venturing*, **4**, 367–86.

Anderson, J.R. (1990), *Cognitive Psychology and its Implications*, New York: W.H. Freeman and Company.

Bhave, M.P. (1994), 'A process model of entrepreneurship venture creation', *Journal of Business Venturing*, **9**, 223–42.

Blossfeld, H.-P. and G. Rohwer (2002), *Techniques of Event History Modeling: New Approaches to Casual Analysis*, Mahwah, NJ: Lawrence Erlbaum Associates.

Carter, N.M., W.B. Gartner and P.D. Reynolds (1996), 'Exploring start-up event sequences', *Journal of Business Venturing*, **11**, 151–66.

Chandler, G.N. and D.W. Lyon, (2001), 'Methodological issues in entrepreneurship reseach: the past decade', *Entrepreneurship Theory & Practice*, **25**(4, Summer), 101–13.

Chandler, G.N., J. Dahlqvist and P. Davidsson (2003), 'Opportunity recognition processes: A taxonomic classification and outcome implications', paper presented at the *Academy of Management Meeting*, Seattle.

Cohen, J. (1994), 'The earth is round (p<.05)', *American Psychologist*, **47**, 997–1003.

Cooper, A.C. (1995), 'Challenges in predicting new venture performance', in I. Bull, H. Thomas and G. Willard (eds), *Entrepreneurship: Perspectives on Theory Building*, London: Elsevier Science Ltd, pp. 109–24.

Dahlqvist, J. and P. Davidsson (2000a), 'Business start-up reasons and firm performance', in P. Reynolds, E. Autio, C. Brush, W. Bygrave, S. Manigart, H. Sapienza and K. Shaver (eds), *Frontiers of Entrepreneurship Reseach 2000*, Wellesley, MA: Babson College, pp. 46–54.

Dahlqvist, J. and P. Davidsson (2000b), 'Initial conditions as predictors of new venture performance: A replication and extension of the Cooper et al. study', *Enterprise and Innovation Management Studies*, **1**, 1–17.

Davidsson, P. (2003), 'The domain of entrepreneurship reseach: Some suggestions', in J. Katz and D. Shepherd (eds), *Advances in Entrepreneurship, Firm Emergence and Growth* (Vol 6), Greenwich, CT: JAI Press.

Davidsson, P. and M. Henreksson (2002), 'Institutional determinants of the prevalence of start-ups and high-growth firms: Evidence from Sweden', *Small Business Economics*, **19**(2), 81–104.

Davidsson, P. and B. Honig (2003), 'The role of social and human capital among nascent entrepreneurship', *Journal of Business Venturing*, **18**, 301–31.

Davidsson, P. and M. Klofsten (2003), 'The business platform: Developing an instrument to gauge and assist the development of young firms', *Journal of Small Business Management*, **41**(1), 1–26.

Davidsson, P. and J. Wiklund (2000), 'Conceptual and empirical challenges in the study of firm growth', in D. Sexton and H. Landström (eds), *The Blackwell Handbook of Entrepreneurship*, Oxford, MA: Blackwell Business.

Davidsson, P. and J. Wiklund (2001), 'Levels of analysis in entrepreneurship research: current practice and suggestions for the future', *Entrepreneurship Theory & Practice*, **24**(4, Summer), 81–99.

Delmar, F. (2000), 'The psychology of the entrepreneur', in S. Carter and D. Jones-Evans (eds), *Enterprise & Small Business: Principles, Practice and Policy*, Harlow: Financial Times, pp. 132–54.

Delmar, F. and P. Davidsson (1999), 'Firm size expectations of nascent entrepreneurs', in P. Reynolds, W. Bygrave, S. Manigart, C. Mason, G.D. Meyer, H. Sapienza and K. Shaver (eds), *Frontier of Entrepreneurship Research 1999*, Wellesley, MA: Babson College, pp. 90–104.

Delmar, F. and P. Davidsson (2000), 'Where do they come from? Prevalence and characteristics of nascent entrepreneurs', *Entrepreneurship & Regional Development*, **12**, 1–23.

Delmar, F. and S. Shane (2002), 'What founders do: a longitudinal study of the start-up process', paper presented at the Babson College/Kauffman Foundation *Entrepreneurship Research Conference*, Wellesley, MA.

Delmar, F. and S. Shane (forthcoming), 'Legitimating first: organizing activities and the survival of new ventures', *Journal of Business Venturing*.

Douglas, S.R. and C.S. Craig (1983), *International Marketing Research*, Englewood Cliffs, NJ: Prentice-Hall.

Fink, A. (ed.) (1995), *The Survey Kit*, Thousands Oaks, CA.: Sage Publications.

Gartner, W.B. (1988), ' "Who is an entrepreneur?" is the wrong question', *American Small Business Journal*, **13**(Spring), 11–31.

Gartner, W.B. (1993), 'Words lead to deeds: Towards an organizational emergence vocabulary', *Journal of Business Venturing*, **8**, 231–9.

Gartner, W.B. (2001), 'Is there an elephant in entrepreneurship research? Blind assumptions in theory development', *Entrepreneurship Theory & Practice*, **25**(4, Summer), 27–39.

Gartner, W.B. and N. Carter (2003), 'Entrepreneurial behavior and firm organizing processes', in A.Z.J. and D.B. Audretsch (eds), *Handbook of Entrepreneurship Research*, Dordrecht, NL: Kluwer.

Gimeno, J., T.B. Folta, A.C. Cooper and C.Y. Woo (1997), 'Survival of the fittest? Entrepreneurial human capital and the persistence of underperforming firms', *Administrative Science Quarterly*, **42**, 750–83.

Hair, J.F., R.E. Anderson, R.L. Tatham and W.C. Black (1998), *Multivariate Data Analysis*, (5th edn), Upper Saddle River, NJ: Prentice Hall.

Kirzner, I.M. (1983), 'Entrepreneurs and the entrepreneurial function: a commentary', in J. Ronen (ed.), *Entrepreneurship*, Lexington, MA: Lexington Books.

Little, R.J.A. and D.B. Rubin (1987), *Statistical Analysis with Missing Data*, New York: John Wiley.

Low, M. (2001), 'The adolescence of entrepreneurship research: specification of purpose', *Entrepreneurship Theory & Practice*, **25**(4, Summer), 17–25.

Muthén, B.O. (1997), 'Latent variable modeling of longitudinal and multilevel data', in A. Raftery (ed.), *Sociological Methodology*, Boston; MA: Blackwell Publishers.

NUTEK (2002), 'Företagens villkor och verklighet 2002. Dokumentation och svarsöversikt' (*Conditions and reality of small firms 2002. Documentation and overview of responses*), Stockholm: NUTEK.

Oakes, M. (1986), *Statistical Inference: A Commentary for the Social and Behavioural Sciences*, Chichester: Wiley.

Reynolds, P.D. (1997), 'Who starts new firms? Preliminary explorations of firms-in-gestation', *Small Business Economics*, **9**, 449–62.

Reynolds, P.D. (2000), 'National panel study of US business start-ups. Background and methodology', in J.A. Katz (ed.), *Advances in Entrepreneurship, Firm Emergence and Growth* (Vol 4), Stamford, CT: JAI Press.

Reynolds, P.D. and B. Miller (1992), 'New firm gestation: conception, birth and implications for research', *Journal of Business Venturing*, **7**, 405–17.

Reynolds, P.D., S.M. Camp, W.D. Bygrave, E. Autio and M. Hay (2001), *Global Entrepreneurship Monitor: 2001 Executive Report*, Kansas, MO.: Kauffman Foundation.

Samuelsson, M. (2001), 'Modeling and nascent venture opportunity exploitation process across time', in W.D. Bygrave, E. Autio, C.G. Brush, P. Davidsson, P.G. Green, P.D. Reynolds and H.J. Sapienza (eds), *Frontiers of Entrepreneuship Research* 2001, Wellesley, MA: Babson College, pp. 66–79.

Sarasvathy, S. (2001), 'Causation and effectuation: towards a theoretical shift from economic inevitability to entrepreneurial contingency', *Academy of Management Review*, **26**, 243–88.

Schumpeter, J.A. (1934), *The Theory of Economic Development*, Cambridge, MA: Harvard University Press.

Shane, S. and S. Venkataraman (2000), 'The promise of entrepreneurship as a field of reseach', *Academy of Management Review*, **25**, 217–26.

Shaver, K.G., N.M. Carter, W.B. Gartner and P.D. Reynolds (2001), 'Who is a nascent entrepreneur? Decision rules for identifying and selecting entrepreneurs in the panel study of entrepreneurial dynamics (PSED)' (summary), in W.D. Bygrave, E. Autio, C.G. Brush, P. Davidsson, P.G. Green, P.D. Reynolds and H.J. Sapienza (eds), *Frontiers of Entrepreneurship Research*, Wellesley, MA: Babson College, p. 122.

Shaver, K.G. W.B. Gartner, E. Crosby, K. Bakalarova and E.J. Gatewood (2001), 'Attributions about entrepreneurship: a framework for analyzing reasons for starting a business', *Entrepreneurship Theory and Practice*, **26**(2, Winter), 5–32.

Thornton, P.H. (1999), 'The sociology of entrepreneurship', *Annual Review of Sociology*, **25**, 19–46.

Ucbasaran, D., P. Westhead and M. Wright (2001), 'The focus of entrepreneurship research: contextual and process issues', *Entrepreneurship Theory & Practice*, **25**(4, Summer), 57–80.

Van de Ven, A.H., H.L. Angle and M.S. Poole (1989), *Research on the Management of Innovation: the Minnesota Studies*, New York: Harper & Row.

Van de Ven, A.H., D. Polley, R. Garud and S. Venkataraman (1999), *The Innovation Journey*, Oxford: Oxford University Press.

Venkataraman, S. (1997), 'The distinctive domain of entrepreneurship research: an editor's perspective', in J. Katz and J. Brockhaus (eds), *Advances in Entrepreneurship, Firm Emergence*, and Growth, Greenwich, CT: JAI Press.

3. The entrepreneurial process: emergence and evolution of new firms in the knowledge-intensive economy

Frédéric Delmar[1]

INTRODUCTION

The purpose of this chapter is to present a framework for a Swedish project aiming at understanding and explaining how new firms emerge and evolve in the sector of the economy that is research intensive. Specifically, we want to follow the process that leads to the identification and exploitation of entrepreneurial opportunities through the creation of new independent businesses in milieux characterized by innovativeness. This means that the identification of the entrepreneurial process, the founding of the new venture and its early development will be followed over time. Of special interest is research-intensive entrepreneurship which encompasses areas such as academic entrepreneurship (that is, how researchers at universities directly take part in the commercialization of their own research) (Henrekson and Rosenberg, 2000) to entrepreneurship in new growth areas that are knowledge intensive, such as mobile internet communication. We define entrepreneurship as the process of how, by whom, and with what consequences opportunities to discover future products and services are discovered, evaluated and exploited (Venkataraman, 1997). Opportunities are defined as those situations in which new goods, services, raw materials and organizing methods can be introduced and sold at a price greater than their cost of production (Casson, 1982).[2] We define research-intensive environments as environments characterized by a high component of new knowledge often originating from research. Such environments are also characterized by a constant introduction of innovation and changes.

The main questions are: how does entrepreneurship develop in such contexts and how does this form of entrepreneurship differ from the entrepreneurship found in the general population? Hence, the project's main focus is not on the entrepreneurship that through its dynamism leads to the creation of new employment (Davidsson et al., 1994; 1996) but the entrepreneurship that leads to economic development through its use of new knowledge and technology. Empirically, the purpose of the project is to use longitudinal data registers of high quality to study the process governing research-intensive entrepreneurship in Sweden. More specifically we aim at:

- Reaching more precise and interesting results through a well-crafted theoretical framework, more homogeneous samples than previous research, and to follow those over time.
- Achieving more precise knowledge about how research-intensive entrepreneurship in new populations differ from other forms of entrepreneurship.
- Achieving new and more precise knowledge about how new organizational forms and populations of organizations emerge and evolve in the sectors of the economy that are research intensive.

The study of new firm creation is specifically in research-intensive environments because we can expect those firms to exploit opportunities with a higher degree of innovativeness and novelty than new firms in general. The reason is that random samples of newly founded ventures will be dominated by relatively simple opportunities with little potential. The absolute majority of new firms are based on the imitation of existing business opportunities, and have very little potential to grow or to contribute to economic development through the introduction of new knowledge on the market. The probability of finding a sample of interesting opportunities diminishes if a pure random sample approach is used. Furthermore new firms evolve differently and are exposed to different risks depending on whether or not they have been started in innovative industries (Audretsch, 1991; Audretsch and Mahmood, 1995). We also know that firms established in innovative industries often exhibit a high geographical concentration (Feldman, 2001; Porter, 1990; Zucker et al., 1998). This is an indication that research-intensive entrepreneurship can be more dependent of the regional (innovation) system than other types of entrepreneurship (Eliasson, 2000).

We can therefore assume that the establishment of a new firm based on a research finding or new knowledge (and consequently exhibiting a high degree of innovativeness) as a process differs from the process of establishing a new firm based on an imitation of an already existing business. Research-intensive entrepreneurship must therefore be studied separately, to allow for large enough sample sizes to be created in order to analyse differences. The consequence is that research, advice and economic policy targeted to foster entrepreneurship in these early phases can be better developed to fit the specific needs of different new firms and entrepreneurs.

We believe that this project will fill an important void in the entrepreneurship research by:

- Using an evolutionary perspective on the entrepreneurial process
- Developing previous studies where only certain parts of the process have been investigated in trying to examine the whole process – from the initiation of the process of trying to start a new firm, through the start-up attempt and the early development of the firm – will enable us to better understand the complex system that affects and is affected by entrepreneurial processes.
- Being able to follow this process over a longer time frame (eleven years) gives us the opportunity to understand the dynamic development of the processes.
- Combining register data from Statistics Sweden with primary data gives us the opportunity to describe the development of these processes from different perspectives and level of analysis.
- Combining different empirical studies we will be able more closely to analyse a number of central factors that are crucial to the development of the entrepreneurial process. Most important are the background of the entrepreneur, the nature of the entrepreneurial opportunity and the development over time.

The rest of the chapter is organized as follows. In the next section we develop the project's theoretical framework. In the third section we present the methods and data to be used. We will also discuss the advantages and disadvantages with longitudinal studies relative to other method alternatives. In the final section we present some final conclusions concerning research in entrepreneurship.

THEORY

The Entrepreneurial Process Revisited

In this section we would like to develop some of the major research questions and challenges facing entrepreneurship research. We are here focusing on the process leading to identification and exploitation of the entrepreneurial opportunity, and consequently on the two main components of the process: (a) the existence of opportunities, and (b) the existence of enterprising individuals. Historically, the literature has explained the process as either the product of reinforcing environments or of personal attributes. However, personal attributes alone or environmental characteristics fail to explain more than a minor part of what is happening in the entrepreneurial process. The major problem is that both approaches are based on an equilibrium model. That is, the equilibrium model assumes that entrepreneurial opportunities are randomly distributed across the population or that they do not exist.

If equilibrium is assumed, individuals cannot discover opportunities that differ in value from those discovered by others, and those that become entrepreneurs do so because they have different attributes (Shane and Venkataraman, 2000). For example, Kihlstrom and Laffont (1979) or Knight (1921) state that only the ability to bear uncertainty differentiates entrepreneurs from non-entrepreneurs, and McClelland (1961; McClelland and Winter, 1969) argues that the need for achievement should be considered as a factor differentiating entrepreneurs from others. We also know that entrepreneurship is episodic. That is, many of us move back and forward between self-employment and employment during their working life (Carroll and Mosakowski, 1987; Evans and Leighton, 1989). This indicates that stable individual differences such as uncertainty acceptance or need for achievement can only explain a minor part of why some choose to exploit an entrepreneurial opportunity. However, we will here argue that these approaches are incomplete because they cannot answer the fundamental question related to the study of entrepreneurship: how are opportunities identified and exploited? To answer that question we have to move from an equilibrium model to a disequilibrium model.

The entrepreneurial process is based on disequilibrium. It is the source of both new opportunities and enterprising individuals prepared to exploit them. A system can be said to be in disequilibrium when we have to depart from the assumptions that individuals try to maximize profits, that information and resources are randomly distributed, and that the process is independent of its historical and cultural context. We have strong evidence that knowledge and resources are historically and culturally specific, and differently distributed across different contexts (Aldrich, 1999; Granovetter, 1985; Shane, 2000). We also know that individuals have bounded rationality and most are not interested in maximizing their profits (Hogarth, 1987). This means that the possibilities of identifying, developing, and exploiting an entrepreneurial opportunity are different in different contexts. These differences or variation in the entrepreneurial process are due to differences in the opportunities themselves, the differences among the entrepreneurial individuals, and the process of organizing. The starting point of the argument is the nexus between the individual and the opportunity, which leads to the initiation of the entrepreneurial process.

The nexus of the two main components of the entrepreneurial process, the entrepreneurial opportunity and the enterprising individual, is the core of entrepreneurship. The process is dependent on both the presence of lucrative opportunities and of enterprising individuals. It is important to consider that the quality of the opportunities identified varies, and that there exists an important variation in the attributes of the individual identifying them. This would not be a problem if the variation of quality of the opportunity and individual attributes were not highly correlated with each other. However, they are. The failure to control for this relationship – for example, by only looking at individual attributes – means that we confound the effect of the influence of the individuals and opportunities (Shane, 2000; Shane and Venkataraman, 2000).

Consider the example of an outstanding surfing run (that is, the successful exploitation of an opportunity). In order to surf we need a wave (which varies as opportunities do with the location and time) and a surfer (which varies in attributes as do the enterprising individual). In order to create an excellent surfing run there has to be a match between the surfer's ability and the wave. Not all waves appear in all locations, and not all surfers, independent of location, can ride every wave. A wave too strong and powerful will only represent something impossible and potentially deadly for the inexperienced surfer, but may represent the run of a life-time for an experienced one. At the same time, we know that we can expect the most talented surfers to emerge from and appear in the locations where the most challenging waves are. Hence, we can conclude that the excellent surfing run is dependent both on the surfer and wave. A good surfer will be more able to recognize a good wave and exploit it. Both still exist independently of each other and can be observed separately, but they only create new meaning (the surf) when combined.

That is, a wave is just a wave, and a surfer is just a person with a board. The surf only comes into existence when the surfer decides that she wants to ride that particular wave. Following the same logic, an opportunity is just a set of industry characteristics, technological know-how and information, until an entrepreneur decides to combine these existing factors with an opportunity to be exploited. While entrepreneurship arises in the nexus of the entrepreneurial opportunity and enterprising individual we must still be able to control for and to separate both factors in order to understand what leads to an outstanding surfing run or to the founding and establishment of new firm.

Third, the organizing process is important because when entrepreneurs identify an opportunity, they do not react automatically by establishing a new venture (Freeman, 1982). The establishment of a new firm cannot be seen as the outcome of a single decision or a single act. On the contrary, entrepreneurs choose to organize their new firms through a series of activities – such as organizing a founding team, creating a legal entity, product development and seeking financing – which are initiated at different times, to different degrees, and in a different order (Carter et al., 1996; Gartner, 1985). Hence, the founding and emergence of a new firm cannot be seen as a linear step-by-step process. Instead the founding and emergence of new firms involve development along several lines, any of which can be stopped well short of a firm's successful establishment (Aldrich, 1999).

We can conclude that the variation in the development of the entrepreneurial process (both how it starts, and how it develops) is high. Depending on people's available resources, experiences and knowledge they will identify different opportunities and also exploit them differently. This variation in who chooses to start a new firm, in the organizing process, and in which of these new firms will survive and grow raises, among others, the following questions:

- How do individuals identify the entrepreneurial opportunity they exploit?
- How do new firms and organizational forms emerge from initiation and go forward?
- How do the entrepreneur's characteristics, the characteristics of the opportunity and the combination of them affect this process?
- How do the entrepreneur, the founding team and other key actors learn, and how does this affect the process and the outcome?
- How do critical institutional characteristics (for example, specific university rules in Sweden about patent rights for researchers, the distribution of 3G rights in Sweden) affect the market relations and the critical relationships among resource providers (for example, venture capitalists)?
- How does the early organization process affect the future development of the firm?
- How does this process differ between innovative (research-intensive) industries and non-innovative industries?

In sum, how does the process evolve from the time when a seed to a new firm is planted until the firm has been established as one among others? And how does the process look that leads to such a large variation in organizational forms? What leads to the survival and growth of certain firms and industries, but to the death of others?

Evolutionary Theory

A general theoretical perspective to understand this dynamism is evolutionary theory. The perspective is evolutionary, not that it is based on a biological model, but on the integration of three cooperating change principles that affect economic development: *variation*, *selection*, and *retention*. The principal themes are:

- The process that determines the range of actual discovered and exploited opportunities introduced in the economy (variation).
- The process that alters the relative importance of the competing alternatives (selection).

- The process that determines how positively selected variations are memorized in order to be duplicated or reproduced (retention).

Hence, the dynamic process is the focus and it is related to the nature of competition as a process of endogenous change: variation drives selection while positive and negative feedback processes mean that the development of variations is shaped by the process of selection (Aldrich, 1999; Carroll and Hannan, 2000; Metcalfe, 1994; Nelson and Winter, 1982). Another distinctive element is the adaptation of the behavioural theory of the firm and the focus on learning process and adaptive behaviour (Kogut and Zander, 1992; 1996). This means that the actors in the system learn to adapt to changes in selection process. They are also assumed to operate under the constraints of imperfect, uncertain and localized information. Moreover, evolutionary theory assumes intentional behaviour from the actors, but separates the issue of what we want to do from what is the result of our actions.[3] This also means that evolutionary theory assumes indeterminacy of outcomes. The theory therefore allows us to better mitigate the problems described above facing entrepreneurship research.

Variation in the entrepreneurial process is generated, among others, by entrepreneurs initiating a number of different activities to establish new firms, and to get the new firm to survive in competition with other already established firms. Some variations are more effective than others in the sense that they fit the surrounding boundaries better, and are selected out for survival. This means that the entrepreneurs who create effective variations will establish their firms and make them survive. The entrepreneurs who fail, have either to abandon their projects or adapt in accordance with the environment's constraints.

The kind and amount of information and resources available to new firms characterize the environment. An analysis which is based on information availability departs from the assumption that information is not distributed evenly across actors. As a consequence variation arises as entrepreneurs use information to make decisions under uncertainty and with bounded rationality. Variation arises as different entrepreneurs have access to different amounts of information and choose to interpret them differently based on past experiences and hopes of future developments (Nelson and Winter, 1982; Weick, 1979). Some combinations of judgements and information are seen as more effective than others and are selected to fit the environment and survive. An analysis based on resource availability in the environment departs from that: firms compete for available resources and the terms under which the resources are made available to them.

Selection arises through relative rather than through absolute superiority in attracting resources. It is the entrepreneurs who are relatively more effective in attracting resources and transforming them who are selected for survival

(Barney, 1991; Nelson and Winter, 1982; Schumpeter, 2000 [1934]). The struggle about scarce resources is consequently central to the evolutionary perspective.

Retention can be compared to a memory function where successful variations are stored and institutionalized to be effectively reproduced. When a firm is established and its actors have found a number of activities or routines that give the opportunity to reach the desired goals, they will try to maintain and reinforce the activities that have previously been effective. For example, some human resource strategies will develop and become dominant (Baron, Burton and Hannan, 1996), while some will be prioritized because history has proved that some combinations are more effective than others. The actors' ability to learn (and unlearn) is therefore central because it is through the observation of their own actions and those of others that they learn which activities or routines have the highest probability of leading to survival.

Figure 3.1 summarizes graphically the evolutionary perspective on opportunity exploitation through the establishment of new independent firms. First, we can observe that the process of variation, selection and retention is present within the firm as well as outside in the environment. The former process represents the firm's ability to adapt to environmental changes. At Time 1, we can observe that a high number of variations are present. At Time 2, only those that have been able to adapt to the environmental constraints have survived. This has either happened by voluntary adaptation (the hexagon turning into a square) or by a variation that from the beginning (Time 1, the square) was fit. That is, the former represents a firm that has been able to change and adapt to new selection forces in order to survive, whereas the latter still remains fit because the changes in the selection criteria represented a menace to its environmental fitness. The inability to adapt leads to the exit of the firm (the triangle). At the same time, new variations are introduced (the circle) that change the selection forces, and thereby forcing existing firms to adapt or exit (Time 3). Hence, the process develops over time as new variations are introduced.

The Advantage of the Evolutionary Perspective

To develop theoretical models for how individuals identify and exploit entrepreneurial opportunities is important because the entrepreneurship literature is fragmented and this process is still largely under-researched. This is especially the case with research-intensive entrepreneurship (Miner et al., 2001). Therefore, there is a great need to develop theoretical models to be tested empirically.

The use of an evolutionary perspective leads to a number of theoretical and empirical advantages. Evolutionary theory can explain why there is a selection between those wanting to start a new firm and those who actually succeed and

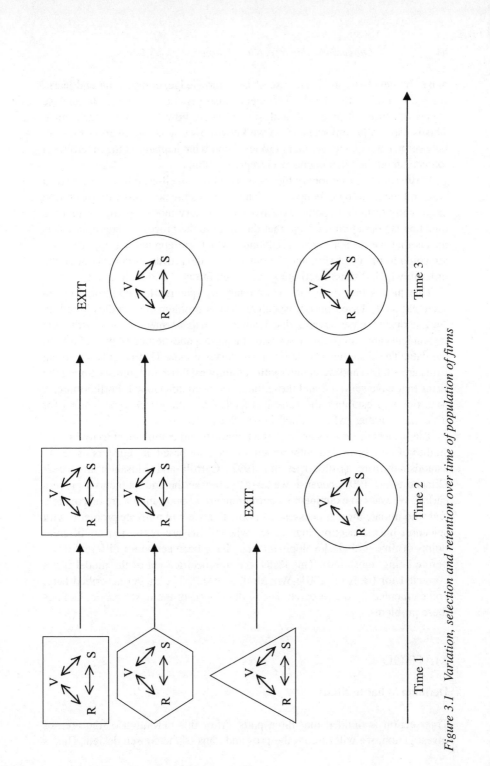

Figure 3.1 Variation, selection and retention over time of population of firms

make the new firm grow. The use of new knowledge, competition and learning are central to the theory. The theory also gives us the ability to analyse events on different levels of analysis and show how they affect each other. This is especially important when we know how crucial the relationships are between what happens on the micro level and what happens at the macro level to understand the phenomena of entrepreneurship.

Furthermore, evolutionary theory is based on a well-established theoretical core and methodological apparatus. This gives us the possibility of generating empirically testable hypotheses. Also, evolutionary models point out that the outcome is not determined and that the order in the process is important. This means that we do not know in advance, which entrepreneurial opportunities are going to be successful, and the outcome of the process is dependent on the order in which different activities have been initiated and their quality.

This means that from the evolutionary perspective the traditional cross-sectional study based on retrospective data is problematic. Studies based on such a design have several disadvantages such as memory loss from the respondents and hindsight biases which lead to a questioning of the validity of the data. These studies also suffer from survival bias. That is, only surviving firms are studied and we cannot with certainty establish differences among the firms that have survived and those that have been abandoned. Furthermore, it is difficult to establish the causal order because they lack time stamps for different activities (Mitchell and James, 2001).

The project represents an important contrast and complement to traditional studies of new firms and entrepreneurs which are based on registers of newly established firms (Brüderl et al., 1992; Carroll and Mosakowski, 1987; Gimeno et al., 1997) because we start to observe the entrepreneurial process earlier. We want to examine how entrepreneurial opportunities are discovered, and who initiate these processes. By doing that we will mitigate problems with selection bias. Selection bias arises when firms are registered at different points of time in their development (they have been active for different times before being registered). This leads to a misspecification of the model if not corrected for (Balgati, 2001; Wooldridge, 2002). The model described here, complemented by the research design developed in the next section, handles these problems.

METHOD

Defining What to Study

This section is divided into three parts. After this definition of the area of investigation, we will discuss the pros and cons of the chosen design. This is followed by a description of the specific studies included in the project. The specific studies cover the three theoretical parts – or areas of investigation – discussed in the previous section:

1. Start of independent firms
2. The early development of the new firm and
3. The evolution of new organizational forms and populations.

In this project we aim to only study emergence and evolution of independent firms as an option to exploit an entrepreneurial opportunity. There are basically two options to exploit an entrepreneurial opportunity. Either an independent new firm can be established or the opportunity can be exploited within an existing firm. The second alternative has been examined in detail in the innovation literature. The possibility to exploit an opportunity effectively differs for the two options. First, new firms and established firms differ in their ability to exploit new innovations and opportunities. Furthermore as Tushman and colleagues (Murmann and Tushman, 2001; Tushman and Anderson, 1986) have shown, different innovations require different organizational settings, depending on their demand for competence. Many innovations need new organizations to be exploited because they cannot be exploited in established organizations, as they are perceived as a threat to the existing competencies and are therefore rejected.

Second, the two options not only differ in what kind of opportunities they can exploit, but also in how they can exploit them. New and small firms differ from older, larger and more established firms when it comes to available human capital, financial resources and legitimacy. Established firms are legitimate because they have been present on the market for a long time and are taken for granted. This means that they have better established routines for resource acquisition and transformation, and have established relationships with stakeholders (for example, investors and customers). Furthermore, because of their size they have relatively more resources available to exploit the full potential of an opportunity in comparison with new and small firms (Aldrich and Auster, 1986; Stinchcombe, 1965).

These three areas of investigation are the base to the entrepreneurial process related to the emergence and evolution of new firms. These three areas are difficult to research using a single database or method. They demand different design to be successfully investigated. However, by combining these three areas in one single project we can escape some of the most important methodological problems normally associated with these kinds of studies and create the prerequisite conditions needed to generate results to be tested under the same theoretical framework. It is also an opportunity to follow how different entrepreneurial opportunities and individual entrepreneurs evolve over time and under different conditions. We therefore start to argue for the pros and cons of longitudinal designs. Thereafter we discuss the design of the separate studies.

Longitudinal Studies in Relation to Other Method Alternatives

One of the major advantages of a longitudinal research design is the opportunity to mitigate a number of methodological problems that have plagued research in entrepreneurship. There are two methods or combinations of those which have dominated: cross-sectional and retrospective studies.

There are several very important advantages with panel data relative to the assumption that entrepreneurship is best understood as a process. First, longitudinal data or panel data gives us the ability to control for individual heterogeneity. That is, panel data can handle the fact that individuals or firms are different from each other and that also develop differently over time and across settings. By following individuals or firms over time, it is possible to differentiate between the effects due to changes over time and the effects due to individual differences. This means for entrepreneurship research that if we only look at a cross-section of individuals trying to start a firm, we will confound the issues of whether the ability to do so is due to (a) individual differences, (b) that they are at different points in the process or (c) that they are in different settings. Hence, the resulting model will not be able to correctly estimate the factors affecting the outcome of being able to start a new firm (Balgati, 2001; Diggle et al., 1994).

The introduction of a time factor also gives the opportunity to achieve better support for causal inference. The fact that we have the opportunity to observe a behaviour before an outcome, gives us a relatively better position to argue for an actual causal relationship (Blossfeld and Rohwer, 1995; Yamaguchi, 1991). This is normally difficult using a cross-sectional design if it is not based on a very strong theory. This is rarely the case with research in entrepreneurship.

The research design proposed here is based on proactive data gathering in contrast to the retrospective studies that tend to dominate. Retrospective studies are prone to several problems. One is the risk of survivor bias. That is, researchers are only able to identify individuals or firms that have been able to survive the process of interest. For example, only start-up attempts that have succeeded are surveyed and conclusions are drawn based on these data. In such a case it is actually impossible to say what factors actually did lead to success and which did not, as we actually do not have any information about those that have failed, and how they differ from survivors. Furthermore, we do not know how many have tried, and how many have in relation succeeded. It is therefore important to start observing the process from the beginning in order to follow the development of all members that participate.

Another problem with retrospective studies is hindsight bias. People's memories of what has happened are seldom in accordance with what has actually happened. People tend not only to forget, but also to have a false recollection of what has happened. They tend to recreate the development of the process by adding and subtracting facts so it will make a more causally oriented story. These two problems have to some extent been dealt with in a longitudinal study of start-ups where the authors have been active (Delmar and Davidsson, 1999; Delmar and Davidsson, 2000; Delmar and Gunnarsson, 2000; Delmar and Shane, 2003).

However, there are some limitations to panel data beside their costs. They include design and data collection problems related to the definition of the population, non-response due to attrition, measurement problems, and the length of the period of observation. By the definition of the population we mean the risks of not targeting the right population. For example, we could be interested in following a population of entrepreneurial opportunities with high growth potential to discover that the potential would never be realized. Also respondents tend to drop out over time because they feel less committed to participate. Another problem is measurement errors that may arise due to, for example, unclear questions, misrecording and inappropriate informants.

Another problem is the length of the period of observation. For how long should the panel be followed? If we follow the panel for too short a time we might miss important outcomes. This can be compared to watching a marathon being run without any information about how much time it takes to run the race, and stopping watching just before the run is over. The consequence is that we miss important information about the development of the contest. On the other hand, we cannot observe the process for infinity (we do not wish to spend all our time watching every contestant finishing the marathon run), because of the cost associated with the observation. Furthermore the longer we observe, the higher is the chance of increasing attrition and measurement errors. In sum, many of the problems that are present in all forms of surveys are present in panel data, but the problems are greater as we repeat the same measurement over time, hence multiplying the potential sources of errors (Balgati, 2001).

Design of the Projects

We have argued that an evolutionary perspective is favourable to study and understand the entrepreneurial process and its effects. The adaptation of the evolutionary perspective has important consequences for the designs of empirical studies. As we argued above, the need to follow the process from its conception and onwards means that longitudinal data have to be collected. We have also argued that entrepreneurship should be understood as the nexus between the entrepreneurial opportunity and the enterprising individual. The consequences for empirical research are that we need better control of these two factors in order to achieve better knowledge of the entrepreneurial process. That is, we advocate for a more homogeneous data set to study.

The author has worked previously with a data set of a random sample of Swedish start-up attempts (Delmar and Davidsson, 1999; 2000; Delmar and Gunnarsson, 2000; Delmar and Shane, forthcoming). A specific limit to this research was the problem of heterogeneity in the analyses as both entrepreneurial opportunities and entrepreneurial individuals varied. That is, that the mix of different entrepreneurial opportunities (different in content, risk exposition and growth potential) and individuals who all differ from each other leads to an inability to draw more detailed conclusions of what factors lead to the establishment of some firms and not others. There are enormous differences in the process between establishing a small family business based on handicraft and the needs of a local market, and the establishment of a computer software firm with ambitions of a rapid internationalization. Hence, more homogeneous samples are needed to study the entrepreneurial process.

The argument for more homogeneous data sets are that while the 'within' variation in a group of individuals sharing the same background is important it is still less important than the 'between' variation among different groups. Furthermore, heterogeneous data sets lead to the inability to control for both the within and between variation as the different populations have not been defined beforehand. This leads to results that are less robust and to results that are too general to be practically applicable in individual settings.

We have also specifically argued that research on knowledge intensive entrepreneurship should study:

- How independent firms are started based on research-intensive knowledge
- How the research- or knowledge-intensive firms develop over time and in different settings
- How new organizational forms and populations based on research-intensive knowledge emerge and evolve (specifically mobile Internet).

This requires different studies or data sets and a combination of methods. We here present the different data sets. It is a combination of two different data sets that will enable us to answer these three major questions. The first data set is composed of a number of registers obtained from Statistics Sweden. In the second data set, we will reconstruct – using interviews among other ways – the emergence and evolution of the population of firms that uses mobile data communication as the technical platform for their business activities.

We have chosen to work with these two data sets because we believe this enables us to answer research questions that have not been answerable previously. Both designs are separately traditional and well proven, but taken together they give us new opportunities. One advantage is the combination of primary and secondary data. Furthermore, the cooperation leads to more researchers having access to a larger set of data at a relatively smaller cost, and to the knowledge among the involved researchers being developed.

Statistics Sweden. Based on data available at the present time to Statistics Sweden, we are able to investigate two main questions: (1) Who start independent firms based on research-intensive knowledge? and (2) How do firms based on research-intensive knowledge opportunities evolve? Statistics Sweden has developed a number of longitudinal databases that give us a unique opportunity to follow both the individual and the firm between the period of 1990 and 2000. This is made possible as tracking is based on the individual person number (the Swedish equivalent to the social security number), which is unchanged during the life of an individual. As a consequence we obtain stable units to follow over time.

The database LOUISE is an example of such a register. It is a longitudinal database where education, income and labour status are the focus. The primary object of the registers is the individual, but we have the opportunity to attach other objects such as, for example, the family, the work place, and the firm (our second main register). Yearly data exists for the period 1990 to 2000 (11 years). As a result, we can follow individuals, groups of individuals and firms over time.

A very important advantage is that we are able to follow the activities of an individual several years before she/he starts a firm, and several years after that, or to follow the development of a new firm during its first 11 years of life. That is, we can follow what an individual does after she/he has finished her/his university degree, what jobs she/he takes and what firm she/he might or might not start. If she/he starts a firm, we can then follow the performance of that firm. In LOUISE, everyone is included who is registered in Sweden and is above 15 years of age. The register covers from an entrepreneurship perspective a very long time period. This is important if we want to be able to understand the dynamic process of entrepreneurship. The register gives us a unique opportunity to follow both individuals and firms from the earliest phase and forward. Consequently, we can investigate how the individual comes into self-employment, and how the firm they have created alone or with others develops over time.

Specifically, we want to create seven different sets based on these two registers (the firm register and the LOUISE register). In the three first sets we will follow individuals over time to examine who chooses to enter or exit self-employment. In the four last ones we follow the firm over time to see how they develop over time (survival, growth, and possibly profitability). As we sample all sets from the same register we can first examine what leads to a specific person's decision to start a firm and then follow that firm's development (with or without the individuals who started it). With the exception of set 1 and set 4 we work with the total populations (all firms and all individuals in Sweden fitting our definitions). The seven sets are presented in Table 3.1.

Data will be arranged as panel data, which enables us to study the development over time. The data sets are not only unique in that they include, from an entrepreneurship research perspective, a long time period (11 years), but also because a large number of interesting variables are measured with great accuracy. For example, we can mention level and direction of education, labour force status, income, wealth, and family status. Furthermore, we will be able on the firm level to attach variables such as financial performance, partnership, employee and hiring forms and their origins, entry and exit. We also hope to be able to attach patent data to the sets. The data structure also gives an opportunity to directly attach information on the firm level to the project on mobile Internet. This is not possible at the individual level because Statistics Sweden will not allow identification. It is the research group's assessment that this data represents a unique opportunity to do international research of the highest quality.

The opportunity to carry out advanced demographic studies of potential firm founders and business dynamics is important, and gives us several interesting results which can be exemplified by Johansson's (2001) study of the Swedish IT sector. Also being able to attach data to the individual level, as has been done by Gratzer (1996) in his studies of the automatic restaurant industry, enables us to explore how different individuals affect the demography of firms through their entrepreneurial behaviour. For example, we can see if there are individuals who are much more active than others, and if there are clusters of individuals who cooperate to start and develop firms. In a similar way to the business demographer who examines how the role of different entry forms (de novo, spin-off from larger firms, mergers, and others) affects the development of an industry, we can examine how different entrepreneurial individuals and their attributes affect the development by being totally new, or having previous start-up experience in another industry, or from the same industry. We can also examine how possible gender differences in firm founders or their belonging to a minority group might affect the development of the firm.

Mobile data communication. Related to the start and development of new firms is the emergence and evolution of new organizational forms and new populations. The process here is different because these new firms establish a new industry and create a new population. The new population has to be integrated into already established populations. As a consequence, these new firms are exposed to other risks than those started in already established populations because they create a new challenge for existing populations as well (cf.

Table 3.1   Description of data sets

Individuals	Firms
Set 1 is composed of a *random sample* of n = 5000 of the Swedish population. The purpose of this sample is to obtain a representative sample of the Swedish population that we can then compare to sets 2 and 3.	Set 4 is comprised of a *random sample* of n = 5000 of start-ups. The purpose with this set is to use it as a control for sets 5, 6 and 7.
Set 2 is comprised of *the population* of individuals who have a university degree or above in natural science or engineering. The purpose is to examine how this population, which has research-intensive knowledge, start firms. In this set we control specifically for the effect of education.	Set 5 is comprised of *the population* of firms started by individuals included in set 2. This gives us the opportunity to not only follow the process leading to the start of a new firm, but also to follow how that firm evolves over time. These firms can be started in different industries that are more or less research intensive.
Set 3 is comprised of *the population* of individuals working in the most interesting research-intensive sectors (for example, pharmaceuticals, biotechnology and information technology). The purpose is to examine how individuals who are active in these areas start new firms. In this case, we control specifically for the effect of the industry.	Set 6 is comprised of *the population* of firms that have been started by persons included in set 3. The purpose is the same as for set 5.
	Set 7 is comprised of *the population* of firms that are started in the most interesting research-intensive sectors (for example, pharmaceuticals, biotechnology and information technology). The purpose is to investigate how these firms emerge and develop. This set differs from sets 5 and 6 in that it does not take the background of the firm founders into consideration.

Schumpeter's 'the gale of creative destruction') (Aldrich and Baker, 2001; Aldrich and Fiol, 1994; Baron et al., 1996; Romanelli and Bird Schoonhoven, 2001; Schumpeter, 2000 [1934]; Stinchcombe, 1965). This type of ecological study which follows the development of a new population or industry has been proven to be an effective way of studying entrepreneurial processes (Carroll and Hannan, 2000; Hannan and Freeman, 1984) because each firm's development can be studied in relation to the development of the whole population.

In this study we will follow the development of all firms established in Sweden in the sector of mobile Internet. This sector is anticipated to be of great importance for the economic development of Sweden. Such a register has already been developed at Chalmers Technological University and includes 167 firms. However, it needs to be complemented with additional data and to be developed longitudinally for the five years to come. The register is in itself important and in combination with the register from Statistics Sweden, its potential is augmented for three reasons.

First, to control for a single population enables us to control for the entrepreneurial opportunity. That is, the prerequisite conditions are the same for all entrepreneurs who enter the population, but, based on differences in experience and knowledge, they will choose to exploit opportunities in different ways (Shane 2000). This gives genesis to different business ideas and models.

The study functions therefore as a natural balance between the first project where we primarily control for individual differences in education and industry experience, and how it affects who is going to become an entrepreneur and which firms are going to survive at macro and meso level. In this project we primarily control for the entrepreneurial opportunity and have access to more detailed information about how firms behave when adapting to and producing changes at the micro and meso level.

Second, research-intensive entrepreneurship originating from universities is only a sub-group of the total population of research-intensive entrepreneurship. Many new growth-oriented technology-based firms originate from different incubator firms (Jacobsson and Lindholm Dahlstrand, 2001). It is important to understand how different organizational forms (universities being one and private firms another) generate new opportunities. It is therefore important to acquire better knowledge of how opportunities in this sector are exploited, and the effect on the population. Third, the population term is probably better sited than the industry term to study how new organizational forms based on new technology evolve, because firms can exploit the same technology for different problems in different industries (Aldrich, 1999). To build a population based on the commercial exploitation of a common opportunity may give insights into how technological and innovations systems develop, that traditional industry studies cannot.

More specifically, we aim to study how different business models evolve in contexts characterized by great turbulence (Eisenhardt and Martin, 2000; Teece, et al., 1997). As new technology is constantly introduced in the population, individual firms and the population as a whole must constantly re-evaluate their business models and their applications. This leads to the fact that variation and selection occurs more rapidly in this type of research-intensive context than in other contexts. The purpose is to better understand how entrepreneurs learn to handle these changes and how they succeed or fail in integrating them in business.

In sum, the combination of the two studies gives us a unique opportunity to study the evolution of the entrepreneurial process from the discovery of the opportunity and forward, and over different contexts. Furthermore, the combination enables us to study different aspects of the entrepreneurial process where research-intensive entrepreneurship and technology represent a major part, not least because of their large and growing importance for economic development, which has become increasingly dependent on the production and the exploitation of knowledge.

CONCLUSION

We have argued that research-intensive entrepreneurship is an important and relevant field of study. It is of practical importance because we have to acknowledge that the entrepreneurial process in research-intensive sectors differs from other forms of entrepreneurship. More knowledge is needed about the special risk and opportunities that practitioners are likely to face when engaging as entrepreneurs or trying to create a supporting environment. From a research perspective, this is an important effort as it aims at trying to better understand entrepreneurship where innovativeness is an important component of the entrepreneurial opportunity. Specifically, the research project will focus on the establishment and evolution of new and independent firms as a form of opportunity exploitation.

Implications for Research

This project will make several important contributions to research on entrepreneurship and business dynamics. First, we argue for the need for empirical research on new venture creation and entrepreneurship to be theoretically grounded. In order to be able to reach interesting and valuable results about research-intensive entrepreneurship we have proposed the use of an evolutionary perspective on the entrepreneurial process. We do so for several reasons.

We do not believe that an equilibrium model can explain more than a minor part in the entrepreneurial process. We have argued that resources and knowledge are historically and culturally specific. Following this line of reasoning, we highlight the problem of nexus of the opportunity and of the enterprising individual. That is, there is a strong bond between the two, where individual background and experience have an effect on what kind of opportunities are identified, but also the nature of the opportunity will affect the choice to exploit it. Hence, a challenge for entrepreneurship research is to handle this nexus, by trying to control for the two phenomena. Finally, we also argue that establishment of a new firm cannot be conceived as a linear step-by-step process.

These arguments lead us to adopt an evolutionary perspective on entrepreneurship because it can handle the dynamism and uncertainty that we see as central components of the entrepreneurial process. Based on the perspective we argue that the entrepreneurial process can be seen as a process affecting economic development based on three change principles: variation, selection and retention. The behaviour of the entrepreneur leads to changes in how the economic system functions as new opportunities are exploited. At the same time, entrepreneurs need to learn how to adapt to changing selection forces, and how to reproduce routines and skills that have been proven successful. The process is endogenous because there are limited resources that actors (including entrepreneurs) compete to obtain. Because the perspective has a well-developed theoretical core and methodological apparatus, we believe in its ability to generate a better understanding of research-intensive entrepreneurship.

Practically, we hope to work with two panel data sets. The first set is based on registers from Statistics Sweden and enables us to study economic activity both at the firm level and the individual level for the period 1990 to 2000. Hence, we can follow the development of single individuals and new firms for a period up to 11 years. This allows us to follow both what happens before the choice to establish a new firm, and what happens during the early days of the firm's development. By being able to follow both the development over a long period of time at the individual and at the firm level, we hope to achieve new insights. Moreover the data concerns populations and not samples and is generally of very high quality lending support for robust results.

The second panel data set aims at reconstructing the population of firms that use mobile Internet as the technological platform for their business activities. The specific aim is to follow how firms in this turbulent environment adapt (or fail to adapt) to and produce changes. The business model is seen as the carrier of the routines and skills that define the survival capacity of the firm. Here we follow the development of all firms created in the industry from its conception and onwards. This will give unique insights into how business models in individual firms co-evolve with the development of the industry. We will be able to study both firm-level processes as well as intra-firm processes.

Implications for Practitioners

Both policy makers, and existing and potential entrepreneurs will find the results valuable. Much of this research has been developed in close cooperation with different practitioners to fulfil their needs for knowledge about the entrepreneurial process.

From a policy maker's perspective this research is of great importance because it gives them detailed information about trends and development in the knowledge intensive sector. This is especially important for Europe, which has become a leader in the commercialization of research-intensive knowledge. For Swedish policy makers, this project is important because it allows them to better understand how investments in education and R&D are transformed into entrepreneurship. This is an important question as Sweden has among the highest investments in R&D per capita in the world but very little output (Andersson et al., 2002).

For managers and entrepreneurs, the analyses at the meso and micro level are perhaps the most interesting. Our project aims at understanding new venture development in contexts that are knowledge intensive and characterized by volatility. Our analyses will help to understand how new ventures are best established, and what factors affect their future growth and survival. We focus on central aspects such as human resource management (for example, founding team composition, hiring of new employees), resource acquisition, business model development, and performance. All these listed factors are known to have an important impact on the venture's ability to survive and prosper.

In conclusion, we hope that by engaging in this work we will attain results and new knowledge that will be of great value for academics and practitioners alike. We also hope that other scholars will join our effort to better understand the nature of the entrepreneurial process.

NOTES

1. The author represents the initiator of the research project, but this chapter has been developed in close cooperation with the other members of the research team. I would like to thank: Per Davidsson, Carin Holmquist, Scott Shane, Sören Sjölander and Johan Wiklund for their commitment and valuable input to the project.
2. As we argue further on in this work, the perception of what is and what is not an opportunity is dependent on the entrepreneur's personal experience and knowledge. The term 'opportunity' does not in any sense include or preclude that opportunities are objective and waiting to be identified. The process of opportunity identification and exploitation is socially constructed and rest in the organization of human and financial resources. Therefore the opportunity itself becomes endogenous to its process of exploitation, but its characteristics can be observed separately from the individuals exploiting it.
3. This is what is meant by separating between the conditions under which variations are produced and the conditions under which they are selectively retained. When we act, we act

both on purpose and unpurposefully (or rather have a priori unknown consequences), but both sorts of acts have consequences for the outcome in the process we are engaged in. Since we are social actors, what we do and how that is to be understood is not fully under our control and 'good' intentions can therefore be misunderstood by other social actors with whom we have to coordinate our life. Therefore, intentional behaviour is not enough to understand societal life.

REFERENCES

Aldrich, H. (1999), *Organizations Evolving*, London: Sage Publications.
Aldrich, H. and E.R. Auster (1986), 'Even dwarfs started small: liabilities of age and size and their straegic implications', *Research in Organizational Behavior*, **8**, 165–98.
Aldrich, H. and T. Baker (2001), 'Learning and legitimacy: enterpreneurial responses to constraints on the emergence of new populations and organizations', in C. Bird Schoonhoven and E. Romanelli (eds), *The Enterpreneurship Dynamics: Origins of Entrepreneurship and the Evolution of Industries*, Stanford, California: Stanford University Press, pp. 207–35.
Aldrich, H.A. and C.M. Fiol (1994), 'Fools rush in? The institutional context of industry creation', *Academy of Management Review*, **19**(4), 645–70.
Andersson, T., O. Asplund and M. Henrekson (2002), *Betydelsen av innovationssystem: utmaningar för samhället och för politiken*, Stockholm: Vinnova: Verket för innovationsystem.
Audretsch, D.B. (1991), 'New-firm survival and the technological regime', *The Review of Economics and Statistics*, **73**(3), 441–50.
Audretsch, D.B. and T. Mahmood (1995), 'New firm survival: new results using a hazard function', *The Review of Economics and Statistics*, **77**(1), 97–103.
Balgati, B.H. (2001), *Econometric Analysis of Panel Data* (2nd edn), Chichester: John Wiley & Sons Ltd.
Barney, J. (1991), 'Firm resources and sustained competitive advantage', *Journal of Management*, **17**, 99–119.
Baron, J.N., D. Burton and M.T. Hannan (1996), 'The road taken: origins and evolution of employment systems in emerging companies', *Industrial and Corporate Change*, **5**, 239–75.
Blossfeld, H.-P. and G. Rohwer (1995), *Techniques of Event History Analysis: New Approaches to Causal Analysis*, Mahwah, New Jersey: Lawrence Erlbaum Associates.
Brüderl, J., P. Preisendörfer and R. Ziegler (1992), 'Survival chances of newly founded business organizations', *American Sociological Review*, **57** (April), 227–42.
Carroll, G.R., and M.T. Hannan (2000), *The Demography of Corporations and Industries*, Princeton, New Jersey: Princeton University Press.
Carroll, G.R., and E. Mosakowski (1987), 'The career dynamics of self-employment', *Administrative Science Quarterly*, **32**, 570–89.
Carter, N.M., W.B. Gartner and P.D. Reynolds (1996), 'Exploring start-up event sequences', *Journal of Business Venturing*, **11**(3), 151–66.
Casson, M. (1982), *The Entrepreneur*, Totowa, NH: Barnes and Nobles Books.
Davidsson, P., L. Lindmark and C. Olofsson (1994), *Dynamiken i Svenkt Näringsliv* (The Dynamics of the Swedish Business Sector), Lund, Sweden: Studentlitteratur.

Davidsson, P., L. Lindmark and C. Olofsson (1996), *Näringslivsdynamik under 90-talet*, Stockholm: Nutek.

Delmar, F. and P. Davidsson (1999), 'Firm size expectations of nascent entrepreneurs', in P.D. Reynolds, W.D. Bygrave, S. Manigart, C.M. Mason, G. Dale Mayer, H.J. Sapienza and K.G. Shaver (eds), *Frontiers of Entrepreneurship Research 1999*, Babson College, MA: Arthur M. Blank Center for Entrepreneurship, pp. 90–104.

Delmar, F. and P. Davidsson (2000), 'Where do they come from? Prevalence and characteristics of nascent entrepreneurs', *Entrepreneurship & Regional Development*, **12**, 1–23.

Delmar, F. and J. Gunnarsson (2000), 'How do self-employed parents of nascent entrepreneurs contribute?' in P.D. Reynolds, E. Autio, C. Brush, W.D. Bygrave, S. Manigart, M.C. and H.J. Sapienza and K.G. Shaver (eds), *Frontiers of Entrepreneurship Research 2000*, Babson College, MA: Arthur M. Blank Center for Entrepreneurship, pp. 150–62.

Delmar, F. and S. Shane (2003), 'Does business planning facilitate the development of new ventures?', *Strategic Management Journal*, **24**, 1165–85.

Diggle, P.J., K.-Y. Liang and S.L. Zeger (1994), *Analysis of Longitudinal Data*, Oxford: Oxford University Press.

Eisenhardt, K.M. and J.A. Martin (2000), 'Dynamic capabilities: what are they?', *Strategic Management Journal*, **21**, 1105–21.

Eliasson, G. (2000), 'Industrial policy, competence blocs and the role of science in economic development', *Journal of Evolutionary Economics*, **10**, 217–41.

Evans, D.S. and L.S. Leighton (1989), 'Some empirical aspects of entrepreneurship', *American Economic Review*, **79**(3), 519–35.

Feldman, M.P. (2001), 'The entrepreneurial event revisited: firm formation in a regional context', *Industrial and Corporate Change*, **10**(4), 861–91.

Freeman, J. (1982), 'Organizational life cycles and natural selection processes', *Research in Organizational Behavior*, **4**, 1–32.

Gartner, W.B. (1985), 'A conceptual framework for describing the phenomenon of new venture creation', *Academy of Management Review*, **10**(4), 696–706.

Gimeno, J., T.B. Folta, A.C. Cooper and C.Y. Woo (1997), 'Survival of the fittest? Entrepreneurial human capital and the persistence of underperforming firms?' *Administrative Science Quarterly*, **42**, 750–83.

Granovetter, M. (1985), 'Economic action and social structure: the problem of embeddedness', *American Journal of Sociology*, **9**(3), 481–510.

Gratzer, K. (1996), 'Småföretagandets villkor: automatrestauranger under 1900-talet', Doctoral thesis, University of Stockholm, Stockholm.

Hannan, M.T. and M.T. Freeman (1984), 'Structural inertia and organizational change', *American Sociological Review*, **49**, 149–64.

Henrekson, M. and N. Rosenberg (2000), *Akademiskt entreprenörskap: Universitet och näringsliv i samverkan*, Stockholm: SNS Förlag.

Hogarth, R. (1987), *Judgment and Choice* (2nd edn), Chichester: John Wiley & Sons.

Jacobsson, S. and Å. Lindholm Dahlstrand (2001), 'Nya teknikbaserade företag och industriell tillväxt', in P. Davidsson, F. Delmar and J. Wiklund (eds), *Tillväxtföretagen i Sverige*, Stockholm: SNS, pp. 116–43.

Johansson, D. (2001), 'The Dynamics of Firm and Industry Growth: the Swedish Computing and Communications Industry', unpublished Doctoral thesis, Royal Institute of Technology, Stockholm.

Kihlstrom, R.E. and J.-J. Laffont (1979), 'A general equilibrium entrepreneurial theory of firm formation based on risk aversion', *The Journal of Political Economy*, **87**(4), 719–48.

Knight, F.H. (1921), *Risk, Uncertainty and Profit*, Boston: Houghton Mifflin Company.

Kogut, B. and U. Zander (1992), 'Knowledge of the firm, combinative capabilities, and the replication of technology', *Organization Science*, **3**(3), 383–97.

McClelland, D.C. (1961), *The Achieving Society*, Princeton, New Jersey: Van Nostrand.

McClelland, D.C. and D.G. Winter (1969), *Motivating Economic Achievement*, New York: Free Press.

Metcalfe, J.S. (1994), 'Evolutionary economics and technology policy', *The Economic Journal*, **104**(425), 931–44.

Miner, A.S., D.T. Eesley, M. Devaughn and T. Rura-Polley (2001), 'The magic beanstalk vision: commercializing university inventions and research', in C. Bird Schoonhoven and E. Romanelli (eds), *The Entrepreneurship Dynamic: Origins of Entrepreneurship and the Evolution of Industries*, Stanford, CA: Stanford University Press, pp. 109–496.

Mitchell, T.R. and L.R. James (2001), 'Building better theory: time and the specification of when things happen', *Academy of Management Journal*, **26**(4), 530–47.

Murmann, J.P. and M.L. Tushman (2001), 'From the technology cycle to the entrepreneurial dynamic', in C. Bird Schoonhoven and E. Romanelli (eds), *The Entrepreneurship Dynamic*, Stanford, California: Stanford University Press, pp. 178–203.

Nelson, R., and S. Winter (1982), *An Evolutionary Theory of Economic Change*, Cambridge, MA: Belknap Press.

Porter, M.E. (1990), *The Competitive Advantage of Nations*, New York: Free Press.

Romanelli, E. and C. Bird Schoonhoven (2001), 'The local origin of new firms', in C. Bird Schoonhoven and E. Romanelli (eds), *The Entrepreneurship Dynamics*, Stanford, California: Stanford University Press, pp. 40–67.

Schumpeter, J.A. (2001[1934]), 'Entrepreneurship as innovation,' in R. Swedberg (ed.), *Entrepreneurship: The Social Science View*, Oxford, England: Oxford University Press.

Shane, S. (2000), 'Prior knowledge and the discovery of entrepreneurial opportunities', *Organizational Science*, **11**(4), 448–69.

Shane, S. and S. Venkataraman (2000), 'The promise of entrepreneurship as a field of research', *Academy of Management Review*, **25**(1), 217–66.

Stinchcombe, A.L. (1965), 'Social structure and organizations', in J.G. March (ed.), *Handbook of Organizations*, Chicago: Rand MacNally, pp. 142–93.

Teece, D.J., G. Pisano and A. Shuen (1997), 'Dynamic capabilities and strategic management', *Strategic Management Journal*, **18**(7), 509–33.

Tushman, M.L. and P.C. Anderson (1986), 'Technological discontinuities and organizational environments', *Administrative Science Quarterly*, **31**, 439–65.

Venkataraman, S. (1997), 'The distinctive domain of entrepreneurship research: an editor's perspective', in J. Katz and R.H.S. Brockhaus (eds), *Advances in Entrepreneurship, Firm Emergence, and Growth* (Vol 3), Greenwich, CT: JAI Press, pp. 119–38.

Weick, K.E. (1979), *The Social Psychology of Organizing*, Reading, Massachusetts: Addison-Wesley.

Wooldridge, J.M. (2002), *Economic Analysis of Cross Section and Panel Data*, Cambridge, MA: The MIT Press.

Yamaguchi, K. (1991), *Event History Analysis* (Vol. 28), Newbury Park: Sage Publications.
Zucker, L.G., M.R. Darby and M.B. Brewer (1998), 'Intellectual human capital and the birth of the US biotechnology enterprises', *The American Economic Review*, **88**(1), 290–306.

4. New firm performance: conceptual perspectives[1]

Tatiana Iakovleva and Lars Kolvereid

INTRODUCTION

One of the central questions in the study of entrepreneurship is concerned with why some new ventures succeed and others do not (Cooper and Gascon, 1992). An understanding of why firms fail or succeed is crucial to the stability and health of the economy (Gartner et al., 1999; Storey et al., 1987). If we can achieve a better understanding of what influences a new venture success, this will have implications for prospective entrepreneurs, as well as their advisors and investors (Cooper and Gascon, 1992). That is why 'understanding how and why some entrepreneurs succeed remains a major challenge for the entrepreneurship research community' (Aldrich and Martinez, 2001, 41).

Performance of the organization is a 'yardstick by which founder measures success' (Chandler and Hanks, 1994a, 78). As we are interested in new and small businesses, we can apply the logic of Chandler and Hanks (1994a), arguing that in a new small venture the performance of the entrepreneur or entrepreneurial team can be measured by the performance of the organization. While the performance of new ventures is widely studied (see for example Capon et al. 1990; Cooper and Gascon, 1992; Lerner et al. 1997; Lussier and Pfeifer, 2000; Wiklund, 1998), there is no consensus regarding the basic constructs that affect a new venture's performance. This can be explained by the presence of different theoretical imperatives, which concern firm/entrepreneur performance from different viewpoints. It is then important to study those imperatives to find out underlying logic in explaining performance.

The second reason for difficulties in determining factors contributing to performance is the multidimensionality of the concept itself. The term 'performance' fails to meet the requirements of convergent and discriminant validity necessary to validate a unidimensional construct (Murphy et al., 1996). There is little consistency in what is meant under the term 'performance' in different studies. Three different measures are most often associated with the concept of performance (Delmar, 2000):

- Survival of the firm – what factors influence the long-term survival?
- Firm growth – what factors affect the expansion of the firm?
- Firm profitability – what factors influence the firm's ability to generate profits?

Relationship between a given independent variable and performance is likely to depend upon the particular performance measure used. It is quite possible for an independent variable to be positively related to one performance measure and negatively related to another (Murphy et al., 1996). It is advised that studies should include the multiple dimensions of performance and use multiple measures of those dimensions (Murphy et al., 1996). Being aware of this fact and taking into consideration the multiple dimension nature of performance, we use the term 'performance' as an aggregate dependent variable and include in our analysis theories that study all the outcomes mentioned above.

The purpose of the chapter is to provide a conceptual framework to explain performance differences among young businesses. In this chapter, a review of theoretical perspectives within entrepreneurship is presented in relation to the notion of performance. This review will seek to highlight how entrepreneurial/organizational performance is explained within population ecology, resource-based perspective, strategic adaptation and the behavioural/psychological perspectives. Based on a literature review a composite model for explaining the performance of new ventures is proposed.

THE POPULATION ECOLOGY PERSPECTIVE

The environment constitutes the initial conditions facing entrepreneurs in any economy (Aldrich, 1999). Environmental factors could be evaluated with the help of the population ecology imperative. The development of a biological system has been regarded as an intellectual model to describe the development of new firms (Hannan and Freeman, 1977). Employing a biological analogy, such a model suggests that those organizations that are well adapted to their environments will survive. Through a selection mechanism the external environmental conditions will determine the characteristics of populations of organizations (Nelson and Winter, 1982). According to Bygrave and Hofer (1991, 81) 'population ecology models predict the probability of birth and death within a population of businesses in a given industry niche'. Ecologists work at four levels of analysis: group, organization, population, community. Within the evolutionary perspective, Aldrich (1990) suggests that the founding of new organizations can be influenced by intra-population, inter-population and institutional factors. This perspective suits best for macro-level interpretation of organizational birth, death and survival (Westhead and Birley, 1994). This stream of research can be labelled deterministic, as it assumes that the external environment predefines those firms that will survive and those that will not.

Empirical Findings

The population ecology perspective presumes that factors including the differential structure of opportunity, location, sectoral activities and socio-political variables (that is availability of government assistance) are critical determinants of performance (Covin and Slevin, 1989). Environmental economic conditions, such as market structure, regional opportunities, investment climate, the availability of labour and other features are related to economic measures of venture profitability, revenues and number of employees (Tsai et al., 1991). In many studies the environmental influence of location or industry on performance is shown (Begley, 1995; Cooper et al., 1994). In these cases environment is analysed at aggregate level – thus, environment is assumed to have the same effect on all firms in a particular industry or location.

In other studies, the influence of the environment on the individual firm has been examined. Such an environment is labelled 'the task environment' (Scott, 1992). Characteristics like munificence, heterogeneity, hostility, dynamics, customer structure and competition have been frequently researched and found to influence performance of the firm (Bamford et al., 1997; Kolvereid, 1992; Tsai et al., 1991). It has been found that resource availability, including venture capital, technical labour force, loans, support services and a favourable entrepreneurial subculture also have a major influence on performance (Lerner et al., 1997).

Macro perspective is mostly about birth/death and survival. According to the population ecology theory, the inertia of firms is sometimes too great for them to be able to adapt to new environmental conditions. As a result, the environment has a direct effect on performance, regardless of the strategy selected by the firm (Aldrich, 1979). This perspective is not so helpful in determining performance differences between firms. The industry factor, however, should be taken into consideration if one studies performance differences within a multi-industry sample. The task environment was also proven to have an influence on firm performance. Based on these findings the following proposition is suggested:

> Proposition 1: Industry structure and characteristics of external environment influence new venture performance

Criticism

The predictive limitations of the population ecology perspective with regard to types of organizations established and their performance have been widely discussed (Aldrich, 1990; Bygrave and Hofer, 1991; Romanelly, 1989). The firm is treated as 'a black box', and the firm or the entrepreneur is not taken into account. That means that the role of the entrepreneur is ignored. Firm behaviour and founder personality may, however, also have an impact on firm survival. Issues related to adaptation, learning, search and resource-dependence are also ignored. The exit (discontinue operations) of the firm is seen as being forced by environmental conditions hostile to the firm. However, a study of Gimeno et al. (1997) showed that organizational survival is also determined by the threshold of performance. Thus organizational exit is considered as a choice of the entrepreneur.

Changes in the Ontology of Population Ecology

Today the population ecology perspective has significantly matured, developing from a simplistic and deterministic biological metaphor into a rich theoretical framework capable of incorporating other theoretical perspectives (Low and MacMillan, 1988). The firm is no longer treated as a 'black box'. A number of attempts have been made to apply evolutionary thinking to firm-level analysis (Burgelman and Rosenbloom, 1989; Covin and Slevin, 1989; Specht, 1993). The role of the owner/manager is taken into consideration. As Aldrich and Martinez (2001, 44) argue:

> today evolutionary approach studies the creation of new organizational structures (variation), the way in which entrepreneurs modify their organizations and use resources to survive in changing environment (adaptation), the circumstances under which such organizational arrangements lead to success and survival (selection), and the way in which successful arrangements tend to be imitated and perpetuated by other entrepreneurs (retention). . . . Organizational survival does not depend on strategic choices or environment forces alone, but rather on the degree of fit between entrepreneurial efforts and environmental forces.

This is in line with the contingency approach as well as with Porter's view on firms' competitive advantage.

The Strategic Adaptation Perspective

Strategic choice theorists maintain that managers have the freedom to choose between different strategic orientations under the same environmental contingencies, which determines firm performance (Child, 1972; Lawrence and Dyer 1983; Sandberg and Hofer 1987; Tsai et al., 1991). The heart of the contingency approach is the notion that managers or entrepreneurs consciously select strategies, and that their choices, at least in part, reflect their views of the optimal strategy in a given environment (Shane and Kolvereid,

1995). Thus strategy may depend on, but is not completely determined by, environment. In order for firms to achieve high performance, they need to adapt their strategies to their environment. With understanding of the complexity of factors that influence the success and survival of the firm, the contingency approach seeks to identify major contingent variables that significantly shape entrepreneurial outcomes (Low and MacMillan, 1988).

Porter's (1985, 1991) strategic model builds on traditional industrial organization theory. Within this framework the firm is viewed as a bundle of strategic activities aiming at adapting to industry environments by seeking an attractive position in the market arena (Spanos and Lioukas, 2001). For Porter, strategy is a consistent array of configuration activities (Porter, 1991). Porter's approach has an 'outside-in' view on market structure and its effect on performance. In Porter's framework, firm performance is first of all a function of industry, and firm effects occupy only a secondary role (Porter, 1991). Resources follow strategic choices, either built within the firm or acquired from the environment. Thus, the environment determines which strategy to follow, and strategic choice in turn determines the resources needed. This means that resources are not valuable as they are attached to strategic activities (Porter, 1980).

Strategy choice then is a 'product of (and response to) a sophisticated understanding of industry structure' (Spanos and Lioukas, 2001, 909). Numerous studies have shown that the choice of strategy affects especially small new venture performance (Brush and Chaganti, 1997; Covin et al., 1990; Covin and Slevin, 1989; Miller and Tolouse, 1988; Spanos and Lioukas, 2001). Thus, both the contingency approach and Porter's competitive strategy approach view strategy as an important element in explaining firm performance.

Based on the discussion of strategic theories the following proposition is made:

Proposition 2. The environment influences the choice of the firm's strategy, which in turn influences new venture performance

THE RESOURCE-BASED PERSPECTIVE

According to the resource-based view (RBV) a firm may be perceived as an aggregation of resources, which are translated by management into strengths and weaknesses of the firm (Lerner and Almor, 2002). Barney described resources as 'all assets, capabilities, organizational processes, firm attributes, information, knowledge, etc. controlled by a firm that enable the firm to conceive of and implement strategies that improve its efficiency and effectiveness' (Barney, 1991,

101). Wernerfelt used the term 'resource' to refer to 'anything, which could be thought of as a strength or weakness of a given firm' (Wernerfelt, 1984, 172).

The resource-based view (RBV) suggests that differences in performance among firms may be best explained through differences in firm resources and their accumulation and usage (efficiency), rather than through differences in industry structure (Andrews, 1980; Barney, 1991; Grant, 1991; Penrose, 1959; Peteraf, 1993). In explaining these differences, resource-based theorists tend to focus on resources that are long-lived and difficult to imitate (Conner, 1991). To sustain long-run competitive advantage, resources should meet four criteria: (1) they must be valuable, in the sense that they exploit opportunities and/or neutralize threats in a firm's environment, (2) they must be rare among the firm's current and potential competitors, (3) they must be imperfectly imitable, and (4) there can not be strategically equivalent substitutes for these resources that are valuable but neither rare nor imperfectly imitable (Barney, 1991).

Resources alone are not sufficient to achieve competitive advantage. In the resource-based perspective managers have to select an appropriate strategy in order to make the most effective use of the firm's resources and capabilities (Grant, 1991). The extent to which core resources and capabilities are identified and exploited in appropriate ways by the firm's strategy will influence its performance. The RBV thus uses an 'inside-out' view on a firm's resources and their effect on performance. Here strategy selection is based on the evaluation of available resources. Because of constant environmental changes, managers do have choices to make about strategic alternatives, but their options might be limited within the established framework of available resources (Spanos and Lioukas, 2001).

Empirical Findings

Numerous studies have shown that different kinds of resources contribute to firm performance. Peteraf (1993) claims a major contribution of the RBV is to explain long-lived differences in firm profitability, which cannot be attributed to differences in industry conditions. Empirical studies show the existence of a relationship between organizational resources and performance, including resources such as competencies and capabilities of the firm (Chandler and Hanks, 1994b; Chasten and Mangles, 1997; Heeley, 1997), availability of capital (Bamford et al., 1997; Cooper et al., 1994), organizational or individual networks (Donckels and Lambrecht, 1994; Hansen, 1995).

Criticism

Despite considerable progress in a relatively short amount of time, the resource-based view suffers from a number of weaknesses. When faced with a real firm, it is often difficult to identify those resources, alone or in combination with others, which account for a firm's success (Foss et al., 1995). The RBV inherited some assumptions of the neoclassical theory – competition is assumed to be Bertrand, factor markets are efficient in a semi-strong sense and the supply side on factor markets appropriate all value when information is symmetric, strategies are 'strategic substitutes'; only 'efficiency-based' strategies are taken into consideration (Foss, 1998). These assumptions are not generally true. Also, the RBV has the problem of isolated resources – a tendency to analyse resources in isolation and thus missing system effects; the problem of resource application – implicitly resources are always taken to be in their best uses; the problem of the environment – primitive simplistic treatment of the environment; the problem of uniqueness – strong emphasis on unique strategies and resources while strategies for example can be 'strategic complements'; the problem of resource creation – the RBV focuses on existing resources and does not take into consideration how new resources are created. A number of other problems are also mentioned in Foss (1998): the problem of value sharing, the problem of tautology, the problem of hard-to-observe variables, and the problem of managerial implications.

Changes in the Ontology

Although resources are crucial to the performance of a venture, resources alone are not sufficient to achieve sustainable competitive advantage (Ucbasaran et al., 2001). In the early version of the RBV there was no distinction between resources and capabilities. This reflected in an absence of distinction between the static and dynamic view of the firm. According to Amit and Schoemaker (1993), however, resources are assets that are either owned or controlled by a firm, whereas capabilities refer to the firm's ability to exploit and combine resources through organizational routines in order to accomplish its targets. Unlike most of the resources, capabilities are not tradable and they are unique, which makes them the source of the competitive advantage (Baden-Fuller, 1995). As Teece et al. (1994) wrote, 'a firm's distinctive competence needs to be understood as a reflection of distinctive organisational capabilities to coordinate and learn. By "organisational capabilities" we mean the capabilities of an enterprise to organize, manage, coordinate or govern sets of activities'. Teece et al. (1997) developed the concept of 'dynamic capabilities', which reflects the dynamic view of the firm and its activities. The process of acquiring, developing, reconfiguring and maintaining internal and external resources over time to form different bundles of resources and capabilities, addressing rapidly changing environments (or to change environments) is called 'dynamic capabilities' (Teece et al., 1997).

The Resource-based View in Entrepreneurship Studies

Entrepreneurship studies using the resource-based approach view the entrepreneur as a firm resource (Penrose, 1959; Dollinger, 1999). Dollinger argues that the resource-based approach is the most appropriate one in order to understand small business creation and management, because it best describes how business owners themselves build their businesses from the resources and capabilities they currently possess or can acquire. He further claims entrepreneurs can create sustainable competitive advantage for their ventures when they possess, or can acquire and control resources that are rare, valuable, hard to duplicate and non-substitutable.

Often human capital characteristics of the entrepreneur or of the members of the founding team provide personal abilities that facilitate small firm growth and performance (Begley, 1995; Bird, 1993; Brush and Chaganti, 1997; Chandler and Jansen, 1992; Davidsson, 1989; Miller and Toulouse, 1988). General human capital characteristics, which include founder's age or level of education, years of work experience and management experience, do affect new venture performance (Gimeno et al., 1997; Cooper et al., 1994). However, the effects those general human capital characteristics have on enterprise performance also 'depend on its relative payoff in the venture versus alternative employment' (Gimeno, 1997, 756). Sandberg and Hofer (1987) found only weak evidence of the impact of biographical characteristics of an entrepreneur on performance, while they found that there is an interactive effect of industry structure, strategy and entrepreneur which is important.

Specific human capital is valuable only if the context of those characteristics are similar to the new venture context. Business similarity was shown to have a positive effect on performance (Cooper et al., 1994). The influence of previous entrepreneurial experience on small businesses performance has been tested in several studies (Cooper and Gimeno-Gascon, 1992; Neiswander and Drollinger, 1986). Ronstadt (1988) found that longer, more successful entrepreneurial careers are a function of earlier career starts and involvement in multiple ventures. According to Box et al. (1993), prior start-ups and years of entrepreneurial experience are significantly correlated with performance. Gaglio (1997) argues that previous entrepreneurial experience may provide a framework or mental schema for processing information. Findings proving the relationship between founder's experience and venture success, however, are often inconsistent (Reuber and Fischer, 1994). The reason for this is the absence of the conceptual basis for the way in which experience is studied. Reuber and Fischer (1999) proposed a model, where previous stock or stream of experience together with the expertise and dominant logic/cognition influence decisions and actions taken by entrepreneurs, which in turn influence performance. If the purpose is to investigate newly founded enterprises, it is more appropriate to speak about stock of experience at the founder's level, rather than about the stream of experience at the venture level. The stock of experience of an entrepreneur (or of a team of founders) influences development of the expertise and skills. Through expertise and dominant logic decisions are made and actions taken that influence venture performance. The duration of experience, the diversity of experience and the time factor should also be taken into consideration (Reuber and Fischer, 1999).

Often competencies of the founder seem to be crucial to venture performance. Those competencies in turn depend upon both general and specific human capital characteristics. The importance of business skills, particularly strength in idea generation and dealing with people, was positively related to performance in Brush and Hisrich's (1991) longitudinal study. In the study by Lerner et al. (1997), it was found that an index of business skills (obtaining financing, budgeting, labour management, and planning ahead) was highly correlated with revenues and performance. Chandler and Hanks (1994a) found the competence of entrepreneurs in identifying business opportunities (entrepreneurial competence) and gathering resources (managerial competence) to be directly related to performance. In addition, they found that the interaction between those competencies and the environment had a moderating effect on the growth and sales volume of emerging manufacturing firms.

Based on the overview of the resource-based theory and its implications for entrepreneurial studies, the following proposition are suggested:

Proposition 3: Firm's internal resources influence new venture performance

Proposition 4: Firm's internal resources and capabilities influence strategic choices, which in turn influence the new venture performance

Proposition 5: Founder's background influences new venture performance

Proposition 6: Founder's background and competencies influence the choice of firm strategy through cognition process, which in turn influence new venture performance

THE BEHAVIOURAL/PSYCHOLOGICAL PERSPECTIVE

The personality of the entrepreneur is often perceived by practitioners as one of the most fascinating topics in the field of entrepreneurship (Delmar, 2000). It is generally believed that a successful entrepreneur is a result of the special set of personal abilities and characteristics, rather than other factors. As a natural consequence of this belief, the psychological perspective in entrepreneurship research has, until recently, concentrated on discovering stable individual characteristics such as personality traits. Personality is often treated as a set of characteristics or traits that are stable across situation and time. Some certain characteristics assumed to be related to entrepreneurs are: risk-taking propensity (Brockhaus, 1980), need for achievement (McClelland, 1961), locus of control (Brockhaus, 1982), desire for autonomy (Collins and Moore, 1964).

Empirical Findings

Need for achievement has been confirmed to have a relationship with entrepreneurship – creation of new enterprise or performance (Begley and Boyd; 1987, Delmar 1996). According to the motivation theory, people with a high need for achievement value particular work-task situations and perform well in these. Recently Miner developed McClelland's achievement motivational theory by developing five motive patterns instead of a single achievement motive. Attitudes towards self-achievement, avoiding risks, seeking feedback, personal innovation, and orientation to the future are important for entrepreneurs. Results show that Miner's scales have consistent validity in that scores correlated significantly with entrepreneurial performance, particularly growth (Miner et al., 1992). Hisrich and Brush, (1984) found that individual motivations and owner/founder goals are related to performance in women-owned businesses. Motivation also showed a strong relationship to performance in the study by Lerner et al. (1997).

The risk-taking propensity was not proven to be significantly correlated with entrepreneurship (Brockhaus, 1980). It was found that knowledge and situational characteristics are more important determinants of risk-taking than personality (Delmar, 2000). Concerning locus of control, empirical studies have shown a low to moderate positive correlation between internal control and entrepreneurs, and there is a weak tendency that a high internal orientation is associated with better performance (Brockhaus, 1982; Miller and Toulouse, 1988). In some studies no significant correlations were reported between entrepreneurs and managers in respect to locus of control (Sexton and Bowman, 1985). Entrepreneurs have proven to have a high need of autonomy (Sexton and Bowman, 1985). However, it is difficult to explain causality with venture creation or performance (Delmar, 2000). That is, do individuals with a high desire for autonomy start a venture because they want autonomy, or do they want autonomy because they do not want others to take control of what they have created?

Criticism

Studies focusing on entrepreneurs' personalities, backgrounds, early experience and traits have been widely criticized and have generally produced disappointing findings (Gartner, 1990). As proven, personality traits cannot explain more than a minor share of entrepreneurial behaviour and differences in business performance (Delmar, 2000). First researchers have not reached a consensus on the relevance of the individual characteristics, their importance and how they vary in different situations. The second problem is that the variables characterizing the entrepreneur and the environment are static. While the environment changes constantly, traits or characteristics alone have very little ability to explain behaviour. Psychological characteristics could have been developed over time. Thus, external validity of the psychological trait approach is low (Delmar, 2000). Third, methods and theory itself are quite obsolete in relation to modern psychological research. The concept of personality is multidimensional – at least five measures of interpersonal evaluation should be included (Hogan et al., 1996). A psychology traits perspective fails to acknowledge the heterogeneous nature of entrepreneurs (Delmar, 2000). Another problem is that traits and needs are distal factors that may explain only general behaviours, while the actual behaviour is better explained by proximal factors (task characteristics). A proximal explanation of behaviour looks at factors defining the situation in which individuals find themselves when choosing certain actions. Another argument against trait theories is that they are not sophisticated enough to account for the complexity of entrepreneurial behaviour (Delmar, 2002).

Changes in the Ontology

As a result of these difficulties, there was a shift from studying the personality of the entrepreneur toward the behavioural aspects of entrepreneurs (Chell et al., 1991; Gartner et al., 1992; Lumpkin and Dess, 1996). The cognitive decision making processes among entrepreneurs have also been explored (Baron, 1998; Manimala, 1992; Palich and Bagby, 1995). Theories trying to explain behaviour by individuals perceiving and interpreting the information around them are cognitive theories. In other words, the field has developed from examining personality traits in isolation to examining the integration between the entrepreneur's perception, intention and ability and the characteristics of the situation (Delmar, 2000). They allow psychological characteristics of entrepreneur's, situational variables and personal background (age, sex, and so on) to be taken into consideration. Two groups of models can be defined: 'attitude based' models and 'motivation based' models.

Attitude models explain how attitudes on entrepreneurship shape people's behaviour. Attitudes are considered to be important determinants of behaviour if certain conditions are met (Bagozzi and Warshaw, 1992). The theory of planned behaviour explains behaviour when the actions of the person are dependent on something or someone else outside one's control (Ajzen, 1991).

The theory postulates that the tendency to engage in a particular behaviour is determined by the individual intention to do so. Intentions in turn are dependent on attitudes and subjective norms. From empirical studies of business start-ups (Davidsson, 1989; Kolvereid, 1996) or growth (Kolvereid and Bullvåg, 1996; Wiklund, 1998) it follows that attitudes or subjective norms alone have little ability to predict intentions. The strongest predictor is perceived behavioural control. Perceived behavioural control is ease or difficulty of performing the behaviour. A person will try to start a business if she/he believes that she/he can do it in terms of possessing the ability and knowledge required to carry it out (Delmar, 2000). If the perceived behavioural control is in accordance with actual behavioural control, they can help to predict the likelihood that intentions will be realized as behaviour (Ajzen, 1991).

The second group is cognitive motivation models. These models offer the ability to explain both highly complex behaviour and differences in choices and performance. The concept of self-efficacy is concerned with 'people's beliefs about their capabilities to produce performance that influence events affecting their lives' (Bandura, 1995, 434). Perceived self-efficacy has been proposed as a central concept in entrepreneurship (Boyd and Vozikis, 1994) because it has been proven to be associated with initiating and persisting in achievement-related behaviours (Wood and Bandura, 1989). Perceived self-efficacy proved to affect the strategies and performance of entrepreneurs. It was found that entrepreneurs with higher perceived self-efficacy achieve higher performance. Performance was measured as profitability, customer satisfaction and ability to survive (Westerberg, 1998).

Self-efficacy is related to perceived behavioural control, but the concept focuses more on the actual functioning of perceived capabilities, that is, how belief in one's capabilities to mobilize the motivation, cognitive resources and courses of action needed to control events in one's life (such as starting and managing the business) affects one's behaviour and subsequent performance (Delmar, 2000). That why it suits best of all the purpose of explaining the influence of motivation toward firm performance. Self-efficacy can be enhanced by some human capital variable, such as previous work experience, entrepreneurial experience and role models (Boyd and Vozikis, 1994).

Within psychological/behavioural theories cognitive models offer the most sophisticated theoretical frame of reference, which incorporates the complexity of entrepreneurial behaviour, and enables the actual test of the model (Delmar, 2000). Those models have a relatively high explanatory power and they are dynamic in contrast to static models of psychological traits. Probably, motivation is the most important psychological characteristic, which helps us understand why individuals act as they do. It is particularly important to understand reasons for firm growth intention (Wiklund, 1998). Motivation, however, does not affect performance unless action is taken. That is why strategy serves as a mediator between psychological characteristics and performance. Based on the overview of the behavioural/psychological perspective, the following propositions are made:

> Proposition 7: Background characteristics of the entrepreneur influence personal self-efficacy

> Proposition 8: Personal motivations, attitudes and perceived self-efficacy influence new venture performance

> Proposition 9: Personal motivations, attitudes and perceived self-efficacy influence the choice of strategy which in turn influence new venture performance

THE RESEARCH MODEL

We have reviewed four theoretical imperatives in an attempt to find factors influencing performance of the firm/entrepreneur/entrepreneur team. There are unavoidable trade-offs in research and there is no single best approach (Davidsson and Wiklund, 2001). The core of the theories are summarized in Table 4.1.

When analysing the causal logic of each perspective, it is obvious that each of the factors is important and contributes to our understanding of performance. In order to fully explain performance, an integration of these perspectives is needed. There have been prior attempts to combine constructs such as environment, strategy, organizational forces and individual characteristics to explain performance (Chandler and Hanks, 1994a; Cooper et al., 1994; Covin and Slevin, 1989; Hofer and Sandberg, 1987; Spanos and Lioukas, 2001; Tsai et al., 1991; Wiklund, 1998). The findings imply that often a combination of factors provides a better explanation than each factor taken alone. However, often the models proposed lack theoretical ground and also do not take into consideration all variables that seem to contribute to the explanation of performance simultaneously. There is a need to develop a more advanced model that can incorporate the latest changes in the ontology of the main streams of research and that can be empirically tested. There have been multiple calls for a combination of the theoretical constructs and different levels of analysis in order to better explain particular phenomena (Low and MacMillan, 1988; Low, 2001; Aldrich and Martinez, 2001; Gartner, 2001). Following their advice we would like to propose a model that we hope can help the concept of performance of newly founded ventures to be understood (see Figure 4.1). The propositions made earlier are marked with the 'P' symbols. This model uses theoretical constructs on a high level of abstraction. That means that the task of operationalization of the model will depend upon the concrete research

Table 4.1   Causal logic in explaining performance of four theoretical perspectives

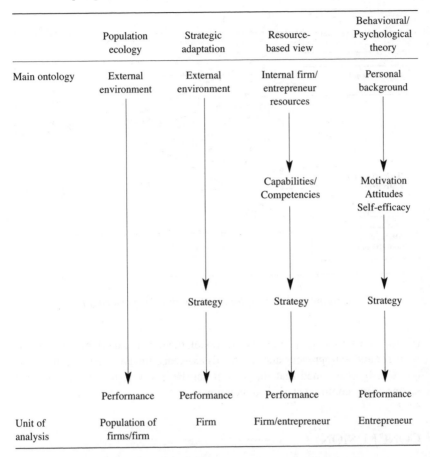

	Population ecology	Strategic adaptation	Resource-based view	Behavioural/ Psychological theory
Main ontology	External environment	External environment	Internal firm/ entrepreneur resources	Personal background
			↓	↓
			Capabilities/ Competencies	Motivation Attitudes Self-efficacy
	↓	↓	↓	↓
		Strategy	Strategy	Strategy
	↓	↓	↓	↓
	Performance	Performance	Performance	Performance
Unit of analysis	Population of firms/firm	Firm	Firm/entrepreneur	Entrepreneur

problem in question. We argue that performance of the new small venture is dependent upon: (1) The environment; (2) The ability of the owner/manager to adopt to this environment (strategy); (3) The internal resources of the firm/entrepreneur characteristics and their utilization through the capabilities/competencies transformed into strategies; (4) The motivation, attitude, self-efficacy of the entrepreneur transformed by the decisions taken by an individual (strategy) through the cognition process.

A model is by definition a simplification of a complex reality and there is always a trade-off between including certain factors and relationships in the model and disregarding them. Simplicity and complexity need to be balanced

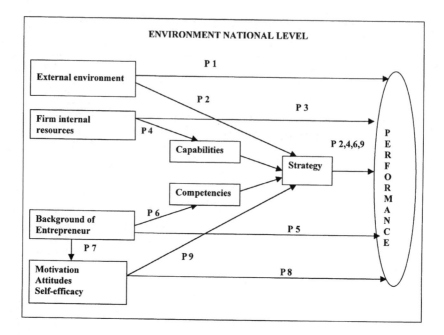

Figure 4.1   A framework for explaining new venture performance

(Ruist, 1990). In order to simplify the model, the reciprocal effects of the environment and entrepreneur and the firm's existence toward the environment is omitted. It is assumed that this model can be easily tested in an empirical setting using common statistical techniques.

CONCLUSION

The purpose of this chapter was to highlight issues associated with new venture performance variations. Understanding what leads ventures to superior performance is viewed as an important task, which has theoretical as well as practical implications. Today a large number of studies exist investigating factors leading to success. However, the results of these studies are often inconsistent. This is due to the several reasons. The most important one is probably the absence of the theoretically grounded models, which can help us to explain findings in a systematic way. It is well accepted that entrepreneurship is a multidisciplinary field. The result of this is that studies published on this broad label stem from different theoretical imperatives and often even disciplines. This variety is often seen as a weakness of entrepreneurship as a science. It is argued that a paradigm of entrepreneurship does not exist because the object of research and the main assumptions of the theories within the field are so different (Gartner, 2001).

However, this diversity results in an opportunity to broaden research horizons. From the overview of the four theoretical imperatives, which are discussed in this study, it is evident that each of them can explain a part of the complex reality. Each of those theories explains how some factors, but not others, contribute to firm/entrepreneur performance. While integrating well defined theoretical constructs from those theories, we can benefit in achieving a more accurate picture of the reality. This results in the development of a model that can explain more than each of the four theories can separately. Furthermore, an attempt is made to develop a model that utilizes variables from multiple levels of analysis, something which has been sought after by other authors (Low and MacMillan, 1988). It is expected that the results from the empirical testing of the suggested model will have theoretical as well as practical implications.

NOTE

1. Helpful comments on earlier drafts of this manuscript from Alain Fayolle and Paul Westhead are greatly acknowledged.

REFERENCES

Ajzen, I. (1991), 'The theory of planned behaviour', *Organisational Behaviour and Human Decision Processes*, **50**, 179–211.
Aldrich, H.E. (1979), *Organizations and Environments*, Englewood Cliffs, NJ: Prentice-Hall.
Aldrich, H. (1990), 'Using an ecological perspective to study organizational founding rates', *Entrepreneurship Theory and Practice*, **14**(3), 7–24.
Aldrich, H. (1999), *Organizations Evolving*, London: Sage Publication Ltd.
Aldrich, H.E. and M.A. Martinez (2001), 'Many are called, but few are chosen: an evolutionary perspective for the study of entrepreneurship', *Entrepreneurship Theory and Practice*, **25**(4), 41–56.
Amit, R. and P.J.H. Schoemaker (1993), 'Strategic assets and organisational rent', *Strategic Management Journal*, **14**(1), 33–46.
Andrews, K. (1980), *The Concept of Corporate Strategy*, Homewood, Ill: Richard D. Irwin.
Baden-Fuller, C. (1995), 'Strategic innovation, corporate entrepreneurship and matching outside-in to inside-out approaches to strategy research', *British Journal of Management*, **6** (Special Issue), 1–14.
Bagozzi, R. and P.R. Warshaw, (1992), 'An examination of the etiology of the attitude–behaviour relation for goal-directed behaviours', *Multivariate Behavioural Research*, **27**(4), 601–34.

Bamford, C.E., T.J. Dean and P.P. McDougall (1997), 'Initial strategies and new venture growth: an examination of the effectiveness of broad vs. narrow breadth strategies', in D. Reynolds, W.D. Bygrave, N.M. Carter, P. Davidsson, W.B. Gartner, C.M. Mason and P. McDougall (eds), *Frontiers of Entrepreneurial Research*, Wellesley, MA: Babson College, pp. 375–89.

Bandura, A. (ed.) (1995), *Self-efficacy in Changing Societies*, New York: Cambridge University Press.

Bandura, A. (1997), *Self-efficacy: The Exercise of Control*, New York: Freeman Press.

Barney, J. (1991), 'Firm resources and sustained competitive advantage', *Journal of Management*, **17**, 99–120.

Baron, R.A. (1998), 'Cognitive mechanisms in entrepreneurship: why and when entrepreneurs think differently than other people', *Journal of Business Venturing*, **13**(4), 101–14.

Begley, T.M. (1995), 'Using founder status, age of firm, and company growth rate as the basis for distinguishing entrepreneurs from managers of small business', *Journal of Business Venturing*, **10**, 249–63.

Begley, T. and D. Boyd, (1987), 'Psychological characteristics associated with performance in entrepreneurial firms and smaller businesses', *Journal of Business Venturing*, **2**, 79–93.

Bird, B. (1993), 'Demographic approaches to entrepreneurship: the role of experience and background', in J.A. Katz and R.H. Brockhause (eds), *Advances in Entrepreneurship, Firm Emergence and Growth*, (Vol. 1). Greenwich: JAI Press Inc, pp. 11–48.

Box, T.M., M.A. White and S.H. Barr, (1993), 'A contingency model of new manufacturing firm performance', *Entrepreneurship Theory and Practice*, **18**(2), 31–45.

Boyd, N. and G. Vozikis, (1994), 'The influence of self-efficacy on the development of entrepreneurial intentions and actions', *Entrepreneurship Theory and Practice*, **18**(4), 63–77.

Brockhaus, R. (1980), 'Risk taking propensity of entrepreneurs', *Academy of Management Journal*, **23**(3), 509–20.

Brockhaus, R. (1982), 'The psychology of the entrepreneur', in C.A. Kent, D.L. Sexton and K.H. Vesper (eds), *Encyclopedia of Entrepreneurship*, Englewood Cliffs, NJ: Prentice Hall.

Brush, C.G. and R. Chaganti, (1997), *Resources in New and Small Ventures: Influence on Performance Outcomes*, paper presented at the 1997 Babson Entrepreneurship Research Conference, Wellesley, MA.

Brush, C.G. and R.D. Hisrich, (1991), 'Antecedent influences on women-owned businesses', *Journal of Managerial Psychology*, **6**(2), 9–17

Bull, I. and G. Willard, (1993), 'Towards a theory of entrepreneurship', *Journal of Business Venturing*, **8**, 183–95.

Burgelman, J. and R. Rosenbloom, (1989), 'Technology strategy: an evolutionary process perspective', in R.S. Rosenbloom and R.A. Burgelman (eds), *Research on Technological Innovation, Management and Policy*, Vol. 4, pp. 1–23.

Bygrave, W.D. and C.W. Hofer, (1991), 'Theorizing about entrepreneurship', *Entrepreneurship Theory and Practice*, **16**(2), 13–22.

Capon, N., J.U. Farly and S. Hoeng, (1990), 'Determinants of financial performance: a meta-analysis', *Management Science*, October, 1143–59.

Chandler, G.N. and S.H. Hanks, (1994a), 'Founder competence, the environment, and venture performance', *Entrepreneurship Theory and Practice*, **18**(3), 223–37.

Chandler, G.N. and S.H. Hanks, (1994b), 'Market attractiveness, resource-based capabilities, venture strategies and venture performance', *Journal of Small Business Management*, **12**(1), 27–35.

Chandler, G. and E. Jansen, (1992), 'Founder's self assessed competence and venture performance', *Journal of Business Venturing*, **7**(3), 223–36.

Chaston, I. and T. Mangles, (1997), 'Core capabilities as predictors of growth potential in small manufacturing firms', *Journal of Small Business Management*, **35**(1), 47–57.

Chell, E., J.M. Haworth and S.A. Brearly, (1991), *The Entrepreneurial Personality: Concepts, Cases and Categories*, London: Routledge.

Child, J. (1972), 'Organizational structure, environment and performance: the role of strategic choice', *Sociology*, **6**, 2–22.

Cole, A. (1986), 'Meso-economics: A contribution from entrepreneurial history', *Explorations in Entrepreneurial History*, **6**(1), 3–33.

Collins, O. and D. Moore, (1964), *The Enterprising Man*, East Lansing, MI: Michigan State University.

Conner, K. (1991), 'A historical comparison of resource-based theory and five schools of thought within industrial organization economics: do we have a new theory of the firm?', *Journal of Management*, **17**, 121–54.

Cooper, A. and F. Gimeno-Gascon, (1992), 'Entrepreneurs, processes of founding, and new-firm performance', in D. Sexton and J. Kasarda (eds), *The State of the Art of Entrepreneurship*, Boston: PWS-Kent Publishing Company, pp. 301–40.

Cooper, A., F.J. Gascon and C. Woo, (1994), 'Initial human and financial capital as predictors of new venture performance', *Journal of Business Venturing*, **9**, 371–95.

Covin, J. and D. Slevin, (1989), 'Strategic management of small firms in hostile and benign environments', *Strategic Management Journal*, **10**(1), 75–87.

Covin, J., D. Slevin and T. Covin, (1990), 'Content and performance of growth-seeking small firms in high- and low-technology industries', *Journal of Business Venturing*, **5**, 391–412.

Davidsson, P. (1989), *Continued Entrepreneurship and Small Firm Growth*, Stockholm: Stockholm School of Economics.

Davidsson, P. and J. Wiklund, (2001), 'Levels of analysis in entrepreneurship research: current research practice and suggestions for the future', *Entrepreneurship Theory and Practice*, **25**(4), 81–99.

Delmar, F. (1996), *Entrepreneurial Behaviour and Business Performance*, Stockholm: Stockholm School of Economics.

Delmar, F. (2000), 'The psychology of the entrepreneur', in S. Carter and D. Jones-Evans (eds), *Enterprise and Small Business: Principles, Practice and Policy*, Harlow: Financial Times.

Dess, G.G. and D.W. Beard, (1984), 'Dimensions of organisational task environments', *Administrative Science Quarterly*, **29**, 52–73.

Dollinger, M.J. (1999), *Entrepreneurship Strategies and Resources*, Upper Saddle River, N.J.: Prentice Hall.

Donckels, R. and J. Lambrecht, (1994), 'Networks and small business growth: an explanatory model', *Small Business Economics*, **7**, 273–89.

Foss, N. (1998), 'The resource-based perspective: an assessment and diagnosis of problems', *Scandinavian Journal of Management*, **14**, 133–49.

Foss, N. and B. Erikson, (1995), 'Competitive advantage and industry capabilities', in C. Montgomery (ed.), *Resources in an Evolutionary Perspective: Synthesis of*

Evolutionary and Resource-based Approaches to a Strategy, Boston/Dordrecht, London: Kluwer Academic Publishers, pp. 43–70.

Foss, N., C. Knudsen and C. Montgomery, (1995), 'An exploratory of common ground: integrating evolutionary and strategic theories of the firm', in C. Montgomery (ed.), *Resources in an Evolutionary Perspective: Synthesis of Evolutionary and Resource-based Approaches to a Strategy*, Boston/Dordrecht, London: Kluwer Academic Publishers, pp. 1–18.

Gaglio, C. M. (1997), 'Opportunity identification: review, critique and suggested research directions', in J. A. Katz (ed.), *Advances in Entrepreneurship, Firm Emergence and Growth*, vol. 3, Greenwich, CT: JAJ Press, pp. 139–202.

Gartner, W. B. (1990), 'What are we talking about when we talk about entrepreneurship?', *Journal of Business Venturing*, **5**(1), 15–28.

Gartner, W. B. (2001), 'Is there an elephant in entrepreneurship? Blind assumptions in theory development', *Entrepreneurship Theory and Practice*, **25**(4): 21–39.

Gartner, W., B. Bird and J. Starr, (1992), 'Acting as if: differentiating entrepreneurial from organizational behaviour', *Entrepreneurship Theory and Practice*, **16**(3), 13–31.

Gartner, W., J.A. Starr and S. Bhat, (1999), 'Predicting new venture survival: an analysis of "anatomy of start up". Cases from inc. Magazine', *Journal of Business Venturing*, **14**(2), 215–32.

Gimeno, J., T.B. Folta, A. Cooper and C.Y. Woo (1997), 'Survival of the fittest? Entrepreneurial human capital and the persistence of underperforming firms', *Administrative Science Quarterly*, **42**, 750–83.

Gist, M. (1987), 'Self-efficacy: implications for organizational behaviour and human resource management', *Academy of Management Review*, **12**(3), 472–85.

Grant, R.M. (1991), 'The resource based theory of competitive advantage: implications for strategy formulation', *California Management Review*, **33**(3), 114–35.

Hannan, M. and J. Freeman, (1977), 'The population ecology of organizations', *American Journal of Sociology*, **82**, 929–64.

Hansen, E.L. (1995), 'Entrepreneurial networks and new organisation growth', *Entrepreneurship Theory and Practice*, **19** (Summer), 7–19.

Heeley, M.B. (1997), 'Appropriating rents from external knowledge: the impact of absorptive capacity on firm sales growth and research productivity', in D. Reynolds, W.D. Bygrave and N.M. McDougall (eds), *Frontiers of Entrepreneurship Research*, Wellesley, MA: Babson College, pp. 390–404.

Herron, L., H.J. Sapienza and D. Smith-Cook, (1991), 'Entrepreneurship theory from the interdisciplinary perspective: volume 1', *Entrepreneurship Theory and Practice*, **16**(2), 7–12.

Hisrich, R. and C.G. Brush, (1984), 'The women entrepreneur: management skills and business problems', *Journal of Small Business Management*, **22**, 31–7.

Hofer, C.W. (1975), 'Toward a contingency theory of business strategy', *Academy of Management Journal*, **18**, 784–810.

Hofer, C.W. and W.R. Sandberg, (1987), 'Improving new venture performance: some guidelines for success', *American Journal of Small Business*, **3**, 11–21.

Hofer, C.W. and D. Schendel, (1978), *Strategy Formulation: Analytic Concepts*, St. Paul, MN: West.

Hogan, R., J. Hogan and B.W. Roberts, (1996), 'Personality measurements and employment decisions', *The American Psychologist*, **51**(5), 469–73.

Kolvereid, L. (1992), 'Growth aspirations among Norwegian entrepreneurs', *Journal of Business Venturing*, **12**, 213–25.

Kolvereid, L. (1996), 'Predictions of employment status choice intentions', *Entrepreneurship Theory and Practice*, **20**(3), 47–57.

Kolvereid, L. and Bullvåg, E. (1996), 'Growth intentions and actual growth: the impact of entrepreneurial choice', *Journal of Enterprising Culture*, **4**(1), 1–17.

Lawrence, P. and D. Dyer, (1983), *Renewing American Industry*, New York: Free Press.

Lerner, M. and T. Almor, (2002), 'Relationships among strategic capabilities and the performance of women-owned small ventures', *Journal of Small Business Management*, **40**(2), 109–25.

Lerner, M., C. Brush, and R. Histich, (1997), 'Israel women entrepreneurs: an examination of factors affecting performance', *Journal of Business Venturing*, **12**, 315–39.

Low, M.B. (2001), 'The adolescence of entrepreneurship research: specification of purpose', *Entrepreneurship Theory and Practice*, **25**(4), 17–25.

Low, M.B. and I.C. MacMillan, (1988), 'Entrepreneurship: past research and future challenges', *Journal of Management*, **35**, 139–61.

Lumpkin, G.T. and G.G. Dess, (1996), 'Clarifying the entrepreneurial orientation construct and linking it to performance', *Academy of Management Review*, **21**(1), 135–72.

Lussier, R. and S. Pfeifer, (2000), 'A comparison of business success versus failure variables between US and Central Eastern Europe: Croatian entrepreneurs', *Entrepreneurship Theory and Practice*, **24**(4), 59–67.

Manimala, M.J. (1992), 'Entrepreneurial heuristics: a comparison between high PI (pioneering innovative) and low PI ventures', *Journal of Business Venturing*, **7**(6), 477–504.

McClelland, D. (1961), *The Achieving Society*, Princeton NJ: van Nostrand.

Miller, R.W. and Toulouse, J.-M. (1988), 'Strategy, structure, CEO personality and performance in small firms', *American Journal of Small Business* (Winter, 1986), 47–61.

Miner, J., N. Smith, and J. Bracker, (1992), 'Predicting firm survival from a knowledge of entrepreneur task motivation', *Entrepreneurship and Regional Development*, **4**, 145–53.

Moyes, A. and Westhead, (1990), 'Environments for new firms formation in Great Britain', *Regional Studies*, **24**(2), 123–136.

Neiswander, D.K. and J.M. Drollinger, (1986), 'Origins of successful start-up ventures', *Frontiers of Entrepreneurship Research*, Wellesley, MA: Centre for Entrepreneurship Studies, Babson College, pp. 328–43.

Nelson, R. and S. Winter, (1982), *An Evolutionary Theory of Economic Change*, Cambridge, MA: The Belknap Press.

Palich, L.E. and D.R. Bagby, (1995), 'Using cognitive theory to explain entrepreneurial risk-taking: challenging conventional wisdom', *Journal of Business Venturing*, **10**(6), 425–38.

Penrose, E. (1959), *The Theory of the Growth of the Firm*, Basil Blackwell.

Peteraf, M., (1993), 'The cornerstones of competitive advantage: a resource-based view', *Strategic Management Journal*, **14**, 179–91.

Porter, M. (1980), *Competitive Strategy*, New York: Free Press.

Porter, M. (1985), *Competitive Advantage*, New York: Basic Books.

Porter, M. (1991), 'Towards a dynamic theory of strategy', *Strategic Management Journal*, Winter Special Issue, **12**, 95–117.

Reuber, R. and E. Fischer, (1994), 'Entrepreneurs' experience, expertise, and the performance of technology-based firms', *IEEE Transactions on Engineering Management*, **42**(4), 1–10.

Reuber, R. and E. Fischer, (1999), 'Understanding the consequences of founders' experience', *Journal of Small Business Management*, **37**(2), 30–45.

Romanelly, E. (1989), 'Organization birth and population variety: a community perspective on origins', in B. Staw and L. Cummings (eds), *Research in Organization Behaviour*, Vol.11. Greenwich, CT: JAJ Press.

Ronstadt, R. (1988), 'The corridor principle', *Journal of Business Venturing*, **3**(1), 31–40.

Ruist, E. (1990), *Modellbygge før empirisk analyse* (Model building for empirical analysis), Lund: Studentlitteratur.

Sandberg, W. and C. Hofer, (1987), 'Improving new venture performance: the role of strategy, industry structure and the entrepreneur', *Journal of Business Venturing*, **3**(1), 5–28.

Schumpeter, J. (1911, 1926, 1934), *Theory of Economic Development: An Inquiry into Profits, Capital, Credit, Interest and Business Cycle*, transl. Redovers Opie, Cambridge: Harvard University.

Scott, W.R. (1992), *Organizations: Rational, Natural and Open Systems*, Englewood Cliffs, NJ: Prentice Hall.

Sexton, D. and N. Bowman, (1985), 'The entrepreneur: a capable executive and more', *Journal of Business Venturing*, **1**(1), 129–41.

Shane, S. and L. Kolvereid, (1995), 'National environment, strategy and new venture performance: a three country study', *Journal of Small Business Management*, April, pp. 37–50.

Spanos, Y. and S. Lioukas, (2001), 'An examination into the causal logic of rent generation: contrasting Porter's competitive strategy framework and the resource-based perspective', *Strategic Management Journal*, **22**(10), 907–34.

Specht, H. (1993), 'Munificence and carrying capacity of the environment and organisational formation', *Entrepreneurship Theory and Practice*, **17**(2), 77–86.

Stevenson H. and J. Jarillo, (1990), 'A paradigm of entrepreneurship: entrepreneurial management', *Strategic Management Journal*, **11**, 17–27.

Stevenson, H., M. Roberts, and H. Grousback, (1985), *New Business Ventures and the Entrepreneur*, Homewood, Ill: Irwin.

Storey, D., K. Keasey, R. Watson, and P. Wynarczyk, (1987), *Performance of Small Firms: Profits, Jobs, and Failure*, London: Croom Helm.

Teece, D., G. Pisano, and A. Shuen, (1997), 'Dynamic capabilities and strategic management', *Strategic Management Journal*, **18** (7), 509–33.

Teece, D., R. Rumel, G. Dosi, and S. Winter, (1994), 'Understanding corporate coherence: theory and evidence', *Journal of Economic Behaviour and Organisation*, **23**, 1–30.

Tsai, W., I. MacMillan and M. Low, (1991), 'Effects of strategy and environment on corporate venture success in industrial markets', *Journal of Business Venturing*, **6**, 9–28.

Ucbasaran, D., P. Westhead and M. Wright, (2001), 'The focus of entrepreneurial research: contextual and process issues', *Entrepreneurship Theory and Practice*, **25**(4), 57–80.

Vesper, K. (1990), *New Venture Strategies*, Englewood Cliffs, NJ: Prentice-Hall.

Wernerfelt, B. (1984), 'A resource based view of the firm', *Strategic Management Journal*, **5**, 171–80.

Westerberg, M. (1998), 'Managing in turbulence: an empirical study of small firms operating in a turbulent environment', Doctoral Thesis, DT 1998: 43, Luleå University of Technology.

Westhead, P., and S. Birley, (1994), 'Environments for business deregulations in the United Kingdom 1987–1990', *Entrepreneurship and Regional Development*, **6**, 29–62.

Westhead, P. and M. Wrighte, (2000), 'Introduction', in P. Westhead and M. Wright (eds), *Advances in Entrepreneurship*, volume I, Cheltenham, UK and Northampton, MA, USA: Edward Elgar, pp. xii–c.

Wiklund, J. (1998), 'Small firm growth and performance', Joonkooping International Business School, Doctoral dissertation, Joonkooping University.

Wilken, P.H., (1979), *Entrepreneurship, a Comparative and Historical Study*, Norwood, NJ: Ablex.

Wood, R. and A. Bandura, (1989), 'Social cognitive theory of organizational management', *Academy of Management Review*, **14**(3), 361–84.

5. The new paradigm of multipolar competition and its implications for entrepreneurship research in Europe[1]

Leo Paul Dana, Mark B. Bajramovic, and Richard W. Wright

INTRODUCTION

The word 'entrepreneurship' refers to the economic undertaking of entrepreneurs. This is based on the classical definition of the word, which can be traced to the German *unternehmung* (literally: undertaking) and to the French *entreprendre* (literally: between taking). The agents of entrepreneurship are entrepreneurs (from the French *entrepreneurs*, literally: between takers). The flagships of entrepreneurship are small and medium enterprises (SMEs), and these are gaining importance across Europe.

The environment for business in the New Europe is changing dramatically. Not long ago, competition in international markets was the realm of large companies, while entrepreneurs typically operated smaller businesses that remained local or regional in scope. However, the removal of government-imposed barriers that segregated and protected domestic markets, and recent technological advances in manufacturing, transportation and telecommunications, allow even the smallest firms access to customers, suppliers and collaborators across Europe.

The New Europe is characterised by two overarching trends: (1) the reduced importance of the nation-state as the relevant unit around which international business activity is organised and conducted; and (2) the diminishing importance of the stand-alone firm as the principal unit of business competition.

While traditional entrepreneurship research focused on individuals within a given country, future research about entrepreneurship in Europe will increasingly need to address issues of internationalisation. In addition, while research approaches to internationalisation focused traditionally on a uni-polar and hierarchical distribution of power and control, we suggest that future research should reflect the new reality that involves a multi-polar distribution of power and control. We will discuss each of these transformations and then illustrate their impact on the future on entrepreneurship research in Europe.

THE DEMISE OF THE NATION-STATE AS THE PRIMARY MACROECONOMIC PLAYER

For centuries, the nation-state was the basic unit around which international economic activity was planned, organised and conducted, regardless of the origin of firms. The *multi-domestic* model of Foreign Direct Investment typified foreign investment by European multinationals such as Ericsson, Nestlé, Philips, and Unilever; each of these large enterprises has managed highly autonomous subsidiaries, each conforming to local or national environments. Traditional research therefore reflected a macroeconomic environment in which international economic activity is moulded and constrained largely by the power of individual nation-states.

The traditional approaches of business involvement, in which business activity is organised largely around the segmentation of factor and product markets into distinct nation-states, is giving way to a new paradigm in which the firm will source, produce and sell without regard to national boundaries. Across Europe, we see examples of the decline in the segmentation of product and factor markets by individual nations as power evolves from nation-states to higher, supra-national units. This occurs in regional trade agreements such as that of the EU, where power is shifting from the individual member nation-states to the pan-European level. This diminution of national power, and its transfer to a supra-national European level, has profound implications for entrepreneurship and entrepreneurship research. Even small-scale entrepreneurs have access to a vastly expanded Europe.

The upward evolution of national powers to higher levels also means that firms everywhere now face increasing competition, without the domestic-market protection formerly afforded by national governments. Even if a small firm prefers not to enter international markets, it must achieve world-scale efficiencies in order to remain competitive and viable in today's open markets. The integration of product and factor markets implies further that any firm operating outside of its domestic environment – or even one seeking to obtain world-scale efficiencies without leaving its domestic market – will increasingly need to interface with suppliers and customers in other national cultures. The firm can no longer operate solely within its domestic environment, nor can it decentralise its activities into discrete national profit centres, in which managers often need be sensitive to a single local economy or culture.

While economic power and sovereignty are clearly seen evolving from national to supra-national levels, we are simultaneously witnessing another important, albeit less obvious, diminution of the traditional powers of nation-states in the opposite direction: from nation-states to local or regional levels. This is especially true in the realm of political and cultural sovereignty.

This trend toward the fragmentation or devolution of national powers is dramatically evident in the abrupt disintegration of the Soviet Union and the former Yugoslav federation. However, devolution of national powers – albeit on a more gradual and rational basis – is seen elsewhere as well, most obviously in Western Europe. In the United Kingdom, significant new legislative and cultural powers are being decentralised to Scotland and Wales. In Spain, the linguistic and cultural assertiveness of regions such as Catalonia, the Basque Region, and Galicia are becoming far more pronounced than before. Despite the unification of East and West Germany, much greater local autonomy is devolving to the individual German *länder*, or states. Even in France – long considered a bastion of centralised power in the nation-state – a new, semi-autonomous status has been granted to Corsica; and there is a notable resurgence of regional languages and culture, such as Languedoc or Provençal in the south, and Breton in the west.

It is our belief that local and regional cultural distinctions are becoming more pronounced in the New Europe, than was the case in the past. While the consolidation of economic power at increasingly high, supra-national levels may enable trans-European firms to achieve new productive efficiencies, the growing devolution of cultural and political sovereignty to local and regional jurisdictions means that large firms may need to rely increasingly on smaller, localised firms to achieve the cultural sensitivities they need for local adaptation, thus providing new niche opportunities for SMEs.

THE DEMISE OF THE FIRM AS THE PRIMARY MICROECONOMIC PLAYER

Traditional approaches to internationalisation focused on a uni-polar and hierarchic distribution of power and control. Internalisation Theory (Buckley and Casson, 1976; Morck and Yeung, 1991, 1992; Rugman, 1979, 1981; and Teece, 1985) showed that, by investing in its own foreign subsidiaries, a firm could expand operations, while maintaining control at head office. Likewise, Dunning's Eclectic Paradigm (1973, 1977, 1980, 1988) focused on ownership-specific advantages and location-specific advantages that a firm can enjoy, while maintaining centralised control. A uni-polar scenario is implicit, as well, in the Stage Models of incremental internationalisation (Bartlett and Ghoshal, 1989; Bilkey, 1978; Bilkey and Tesar, 1977; Buckley et al., 1988; Cavusgil, 1980, 1984; Cavusgil and Nevin, 1981; Johanson and Vahlne, 1977, 1990; Johanson and Wiedersheim-Paul, 1975; Leonidou and Katsikeas, 1996; and

Newbould et al., 1978). Internationalisation could be achieved without giving up power and control; the internationalising firm could maintain its uni-polar distribution of power and control, albeit at a heavy capital cost. Internationalisation under this model was expensive because ownership and uni-polar (centralised) decision-making led to huge, integrated factory complexes. This model is losing relevance in the New Europe.

The profound change occurring at the microeconomic level is the demise of the stand-alone company as the primary unit of competition. In the past, emphasis has been on *internalising* value-added functions, to bring them more fully within the control of the firm's management, and on building walls around the firm to help secure the retention of its internal proprietary advantages from competitors. As firms of all sizes decide not to control the full range of value-added functions on their own, we increasingly see firms forming collaborative alliances with other firms.

An alternate to the uni-polar paradigm of internationalisation assumes a multi-polar distribution of power and control. Rather than focusing on the internationalisation of an individual centralised firm with a uni-polar distribution of power and control, we can focus on a multi-polar network of firms. Power and control are divided among independent firms that co-operate voluntarily for increased efficiency and profit. Networks result in the demise of the stand-alone firm as the principal unit of business competition. Literature pertaining to this networking perspective includes Acs and Dana (2001); Axelsson and Easton (1992); Bodur and Madsen (1993); Brüderl and Preisendörfer (1998); Chetty and Blackenburg-Holm (2000); Coviello and Munro (1997); Dana (2001); Etemad et al. (2001); Fontes and Coombs (1997); Gomes-Casseres (1996); Gynawali and Madhavan (2001); and Holmlund and Kock (1998). Stabell and Fjeldstad (1998) discuss reciprocal interdependence; while Casti and Karlqvist (1995); Jarillo (1993); Webster (1992) and Zineldin (1998) further illustrate the possiblity of a non-zero sum game.

THE NEW PARADIGM OF MULTI-POLAR COMPETITION

Mutually beneficial relationships have always been at the core of competitiveness. Increasingly, however, firms are finding that networks of relationships need not necessarily be controlled by direct ownership to be effective. Today's competitive business environment is witnessing a paradigm shift from traditional forms of collaboration, in which the locus of power and influence reside in internal hierachical structures, to newer forms of resource-based collaboration, resulting in mutual interdependence through which greater economies of scale can be established. In this newly-emerging competitive paradigm shift, the unit of competition is no longer the individual firm; but rather a network of firms collaborating interdependently. In such resource-centric trans-industry systems, each SME has the opportunity to specialise in a set of capabilities, competencies and skills much needed by the network, in order to generate greater benefits both for itself and in turn for its networked partners; more so than any of them could by operating independently of each other. Each participating member of such resource-based networks – often regardless of size – specialises in a different part of the value chain, which may be located in different parts of the world.

A rich literature has been developed on collaboration among large firms. Among the most prominent contributions are Doz and Hamel (1997), Forrest (1992), Gomes-Casseres (1994), Kanter (1994), Parkhe (1997), Stafford (1994), and the three-volume series edited by Beamish and Killing (1997). What is new is the alliance imperative for small firms. For small firms, perhaps even more than for large ones, partnering with other firms through various forms of collaborative arrangements is becoming imperative. As a consequence of these new imperatives, small firms are benefiting increasingly from mutual interaction with other similar sized firms. This is documented by Bartels (2000); Chetty and Blackenburg-Holm (2000); Coviello and Munro (1995; 1997); Holmlund and Kock (1998); Perrow (1992); Sadler and Chetty (2000); and Welsh et al. (2000). An even newer trend is toward mutually-supportive networks that include small firms and large firms working together for mutual reward. This trend is illustrated by Etemad et al. (2001); and by Wright and Dana (2003).

To facilitate the discussion that follows, we propose a typology of networks:

- *Horizontal networks*, which transform competitors into allies;
- *Vertical networks*, integrating buyers and suppliers; and
- *Trans-industry networks*, which relate or connect otherwise seemingly independant value chains by linking them through mutually inclusive resource-based needs in order to achieve greater economies of scale in a single functional unit.

Current value chain models depict the firm as an individual self-contained linear series of functional units. This is shown schematically in Figure 5.1. When these value chains are examined relationally with other firms, integration is historically depicted to occur Horizontally and Vertically. As we enter into an age of networks, horizontal integration transformed competitors into allies, while vertical networks integrated buyers and suppliers. This is illustrated in Figure 5.2.

These forms of integration can further be conceptualised in a three-dimensional plane as illustrated in Figure 5.3.

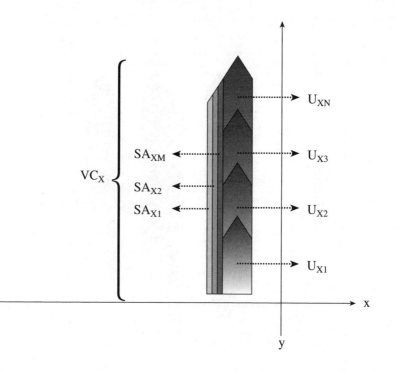

Notes:
VCx   =   Value chain for product x.
U_{x1} =   Product x primary value chain activity 1 for transforming inputs into outputs for consumers (i.e. Research & Development).
U_{x2} =   Product x primary value chain activity 2 (i.e. Production).
U_{x3} =   Product x primary value chain activity 3 (i.e. Marketing & Sales).
U_{xN} =   Product x primary value chain activity 4 (i.e. Service).
SA_{x1} =   Product x value chain support activity 1 (i.e. Company Infrastructure).
SA_{x2} =   Product x value chain support activity 2 (i.e. Human Resources).
SA_{xM} =   Product x value chain support act.

Figure 5.1   Artisan value chain model

A more accurate representaion of firms interacting in their given environ-ments can be created by re-orienting firms' value chains from a three-dimen-sional linear plane to a three-dimensional non-linear perpective. This is illustrated in Figure 5.4 and Figure 5.5.

Resource-based trans-industry integration results in economies of scale otherwise beyond the capacity of a single firm. Formerly segmented specialised elements of a firm's value chain are now presented with the oppor-tunity to operate as larger units within the context of their environment. This change is due to several factors, including economies of scale, as well as both

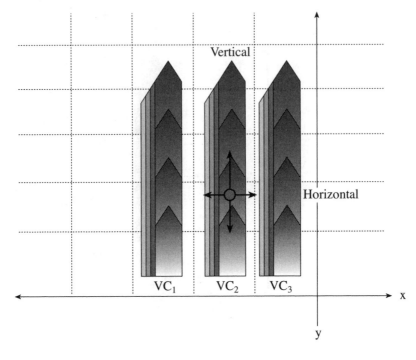

Figure 5.2   Vertical and horizontal integration

comparative and absolute cost advantage. Resource-based trans-industry integration is thus a *function* of:

1. Market forces of competitive divergence causing consumer product specialisation vs. a set of related firm's internal forces of the converging network economies of scale.
2. Market forces of *converging consumer needs* (function of globalisation as the nation-state loses importance to a larger entity) vs. market forces of *diverging consumer needs* (function of regionalism, as the nation-state loses importance to smaller units).
3. Factors determining the rate of exchange between the consumer and the firm, both on a tangible level (physical product distribution) and intangible level (media and communication).

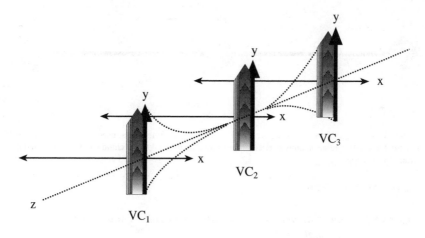

Notes:
VC$_x$ = Value chain for producing good x.
X   = Plane of horizontal integration.
Y   = Plane of vertical integration.
Z   = Plane of trans-industry integration.

Source: Mark B. Bajramovic.

Figure 5.3   Three-dimensional linear depiction of horizontal and vertical integration

We define trans-industry integration, as networks which relate or connect otherwise seemingly independent value chains by linking them through mutually inclusive resource-based needs in order to achieve greater economies of scale in a single functional unit (for example the purchase of a ranch to produce leather for three unrelated goods: Camera Bags (VC$_1$), Cars (VC$_2$) and Shoes (VC$_3$)). This systems unit is illustrated cross-sectionally in Figure 5.6, and longitudinally in Figure 5.7. The unit of analysis then becomes a *systems unit*, as opposed to a simple value chain. When the unit of analysis changes, then we suggest that research must reflect this.

IMPLICATIONS FOR ENTREPRENEURSHIP RESEARCH IN EUROPE

This chapter has explained how the demise of nation-states and individual firms has led to international multi-polar business networks. We have discussed collaborative imperatives as they relate to small and medium enterprises, and we have provided a summary of ideas about networks and value

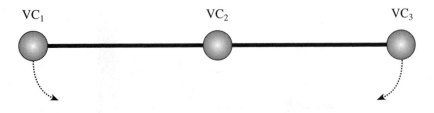

Note: Linear depictions, irrespective of the number of dimensions used, do not accurately portray the relative relationships between inter- and intra-related value chain elements involved in Trans-Integration.

Source: Mark B. Bajramovic.

Figure 5.4   Linear depiction of three unrelated value chains (cross-sectional view)

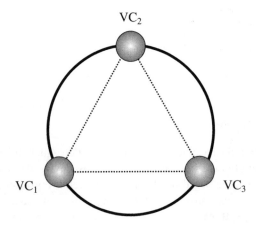

Source: Mark B. Bajramovic.

Figure 5.5   Non-linear organic depiction of three unrelated value chains (cross-sectional view)

chains. The strategic alternatives facing small firms have thus changed dramatically.

We have noted a trend toward larger units both at the macroeconomic level and at the micro-economic level – perhaps more pronounced in Europe today than anywhere else. Both the state and the firm have yielded control, in exchange for the advantages inherent in being a part of a larger entity. Simultaneously, at both the macro and micro levels, there is a trend toward

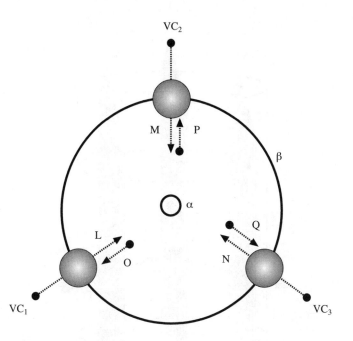

Notes:

VC_x = Value chain for product x.

α   = Centralized trans-integrated hub, apex of convergence for network where value chains VC_1, VC_2 and VC_3 non-value chain related activities overlap in a state of parity with respect to formative effects and contributions.

β   = Maximum extremity of overlapping similarity of resource-based trans-integrated non-value chains VC_1, VC_2 and VC_3. Within this interior spherical area at any given set of three-dimensional coordinates x-y-z exists a potential area for the development of a mutually inclusive, but unrelated value chain activity constrained by the limitation that the non-primary activities does not overlap with the linear fields of three-dimensional horizontal (0,y,z) or vertical (x,0,z) integration (where the dimension of z is not used to depict a level of integration in itself, but is representatives of all 360 degrees of integration. As such, integration on a trans-level may represent a new form of expansion in the vertical and horizontal realms as opposed to a new variable dimension in itself.

L,M,N = Force vectors directing the integration of increasing similar unrelated value chain activities (forces of convergence). Converging forces lead to the cost/benefit maximisation of unrelated value chain activities via:
1. Standardization of production (as a function of consumer directed market forces)
2. Attainment of economies of scale through maximisation of productivity by the intermediary activity relating to the product and its consumption by the consumer.

O,P,Q = Force vectors of competition directing the segregation of unrelated value chain activities. As a result of the development of unique core competencies any vector departure from the point of parity of convergence, ∞ (0,0,0), can be deemed to be a dominant influence of competitive divergence (or dominant force of convergence) by any given value chain (VC_x), and can be quantified by the discrepancy between the *non-central trans-integrated* hub, ∞' (where x≠0 and y≠0) and the optimum centre of similarity value is α(0,0,0).

Source: Mark B. Bajramovic.

Figure 5.6   Systems unit with trans-industry integration (cross-sectional view)

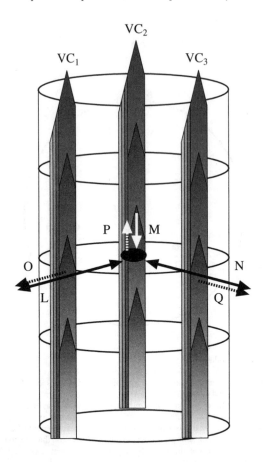

Notes:

VC$_x$ = Value chain for product x.

α   = Centralized trans-integrated hub of unrelated value chain activities.

β   = Area of non-value chain related activity *trans-convergence* between value chains VC$_1$,VC$_2$ and VC$_3$.

L,M,N = Force vectors directing the integration of increasingly similar unrelated value chain activities (forces of convergence).

O,P,Q = Force vectors of competition directing the segregation of unrelated value chain activities (forces of divergence). Any vector departure from apex α(0,0,0) can be deemed to be a dominant influence of competition by any given value chain, VC$_x$.

Source: Mark B. Bajramovic.

Figure 5.7   Systems unit with trans-industry integration (longitudinal view)

greater specialisation and local expertise. Governments feel increasing pressure to delegate political and cultural powers to local jurisdictions, while firms benefit from increased focus and specialisation in their business activities. As the business environment of Europe changes, research should reflect the new realities.

We suggest that priorities for future entrepreneurship research in Europe should include the following:

1. Research on entrepreneurship in Europe should reflect the context of networks rather than focusing solely on the firm or the individual entrepreneur. Subjects of interest for future research include: causal variables of why networks form the way they do; why entrepreneurs enter particular networks; dealing with goal confluence and conflict resolution in international, intercultural alliances; the dynamics within a network; the success factors; and the dynamics among networks. This includes horizontal, vertical and trans-industry integration.

2. In particular, we note a dearth of published research on relationships between smaller, entrepreneurial firms and larger ones. Increasingly, small firms across Europe are entering directly into the value chains of large firms, often becoming indispensable to the ongoing success of the larger firms. Research has focused mainly on strategic alliances among large enterprises and more recently on clusters of small firms, but very little on the interaction between small and large firms.

3. In the past, entrepreneurs were perceived as being either independent, or else being dependent on larger firms. Future research might show that it is possible to trade off independence for *interdependence*. Additional research is needed to define and measure levels of dependence and interdependence among firms. However, this may be a particularly daunting challenge for researchers, as we are unaware of any instrument designed to accomplish this.

4. Whereas the locus of regulatory power formerly resided with individual nation-states, power throughout much of Europe is evolving to a higher, supranational level, as well as devolving to local and regional levels. Given the vast regulatory changes taking place in the EU, future research should examine how entrepreneurs adapt to the changing regulatory environment of the New Europe – both to the evolution of regulatory powers at the pan-European level and to the devolution of powers to local and regional levels.

5. An emerging opportunity for entrepreneurship research lies in the ten new members of the EU, particularly in those countries where entrepreneurs have emerged only recently from centralized planning under communist regimes. Entrepreneurship research could help re-kindle entrepreneurial

values and an entrepreneurship culture, in European regions where communist rule and nationalizations extinguished the entrepreneurial spirit.

6. The fact that English is becoming the predominant language of business across Europe may facilitate the conduct of research across Europe in a single language, thereby avoiding the problems inherent in translation and back-translation. It is important, however, for researchers to keep in mind the fact that cultural nuances still remain. Rather than using several versions of a questionnaire in different languages, it is becoming easier for researchers to use a single, English-language version throughout. The risk, however, is that questions may be interpreted differently in different cultures, despite the ability of people to speak English. For this reason, we recommend that quantitative research be supplemented by qualitative methodologies.

NOTE

1. This chapter is based on the keynote lectures presented by Leo Paul Dana at the McGill University Conference on International Entrepreneurship, in Montreal, Canada, September 2002, and at the First European Summer School in Valence, France, September 2002, and on a lecture by Richard W. Wright at the Indiana University Conference on International Business, in Bloomington, Indiana, October 2002. The ideas are elaborated in Richard W. Wright and Leo Paul Dana, 'Changing paradigms of international entrepreneurship strategy', *Journal of International Entrepreneurship*, **1**(1), March 2003, pp. 135–52. The conceptual models and diagrams included within this document were designed and created by Mark B. Bajramovic.

REFERENCES

Acs, Zoltan J., and Leo Paul Dana (2001), 'Contrasting two models of wealth redistribution', *Small Business Economics*, **16**(2), March, 63–74.

Axelsson, Bjorn, and Geoff Easton (eds) (1992), *Industrial Networks: A New View of Reality*, London: Routledge.

Bartels, Frank L. (2000), 'International competition and global cooperation', in Leo Paul Dana (ed.), *Global Marketing Cooperation and Networks*, Binghamton, NY: International Business Press, pp. 85–98.

Bartlett, Christopher A. and Sumatra Ghoshal (1989), *Managing Across Borders: The Transnational Solution*, Boston: Harvard Business School Press.

Beamish, Paul W. and J. Peter Killing (eds) (1997), *Cooperative Strategies: European Perspectives/Asian Pacific Perspectives/North American Perspectives*, San Francisco: The New Lexington Press.

Bilkey, Warren J. (1978), 'An attempted integration of the literature on the export behavior of firms', *Journal of International Business Studies*, **9**(1), 33–46.

Bilkey, Warren J. and George Tesar (1977), 'The export behavior of smaller sized Wisconsin manufacturing firms', *Journal of International Business Studies*, **8**(1), Spring/Summer, 93–8.

Bodur, Muzaffer and Tage Koed Madsen (1993), 'Danish foreign direct investments in Turkey', *European Business Review*, **93**(5), 28–43.

Brüderl, Josef and Peter Preisendörfer (1998), 'Network support and the success of newly founded businesses', *Small Business Economics*, **10**(3), 213–25.

Buckley, Peter J. and Mark Casson (1976), *The Future of the Multinational Enterprise*, London: Macmillan.

Buckley, Peter J., Gerald D. Newbould and Jane C. Thurwell (1988), *Foreign Direct Investment by Smaller UK Firms*, London: Macmillan.

Casti, John L. and Anders Karlqvist (eds) (1995), *Cooperation and Conflict in General Evolutionary Process*, New York: Wiley.

Cavusgil, S. Tamer (1980), 'On the internationalisation process of firms', *European Research*, **8**, 273–81.

Cavusgil, S. Tamer (1984), 'Differences among exporting firms based on their degree of internationalisation', *Journal of Business Research*, **12**(2), 195–208.

Cavusgil, S. Tamer and John R. Nevin (1981), 'International determinants of export marketing behavior', *Journal of Marketing Research*, **28**, 114–19.

Chetty, Sylvie and Desirée Blackenburg-Holm (2000), 'Internationalisation of small to medium-sized manufacturing firms: a network approach', *International Business Review*, **9**, 77–93.

Coviello, Nicole E. and Hugh J. Munro (1995), 'Growing the entrepreneurial firm: networking for international market development', *European Journal of Marketing*, **29**(7), 49–61.

Coviello, Nicole E. and Hugh J. Munro (1997), 'Network relationships and the internationalisation process of small software firms', *International Business Review*, **6**(2), 1–26.

Dana, Leo Paul (2001), 'Networks, internationalization and policy', *Small Business Economics*, **16**(2), 57–62.

Doz, Yves and Gary Hamel (1997), 'The use of alliances in implementing technology strategies', in Michael L. Tushman and Philip Anderson (eds), *Managing Strategic Innovation and Change*, Oxford: Oxford University Press, pp. 556–80.

Dunning, John H. (1973), 'The determinants of international production', *Oxford Economic Papers*, November, pp. 289–336.

Dunning, John H. (1977), 'Trade, location of economic activity and MNE: a search for an eclectic approach', *The International Allocation of Economic Activity: Proceedings of A Nobel Symposium Held at Stockholm*, London: Macmillan, pp. 395–418.

Dunning, John H. (1980), 'Toward an eclectic theory of international production: empirical tests', *Journal of International Business Studies*, **11**(1), 9–31.

Dunning, John H. (1988), 'The eclectic paradigm of international production: a restatement and some possible extensions', *Journal of International Business Studies*, **19**, Spring, pp. 1–31.

Etemad, Hamid, Richard W. Wright and Leo Paul Dana (2001), 'Symbiotic international business networks: collaboration between small and large firms', *Thunderbird International Business Review*, **43**(4), 481–99.

Fontes, Margarita and Rod Coombs (1997), 'The coincidence of technology and market objectives in the internationalisation of new technology-based firms', *International Small Business Journal*, **15**(4), 14–35.

Forrest, Janet E. (1992), 'Management aspects of strategic partnering', *Journal of General Management*, **17**(4), 25–40.

Gomes-Casseres, Benjamin (1994), 'Group versus group: how alliance networks compete', *Harvard Business Review*, **72**, July–August, 62–74.

Gomes-Casseres, Benjamin (1996), *The Alliance Revolution: The New Shape of Business Rivalry*, Cambridge, Massachusetts: Harvard University Press.

Gynawali, Devi R. and Ravindranath Madhavan (2001), 'Network structure and competitive dynamics: a structural embeddedness perspective', *Academy of Management Review*, **26**(3), July, 431–45.

Holmlund, Maria and Soren Kock (1998), 'Relationships and the internationalisation of Finnish small and medium-sized companies', *International Small Business Journal*, **16**(4), 46–63.

Jarillo, Carlos J. (1993), *Strategic Networks – Creating the Borderless Organization*, Oxford: Butterworth-Heineman.

Johanson, Jan, and Jan-Erik Vahlne (1977), 'The internationalization process of the firm – a model of knowledge development and increasing foreign market commitments', *Journal of International Business Studies*, **8**(1), Spring/Summer, 23–32.

Johanson, Jan, and Jan-Erik Vahlne (1990), 'The mechanism of internationalisation', *International Marketing Review*, **7**(4), 11–24.

Johanson, Jan, and Finn Wiedersheim-Paul (1975), 'The internationalisation of the firm: four Swedish cases', *Journal of International Management Studies*, **12**(3), October, 305–22.

Kanter, Rosabeth Moss (1994), 'Collaborative advantage: the art of alliances', *Harvard Business Review*, **72**, July–August, 96–108.

Leonidou, Leonidas C. and Constantine S. Katsikeas (1996), 'The export development process', *Journal of International Business Studies*, **27**(3), 517–51.

McMillan, John (2002), *Reinventing the Bazaar: A Natural History of Markets*, New York & London: W. W. Norton & Company.

Morck, Randal and Bernard Yeung (1991), 'Why investors value multinationality', *Journal of Business*, **64**(2), 165–87.

Morck, Randal and Bernard Yeung (1992), 'Internalization: an event study test', *Journal of International Economics*, **33**, 41–56.

Newbould, Gerald D., Peter J. Buckley and Jane C. Thurwell (1978), *Going International – The Enterprise of Smaller Companies Overseas*, New York: John Wiley and Sons.

Parkhe, Arvind (1997), 'Strategic alliance structuring: a game theoretic and transaction cost examination of inter-firm cooperation', *Academy of Management Journal*, **36**(4), 794–829.

Perrow, Charles (1992), 'Small firm networks', in Nitin Nohria and Robert G. Eccles (eds), *Networks and Organizations: Structure, Form, and Action*, Boston: Harvard Business School Press, pp. 445–70.

Rugman, Alan M. (1979), *International Diversification and the Multinational Enterprise*, Farborough: Lexington.

Rugman, Alan M. (1981), *Inside the Multinationals: The Economics of Internal Market*, New York: Columbia University Press.

Sadler, Aaron and Sylvie Chetty (2000), 'The impact of networks on New Zealand', in Leo Paul Dana (ed.), *Global Marketing Co-Operation and Networks*, Binghamton, New York: International Business Press, pp. 37–58.

Stabell, Charles, and Øystein Fjeldstad (1998), 'Configuring value for competitive advantage: on chains, shops and networks', *Strategic Management Journal*, **19**, 413–37.

Stafford, Edwin R. (1994), 'Using co-operative strategies to make alliances work', *Long-Range Planning*, **27**(3), 64–74.

Teece, David J. (1985), 'Multinational enterprise, internal governance and economic organization', *American Economic Review*, **75**, 233–38.

Webster, Frederick E. (1992), 'The changing role of marketing in the corporation', *Journal of Marketing*, **56**, October, 1–17.

Welsh, Denice, Lawrence Welsh, Ian Wilkinson and Louise Young (2000), 'An export grouping scheme', in Leo Paul Dana (ed.), *Global Marketing Cooperation and Networks*, Binghamton, New York: International Business Press, pp. 59–84.

Wright, Richard W. and Leo Paul Dana (2003), 'Changing paradigms of international entrepreneurship strategy', *Journal of International Entrepreneurship*, **1**(1), xx.

Zineldin, Mosad Amin (1998), 'Towards an ecological collaborative relationship management', *European Journal of Marketing*, **32**(11/12), 1138–64.

PART II

European Research Methodologies in
Entrepreneurship: Is There Some Place for
Newness and Innovation?

6. Current state of methodology in entrepreneurship research and some expectations for the future[1]

Paula Kyrö and Juha Kansikas

NEED FOR ENTREPRENEURSHIP SPECIFIC METHODOLOGY

The need to advance methodology in entrepreneurship research has varied from a very philosophical basis to more practical recommendations (for example Bygrave, 1989a, 1989b; Davidsson, 2001; Sexton and Smilor, 1986). Among contemporary contributors representing a philosophical perspective we can mention William D. Bygrave (1989a; 1989b) with his two articles 'The entrepreneurship paradigm I and II' in the *Journal of Entrepreneurship Theory and Practice*. The basic argument behind his thought is that advancing methodology relates to its ability to describe and understand human behaviour.

The contemporary paradigm debate also combines methodological considerations with the conceptual needs, claiming that both discipline-specified theories and methodology are needed (for example Bygrave, 1989a, 1989b; Davidsson, 2001; Sexton and Smilor, 1986). Often it is recommended that methodological solutions be sought from other fields of science, as suggested by Macmillan and Katz (1992) from epidemiology, criminology, history, archaeology and palaeontology, and by Stewart (1991), from anthropology.

The empirical studies depicting the current outlook of methodological choices, as interplay between methods and theories, can be found in the 1980s and at the beginning of the 1990s. Among these we can mention the studies of Wortman (1986), in the interface between entrepreneurship and small businesses, of Churchill and Lewis (1986), borrowing 'lenses' from the younger though somewhat more mature fields of strategy and marketing and of Brush (1992) in women entrepreneurship. Their data have consisted of journal articles and conference papers.

This study is participating in this methodological discussion by suggesting that, even though methodological considerations have been discussed and even though a consensus for the need to develop entrepreneurship specific methodology seems to prevail, little has actually happened in this respect. It is also argued that one reason for this might be due to the tendency to distinguish philosophical discussion from the actual methodological choices. A structural approach employing the concept of the paradigm as a mediator between these two is introduced in order to advance this discussion. However, since defining the concept of a paradigm is problematic, this study examines it by defining its nature, characteristics and elements as well as their relationships as a part of the entrepreneurship research and the dynamic debate of a scientific inquiry rather than searching for strictly defined sentences for its meaning. How this is done is explicated through methodological choices.

METHODOLOGICAL CHOICES

Methodologically, this study belongs to the field of interpretative concept research and more specifically, it applies the descriptive interpretative method introduced by Lämsä and Takala (2001). The output of the conceptual study is further adopted to depict the current outlook of methodological choices. The aim of the latter is two-fold: on the one hand it aims to test the applicability of the constructed conceptual frame as an analysing tool and on the other hand, it aims to reveal the current outlook of the methodological state in entrepreneurship research.

Conceptual methodology consists of two basic branches – analytical and interpretative. The interpretative branch aims to find meanings included in concepts, and their definitions, in order to expand the understanding of that concept. It looks for the meanings related to the concepts and the interpretation is linked with the contextual factors. Contextuality and a theoretical thematisation distinguish the interpretative branch from the analytical study, and justify it as a methodological alternative in the human sciences. Contextuality in this study emerges in two respects: firstly, the methodological discussion is anchored to and guided by the entrepreneurship debate and, secondly, the paradigm discussion is anchored to the dynamic debate of a scientific inquiry that provided the concept of a paradigm.

Among its four categories, that is, heuristic, theory-bounded, descriptive and critical, the descriptive method aims to increase the understanding of a concept by finding, describing and interpreting the entity of meanings. (Lämsä and Takala, 2001) It emphasises the further development of the concepts and their definitions, found in other writers' written texts. Lämsä and Takala (2001) suggest that, at best, the descriptive conceptual study might provide 'a fertile re-interpretation from a completely new perspective'. In this study, this effort is focused on a structural view that explicates conceptually the gap between the philosophical basis and methodological choices.

Lämsä and Takala (2001) argue that the validity of this method is analogous to the adopted assumption of reality at the particular time, since the use of method always includes a set of commitments from the philosophy of science. The concepts and their meanings must be seen as ever-changing, dynamic processes. They are ambiguous, changing, as well as socially and culturally constructing. Therefore, it can be considered that the interpretative study of concepts already commits itself to basic assumptions at the very beginning, and always gives us information in limited frames.

In this study, these assumptions are based on a pragmatism that aims to find a solution to non-dualistic ideas of reality. Instead of claiming that reality consists of two disparate parts such as appearance and reality, the mind and body, spirit and nature and consequently knowledge are guided by binary thinking; as for example, realism assumes, pragmatists strive to understand reality through action. For them, truth is an acquired quality. For Dewey (1951), it is something that is happening to an idea while verifying it and for James (1913); it is the same as a process of verification. According to Sarvimäki (1988), 'in his action, interaction and co-action with the world man gets to know the world and his knowledge guides his further action'. Consequently, pragmatist knowledge is situational and contextual, as the descriptive, interpretative concept method assumes.

Adopting pragmatism to the research process requires parting from the traditional way of describing it as theoretical and empirical parts and instead views it as a process, in which the previous step creates presumptions and leads to the next step. In scientific inquiry, each of these steps is explicated and defended, based on previous experiences. Usually, the interpretative research process is regarded as a hermeneutic spiral. Pragmatism supplements this with explicating the nature of action involved in this process.

Thus, the pragmatist view to a research process aims to construct the entity of concepts that might be applied as a tool to increase knowledge in actual research processes. In other words, it proceeds through action for further action. Consequently, this study can be described as consisting of four steps, delineated in Figure 6.1.

The process, as Alasuutari (1994) suggests, starts with the interpretation of hints and an active production of new clues. The researcher uses the hints and clues in concluding something that is not apparent. In this study, the hints from the methodological debate of entrepreneurship research led to the conclusion that a tendency to separate the philosophical debate from the actual method-ological choices seems to prevail. Step 1 follows this hint and identifies these two discussions in the entrepreneurship context. This leads to the second step, which seeks a solution, from a paradigm context, that can be identified in the dynamic discussion of a scientific inquiry. Further experiences from this step address attention towards the links between methods and paradigms. This is

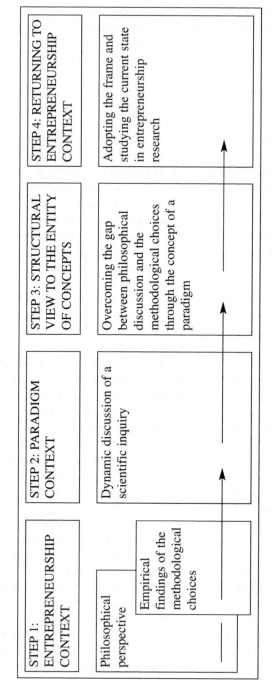

Figure 6.1   The steps in this research process

focused on in Step 3, by finding the structural view to the entity of these concepts. Finally in Step 4, these experiences are returned to the entrepreneurship context with a new perspective. More ordinary studies call this last step 'the empirical part'. The conceptual study can precede the empirical study, or be a study of its own. In this study it is one part, that is, a step, even though not in the traditional binary sense.

The data in this method might be focused either on the actual writings or, more generally on the ideas of the authors. This study emphasises the latter. The focus is on identifying and choosing the authors that represent the valid discussions that might advance this methodological debate. In Steps 1 and 2, instead of looking for the sources according to a certain term, we try to find those contributors who genuinely ponder over the basic problems of methodological choices and development. These authors are listed in Table 6.1. These kinds of choices are always open to criticism, since there most certainly are other contributors who might provide a different approach to this same problem.

The ideas of the contributors interplay dialectically with each other leading from ideas and vague concepts, through reflective thinking, to a new conceptual frame. At the same time, this process is intuitional and rational (Lämsä and Takala, 2001). The difference between analytical and interpretative concept analyses emerges in this dialectical interpretative process.

In this methodological part, we have first identified and positioned the interpretative, descriptive concept method in the field of concept methods. Then, we have described its content and process with philosophical commitments and applied these to this research. Finally, we specified the data, and in

Table 6.1   The sources of data

Step	Contributor
Step 1: Entrepreneurship context	
Identifying philosopical perspective	W.D. Bygrave, P. Davidsson, H. Stevenson and S. Harmeling, L. Von Mises, E. Von Böhm-Bawerk
Identifying empirical findings of the methodological choices	C. Brush, N.C. Churchill and V.L. Lewis, M.S. Wortman Jr.
Step 2: Paradigm context	G. Bachelard, P. Feyerabend, T. Kuhn, K.R. Popper
Step 3: Synthesis of previous steps	
Step 4:	377 refereed journal articles published in 1999 and in 2000

this case specifically the contributors, and the nature of analysing method described. Thus, we have described all three parts, the research method, the data-gathering and the analysing method. The details of Step 4 will follow after presenting the three previous parts.

STEP 1:   PARADIGM DISCUSSION IN ENTREPRENEURSHIP RESEARCH

Philosophical Perspective to Entrepreneurship Research

Bygrave (1989a, 1989b) argues that 'entrepreneurship as an emerging para-digm, in the pre-theory stage' needs more inductive methods, based on empir-ical observations, than on deductive reasoning with statistical analyses. He leads us to this conclusion by comparing the needs of entrepreneurship to physics. He argues that, since entrepreneurship involves 'a disjointed, discon-tinuous, non-linear and usually unique event that cannot be studied success-fully with methods developed for examining smooth, continuous, linear and (often repeatable) processes', there is a need for its own methodology. Per Davidsson (2001) argues for the need for both inductive and deductive stud-ies. Davidsson's arguments evolve from different research areas of new economic activities, without explicit epistemological considerations. Both of these authors use the concept of a paradigm, without explicitly defining what they mean by it.

Stevenson and Harmeling (1990) had thoughts similar to Bygrave when they argued that the theory of change and the theory of equilibrium are both needed and internally consistent. They also claimed that most of the present theory used to explain corporate entrepreneurship is based upon an implicit assumption that we are examining a set of equilibrium-based phenomena. Its goal is in describing the world as it is. Assuming that critical phenomena repeat themselves, the relevant phenomena are those that most closely repre-sent the central tendencies of the universe. These phenomena can best be captured through examination of large numbers with the goal of discovering their distribution. They suggest, however, that knowledge must be understood as behavioural processes rather than as outputs. According to them, individual differences in this respect make a difference.

However, this discussion is as old as entrepreneurship discussion itself. As one of the early contributors, we can consider Ludwig von Mises and his writ-ings on subjectivity. Mises called his approach a praxeology, the science of human intentional action (Böhm-Bawerk, 1890–91; Buchanan 1982; Rizzo, 1982).

These recommendations are examples that lead to a philosophical discussion. It seems to be an interplay between two choices – deductive and inductive reasoning. However, both Davidsson and Bygrave also raise the question of the difficulty of expecting a new paradigm to emerge without accidental discoveries or inventions. This thought is also very fundamental to the origin of economic thought. The roots for it can be identified as early as in the 19th century through the large methodological debate between the German Historical School and the Classical School (for example, Böhm-Bawerk, 1890–91). The abstract-deductive method was offered at that time as a solution.

Choi's dissertation (1993) 'Paradigms and conventions: uncertainty, decision-making and entrepreneurship' can be mentioned as an example of a more extended conceptual approach to a paradigm. He uses the concept of a paradigm, instead of 'ideas' or 'understandings', in order to describe what we use to reflect on our realities. According to him, it relates to all human action. People need paradigms to manage their lives. A paradigm always precedes action. This view might relate to the pragmatist tradition in philosophy that claims that paradigm as it is used in Choi's study is not preceding action, but is formed and is changed through action. For Pierce a preceding phenomenon was belief and for James, it was subjective interest. In general, pragmatism is a tradition born out of the criticism towards dualism; truth is born through action and justified through the consequences. How this happens and what precedes it differs according to the contributor. (Dewey 1951; James, 1913; Rorty, 1986; Thayer, 1968)

This paradigm discussion deals with many basic philosophical questions, from the actual worldview and human existence, to the nature and or the concept of entrepreneurship and its demands on the reasoning, and further to the practical recommendations for advancing methodologies in this field. Thus, the concept of a paradigm, even though not explicitly defined, seems to move from the worldview to the methodological choices; in other words, what we think about the world and human existence and how we are supposed to gain knowledge from it.

On the other hand, the introduced ideas of the reality seem to vary from dualism to a non-dualistic position in philosophy. This indicates that there is no consensus over the very basic assumptions of the nature of entrepreneurship. Also, it is evident that this discussion is not new, but rather has followed throughout the history of entrepreneurship, indicating that perhaps it is at the core of the whole phenomenon. Thus, contextuality of the methodological discussion in entrepreneurship ranges from the past to the present.

The problem of this paradigm discussion, however, is that even though it combines paradigm discussion with methodological considerations, it does not define the basic concept of a paradigm. Thus, it seems to leave the reader with so many loose ends that unravelling them leads to confusion. Therefore, it might be beneficial to explicitly open up the concept of paradigm in order to help the reader in following the reasoning.

Empirical Findings of Methodological Choices

The empirical findings approach the methodological debate from another perspective. They depict the outlook of concrete methodological choices in journal articles and conference papers. The focus is on the interplay between chosen theoretical perspectives and methods without any effort to combine them with deeper levels of knowledge creation.

Churchill and Lewis (1986) studied the interaction between methodology and the area of inquiry, as well as whether the contribution aimed to improve practice, theory or methodology. They had two sets of data: 298 abstracts from ten journals and 150 conference papers. They divided methodologies into seven categories: observational or contemplative theory building, survey, survey using public data, field study, computer simulation/modelling and vignette or 'reportage'. Among these they found that journal articles focused more on the first category, and conference papers on surveys. In total, 77.1 per cent consisted of these two categories. When they analysed the objective of the research, whether it was theory, practice or methodology, they found that the major part of the journal articles (75.5 per cent) concerned practice and 58 per cent of the conference papers referred to theory. Only six conference papers aimed to improve methodology, for the most part building data bases.

These findings indicate that, at that time, studies showed no interest in methodology, especially those papers presented in blind referee journal articles. On the other hand, the concept of methodology seems to be quite problematic. Instead of an explicit definition for it, they give us different categories, focusing on data-gathering methods rather than on the actual methodology or research method. Even though in many cases these are closely related to each other, they cannot be used as synonyms.

Wortman's study, in 1986, consisted of 52 journal articles and conference papers relating to entrepreneurship, and 70 to small businesses. From a methodological perspective, this study had several limitations. It excluded case studies, arguing that 'the small business field has been overwhelmed by exploratory studies and the field has passed the time for mass use of the case study'. Its geographical area was restricted to the United States and Canada. Finally, it only included data-oriented studies. The studies were classified by type of organisation, sample size, research methods and/or instruments employed, statistical methods used, issues studied and content of the study. The results indicated that when statistical methods were used, they generally were at a relatively unsophisticated level, such as means, standard deviations, ranking, t-tests and linear correlation. On the other hand, some developments took place between 1980 and 1984, in the studies on small businesses, towards more sophisticated statistical analysing methods. As a recommendation, the author suggested that more sophisticated statistical analyses would be needed.

The results indicate that advancing methodology is regarded as a matter of using more sophisticated existing statistical analysing methods. From a methodological conceptualisation perspective, the classification of methods in this study is quite confusing. The author seems to divide them into two categories, statistical analyses and case studies. This might imply two directions – either there were only those two choices or the author did not identify different methods in the qualitative field. On the other hand, the study aims to differentiate between a research method, a data-gathering method and an analysing method, which might be regarded as a more advanced approach than Churchill and Lewis's study.

Brush's study was restricted to women business owners. She used 57 conference papers and articles as her data, published during 1977–91. From a methodological perspective, she studied 'research design' referring to a data-gathering method, and a research analysing technique. The findings show that 63 per cent used mail surveys and 21 per cent personal interviews. Forty-four per cent used descriptive statistics and 30 per cent also used chi-square tests, correlation or t-tests. Only 18 per cent used more sophisticated statistical analyses. Qualitative analyses were used in only four studies.

The findings seem to support Wortman's results as to the use of sophisticated statistical methods. On the other hand, results indicate that qualitative methods have not increased interest among women entrepreneurship researchers or they have not been reviewed as a valid choice to be examined. In this study, as in the previous examples, there seems to be little or no interest to advance methodological development. From a conceptualising perspective, the research design and the data-gathering method seem to be synonymous.

These empirical studies may verify the validity of the recommendations to advance methodology in entrepreneurship research. The results indicate that there has been very little interest, either towards methodological development per se or innovative learning, from other fields of science. Also, methodologies used or studied were mainly concentrated on quantitative methods, neglecting expanding potentials in the qualitative field.

The studies seem also to be as conceptually confusing as the concepts of the research method, data-gathering method and analysing method. The suggestion made at the beginning, that actually little that is concrete has happened in methodological development, seems to be valid for empirical studies dating back to the early 1990s. Even though there are limitations regarding the scope of these studies, this general conclusion seems to be obvious.

Combining these two approaches, paradigm discussion with more general recommendations and empirical findings to depict the actual methodological choices, we can conclude that both of them indicate the need to advance methodologies in entrepreneurship research and to support each other. On the other hand, both of them also indicate that there is a need to clarify and sharpen conceptualisation regarding the bases of such concepts as a paradigm and methodology, and methods.

In addition, both of these, philosophical and empirical studies, indicate that there rarely seem to be explicit efforts to combine the methodological discussion with the philosophical bases. However, the examples we have found mainly concern the situation before the 1990s. Since then, there has been an identified increase in entrepreneurship studies that might make a difference in this respect. In order to study this possibility, but also in order to make an effort to advance and participate the paradigm discussion and its conceptualisation from a methodological perspective, we first attempt to study the interplay between methodological choices and philosophical bases, and then study methodological choices in more recent entrepreneurship studies in leading journals.

STEP 2:   THE DYNAMIC DEBATE OF A SCIENTIFIC INQUIRY LEADING TO THE PARADIGM DISCUSSION

The etymological roots for a paradigm can be found from the Greek 'paradeigma', 'to set up as an example'; 'para' referring to beside and 'deiknynai' meaning to show a paradigm that is a model or a pattern (Choi, 1993, 32).

As a concept, however, 'paradigm' is an outcome of an intensified discourse of the dynamics in science that has gained strength, especially in the latter decades of the 20th century. A tremendous growth of scientific knowledge has generated different suggestions about its nature, its relationship to surrounding reality and, on the other hand, to propositions on how this or relevant and valid knowledge, in general, is supposed to be acquired or created (Audi, 1995; Feyerabend, 1997, 1999; Kuhn, 1962; Popper, 1992[1959]; Rorty, 1986). This search has also produced new concepts or conceptual units larger than a theory or a method, helping us to take into account, for example, the school system and structure and the time span of the theory building. (e.g. Kuhn, 1962, 247–8; Popper, 1992; Rorty, 1986). Paradigm and tradition, for example, are among the concepts generated for that purpose (Niiniluoto, 1984). The concept of methodology also relates to these efforts.

A larger context for this debate is the philosophy of science that is centred, on the one hand, on methodology closely related to the theory of knowledge, and on the other hand, on the meaning and content of the posited scientific results closely relating to metaphysics. The philosophy of the social sciences in this field consists of social phenomena as distinct from natural phenomena. It ponders over what is a good social explanation: is there a distinctive method for social research and, for example, what is the relationship between social and individual facts? It has both descriptive and prescriptive qualities. (for example Audi, 1995).

Assuming that entrepreneurship is a part of this field, we can say that its paradigm debate ponders over the role and nature of a human being and of action in the field of entrepreneurship: is there a special methodological base for studying that, and what is the relationship between an individual entrepreneur, a firm/business, the economy and the environment? In short, the entrepreneurship research seems to be looking for its own philosophical bases. Even though a conceptual debate has not found any definite answer, we can say that some philosophical agreement seems to prevail; for example, that entrepreneurs are human actors, whose action relates such phenomena as a new venture creation, innovation and opportunity recognition, and also that entrepreneurship, in general, relates to these phenomena. The paradigm discussion also often seems to take as examples the distinction between the natural sciences and social phenomena, and ponders over the differences between stability and change.

In order to study the nature of a paradigm, we can learn from this dynamic debate of the development of scientific inquiry that basically has

> challenged the empiricists' view towards the theory change 'as an ongoing smooth and cumulative process in which empirical facts, discovered through observation or experimentation, forced revisions in our theories and thus added to our ever-increasing knowledge of the world. It was claimed that, combined with this process of revision, there existed a process of intertheoretic reduction that enabled us to understand the macro in terms of micro, and that ultimately aimed at a unity of science (Audi, 1995, 557).

The paradigm discussion of entrepreneurship also seems to get impetus from this challenge.

Popper (1992 [1959]) examined this problem in his world-famous book *The Logic of Scientific Discovery*. He claimed that, from an epistemological perspective, science is not a system of certain, or well-established, statements; nor is it a system which steadily advances towards a state of finality. Our science is not knowledge (episteme): it can never claim to have attained truth, or even a substitute for it, such as probability. According to him the old scientific ideal of episteme – of absolutely certain, demonstrable knowledge – has proved to be an idol. He used the expression, a theories theory, describing the advance towards theories of an ever-higher level of universality. As a theory of rules for scientific method he applied the term 'quasi-inductive'. It refers to a sort of interplay between a deductive and an inductive method. The idea of a theories theory and a quasi-inductive process are his proposition of scientific dynamics and structure (Popper, 1992).

It should be noted that Popper's main concern was the problem of cosmology: the problem of understanding the world – including ourselves, and our knowledge, as part of the world (Popper, 1992, 15). However, his main point in this context on one hand, is the idea of science as a dynamic open-ended and open-minded process, and on the other, it explicates a need for larger conceptual units. As he expressed it, a theories theory or, from a methodological perspective, a theory of rules of scientific method.

Somewhat different, and perhaps an even more dynamic approach, concentrating more on the nature of the process, can be depicted in the writings of one of Popper's earlier contemporaries, Gaston Bachelard (1884–1962), a French philosopher of science and a literary analyst. In his books *The New Scientific Spirit*, 1934, and *Rational Materialism*, 1953, he generated a dialectical and cyclical approach. For him, scientific knowledge proceeded through a dialectical process of reason and experience. He claimed that new scientific knowledge may lead to a fundamental reformulation of reality (The Columbia Encyclopedia, 2002). He viewed science as developing through a series of discontinuous changes (epistemological breaks). Such breaks overcome epistemological obstacles: methodological and conceptual features of common sense or outdated science that block the path of inquiry (Audi, 1995, 59). Bachelard offers us a dialectical process with reason and experience. This suggests that scientific knowledge is a cultural product, both describing and creating reality. The experience also binds his claim to reality and content. The problem is how can we identify the criteria for those phenomena in this cyclical process that are valuable enough to be further investigated, unless the experience itself defines it?

These discontinuities were moulded in Kuhn's hand, years later, into the idea of a revolutionary development of paradigms. For Kuhn, the paradigm is a key component in the development of scientific knowledge. In his world-famous book, *The Structure of Scientific Revolution*, he argues that scientific work and thought are defined by paradigms consisting of formal theories, classic experiment and trusted methods. Paradigms are conceptual worldviews. (http://www.anova.org/kuhn.html, Kuhn, 1992). Thus Kuhn was the scientist formulating the idea of a paradigm.

The starting point for Kuhn was the difficulties between the natural and social sciences, as it seems to be also in entrepreneurship discussion. He explains it as follows:

Particularly I was struck by the number and extent of the overt disagreements between social scientists about the nature of legitimate scientific problems and methods. Both history and acquaintance made me doubt that practitioners of the natural sciences possess firmer or more permanent answers to such questions than their colleagues in social science. Yet, somehow the practice of astronomy, physics, chemistry, or biology normally fails to evoke controversies over fundamentals that today often seem endemic among, say psychologists or sociologists. Attempting to discover a source of this difference led me to recognise the role in scientific research of what I have since called 'paradigms'. These I take to be universally recognised scientific achievements that for a time provide model problems and solutions to a community of practitioners. Once that piece of my puzzle fell into place, a draft of this essay emerged rapidly. (Kuhn, 1996, x)

As regards the philosophical bases it should be noted that Kuhn seems to found his concept of paradigm on the third branch within the philosophy of science, namely specific foundational questions arising out of the specific results, such as space–time theories and explanations in evolutionary biology (the branches of the Philosophy of Science (Audi, 1995, 611)). His explanation of the dynamics of science also excludes the role of technological advance or of external social, economic and intellectual conditions that might make a difference in a paradigm discussion (Kuhn, 1996). It could be argued that this might be important, especially with such a phenomenon as entrepreneurship which seems to emerge under or create certain economic and social conditions.

On the other hand, his conclusions regarding the questions that should be asked before science can reach a mature state, relate to two other basic branches of the philosophy of science:

> Effective research scarcely begins before a scientific community thinks it has acquired firm answers to questions like the following: What are the fundamental entities of which the universe is composed? How do these interact with each other and with the senses? What questions will legitimately be asked about such entities and what techniques employed in seeking solutions? At least in mature sciences, answers (or full substitutes for answers) to questions like these are firmly embedded in the educational initiation that prepares and licenses the student for professional practice. (Kuhn, 1996, 5)

The results of Step 1, in this research, indicated that such questions in entrepreneurship research are still unanswered and vary considerably between authors.

Kuhn's ideas were not approved without criticism. Perhaps one of the most extreme was presented by Feyerabend. His main thesis concerning the structure of science was that 'the events and results that constitute the sciences have no common structure; there are no elements that occur in every scientific investigation but are missing elsewhere' (Feyerabend, 1997, 280). Successful research does not obey general standards: 'it relies now on one trick, now on another, and the moves that advance it are not always known to the movers.

He was concerned about science's ability to catch the reality. He claimed that philosophers complicated their doctrine, but they did not bring it closer to reality' (Feyerabend, 1999, 282). Similar confusion seems to guide the work of pragmatists. They try to approach it and at the same time to overcome the problem of dualism through action.

Even though these representatives of the dynamic approach to a scientific inquiry and a paradigm development have different views, all of them still believe that there is not only one true and stable knowledge or one way of achieving that knowledge, but rather the reality and hence the way to acquire knowledge about it changes. Thus it seems to follow the very basic arguments presented to delineate the phenomenon and the paradigm discussion in entrepreneurship research, as the examples of Bygrave and Stevenson and Harmeling indicate. On the one hand, these entrepreneurship authors look at the interplay between theories and methodological choices, and on the other hand, they ponder over what kind of reasoning lead to new knowledge.

The core of this paradigm discussion seems to relate to the complex interplay between scientific inquiry and its relationship to knowledge creation, that is epistemology, and to our ideas of the world and existence in it, that is ontology. As Niiniluoto suggested, it is a larger concept that seems to gather, on the one hand, the philosophical bases for the phenomenon or a field of science being studied. Thus, it seems to deal with both the very basic ideas of the world, human existence and knowledge, and methodological considerations that are deduced from these bases. As Kuhn suggests, a paradigm means conceptual worldviews, consisting of an agreement on formal theories, classic experiment and trusted methods. Concepts used by Popper were a theories theory and a theory of rules for a scientific method, while Bachelard concentrated more on an actual process of knowledge creation.

Thus, the paradigm seems to play a certain role as a mediator between philosophical bases and actual methods, and individual theories. It contains the theoretical bases defining the very nature of a phenomenon and the rules to gain knowledge about that phenomenon. Thus, a paradigm is manifested as a group of theories and definitions suitable for describing the field of study, or more broadly the phenomenon and a group of methods, suitable for studying this field.

From this perspective, the claims that entrepreneurship should have a unified definition and that it is the responsibility of every researcher to state clearly what is meant when the term is used, as, for example, Bygrave and Hofer (1991, 13) present it, might lead to unintended results, unless it is deduced from philosophical bases. The reality emerging implicitly in conceptual and methodological choices might be quite different or even contrary to the actual intentions of the author. Perhaps the paradigm understood as a mediator and a gathering link between the philosophical bases and the actual definitions and methods, might serve as a tool to help advance the development of the entrepreneurship specified methodologies and conceptualisation.

We can also argue for the need to define philosophical bases by looking at the actual content of the paradigm and methodological discussion. There seems to be a tendency to deduce the argumentation from dualism and disregard as a starting point non-dualistic traditions in philosophy. We have tried to demonstrate this both by analysing the contemporary paradigm debate in entrepreneurship research and by introducing the dynamic discussion generating the concept of a paradigm. By looking at the whole chain of choices from philosophical bases to actual methods, there might be an easier access to the non-dualistic assumption of reality.

In order to go forward with this suggestion, we will make an effort to construct the structure of a paradigm as a mediator between philosophical bases and methodological choices.

STEP 3:   A STRUCTURAL VIEW DELINEATING THE PARADIGM DISCUSSION

The concepts dealing with the philosophical bases related to the paradigm are ontology and epistemology. Etymologically, 'logos' refers to 'explanation' or 'the word by which the inward thought is expressed, the inward thought itself' (Audi, 1995; McKechnie, 1977). In Greek philosophy, it took on the meaning of 'reason, thought of as constituting the controlling principle of the universe and as being manifested by speech' (McKechnie, 1977). The suffix ' "-logy" refers to a specific kind of speaking like a doctrine, science, theory of' (ibid.); and 'onto-' in Greek means existence or being. Ontology originally referred to the branch in metaphysics dealing with the nature of being and reality (for example McKechnie, 1977). In short, ontology refers to our ideas of reality and how it is constituted.

Epistemology, in turn, is interested in how we can acquire knowledge about that reality. The Greek word, 'episteme', refers to knowledge (for example McKechnie, 1977). Epistemologists try to identify the essential, defining components of knowledge (Audi, 1995). Thus, both of these provide the bases for a paradigm or, vice versa, what we understand by a paradigm leads to ontological and epistemological assumptions. The problems of defining, but at the same time the need to define epistemology in the context of paradigm and methodology, can be demonstrated through its 'tripartite definition', called 'standard analyses' (for a description of epistemology see, for example, Audi, 1995). It means that epistemology consists of three elements, namely justified true beliefs, each of them having several different explanations. Basically, the belief condition means that the knower must be related to the object of knowledge, with the idea, I know that, I believe that. The truth condition has at least three basically different explanations: 1) Truth as a correspondence = agreement, of some specified sort, between a proposition and an actual situation; 2) Truth as coherence = interconnectedness with the proposition with a specified system of propositions; and 3) Truth as pragmatic cognitive value = usefulness of a proposition in achieving a certain intellectual goal. Finally, the justification condition refers to the idea that the knower must have an adequate indication that a known proposition is true. Again we have different, controversial explanations for this. For example, we can regard justification as evidence, epistemically permissible or epistemically good or in a large epistemical justification might simply mean 'evidential support' of a certain sort.

Looking at the concept of ontology and epistemology, we can see that they are some kinds of 'rules of the game', and we have different games with different rules. These rules are interconnected within each game, as for example Stevenson and Harmeling (1990) suggested. What we believe is reality or being, gives us the limits to what we can believe, what we are able to know about that reality and how we are supposed to argue for our knowledge about that reality. What we believe exists, and how it exists leads to the rules of justification, that is how to find adequate justification. These kinds of decisions are already methodological choices, leading to a specific method and further defining what kind of data we can lean on and how we are supposed to analyse it.

If we assume that knowledge is not one entity but many and it changes, it is reasonable to assume that we have different ways of studying it, or as Kuhn suggests, an immature paradigm is engaged in competing schools of science or neighbouring sciences. As the entrepreneurship paradigm discussion indicates, that is the case in this field, and instead of one definition, it has several different definitions which might lead to different epistemological and ontological assumptions. Thus, explicating this chain of arguments might add new aspects to the entrepreneurship discussion, and thus, advance the development of entrepreneurship-specified methodology.

To demonstrate this chain and the relationship between these choices, we can apply a hierarchical approach. Ontology is the largest and deepest level. Simply, we cannot study something we do not believe exists. The essential questions of how we believe that what we believe exists can be: do we believe that what exists is stable, or do we believe that it changes, or is it unique or universal, and what is the relationship between human existence and the world?

Epistemology is the second level deduced from ontology and, further, we have different ways of attaining knowledge that refers to methodology. These bases lead us also to theories about the phenomenon; thus theories and

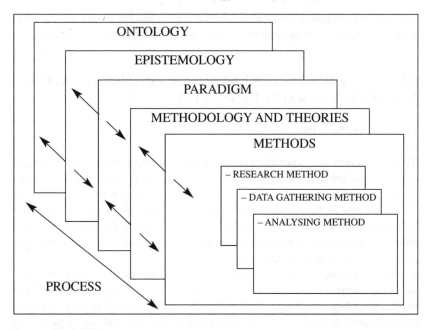

Source: Kyrö (2003).

Figure 6.2   Structural approach to a paradigm

methodology are interconnected. Further, each methodological choice consists of several specific methods. Within these methods we might have several alternatives for data-gathering. This structure is delineated in Figure 6.2.

This kind of a construction is not actually new in entrepreneurship studies, since a similar description of ontology, epistemology and methodology can be found in Hill and Wright's (2001) article, 'A qualitative research agenda for small to medium-sized enterprises'. The difference between their description and this construct is that here it is combined with a paradigm discussion, problematized and argued from two angles: entrepreneurship-specified and a more general philosophical debate, as well as supplemented with more specified methodological choices.

A hierarchical approach positions the paradigm discussion and gives us a tool for analysing methodological choices. It might also advance the paradigm discussion itself, since it positions and specifies the place and the role of the paradigm in a scientific inquiry, thus further developing Kuhn's original idea of its essence. On the other hand, it is a quite simplistic view of an extremely complex phenomenon, and thus easily exposed to criticism, that might further advance the paradigm debate in entrepreneurship.

In order to follow this frame, in Step 4 we will continue by making an effort to apply it to the current methodological state in entrepreneurship studies.

STEP 4:   THE CURRENT STATE OF METHODOLOGY IN ENTREPRENEURSHIP RESEARCH

Conducting the Study

This step adopts the structural frame and examines how studies argue for and explicate the ontological and epistemological commitments. Further, it looks at the kinds of methods that are used and how they are described, considering all three parts of the methodological choices, that is the research, the data-gathering and the analysing method. Finally, it depicts the context of these studies by examining what the target of the study is and how it covers the time span, that is past, present and future.

The data consisted of 337 refereed articles published in leading entrepreneurship journals in 1999–2000 (four entitled the Big 4, covering 72 per cent of this population and supplemented with *Entrepreneurship and Regional Development*, as well as those management journals that are regarded as important in this field). All articles from the entrepreneurship specific journals, and those dealing with entrepreneurship in management journals, were chosen for the analyses. These are specified in Table 6.2. Since this data

Table 6.2   Data distribution of articles by journals

Journal	Frequency of articles			
	1999	2000	Total	Per cent
Journal of Business Venturing	25	22	47	14
Small Business Economics	47	35	82	24
Entrepreneurship: Theory & Practice	21	25	46	14
Journal of Small Business Management	36	33	69	20
Entrepreneurship & Regional Development	19	16	35	10
Organization Science	–	8	8	2
Administrative Science Quarterly	3	–	3	1
Academy of Management Journal	1	11	12	4
Academy of Management Review	1	8	9	3
Academy of Management Executive	–	3	3	1
Strategic Management Journal	8	9	17	5
Journal of Management	4	2	6	2
Total	165	172	337	100

Table 6.3   Editors and publishers of the journals

Journal	Editor	Publisher
Journal of Business Venturing	USA	Elsevier
Small Business Economics	USA	Kluwer Journals
Entrepreneurship: Theory & Practice	USA	Baylor Business
Journal of Small Business Management	USA	Blackwell Publishing
Entrepreneurship & Regional Development	Sweden	Routledge
Organization Science	USA	University of California (USA)
Administrative Science Quarterly	Canada	Cornell University (USA)
Academy of Management Journal	USA	Academy of Management (USA)
Academy of Management Review	USA	Academy of Management (USA)
Academy of Management Executive	USA	Academy of Management (USA)
Strategic Management Journal	USA	John Wiley & Sons, Inc.
Journal of Management	USA	The Southern Management Association

consists of and covers a specific population representing the legitimated scientific consensus of methodological excellency in this field, there is no reason to test its statistical significance. Thus, the direct and proportional distributions and cross tabulations are analysed as such. Data was coded through a SPSS statistical programme and combined with the virtual Flash installation (Kyrö, et al., 2002, http://www.uta.fi/laitokset/aktk/entrenet). The detailed data of articles can be studied at this address, since only the summaries are presented here.

Geographical distribution of the journals and their editors in Table 6.3 indicates that the USA seems to dominate the legitimated scientific consensus of methodological excellency. The editors and publishers of the journals were mainly Anglo-American. Editorial boards in particular are from the United States. Publishers are international or American. European scientists are not well represented among publishers and chief editors. This might make a difference when it comes to the paradigm discussion, since the dynamic debate of a scientific inquiry identified in this study is based on the European view. Thus the results of this study might be partly based on cultural differences, which actually rather manifests different approaches to methodological problems, rather than giving a general view of entrepreneurship research. However, this is only an assumption that should be kept in mind, but its verification would need further studies.

Results

Looking at the targets this discussion focuses on (Figure 6.3), we can say that the main part deals with the firm/business (52 per cent) and its relationship to

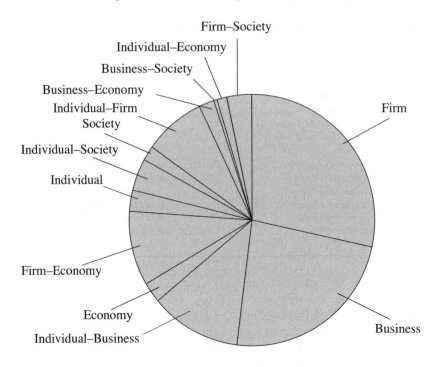

Figure 6.3   Studies divided according to the targets

the individual (19 per cent). All together the firm/business is involved in 85 per cent of the studies. The individual including his/her relationship to other levels of analyses, comprises 28 per cent of the studies. Macro-level phenomena, the society and the economy are marginal as research targets. Thus, the main focus in entrepreneurship research is on the firm/business.

Examining the methodological choices and their relationship to epistemological and ontological commitments, it is easy to summarise the findings. None of these articles seemed to explicate the ontological and epistemological levels relating to their methodological choices.

Research methods were divided into eight different groups (see Table 6.4). Sixty-four per cent used some kind of statistical method, 22 per cent a qualitative method or approach and 6 per cent used econometrics etc., methods typical for macro-level studies. The methodological choice for 8 per cent of the studies was missing. In the main the statistical methods can be regarded as sophisticated, since only 16 articles used descriptive statistics.

Eleven per cent of the studies used qualitative methods, and eleven per cent used a qualitative approach. Discursive methods were represented most,

Table 6.4   Distribution of research methods in journal articles

Research method	Frequency	Per cent	
Descriptive statistics	16	5	
Different regression analyses	90	27	
Different variance analyses	30	9	} 64
Other statistical analyses	77	23	
Qualitative methods	38	11	
Theoretical or building a model or frame	40	11	} 22
Econometric etc. models	19	6	
Missing	27	8	
Total	337	100	

Table 6.5   The division of qualitative methods

Qualitative method	Frequency	Per cent
Ethnography	1	3
Discursive method	26	68
Case	8	21
Historical method	1	3
Narrative	2	5
Total	38	100

followed by case studies (see Table 6.5). Ethnography and historical approaches were used in one article and narrative in two articles.

Research methods were further divided into research, data-gathering and analysing methods (see Table 6.6). In the statistical methods, the data-gathering method consisted of three parts: defining the population, describing the sampling and the actual data-gathering. The criteria for defining the population were very loose. The lowest criterion was that the authors defined the database they used. The results indicate that only 22 per cent were able to do this. On the other hand, the majority of the methodological descriptions were reasonably well covered.

Conclusions

The results indicate that the dominating interest is focused on the firm/business, that is, on a micro-level and that the most popular methods used are statistical methods. Also, it is evident that there is no explicit effort to open up

Table 6.6 Distribution of research, data-gathering and analysing methods in statistical studies

Statistical method	Research method (Per cent)	Population (Per cent)	Sampling (Per cent)	Data-gathering (Per cent)	Analysing method (Per cent)	Total (No.)	Total (Per cent)
Descriptive statistics	3	1	7	6	8	16	8
Different regression analyses	41	14	37	32	41	90	42
Different variance analyses	14	2	14	12	14	30	14
Other statistical analyses	31	6	32	31	35	77	36
Total	90	22	89	81	97	213	100

the link between ontological and epistemological choices. These issues might relate to each other, since the agreement on methodological choices decreases the pressure to ponder the philosophical bases.

On the other hand, the actual research process seems to be well justified in statistical analyses. Compared to previous studies made by Churchhill and Lewis, and Wortman and Brush, we can say that the level of sophistication in statistical methods increased towards the end of the 1990s. Furthermore, the description of the research process seems to be satisfactory with one exception, namely the population. This might be interpreted as indicating the difficulties of defining the phenomenon itself and/or the lack of proper data bases. Thus, it is a signal opposite to a methodological consensus.

The position of qualitative studies is quite interesting. Their role is minor and focused on either case or discursive methods. On the other hand, compared to Wortman's claim of the domination of case studies and Brush's findings of their marginal position in women entrepreneurship studies, their proportion has increased, indicating an established position in methodological choices. In addition, the number of discursive methods might mean an effort or a need for re-interpretation. This is also a signal opposite to a methodological consensus.

On the other hand, alternative methods seem to be almost invisible: one history, one ethnography and two narratives. The recommendation to borrow methodological solutions from other fields of science has not generated many results so far.

If we look at the methodological choices from a time perspective, there are no methods for future studies and only one for history. Basically, this means that the focus is on the present. However, if we have a more extensive definition for a time perspective, than being merely a method, there might be more findings for future and past orientations.

In general, the suggestion made at the beginning, that actually little has happened in the concrete methodological development, seems to be valid in some respect. There are only a few openings to borrow methodological solutions from other scientific fields. The suggestion that entrepreneurship should develop a methodology of its own seems to be far in the future. No apparent efforts towards that direction can be found. Advancement has taken place in statistical methods, as well as in the field of discourse methods.

The dominating contemporary profile of entrepreneurship research seems to concentrate on studying entrepreneurship as a micro-level phenomenon at the present time through statistical methods. The interesting question is whether this profile refers to some kind of consensus on the nature of this phenomenon, and what it tells us about the nature of epistemological and ontological levels. The demand for opening the methodological choices towards other fields of science or towards a methodology of its own, as Bygrave suggested, has not really been taken seriously.

With some reservations, this step in the research process has achieved its goals. We have depicted the current outlook of the methodological choices. In this respect, the major problem consists of the criteria for categorising the methods and analysing different parts of the methods. In other words, we think that we should have been more precise in order to make solid conclusions. The differences between categories were not always obvious, and the identification of the different methodological parts in data-gathering would have demanded co-evaluation. On the other hand the main lines in methodological development were quite apparent, and the conclusions could be regarded as reliable.

The other aim to test the applicability of the constructed conceptual frame as an analysing tool has been partly reached, since it seems to reveal the obvious lack of arguing for deeper levels of analysis. On the other hand, that finding could also be made quite easily without that tool. To really see its usefulness as an analysing tool would have required a further interpretation of each article from an epistemological and ontological perspective. Only then could we say something about the actual situation in this respect. It is difficult to achieve this goal, since further interpretation has not been explicitly done.

FINAL CONCLUSIONS AND EVALUATION

The aim of this study was to advance the methodological debate in entrepreneurship research by introducing a structural approach that combined philosophical bases with actual methodological choices, through the paradigm discussion. It was also suggested that actually little has happened, in the concrete methodological development, either by borrowing methodological solutions from other fields of science or by developing entrepreneurship specific methodology.

The findings indicated that the development that has taken place concentrated more on sophisticated statistical methods, and in some respect employing discursive methods, rather than extensively borrowing ideas and solutions from other fields of science. There were hardly any signs of creating an entrepreneurship specific methodology, and the interest towards defining ontological and epistemological commitments was non-existent. The idea that we might benefit from re-evaluating these commitments, in order to provide new insights into entrepreneurship specific methodology, is still waiting for further studies. On the other hand, we have indications that these issues have also been unsolved for the very early contributors in this field and that the most profound questions on the nature of entrepreneurship relate to them. Thus, this at present unstudied field might offer new prospects for advancing both the conceptual and the methodological debate. This was supported by the finding that there seems to be a tendency to deduce the argumentation from dualism, and to disregard, as a starting point, non-dualistic traditions in philosophy. Reconsidering the geographical distribution of the journals and their editors makes one wonder if this is partly due to the cultural differences. And furthermore, if we actually have geographically and culturally different approaches to methodological questions in the USA and in Europe is this manifested as a paradox between the explicated needs to advance entrepreneurship-specific methodology and the actual outcome of this discussion? Otherwise this obvious paradox seems like a hidden agenda – a paradigm itself as Kuhn defined it: 'recognise *the role in scientific research of what I have since called "paradigms"*. These I take to be universally recognised scientific achievements that for a time provide model problems and solutions to a community of practitioners' (Kuhn, 1996, x, italics original).

The effort of this study to identify the role of the paradigm in a scientific inquiry and its relationship between the ontology, epistemology and the actual methodological choices, thus gives an explicit form and a tool to both advancing Kuhn's basic idea and definition of a paradigm and to explicating the current methodological state of entrepreneurship research. Applying the structural approach that defines a paradigm as a mediator between philosophical bases and methodological choices and as a concept explicating the relationships between these two, also brought some new light to something that has not been apparent through descriptive method, thus increasing the understanding of a concept by finding, describing and interpreting the entity of meanings, which is in the core of the interpretative concept method. It also, however, suggests that perhaps we could also apply this approach to the theoretical debate of the concept of entrepreneurship and put less effort on restricting it to specific sentences. Consequently this study encourages us to expose and define our own ideas and position in this system of philosophical concepts in each study, and more collectively in the field of entrepreneurship research.

Thus methodologically the quite recently launched descriptive, interpretative concept method turned out to be a valid choice. In addition, supplementing it with pragmatism that led to the action-bound research process consisting of several steps seemed to work well. However, criticism should be addressed to the dialectical nature of this process that was supposed to be at the same time intuitional and rational. The general feeling, after adopting this idea, is that it is very hard to argue solidly for such a process. These experiences suggest that there is a need for further development of this method, especially its process. In this respect, in the field of pragmatism, Pierce's system of reasoning might offer some help.

Kuhn's definition of a paradigm challenges us, however, also to give faces to those 'model problems and solutions of a community of practitioners' that dominate the field of entrepreneurship research. The results of the current state of methodological choices and the dominating target of the studies indicate that the focus is on the current problems of businesses and firms. As scientists, this leaves us to wonder where the history and future of entrepreneurship are and what is the role and impact of entrepreneurship to the surrounding society and environment. Are our model problems and solutions focused mainly on the contemporary problems and are we able or interested in studying only what seems to be immediate and obvious in the surrounding reality? This challenges us also to include in the future the axiological problems to the structural approach. Finally the sophistication of statistical methods has not led us to question their ability to describe a complex and non-linear reality. In this respect the findings indicated that there were no efforts, for example, to apply fuzzy logics and Bayesian non-linear modelling (for example Niskanen, 2003 http://www.metodix.com; Nokelainen et al., 2003).

IMPLICATIONS

The implications of this study lead more generally to a methodological development, specifically to entrepreneurship research and finally to the debate on advancing conceptual development. First there seems to be an urgent need to be more innovative in order to find new insights into methodological questions. This involves the human mind and behaviour that leads to a non-dualistic rather than a dualistic position in philosophy. The current outlook of the methodologies and their position in this respect was not very promising, even though some silent signals could be identified. Perhaps we might benefit from employing methods that concentrate both on the past and the future instead of on the present, as well as applying methods that reveal action instead of stable descriptions. These suggestions lead to two directions: on the one hand, to the pragmatism originally invented in the USA and to the critical paradigm originally developed in Germany. Perhaps some ideas from these schools in philosophy could be combined in an innovative way in order to advance the entrepreneurship specific methodology. In entrepreneurship research this requires that we both recognise opportunities in other fields of science and combine resources in a novel way for new inventions. This is something that lies at the core of the phenomenon of entrepreneurship. Finally the structural view of the concept of a paradigm suggests that we might benefit from viewing concepts also as developing entities of different elements and their relationships rather than demarcating the definitions into strictly defined sentences.

NOTE

1. Paula Kyrö is responsible for the conceptual part of this study as well as the analyses, conclusions and writing the report. Juha Kansikas has gathered the data and provided most of the distributions. The responsibility for the results is divided accordingly. Both of us are indebted to Maarit Liimatainen for coding the data to SPSS and to Pearl Lönnfors for language proof reading. Above all, however, we are indebted to Jönköping International Business School for offering excellent research possibilities and data bases for conducting this study. The first version of this paper was presented at 1st European Summer University, Valence, France, 19–21 September 2002.

REFERENCES

Alasuutari, P. (1994), *Laadullinen Tutkimus*, Jyväskylä: Vastapaino.
Audi, R. (gen. ed.) (1995), *The Cambridge Dictionary of Philosophy*, Cambridge: Cambridge University Press.
Brush, C.G. (1992), 'Research on women business owners: past trends, a new perspective and future directions', *Entrepreneurship Theory and Practice,* **16**(4) Summer, 5–30.
Buchanan, J.M. (1982), 'The domain of subjective economics: between predictive science and moral philosophy', in I. E. Kirzner (ed.), *Method, Process and Austrian Economics. Essays in Honour of Ludwig von Mises*, Toronto: Lexington Books, pp. 7–20.
Bygrave, W.D. (1989a), 'The entrepreneurship paradigm (I): a philosophical look at its research methodologies', *Entrepreneurship Theory & Practice*, **14**(1), 7–26.
Bygrave, W.D. (1989b), 'The entrepreneurship paradigm (II): chaos and catastrophes among quantum jumps?', *Entrepreneurship Theory & Practice*, **14**(2), 7–30.
Bygrave, W.D. and C.W. Hofer (1991), 'Theorizing about entrepreneurship', *Entrepreneurship Theory & Practice*, **16**, 13–22.
Von Böhm-Bawerk, E. (1890–91), 'The historical vs. the deductive method in political economy', Translated by Henrietta Leonard, *Annals of the American Academy*, Volume 1, http://socserv2.mcmaster.ca/econ/ugcm/3113/bawerk/bohm001.html
Choi, Young Back (1993), *Paradigms and Conventions – Uncertainty, Decision Making and Entrepreneurship*, The University of Michigan Press.
Churchill, N.C. and V.L. Lewis (1986), 'Entrepreneurship research. Directions and methods', in D.L. Sexton and R.W. Smilor (eds), *The Art and Science of Entrepreneurship*, Cambridge: M.A. Ballinger, pp. 333–66.
The Columbia Encyclopedia, (2002), 6th edn, New York: Columbia University Press, www.bartleby.com/65/.
Davidsson, P. (2001), 'Towards a paradigm for entreprenurship research', Conference proceedings, Vol. 1. *Rent XV Research in Entrepreneurship and Small Business*, 22–23 November, Turku, Finland, Small Business Institute, Turku School of Economics and Business Administration.
Dewey, J. (1951), *Experience and Education*, 13th edn, New York: The MacMillan Company.
Ehrencrona, A. (2000), *Thomas Kuhn*, http://cgi.studen.nada.kth.se(cgi-bin/d95-aeh/get/kuhneng. 12.4.2000.
Feyerabend, P. (1997), *'Against Method'*, 3rd edn, London and New York: Verso.

Feyerabend, P. (1999, first published 1987), '*Farewell to Reason*', London and New York: Verso, http://www.anova.org/kuhn.html.

Gunning, J.P. (2001), '*The Praxeological Entrepreneur*', http://www.fortunecity.com/meltingpot/barclay/212/subjecti/workpape/praxent.htm, 16.1.2001. Loaded 27.8.2002.

Hill, J. and L.T. Wright (2001), 'A qualitative research agenda for small to medium-sized enterprises', *Marketing Intelligence & Planning*, **19**(6), 432–43.

James, W. (1913), *Pragmatism*, Helsinki: Otava.

Kirzner, I.E. (ed.) (1982), *Method, Process and Austrian Economics, Essays in Honour of Ludwig von Mises*, Toronto: Lexington Books.

Kuhn, T. (1962), *The Structure of Scientific Revolutions*, Chicago: University of Chicago Press.

Kuhn, T.S. (1992), *De vetenskapliga revoltionernas struktur*, Stockholm: Thales.

Kuhn, T.S. (1996), 3rd edn, *The Structure of Scientific Revolutions*, Chicago: The University of Chicago Press.

Kyrö, P. (2003), 'The paradigm and methodological choices in scientific research', http://www.metodix.com.

Kyrö P., J. Kansikas, M. Liimatainen and T. Mäkelä (2002), *Method Space in Entrepreneurship Research*, http://www.uta.fi/laitokset/aktk/entrenet.

Lämsä, A-M and T. Takala (2001), *Interpretative Study of Concepts*, http://www.metodix.com.

Macmillan, I.C. and J.A. Katz (1992), 'Idiosyncratic milieus of entrepreneurial research: the need for comprehensive theories', *Journal of Business Venturing*, **7**(1) (January), 1–8.

McKechnie, J.L. (ed.) (1977), *Dictionary of the English Language*, unabridged, 2nd edn, USA: The World Publishing Company.

Niiniluoto, I. (1984), *Johdatus Tieteen Filosofiaan. Käsitteen ja Teorianmuodostus*, Helsinki: Otava.

Niskanen, V.A. (2003), *A Brief Introduction to Fuzzy System Modelling*, http://www.metodix.com.

Nokelainen, P., T. Silander, P. Ruohotie, and H. Tirri (2003), 'Investigating Non-linearities with Bayesian Networks', paper presented at 111th Annual Convention of the American Psychology Association, August, Toronto, Canada.

Popper, K.R. (1992), *The Logic of Scientific Discovery*, USA & Canada: Routledge, (first published in English 1959 by Hutchinson Education).

Rizzo, M.J. (1982), 'Mises and Lakatos: a reformulation of Austrian methodology' in I.E. Kirzner (ed.), *Method, Process and Austrian Economics*, Toronto: Lexington Books, pp. 53–74.

Rorty, R. (1986), *Consequences of Pragmatism* (Essays: 1972–80), 3rd edn, Minneapolis: University of Minnesota Press.

Sarvimäki, A. (1988), *Knowledge in Interactive Practice Disciplines: An Analysis of Knowledge in Education and Health Care*, Research Bulletin 68, Helsinki: Department of Education, University of Helsinki.

Sexton, D.L. and R.W. Smilor (eds) (1986), *The Art and Science of Entrepreneurship*, Cambridge: M.A. Ballinger.

Stevenson, H. and S. Harmeling (1990), 'Entrepreneurial management's need for a more 'chaotic' theory', *Journal of Business Venturing*, **5**, pp. 1–14.

Stewart, A. (1991), 'A prospectus on the anthropology of entrepreneurship', *Entrepreneurship Theory and Practice*, Winter, pp. 71–91.

Thayer, H.S. (1968), *Meaning and Action. A Critical History of Pragmatism: The Bobbs-Merrill Company*, New York: The City College, University of New York, USA.

Wortman, M.S. Jr (1986), 'A unified framework, research typologies, and research prospectuses for the interface between entrepreneurship and small business', in D.L. Sexton and R.W. Smilor (eds), *The Art and Science of Entrepreneurship*, Cambridge: M.A. Ballinger, pp. 273–332.

7. The origins, lessons and definition of entrepreneurial achievement: a multi-paradigm perspective via the case method

Ajay Bhalla, Steven Henderson and David Watkins

INTRODUCTION: CASES AND CONSTRUCTS IN ENTREPRENEURSHIP RESEARCH

The narration of stories is an ancient form of imparting knowledge. A well told story holds the attention of the reader and allows the sharing of wisdom and meaning with the inexperienced. It allows the imaginative listener to march with Agamemnon, feast with Jamshed or sail with Noah, absorbing cultural messages and experiences. Freer thinkers and intellectuals may periodically reassess and reinterpret these messages, and review the consequences of alternative actions.

One modern descendent of the story is the case study, which, for a variety of reasons, is central to teaching within several different disciplines, particularly those of an overtly vocational and professional nature. Thus, Law has been taught at Harvard using the case method since the middle of the 19th century (Gue, 1997). This seems inherently reasonable, since cases are not only a pedagogic resource but actually constitute much of the discipline's lifeblood, not least because under Common Law the 'case' is the key unit of progression for the law itself. In other disciplines, such as medicine, cases are used both as an illustration of established general principles, and to simulate practice for diagnosis and application of these principles to patients in later professional life.

It is less easy to explain the use of the case method in management and business research and education. Management processes and organizations, like life itself, are not experienced or particularly well explained as a 'case study', and thus are not part of the discipline itself. In particular, the constraints of detail, perception, interaction and time are lost in the narrative discipline imposed by the presentation. The difference between the recording of a case and the events themselves are well elucidated by Sartre when describing the difference between the muddle and dislocation of events as they are experienced and the ordered consequences and reactions recorded in a biography (Sartre, 1963).

Furthermore, there are few firmly grounded principles within management generally – and within entrepreneurship in particular – that can be comfortably and unambiguously elicited from cases. However, it is frequently possible to identify interesting situations, and subsequently produce cases, which narrate a sequence of events from one principle or perspective. Indeed, the selection of cases to be studied in an entrepreneurship programme might be made precisely for this reason, given the prescriptive nature of many of the teaching notes produced with such cases. However, Kay (1991) argues that it is the *lack* of such generalizable business principles which necessitates the widespread use of the case study: that is to say, researchers and teachers use the vehicle looking for general patterns and possibilities in the case which may not have been evident (or even present, cynics might observe) to those experiencing the matters under consideration. Seen in this context, cases become a contributory part of truth – or principle – creation, rather than dissemination or clarification of an external, objective, understood reality.

Certain entrepreneurship journals, in particular *Entrepreneurship Theory and Practice* and *Journal of Small Business and Enterprise Development*, have at different times made particular efforts to increase the number and diversity of well constructed entrepreneurship cases in general circulation (Cf. Chrisman, 1994; Watkins and Reader, 2003 and 2004). Unlike some other sub-fields of business and management, the number and quality of entrepreneurship cases in case repositories such as the *European Case Clearing House* (ECCH) is some-what limited.[1] Similarly, the debate on the validity and use of case studies in management education which surfaces from time to time in such fora as the *Academy of Management Review* (for example that between Eisenhardt (1989, 1991) and Dyer and Wilkins (1991)) is only rarely echoed in the entrepreneur-ship literature. Romano (1989), Chrisman (1994), Gill (1995) and Chetty (1996) are rare examples of scholarly reflection on the case method in this context.

Here, our principal purpose is to use a well-regarded and high profile case study, recently published, to demonstrate the way in which even narratives constructed within a narrow paradigmatic frame may be used to *challenge* that frame and generate alternative perspectives on entrepreneurial processes. However, a by-product of this is to open up possibilities for the more creative uses of the case method more generally. For, if we are open to the possibility that cases *create* stories and interpretations about what happened, rather than *reflect* a given sequence of events, we are obliged to face particular implica-tions about how cases are used and how they are created.

Far from *limiting* the role of the case study, awareness of its interpretative origin should rather be emancipatory. Argyris (1980), focusing on organizational learning, urged the use of the case for such behavioural development as decision-making, exploring different interpretations, confrontation and reconciliation in the context of organizational problems and solutions. Limitations, they argued, tend to be found in the role of teachers who use these cases to amplify or illustrate a predetermined learning experience. Naturally, their less iconoclastic critics wished to preserve doctrinal pedagogies (Romm and Mahler, 1991).

Before carrying out this case reinterpretation, we need to expound, expand and synthesize two frameworks of analysis developed in the wider contexts of strategic management and organizational behaviour so as to be able to apply these to cases developed within the entrepreneurship domain.

DEVELOPING THE FRAMEWORK OF ANALYSIS 1: WHITTINGTON

In the next two sections we examine paradigmatic frameworks developed by Whittington (1993) and by Burrell and Morgan (1979). We would not wish to canonize either. Our purpose is not to contribute to debates about the ontology of meta-theories, but rather to *use* them to generate alternative perspectives and counter narratives of processes in entrepreneurial firms. One may thereby enhance the richness of a case and present alternative, latent, implications and lessons. Once these counter narratives have been developed, it is possible, even desirable, to discard their paradigmatic origins and treat each as a contentious account in its own right.

Scholars from Sandberg (1992) to Verstraete (2003) have identified aspects of strategic management as a key input to understanding entrepreneurship. Yet strategic management is not a unitary body of theory, but contested ground. Thus Whittington's framework of paradigms was developed as a means of untangling the various schools of thought within strategic management, (although once defined they can be seen to have wider applicability). Like much of the strategy literature, the key ideas can be summarized within a two-by-two grid (see Figure 7.1).

Classical Approach

What Whittington characterizes as the Classical School is usually adopted by those who intend to research and write on topics which should be helpful to managers. This paradigm is most readily associated with such writers as Ansoff (1965) and Porter (1980) in that managerial activity is assumed to be rational, deliberate and focused on achieving some long-term objectives that

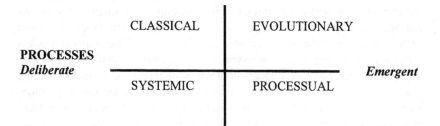

OUTCOMES

Profit-Maximizing

CLASSICAL	EVOLUTIONARY
SYSTEMIC	PROCESSUAL

PROCESSES
Deliberate ——————————————————— *Emergent*

Pluralistic

Source: Whittington (1993).

Figure 7.1   'Schools' of strategic management after Whittington

can usually be subsumed into return on assets. The environment is seen to be dynamic, but essentially predictable if only the right techniques are intelligently applied. Consequently, the strategic planning process is based upon establishing organizational objectives, environmental scanning, strategy formulation and implementation. Monitoring and control underpin the process of managerial activity. Failure is seen as resulting from deviations from this process leading to the selection of poor strategies, that is those which do not enable the organization to develop a competitive advantage, or lead to superiority in a market that is incapable of satisfying corporate objectives. Cleverness in analysis and development of appropriate competencies during implementation ensure success.

This perspective would appear to offer a practical approach likely to appeal to entrepreneurs. It sees the proprietor(s), or senior manager(s), as the central actor(s), and examines decision making processes and implementation problems accordingly. The perspective can draw upon a wide range of research techniques. Survey techniques have been widely used in the field to examine such key issues as the relationship between formalization of planning methods and performance in entrepreneurial ventures and succession planning as a tool assisting profitable exit. It is within this paradigm in particular that a small business is naively seen as a 'little big business', although the problem has been long recognized (Welsh and White, 1981) and addressed by Jennings and Beaver (1997), among others.

Less formal methods using a case study approach have also been used to elicit information regarding particular problems where questionnaires alone would have been insufficiently sensitive to pick out pertinent details. Recent examples include Fuller-Love and Scapens's (1999) study of difficulties in implementing a performance-related pay scheme in a small shipyard. As managers tried and retried to get their scheme to improve productivity and reduce costs, the researchers were able to re-interview all the actors and assess the changing organizational processes. Similarly, Dodge and Robbins's (1992) study of businesses which appeared to eschew planning and formal marketing – and which would certainly have indicated that, if studied using question-naires only – revealed that effective marketing and, to a lesser degree plan-ning, can be prevalent and continually debated and acted upon without the formality of organizational processes, job titles and documentation.

In short, this particular approach offers much to the researcher. It draws upon a wide variety of research techniques to explore the role of managers in developing and directing their organizations. Many interesting and useful things have been learned along the way. However, it must be accepted, some-what ruefully, that very few controversies have been resolved by these tech-niques and the approach has often been criticized for its failure to deliver a series of empirically robust axioms that could form the basis of an undisputed management science. Indeed, such studies frequently push management theory ever further from a degree of self-confidence. One such study of the relationship between business performance and the proprietors' understanding of the business environment in small retail businesses showed no particular association: that is to say, that building up a detailed picture of the business environment did not seem to be associated with superior performance, contrary to what one might have thought, given the extensive literature on business and SME strategy (Jenkins, 1994; 1997).

Evolutionary Approach

In this paradigm, environmental forces predominate, causing firms to adapt if they are to survive. The difficulty is that organizations are generally unable to predict environmental change in advance, and in consequence cannot gener-ally devise appropriate managerial actions. Management in this paradigm is thus a question of ensuring survival and adaptation by flexibility (Hannan and Freeman, 1988). Rigid strategies and optimization attempts are likely to lead to longer run disasters. The evolutionary approach to management studies would have few problems with the conclusions from – for example – Barton and Matthews's (1989) study regarding SME approaches to financial planning and raising finance.

Management is characterized by 'arbitrary' production, replication and optimization of strategic fit with the environment in the short term. Several such optimizations over a period of time would approximate to a long-term strategy, which Mintzberg (1978) might characterize as 'strategy as pattern'. Successful firms tend to replicate and resemble each other as they adapt toward the few feasible organizational forms and strategies.

Within this paradigm, enquiry into cognitive processes is seen to have less relevance than in other approaches. Rather, researchers will often treat managerial processes as a 'black box' and simply relate outcomes to environment. Economic and cybernetic studies tend to predominate in this field, closely examining both managerial agency and transaction cost implications of strategic ventures (Williamson, 1974).

Processual Approach

In the Processual School, the environment is seen as arbitrary and unpredictable, but not as harsh or punitive as in the Evolutionary School. Poor and sub-optimal performance continues unpunished, both within organizations and by the marketplace. Strategies and change are a consequence of wide ranging political activities within the organization. Satisficing, rather than achieving grand objectives, will be the predominant motivation. Organizational life will be characterized by a multiplicity of interests and political compromises.

Studies adopting this paradigm are inevitably less prescriptive than those previously discussed. If managerial decision-making is seen as a dependant variable of unfathomable and unpredictable organizational processes, then the scope for improving its quality becomes somewhat problematic. It may, however, be possible to make some generalizations about organizational activity and culture, to critique the prescriptive approaches of other works, and to offer some processual advice of humble, rather than ambitious, scope and direction.

A good example of exploring processual generalizations can be found in Poza et al. (1997). The researchers were keen to investigate the sensitive relationship between family and non-family managers in small family businesses. Questionnaires were sent to 229 executives – family and non-family – from 26 family businesses, with additional questionnaires to family members inside and outside the firm. The questions were of a general nature, as no specific hypotheses were under review. A wide range of statistically significant differences in perception emerged between family and non-family members – for example, the latter were less optimistic about the future of the business and their own career prospects within it than the former. Although not particularly surprising to outsiders, awareness of these tendencies might aid family members in decision making.

A further example is given by Miller et al. (1982) who argue that crucial decisions in SMEs concerning strategy and structure are not made by managers seeking to maximize return on investment (as the classical school would suppose) or the result of fortune or mimicry (as the evolutionary school might hold), but rather the personality of the entrepreneur. They do not claim that their model demonstrates good practice, but they do hold that their work is indicative of common (one hesitates to say 'normal') organizational behaviour.

Systemic Approach

The Systemic School holds that it is pointless to examine an organization as a discrete unit in isolation from wider social forces, culture and institutions that facilitate and impinge upon business activity. It is argued that wider social roles and political constraints prevent deliberative managerial strategies developing, or anything like profit maximization to occur.

As with the processual view, it may appear that this approach is less overtly helpful to practitioners. Supporters may argue that in fact it explains a great deal about what are airily described as 'implementation' problems in the literature, and understanding is presumably a precursor to more actions. Furthermore, appreciating these political constraints to effective behaviour is at least as important as comprehending financial constraints, which achieve a much higher profile. Lastly, this view has some cachet at the moment with the so-called 'stakeholder' approach to managerialism.

The importance of gender in business is also a fertile area for research within this kind of framework. Cole (1997) examined the role of women within family businesses, and was particularly interested in exploring the prevailing view that women are in a 'double bind' of having to combine business and family roles; that women have particular business roles based on gender; and are disadvantaged in succession. Her results would question this view, suggesting that men and women seem to have similar, rather than different roles in business; that women are often as unfair to other women as are men; and that gender related succession issues seem less of a problem than generally supposed.

Although the four paradigms that Whittington identifies are very different, and produce distinct yet convincing explanations of the same phenomena (Henderson and Zvesper, 2002) they share a common cultural heritage. They do not, for example, challenge the precept that organizations are goal-directed and that their behaviour is explicable in those terms. The notion that it is *right* for managers to organize towards formal organizational goals is not challenged. Other behaviours in organizations are only really examined in so far as they retard or accelerate the workings of the organization in relation to these goals. Many writers on organizational behaviour point out that the Whittington models may help to identify some key relationships pertaining to the functioning of a business, (and to be fair, Whittington does not claim anything more of his work), but do not capture the experience of working in organizations; neither do they enable non-managerial interests to be represented in their own terms.

DEVELOPING THE FRAMEWORK OF ANALYSIS 2: BURRELL AND MORGAN (1979)

An alternative and broader set of paradigms as presented by Burrell and Morgan (1979) is helpful in showing the effects of paradigm choice in determining: what can be understood; what puzzles will be regarded as important; and, what elements of real life should be disregarded. This framework has been extremely influential in organizational studies generally and has recently been applied in the entrepreneurial domain. Grant and Perren (2002) reviewed current entrepreneurship research published in leading journals. They judged that the vast majority of the 36 articles reviewed were presented from a functionalist perspective, 'a dominance of the Functionalist Paradigm that pervades the elite discourse of research in leading journals *and acts as a potential barrier to other perspectives*' (emphasis added). Perren et al. (2001) further discuss the interesting paradox of a field which is often described as 'pre-paradigmatic' nevertheless presenting it as one with an apparent unifying framework, ascribing this as being likely to result from academics playing to practitioners' agendas (Tranfield and Starkey, 1998). This begs the question of what is lost by constraining entrepreneurship to its functionalist approach.

For an answer, we follow Grant and Perren (2002) and look at Burrell and Morgan's (1979) characterization of sociology as four competing paradigms based upon another two-by-two grid, of which the Functionalist Paradigm is only one possibility (see Figure 7.2).

Functionalist Paradigm

In this paradigm, society is presumed to be as concrete and real as the physical world. The social scientist attempts to determine and understand empirical relationships within society. Whittington's Schools all have an essentially functionalist basis according to Burrell and Morgan's (1979) framework. This is a consequence of structuring around the strategic choice literature, which considers the decisions and processes that an organization goes through in order to fit with its environment. Both organization and environment are understood as real entities, rather than constructs. Such disruptions to the status quo as entrepreneurial activity rupture established interactions between

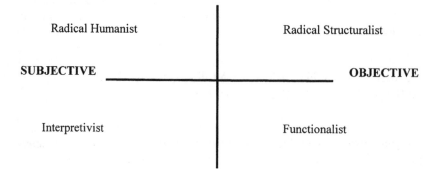

Figure 7.2   *Burrell and Morgan's (1979) paradigmatic framework*

organizations, households, factors of production and institutions. Organizations go through a sequence of mutual adjustments to restore strategic fit. That is to say that the nature of the organization and the environment are not understood in any aspect other than their reciprocity and the conservation and reproduction of wider social relationships, although it is worth pointing out the theoretical possibility that the Systemic School could be used to promote societal reforms that go beyond business (Whittington, 1992).

The justification for researching organizations and management in this way is that it supposedly helps management to perform better. This, the argument runs, ultimately makes everyone better off. Indeed, one would think that such research would *have* to say this, or it would be otherwise unpardonable. However, Burrell and Morgan's three remaining paradigms problematize assumptions about the ontology of society and the desirability of social stability, thereby challenging comfortable technical debates about entrepreneurship.

Interpretative Paradigm

This paradigm does not accept that the social world is real or fixed, but attempts to determine how social truths are created and subscribed to: that is to say, the researcher attempts to learn how actors in the organization create meaning. Research would require contemporaneous study that looked at the way decisions were reached, the extent to which they were implemented and the causal links between specific actions and specific outcomes. These would have to be interpreted from a wider range of perspectives to understand how sense and truth were established and, of course, the results could not be aggregated across organizations.

Recent good examples include Fortado's (1998) study of jokes and nicknames in a small law firm. Apparently trivial interactions and incidents are shown to have a major impact on how individuals see themselves and their roles, as well as moderating formal relationships between business functions and the relationships between legal and support staff.

Ashcroft and Pacanowsky (1996) studied the behaviour of a consciously female-dominated organization, less interested in the business efficacy of this than the interactions between the women. The authors were able to document and explain, among other important things, what they called the 'unique tension of female divisiveness, such as cattiness or pettiness'.

In classic ethnography, a study of interpretation and meaning is an end in itself. However, managerial writers have frequently used ethnographic ideas to generate managerial programmes and initiatives in a rather Functionalist fashion. Perhaps most sinister of these are studies that purport to interpret the low morale of downsizing survivors, those *not* made redundant, and devise appropriate managerial responses to restore individual productivity (Vaara and Tienari, 2002).

Radical Humanist

This paradigm examines how social forces, such as management, act as a means of controlling and directing human activity, thought and experience. It does not accept social constructions as being real in any objective sense, and is usually critical of management theory. It is similar, in parts, to the systemic approach of Whittington, (for example, on leadership) although the Radical Humanist Paradigm would look at the subjugation of individuals as a process in its own right, rather than the business efficacy of this.

Recent work in this area has examined the rhetoric of empowerment, and shown how this apparently liberating idea is commonly experienced as a change in the style of control rather than the diminution of it. Ezzamel et al. (1997) eloquently show the role of the accounting function in the process in a non-judgmental fashion. More painful accounts are described by Abbott and Evans (1995), who relate how a cruel and cavalier management style at a small brewery, apparently based on management by objectives and empowerment, overworked and eventually broke junior staff; and by McCabe (2000) in a factory setting.

An alternative way of using this paradigm is to question relationships espoused by functionalist writers. A good example of this approach is shown in a classic study by Delbridge et al. (1992), which revisits such modern manufacturing processes as JIT, TQM, and so on in a car plant, and argues that the principal source of improved productivity comes from work intensification and stress on the workforce, rather than the technology itself. This opens modern manufacturing to a wide variety of contested value judgements that would be invisible seen from within Functionalist Paradigms.

This way of thinking and researching should not be confused with functionalist writers who simply argue for a more humane management style on the grounds of business efficiency – such as the ubiquitous exhortations of Thomas J. Peters. The point of radical humanism is not that it makes more profitable or efficient organizations than traditional managerialism – although this may be the case (Actouf, 1992) – but that it is a better way for people to live.

Radical Structuralist

This paradigm takes the view that social life is real, as the functionalists hold, but differs in that it sees social dynamics as resulting from contestation of political groups and power structures. Although sharing the concerns of the humanists for freedom and humanity, it tends to look at these in a socio-political context.

SME literature has rarely troubled itself with reflections of this kind. There has been a prevailing, perhaps rhetorical view, that 'SMEs are good things' in the mainstream literature, while critics might hold that capitalist relationships in SMEs are not substantially different from those in larger organizations.

Here, we would argue that there is considerable scope for research within this framework, even if one does not particularly wish to champion an alternative society or philosophy, since such an approach readily discovers discomforting explanations and interpretations of organizational behaviour. Fearful (1996) examined the practice of deskilling in clerical work and found that far from becoming deskilled, workers had learned and developed an *alternative* range of skills to increase their own effectiveness. However, since these skills were not formally recognized by management, or the workers themselves in many cases, they were not rewarded. Fearful goes on to use trait theory to suggest that effective clerical workers were likely to be women, who might further weaken the bargaining position of labour.

Similarly, Holmes and Grieco (1991) describe how pressures from funding agencies progressively undermined and annihilated small-scale, community-based enterprises – including a bus garage and a training agency.

In all the research examples used above, it would have been possible to reinterpret research evidence according to a different paradigm, creating new conclusions and undermining, generally, those put forward by the researcher. Henderson and Zvesper (2002) have shown how this can be carried out with reputable empirical studies. Below, we wish to show how Whittington's Schools and Burrell and Morgan's (1979) Paradigms can be applied to a reputable and high profile case study of entrepreneurial activity to produce new lessons, understandings and interpretations. The case is interpreted by using a vignette that illustrates the lines along which each argument would be developed. The Interpretive Paradigm creates a methodological problem as the lack of verbatim dialogues and interactions drains the approach of its lifeblood.

SCHOOLS, PARADIGMS AND ENTREPRENEURSHIP CASE STUDIES

The case selected for this example of multi-paradigm analysis is ChocExpress Ltd (Brown and Molian, 2001). This case was chosen so as to reduce accusations of selector bias, being the winner in the most recently determined year (2001–02) of the Entrepreneurship category of the annual EFMD European Case Writing Competition, organized by the *European Foundation for Management* and distributed by the *European Case Clearing House*. Briefly, this case gives a comprehensive account of the start-up, travails and ultimate success of a chocolate merchandising company by two friends. This business began as a partnership supplying mints, and later chocolates, to blue chip companies for use as promotional and corporate gifts. All production and design work was factored out – Thorntons being the chief supplier of the chocolate products. The firm expanded into supplying large supermarket chains and used Thorntons' shops to sell to 40 000 households by mail order. It ceased both these arrangements after a time, and developed a more profitable household distribution system using catalogues, mail order and its own Chocolate Tasting Club. Each new stage of the business was characterized by a new business identity (Geneiva Chocolates Ltd., Mint Marketing Company, and so on), and these are shown on the time-line of major developments in the history of the firm (Table 7.1). ChocExpress is the firm based on mail order to households. The two friends remained in control of the business throughout.

The case study stresses the decisions taken by the two founders at each point. It explores the information available at the time, and the personal motivations at each point. It is clear that lifestyle aspirations and notions of freedom motivated the two entrepreneurs, rather more than pecuniary desires. They were also evidently determined to do things properly – there is no direct evidence of cutting corners or sloppy management reported.

Table 7.1   Time-line of key events in history of ChocExpress Ltd

Year	Key Event
1988	Angus Thirlwell and Peter Harries form Mint Marketing Company to supply promotional sweets with customized corporate logos
1990	Geneiva Chocolates Ltd formed by Angus Thirlwell and Peter Harries to supply quality chocolates targeted at the same corporate market as Mint Marketing Company
1991	Geneiva Chocolates Ltd moves into purpose-built premises
1993	Geneiva Retail Chocolates set-up by Angus Thirlwell and Peter Harries to supply chocolates to supermarkets under their own label
1993	ChocExpress set up by Angus Thirlwell and Peter Harries as a mail order chocolate gift company with Thorntons Ltd as a supplier. Thorntons is a traditional family business that manufactures high quality chocolate which it distributes mainly through its own retail stores
1994	ChocExpress forms an alliance with Thorntons to promote its products in their retail stores
1997	Geneiva Retail Chocolates operations abandoned due to low margins and difficult relationship with supermarkets
1997	ChocExpress terminates its alliance with Thorntons Ltd due to disagreements about promoting ChocExpress
1998	ChocExpress launches a mail order catalogue business to supply higher-value customers – based upon the mailbase created with Thorntons
1999	ChocExpress invests in new internet site and begins a faster growth trajectory
2001	ChocExpress builds on its success by setting itself ambitious growth targets and aims to reorganize the logistics side of the business

Source: Based on information taken from ChocExpress Case.

WHITTINGTON'S SCHOOLS AS INTERPRETATIONS OF CHOCEXPRESS LIMITED

Classical Interpretation

This case is written from a classical perspective. It is structured around key decisions made by the proprietors, and focuses on the impressive growth and financial consequences of their actions. The teaching note is structured around three key strategic decisions, SWOT analysis, critical success factors and Greiner's (1972) stages of growth, always stressing managerial control and environmental fit.

Evolutionary Interpretation

The evolutionary view would tend to focus on the transaction cost elements of this business, rather than any notion of the broader business strategy. The low start-up costs – some £50 000 – were achieved by factoring out much of the operational activity, although it is worth noting that the firm's failures with wrapping were at the heart of this, rather than great foresight.

The early corporate clients were targeted on the basis of low maintenance. Blue chip firms could be approached directly, and targeted individually by using photocopies of their logo on the packaging of the promotional mints. The relatively small number of large clients also made invoicing and debt collection comparatively straightforward. The wisdom of factoring manufacture is not in question, but the choice of Thorntons for their chocolate making *was* questionable; only when links with the supplier were severed did ChocExpress discover that it was possible to buy better quality more cheaply elsewhere. The principal benefit of the link with Thorntons was the leveraging of their retail resources, rather than their production prowess, which might not have been predictable at the time the arrangements and decisions were made. The result was that the firm developed an active customer base and brand name at low cost. Much of the subsequent profitability and growth came from this resource.

In short, we see that ChocExpress did not succeed through the execution of effective decisions. Rather, the mistakes of the company were not fatal and had unpredicted (unpredictable) beneficial consequences on the firm's cost structure. The success of the firm depended upon such fortuitous outcomes; the difficult decisions and heroic actions of the proprietors, though no doubt brave, were in trying again rather than getting things right.

Systemic Interpretation

A firm cannot have a strategy independent of the wider cultures and networks in which it is part. The ChocExpress story is one of a small firm in a market in which it had no expertise or history, struggling against the hand of its associates.

The firm's first customer was the entrepreneurial father of one partner, who found that the supply of his own corporate confectionery was disrupted by the failure of existing contractors. It was therefore possible to sell very quickly without promotional expenditure. There is quite a literature on entrepreneurs and their fathers, but in this case the relationship seems to have been encouraging and supportive.

Expansion of the product range to include chocolate was induced by the requirements of their existing customers – the question: 'What else do you do?' It did not seem to come about through any kind of entrepreneurial insight or internal management processes, although the proprietors undoubtedly acted promptly to secure relationships with suppliers of complementary products – Thorntons in particular.

Thorntons is a traditional family company, and this is reflected both in its operations and the identity of its brand. ChocExpress had great difficulty in getting Thorntons to produce what it wanted, or in persuading them to try out new ideas. This was a particular source of tensions, and when the relationship became strained, Thorntons used its financial resources to try to buy the smaller company.

The firm's involvement with supermarkets was also seen as oppressive and restrictive. Chocolate suppliers and supermarkets could have chosen to trade directly, but used intermediaries because the precarious nature of demand and short lifespan of novelty products made both wish to defray some of the risk. This, rather than any innovation or quality issues led to the involvement of Geneiva Chocolate. Consequently, the firm found its margins squeezed and activities restricted by the limited scope of the relationships involved.

The success of the firm depended upon using its relationships to establish the firm in the earlier period, but breaking free of these to develop new relationships conducive to its own development and core skills was the most significant issue.

Processual Interpretation

Processual dynamics turn upon the negotiations, conflicts and legitimacy of conflicting pressures. The ChocExpress case study contains very little information on these issues. Areas that could have been usefully examined are conflicts between functions, professional bodies of knowledge and particular types of strategy.

BURRELL AND MORGAN'S PARADIGMS AS INTERPRETATIONS OF CHOCEXPRESS LIMITED

Radical Humanist Interpretation

The origins of ChocExpress are not found in the entrepreneurial gusto of its founders. Rather, the zest for founding that business comes from a pragmatic response to the feelings of oppression and restriction that they both experienced while working for large firms. This is particularly exemplified by the elation they felt at discontinuing the Geneiva Chocolate operations, the profitable business that supplied chocolate to supermarkets, since it had forced them to behave 'outside their value set'. Severance enabled them to act in the way that they wanted to, as exemplified by their 'company culture chart' reproduced from the case as Table 7.2. Similarly, the opportunity to sell ChocExpress to Thorntons and stay on as managers was rejected, in part at least, for the same reasons.

One line of enquiry open to a radical humanist approach is to consider the experience of others involved in the founders' emancipatory vision and goals. Presumably those who lost their jobs when Geneiva Chocolate closed were not so elated. There were similar issues in the relationship between Thorntons and ChocExpress over the reluctance of Thorntons' store managers to promote the mailorder business. Such reluctance is understandable, since few direct benefits for the store would result, and mail order might actually reduce store sales. ChocExpress was exasperated by the unwillingness of Thorntons to undermine the autonomy of retail managers by insisting that greater emphasis be placed on the line.

Although evidence is naturally limited, there is enough here to speculate that the efforts of the founders to escape the stifling and limiting circumstances that they had experienced previously were successful, but were, occasionally at least, sustained at the expense of reproducing some of those conditions for others inside and outside their firm. Kelly and Kelly (1998) are amongst those to have observed similar patterns in other contexts. Consequently, the 'we' referred to in Table 7.2 seems to be the entrepreneurs, and not a statement about values they wish to propagate throughout their business and business dealings.

Table 7.2   ChocExpress 'company culture chart'

We are	We are not
Leaders	Followers
Adders of value through ideas	Wage slaves to other companies
Always seeking to improve	Red tape merchants
Exciting, excited and excitable	Dull and predictable
Building something worthwhile	Short-termist
Driven by vision and teamwork	Driven by fear and politics

Source: Brown et al. (2001).

Interpretivist Interpretation

The table of cultural values in Table 7.2 above is largely individualistic and hedonistic. It does not refer to the treatment of others, or give any clue regarding how business relationships with other firms will be developed. The elasticity of such terms as 'vision', 'leadership' and 'worthwhile' would also allow a flexibility of interpretation that may be revealing if through an appropriate research design we were able to study how decisions were reached and actions taken.

There is a particular schism between ChocExpress's founders and Thorntons that would be interesting to explore further from this point of view. ChocExpress clearly outmanoeuvred Thorntons, but less by deception than Thorntons' own construction of the relationship between the two firms. It is possible to believe that Thorntons' managers interpreted the relationship as one of mentoring or nurturing; helping an innovative new business led by inexperienced entrepreneurs to establish a customer base and brand in a concentrated industry with extremely high barriers to entry. If this were so, then Thorntons' managers did not appreciate how circumstances were changing: the case puts the ChocExpress view as: 'The child (upstart) had outgrown its parent (mentor)'. When matters came to a head at a meeting to discuss ending the relationship, Thorntons' management was 'surprised and flummoxed'. Even after the shock, Thorntons continued to misunderstand the pragmatic approach of ChocExpress by giving the owners three months to consider their offer to buy the company – ample time to develop and implement an alternative strategy.

An interpretivist scholar would wish to describe how the Thorntons' team came to misunderstand the situation so pitifully, and how the ChocExpress team convinced itself that the firm had the means to prosper alone.

It is worth mentioning in passing that when the original authors of the ChocExpress case were asked to comment on our reinterpretations, they suggested that this interpretation does not reflect the true situation, even though it draws accurately from the text of the case study. In later versions of the case an additional footnote clarifies the issue in a different way. We retain the original interpretation here to reinforce our earlier comments about case study as truth creation. All other reinterpretations were judged reasonable.

Radical Structuralist Interpretation

ChocExpress are merchants, working at various times between manufacturers and retailers. There is an apparent economic oddity in that the product is frequently given free to consumers through the corporate gifts market. From a radical perspective, none of this activity creates profit.

Value is created by labour. Surplus value is the difference between what a worker receives in the form of wages, and the value of their labour. Profits, rents and interest come from this surplus value. However, much of the labour involved in merchant activity influences only the distribution of the surplus value between various economic agents. It does not directly contribute to the value of the product as such. The dynamics of competitive capitalism and specialization relocate the manifestation of surplus value through extraction manufacturing and merchant activities (Marx, 1959).

From this perspective the crux of the case and the turning point in the business is the discovery in 1997 that chocolate could be obtained more cheaply elsewhere than if supplied by Thorntons. The year is particularly significant: this was the year that international financial pressure on the Ivory Coast ended the price fixing arrangements that guaranteed a minimum price for cocoa beans. The consequent collapse in bean prices and the wages of those engaged in cultivating them have not been accompanied by a similar fall in the retail prices of chocolate products – creating additional surplus value. Many companies (like Thorntons) that buy cocoa beans or chocolate on the world markets have expressed surprise and disbelief in allegations that cocoa growers, farmers and labourers might be particularly impoverished by the standards of the region, or that children might be used as slaves on cocoa plantations (Millman, 2001).

From a radical point of view, the story is not about how two entrepreneurs have broken free from restrictive institutional relationships and developed exciting new products, although these facts would not be disputed. Rather the narrative would seek to explain how the profits from these quality products, frequently given away as gifts, have their origins in international capitalist relations of production that exploit and impoverish those prevented from organizing and protecting themselves.

DISCUSSION AND CONCLUDING REMARKS

The case study of ChocExpress is rightly celebrated as a good case that reveals many aspects of successful entrepreneurship in its straightforward narrative. However, by approaching the story from a variety of different schools and paradigms, we are able to draw wider inferences about the source of the firm's success. Within the framework of Whittington's Schools we can alternatively judge the performance of the firm to be: visionary, demonstrating courageous decision making and risk taking within the Classical School; fortuitously successful and dependent on often unintended outcomes in developing a low-cost operation within the Evolutionary School; and resulting from the struggle against debilitating social relations within the Systemic School.

The non-functionalist paradigms from Burrell and Morgan's (1979) framework allow us to pose other questions and make ethical judgements about factors that are normally invisible in mainstream thinking about entrepreneurship. The Interpretive Paradigm reminds us that the logical relationship between actions, events, decisions and outcomes normally presented in a case study are a function of hindsight. Events in progress are not well understood by the actors, and not merely because information is limited and rationality bounded. Rather, we construct meanings on the basis of signals and preconceptions that are rarely articulated, and frequently turn out to be misleading guides both to the actions of others and the consequences of our own endeavours. A Radical Structuralist approach gives both an alternative explanation of the important business dynamics involved, and forces a reappraisal of the largely unspoken view that production, entrepreneurship and customer focus are unequivocally good things. Similarly, the Radical Humanist Paradigm helps us to bring to the surface issues of the commodification of labour within an entrepreneurial business; that is, the transformation of people into parts of a production system that can be defined by the requirements and objectives of the firm and disposed of when inconvenient.

We would argue that our approach to examining the ChocExpress case, and other such entrepreneurial cases, is an important adjunct to the literature on our subject. It is worth considering views from multi-paradigms at an early stage in a research methodology. By adopting a singular view – predominantly functionalist and frequently classical – we may well be able to specify research questions accurately, but at the expense of closing off a large number of insights and judgements.[2] Much the same argument holds true for the choice of a pedagogical strategy.

At the very least our approach should make scholars less confident about their conclusions and prescriptions. For example, the ubiquitous recommendations for succession planning do not come from a rounded literature on the topic. A processual view could usefully focus on the role of the leader as a fulcrum for internal conflict, and the impossibility, in many cases, of finding an effective, politically acceptable leader before the issue is forced on the firm. Similarly, the leader may have a systemic role in terms of business contacts and relationships that may be more important than any executive role he or she performs. An interpretive study, of course, would not take the view that there is a 'correct' time to replace senior managers, but may focus on the signals and interactions that lead some to believe that such a time is or is not approaching, and how these behaviours are interpreted by the various actors. A radical humanist may focus on such things as the association of job role and work with identity and community, and the sense of loss that succession and change carry with them.

We do not, however, recommend that scholars use a mix and match approach in their work. Research questions are best answered when they are unambiguously put and focused methodologically. Our anxiety is that researchers and users of research frequently mistake the answers to such questions for correct or true statements. It is important to recall that useful research questions necessarily *exclude* ways of thinking and learning about entrepreneurship, from whichever School or Paradigm one starts. We justify this conclusion by referring to the ontologies of a case narrative – particularly one that purports to be based upon the decisions taken. From Brown (1979) and Chia (1994), making distinctions is the ontological act that brings forth reality. We would argue that critical decisions in a case study are usually identified after the event as contingency reducing distinctions. That is to say, they are judgements about the point at which many decisions and outcomes that could have occurred in the case were reduced to the retrospectively identified outcome. As Sartre observes, a story is created by its outcome, but written as from its origin.

The Whittington framework, grounded in its theory of strategic choice, naturally depends upon such distinctions about the objectives of the decision on the vertical axis, and the relationship between decision and outcome on the horizontal. The problem is compounded in the case of Burrell and Morgan (1979) since there is an explicit ideological loading to the distinctions made on the vertical axis, and explicit ontology on the horizontal. Any attempt to mix and match will generate paradox and ambiguity, rather than a single, coherent narrative. Therefore we *must* remember that a set of distinctions that create a single, meaningful story may well be important and interesting, but do not represent the truth of the events, since a multitude of other distinctions can always be made, even starting from the distinctions in the story rather than the events themselves.

This result is not trivial in the formation of the subject of entrepreneurship – itself created by making distinctions between itself and other literatures. The point is that these distinctions between Schools can only be made by suppressing, or failing to adequately formulate, the tensions between what we derive from our distinctions and what is ignored. By habitually assuming the functionalist paradigm, and frequently only the Classical School within that, we create a subject founded more upon the coherences between our distinctions than correspondence with the topic we assume to exist and purport to explain and improve. In our view, this implies that the conclusions that can be drawn from Grant and Perren's (2002) observations are more critical than they suggest themselves. The functionalist paradigm does more than limit the influence of alternatives; it actually defines the subject in terms thought to be amenable to policy makers who regard supporting the activity as unequivocally desirable. This strengthens our view that practitioners and future practitioners should be exposed to alternative interpretations of case situations as part of their induction and development.

We hope to have shown that the case study described in this chapter is created by the paradigm assumed, not by the events in the world that are assumed to generate the tale. Our belief is that we are not doomed to fool ourselves if we do not wish to do so. Good case studies can be analysed as we have done here because the author created a strong story along the lines that he wished to tell, yet provided sufficient detail to point to the losses that such a narrative inevitably requires. Consciously generating alternative interpretations of existing cases can make students, and more experienced scholars, sensitive to the broader range of methodological perspectives available for the conduct of entrepreneurship research and the pedagogy of the subject.

NOTES

1. The ECCH (at www.ecch.cranfield.ac.uk) is the world's largest distributor of case studies, teaching notes and associated support materials for business and management education. In excess of 20 000 items are listed on its database as available for supply, of which an all-fields search on the term 'Entrepreneur' generates about 1100 items; at mid-2002, 150 of the latter date from 2001 onwards, suggesting a current generation rate of only 100 items per year.
2. Grant and Perren (2002: Table 6), quoted above, do not break down the functionalist paradigm into the sub-categories identified by Whittington. However, they do categorize the vast majority of the 36 articles as being presented from a functionalist perspective; indeed, much of their discussion – including inter-rater dialogue – is about deviations from this norm. They further discuss the interesting paradox of a field which is often described as 'pre-paradigmatic' (Perren et al., 2001) nevertheless presenting as one with an apparent unifying framework, ascribing this as being likely to result from academics playing to practitioners' agendas (cf. Tranfield and Starkey, 1998). This strengthens our view that practitioners and future practitioners should be exposed to alternative interpretations of case situations as part of their induction and development, since it may make users and funders of entrepreneurship research more sensitive and susceptible to a wider definition and appreciation of the field.

REFERENCES

Abbot, S. and J. Evans (1995), 'From ram to black sheep', *Dissent in Management Thought Conference*, London: Henry Stewart.
Actouf, O. (1992), 'Management and theories of the 1990s: toward a critical radical humanism', *Academy of Management Review*, **17**, 407–32.
Ansoff, I. (1965), *Corporate Strategy*, New York: McGraw-Hill.
Argyris, C. (1980), 'Some limitations of the case method: experiences in a management development programme', *Academy of Management Review*, **5**(2), 291–8.
Ashcroft, K.L., and M.E. Pacanowsky (1996), 'A woman's worst enemy, reflections on a narrative of organizational life and female identity', *Journal of Applied Communication Research*, **24**, 217–30.
Barton, S.L., and C.H. Mathews (1989), 'Small firm financing: implications from a strategic management standpoint', *Journal of Small Business Management*, **27**(1), 1–7.
Brown, R. and D. Molian (2001), *ChocExpress Ltd*, Item 501–066–1, Cranfield: European Case Clearing House.

Burrell, G. and G. Morgan (1979), *Sociological Paradigms and Organizational Analysis*, London: Heinemann Educational.

Chetty, S. (1996), 'The case study method for research in small and medium-sized firms', *International Small Business Journal*, **15**(1), 73–85.

Chia, R. (1994), 'The concept of decision: a deconstructive analysis', *Journal of Management Studies*, **31**(6), 781–806.

Chrisman, J.J. (1994), 'Writing cases for "Entrepreneurship Theory and Practice"', *Entrepreneurship Theory and Practice*, **19**(2), 89.

Cole, P.M. (1997), 'Women in family business', *Family Business Review*, **10**(4), 353–71.

Delbridge, R., P. Turnbull, and B. Wilkinson, (1992), 'Pushing back the frontiers: management control and work intensification under JIT/TQM factory regimes', *New Technology, Work and Employment*, **7**(2), 97–106.

Dodge, H.R., and J.E Robbins (1992), 'An empirical investigation of the organizational life cycle model for small business development and survival,' *Journal of Small Business Management*, **30**(1), 27–37.

Dyer, W.G., Jr and A.L. Wilkins (1991), 'Better stories, not better constructs, to generate theory: a rejoinder to Eizenhardt', *Academy of Management Review*, **16**(3), 613–19.

Eisenhardt, K.M. (1989), 'Building theories from case study research', *Academy of Management Review*, **14**(4), 532–50.

Eisenhardt, K.M. (1991), 'Better stories and better constructs: the case for rigor and comparative logic', *Academy of Management Review*, **16**(3), 620–27.

Ezzamel, M., S. Lilley, and H. Wilmott (1997), 'Accounting for management and management accounting: reflections on recent changes in the UK', *Journal of Management Studies*, **34**, 439–64.

Fearful, A. (1996), 'Clerical workers, clerical skills: cases from credit management', *Technology, Work and Employment*, **11**, 55–65.

Fortado, B. (1998), 'Interpreting nicknames: a micro portal', *Journal of Management Studies*, **35**, 13–34.

Fuller-Love, N. and R.W. Scapens (1999), 'Performance related pay – a case study of a small business', *International Small Business Journal*, **15**(4), 48–63.

Gibb, A. (2000), 'SME policy, academic research and the growth of ignorance: mythical concepts, myths, assumptions, rituals and confusions', *International Small Business Journal*, **18**(3), 13–35.

Gill, J. (1995), 'Building theory from case studies', *Small Business and Enterprise Development*, **2**(2), 71–6.

Grant, P. and L. Perren (2002), 'Small business and entrepreneurship research: meta-theories, paradigms and prejudices', *International Small Business Journal*, **20**(2), 185–210.

Greiner, L. (1972), 'Evolution and revolution as organisations grow', *Harvard Business Review*, **50**(4), 37–46.

Gue, L. (1997), *An Introduction to Educational Administration in Canada*, Toronto: McGraw-Hill Ryerson.

Hannan, M.T. and J. Freeman (1988), *Organizational Ecology*, Cambridge, MA: Harvard University Press.

Henderson, S. and A. Zvesper (2002), 'Narratives of transformation, a strategic decision-makers guide', *Management Decision*, **40**(5), 476–85.

Holmes, L. and M. Grieco (1991), 'Overt funding, political goals, and moral turnover: the organizational transformation of radical experiments', *Human Relations*, **44**, 463–85.

Jenkins, M. (1994), 'Thinking about growth: a cognitive mapping approach to understanding small business development', *Small Business and Enterprise Development*, **1**, 29–37.

Jenkins, M. (1997), 'Linking managerial cognition and organizational performance: a preliminary investigation using causal maps', *British Journal of Management*, **8**, 577–91.

Jennings, P. and G. Beaver (1997), 'The performance and competitive advantage of small firms: a management perspective', *International Small Business Journal*, **15**(2), 63–75.

Kay, J. (1991), 'Economics and business', *The Economic Journal*, January, 55–63.

Kelly, J. and L. Kelly (1998), *An Existential Systems Approach to Managing Organizations*, Westport, CT: Quorum Books.

Marx, K. (1959), *Capital: A Critique of Political Economy – III. The Capitalist Production Process as a Whole*, London: Lawrence and Wishart.

McCabe, D. (2000), 'Factory innovations and management machinations: The productive and repressive relations of power', *Journal of Management Studies*, **37**(7), 931–53.

Miller, D., M.F.R. Kets de Vries and J.M. Toulouse (1982), 'Top executive locus of control and its relationship to strategy-making, structure, and environment', *Academy of Management Journal*, **25**(2), 237–53.

Millman, S.R.L. (2001), 'Child slaves may be making your chocolate', *Radical Thought*, Retrieved from http://www.parliament.the-stationery-office.co.uk/pa/cm200102/cmhansrd/cm020520/debtext/20520–34.htm on 20 July 2002.

Mintzberg, H. (1978), 'Patterns in strategy formation', *Management Science*, **24**(9), 934–48.

Perren, L., A. Berry and R. Blackburn (2001), 'The UK small business research community and its publication channels: perceptions and ratings', *Journal of Small Business and Enterprise Development*, **8**(1), 76–90.

Porter, M.E. (1980), 'Competitive strategy: techniques for analyzing industries and competitors', New York: The Free Press.

Poza, E.J., T. Alfred and A. Maheshwari (1997), 'Stakeholder perceptions of culture and management practices in family firms', *Family Business Review*, **10**(2), 135–55.

Romano, C. (1989), 'Research strategies for small business: a case study approach', *International Small Business Journal*, **7**(4), 35–44.

Romm, T. and S. Mahler (1991), 'The case study challenge – a new approach to an old method', *Management Education and Development*, **22**(4), 292–301.

Sartre, J. (1963), *Nausea*, London: Penguin.

Sandberg, W. (1992), 'Strategic management's potential contributions to a theory of entrepreneurship', *Entrepreneurship Theory and Practice*, **16**(3), 73–90.

Spencer-Brown, G. (1979), *Laws of Form*, New York: E.P. Dutton.

Tranfield, D. and K. Starkey (1998), 'The nature, social organization and promotion of management research: towards policy', *British Journal of Management*, **9**(4), 341–53.

Vaara, E. and J. Tienari (2002), 'Justification, legitimization and naturalization of mergers and acquisitions: a critical discourse analysis of media texts', *Organization*, **9**(2), 275–304.

Verstraete, T. (2003), 'A French perspective on the singularity of entrepreneurship as a research domain: annual review of progress in entrepreneurship, 2000–2001', *European Foundation for Management Development*: Brussels, pp. 10–65.

Watkins, D. (1995), 'Changes in the nature of UK small business research, 1980–1990. Part Two: Changes in the nature of the output', *Small Business and Enterprise Development*, **2**(1), 59–66.

Watkins, D. and D. Reader (2003), 'Using bibliometrics as a tool to understand the literature of entrepreneurship: a review and framework for a research agenda', RENT XII Conference, Lodz, Poland, November.

Watkins, D. and D. Reader (2004), 'Identifying current trends in entrepreneurship research: a new approach', in D. Watkins (ed.), *ARPENT: Annual Review of Progress in Entrepreneurship, 2002–2003*, Brussels: European Foundation for Management Development, pp. 311–24.

Welsh, J. and J. White (1981), 'A small business is not a little big business', *Harvard Business Review*, **59** (July/August), 18–32.

Whittington, R. (1992), 'Putting Giddens into action: social systems and managerial agency', *Journal of Management Studies*, **29**(6), 692–712.

Whittington, R. (1993), *What is Strategy, and Does it Matter?*, London: Routledge.

Williamson, O. (1974), *The Economics of Discretionary Behaviour: Managerial Objectives in the Theory of the Firm*, London: Kershaw.

8. From forecast to realisation – a systemic approach to understanding the evolution of high-tech start-ups

Michel Bernasconi and Franck Moreau

INTRODUCTION

Management researchers have been interested in the analysis of the development of new enterprises for many years. Work on new enterprises in general has been supplemented progressively by a research stream directed at high-tech start-ups, of which the current research study forms part.

The difficulties inherent in the creation of high-tech start-ups are a burden for entrepreneurs, investors and public actors. Research shows that the development process during the first years is critical and that many promising projects fail in spite of their use of competitive technology, relevant business models and skilled entrepreneurs. The objective of this work is to deepen our understanding of how in practice, high-tech start-ups evolve during their initial years.

The first issue that arises is one of definition. Numerous definitions of entrepreneurship exist, but not all of them are necessarily useful or relevant in terms of the observation of the phenomenon of project evolution. If we define entrepreneurship as 'a new economic activity' (Davidsson, 2001), we have a broad and dynamic definition that suits the subject of our research, that is enterprises building a new economic activity based on technological innovation. The choice of the definition of an enterprise in the specific case of a new venture is important for the research positioning and the methodological design. We have selected the definition of an enterprise as 'the implementation of a project' as proposed by Bréchet (1994) as it gives a systemic and dynamic paradigm of the new enterprise that is practical for research purposes.

The next issue is the selection of the approach for the research design. Given the former definitions of entrepreneurship and enterprise, together with the purpose of the research, we agree with the observations of many other researchers (Verstraete, 2003), that strategic management is a helpful perspective from which to approach entrepreneurship research. It is therefore possible to position our research within Wittington's paradigm framework of strategic management, presented by Bhalla et al. in the current book (Chapter 7). Most of the research undertaken to understand the creation and development of new enterprises falls under the processual approach. More recent works have used the alternative systemic approach, and it is this approach, that we have adopted for our study. As Bhalla et al. remark, 'the systemic schools hold that it is pointless to examine an organisation as a discrete unit in isolation with social forces, culture and institution that facilitate and impinge upon business activity'. This broad scope perfectly reflects the richness of the stakeholders influencing the decisions and the evolution of high-tech start-ups, such as venture capitalists, local and national innovation support agencies, and founders.

Furthermore, the systemic approach 'explains a great deal about what are airily described as "implementation" problems in the literature, and understanding is presumably a precursor to more actions' (Bhalla et al., Chapter 7, this volume). This characteristic is apt to the research objective – understanding the evolution of an enterprise based on the implementation processes rather than the decision processes. In such an approach, using business case studies to collect information is both appropriate and legitimate (Yin, 1990; Hlady-Rispal, 2000; Thiétart et al., 1999). Three high-tech enterprises in the Sophia Antipolis area of France were observed to create the case studies.

UNDERSTANDING THE EVOLUTION OF START-UPS: FROM THE PROCESSUAL TO THE SYSTEMIC APPROACH

While management literature has long been interested in the analysis of the evolution of enterprises (Chandler, 1962), research on the creation and development of high-tech start-ups specifically is quite recent. Based on existing work on technological entrepreneurship, both academic and practical, we define the term 'high-tech start-up' as a company less than eight years old, initiated originally by individuals, developing in an incremental or radical way an innovation which is primarily technical, but also commercial or organisational in terms of products, services or processes. (Existing work see, for example, Roberts, 1991; Blais and Toulouse, 1992; Nesheim, 1992; Bernasconi and Monsted, 2000; During, et al. 2001; Davier, 2001; Basso and Bieliczky, 2001)

The processual approach has been widely used historically to describe the evolution of new enterprises. Many works, both descriptive and normative, have dealt with development, evolution, growth patterns and growth paths of new enterprises in general, technological enterprises, or high growth enterprises (for example, for new enterprises: Steinmetz, 1969; Greiner, 1998; Stanworth and Curran, 1976; Adizes, 1999; Galbraith, 1982; Churchill and Lewis, 1983; Quinn and Cameron, 1983; Miller and Friesen, 1984; Flamholtz, 1986; for technological enterprises: Kazanjian, 1988; McCann, 1991; Hansen and Bird, 1997; for high growth enterprises: Delmar and Davidsson, 1998).

Few have dealt specifically with young technology-based enterprises with high growth potential (for example Carter et al., 1996; Garnsey and Heffernan, 2001; Julien et al., 2001).

These different works have resulted in the emergence of an approach that, in summary, proposes the concept of enterprise development as a series of different steps or phases, and the more than metaphorical use of the concept of a life cycle (birth, growth, maturity and so on). These models can be organisational in type (for example Churchill and Lewis, 1983), operational or practical (for example C. Gordon Bell and J. McNamara, 1991) or, much more rarely, conceptual or theoretical (for example Garnsey, 1998).

This approach has yielded undeniable results and has allowed the common traits in the evolution of enterprises to become visible. In particular, it has underlined the most important managerial concerns in terms of different phases, the strategic questions specific to each period and the organisational choices that are associated with each one. However, these stage-based models have also been the subject of numerous criticisms. Without rejecting outright the possibility of building a global explicative and predictive model, critics observe that:

- the models have the disadvantages of being, in general, unrepresentative because they are reductionist and simplified (McCann, 1991; Albert et al., 1994; Sammut, 1998),
- they are imperfect and imprecise (Saporta, 1994; Slevin and Covin, 1995; Levie and Hay, 1998),
- they erroneously define the development of enterprises as singular, linear and sequential (Stanworth and Curran, 1976; Vesper, 1990; Storey, 1994) or at the other extreme as almost random, that is a chain of unordered and non-sequential tasks (Reynolds and Miller, 1992; Hansen and Bird, 1997),
- they are difficult to put into operation due to the diversity of definitions and the difficulty in identifying the phases (O'Farrell and Hitchens, 1988; Hanks et al., 1993; Chell, 2001),
- they are even 'under-conceptualised' due to the lack of supporting theoretical analysis (Garnsey and Heffernan, 2001; Bhidé, 2000).

The systemic approach adds to, and complements, the processual approach. In reality, it allows us to take into consideration the complexity of the start-up by focusing in particular, on the evolution of the relationships between the components rather than on the components themselves. In short, the evolution of the enterprise is dependent on the interaction of the elements. Sammut (1998) defines a system of dynamic management composed of the following elements: the entrepreneur, the activities, the environment, the financial resources and the organisation. The evolution of the system is driven by the evolution of the relationship between the elements.

Bréchet's proposal to approach the enterprise as 'the implementation of a project' is particularly apt to the objective of our research and supports the systemic approach. According to Bréchet, the project of setting up a business cannot be regarded as a vision or an intention, but must necessarily take into account its implementation. He relies on an idea of a 'profession', and the marketplace of skills which it encompasses. 'The project of setting up a business is an evolutive concept since every initial business project becomes concrete if it reaches this point, under the form of an organisation which partially determines its model later to adapt it to the demands of its internal and external environments.' (Bréchet, 1994)

This perspective is an invitation to approach strategy without separating the aims from the implementation. Strategy is evolutive, through the ongoing interaction among the components, and the basic concept is not the end, but the means. Bréchet's proposal also fits well with entrepreneurial strategy defined by Mintzberg et al. (1998) as

> characterised by a visionary process: strategy exists first of all in the leader's mind as a long-term direction, a vision of the future and of the results of the organisation. Such a strategic vision tends to be malleable, and due to this, entrepreneurial strategy often appears to be both deliberate and emergent, deliberate from the point of view of its global vision, and emergent in the way in which the details of the vision evolve.

According to Garnsey (1998) 'The organisation of these businesses is equally malleable, since few businesses are capable of anticipating the resources necessary to their development' (p. 535).

Moreover, this approach allows us to decide not only on the strategic modalities of development, but also to enhance the knowledge of the strategic process of these businesses, the latter being defined as an ongoing project. Bréchet encourages us along this road, by recommending

> that we distance ourselves from a neo-classical methodology which emphasises the 'disembodied' viewpoint of the observer . . . by adopting the point of view of the actor confronted with the demands of his action. . . . The enterprise defined as the implementation of a project, abandoning the end for the sake of the means, is a throwback not only to descriptive and static categories, but to the standard understanding of motives and conditions of collective action. (Bréchet, 1994)

The processual approaches alluded to at the beginning have certainly facilitated the naming and definition of the strategic practice of enterprises at the different phases of the start-up's life. Nevertheless, they appear to be insufficient to help in understanding the reality of the evolution of high-tech start-ups. This is why, without undermining such approaches, but rather in a complementary manner, it is interesting to analyse the modes of development from a systemic perspective. The enterprise as the implementation of a project, offers a framework adapted to the present research study. Based on Bréchet's proposal, the aim of this study is to deepen the understanding of the evolution of high-tech start-ups. The approach consists in analysing the businesses, not by making comparisons between them, nor evaluating them relative to existing models, but rather by analysing each with respect to its own evolution. Hence, the comparison at two moments in the life of a project, distinct as initially planned, but in fact carried out simultaneously, will make it possible to identify the eventual differences. Analysis of these differences should make it possible to identify the premises upon which founders made their projections, the events that have affected the enterprises, and the way in which managers have since reacted.

METHODOLOGICAL CONSIDERATIONS: LONGITUDINAL CASE STUDIES

As our research objective was to achieve a better understanding of the real road travelled by high-tech start-ups, we used the longitudinal case study approach to collect and analyse data. In such an approach, iterative interpretation is commonly accepted as a satisfactory means of developing an understanding of the phenomenon from inside, including the motivations and rationality of actors. Such an approach fits with Bréchet's methodological recommendation.

Description of the Evolution

If we accept the definition of the enterprise as the implementation of a project, we face the problem of how to describe the project. Bréchet states:

> what the different phases in the life of an organisation have in common is not the structures, nor their functioning, which have evolved considerably; it is the project of setting up a business defined by its evolutive characteristics which are bound to arise, if only partially, 1) from the desires and objectives of the originators of the project (as much in the order of the ends as in the means); 2) from the triplet technology–product–market; 3) from the internal and external constraints of its implementation' (1994, 19).

The three evolutive characteristics of Bréchet are in fact strategic elements, which can easily be described and observed as 1) the ambition of the project, 2) the strategic positioning and 3) the implementation. Observing the state of these evolutive characteristics at different moments in the life of the project will allow us to describe and understand the evolution of the project. In order to achieve this, we analysed each characteristic, as shown in Table 8.1.

Table 8.1   Project characteristics and factors analysed

Characteristics	Factors
Precision of strategic positioning	– segmentation: choice between presence in a micro-segment, in several associated micro-segments or not, mass market (industry and/or private);
• Strong	– value chain: choice of specialisation in one or several functions of the chain, or in the totality;
• Medium	– the offer: choice of offer in terms of products, services, and geographic reach;
• Weak	– type of innovation: choice of innovation, incremental, major or radical.
Level of Ambition	– explanation of the vision: explicit or implicit indication of hoped-for future state;
• High	– Evolution of the capital: stock market launch, trade sale, independence;
• Medium	– hoped-for leadership: local, regional, national, international;
• Limited	– speed of achievement of fixed objectives: from 1 to x years.
Anticipation of implementation	– managerial resources and skills: functional skills (financing, technological, marketing, strategic and organisational), transversal (negotiation, managing relationships, contracting, project management, internationalisation);
• Strong	– organisational resources and skills: structuring,
• Medium	role of network, responsibilities and decision-taking, information systems, etc.
• Weak	– technological resources and skills: acquisition, development, construction, protection.

In addition to these characteristics, we also had access to quantitative indicators relating to the way in which the entrepreneurs anticipated the evolution of their business in terms of staffing, turnover, and so on. Such indicators facilitated the evaluation of both the level of development and the compliance with the forecast, as well as, to some extent, the success of the project, even though this latter outcome was not one of the aims.

For each of the three enterprises, the indicators were compared at the two different stages. The differences found were categorised according to their importance: none, minor, significant and major. We did not 'evaluate' their incidence (neutral, negative or positive) due to the complexity of the analysis of differences and the initial position we had adopted of not 'judging' the evolution of each project.

Data Collection and Data Analysis

In order to identify the initial characteristics of the project, we used the first Business Plan formulated by the company, complemented with secondary data and interviews with the founding team. To assess the present status of the business several years after its start-up, semi-directive interviews with members of the management team were conducted.

Defining and describing the project as it was conceived at the outset by the founding team raises problems in areas such as the relevance of the information and the risk of distortion of facts from the interviews with the founding teams. The Business Plan enables us to have a formal written record of the anticipated market positioning strategy, the aims and objectives, as well as the principal modalities of implementation over a period.

In order to assess the current state of the project, we carried out semi-directive interviews with the founder-manager of each business. Factual data was the most important element, but the interviews enabled each manager to provide explanations relating to the evolution of the project. Such factual data and the explanations provided were enhanced by secondary information such as press releases, financial databases, and case studies undertaken by CERAM students on the three enterprises.

Data Reliability

While the use of the business plan as a formal forecasting tool in the definition of strategy and organisational choices is central to our research methodology, we have nevertheless attempted to limit the potential risks that arise from its other functions as a tool of communication for the promoters and evaluation by third parties. For different reasons (confidentiality, negotiation, and so on) the business plan can in fact be the cause of omission, addition, or transformation of information. Furthermore, since we are conscious of the relative reliability inherent in the utilisation of the Business Plan as the single source of information for definition and description of the project, we verified key data with the management team against secondary internal and external data (reports, press releases, articles, and so on).

Data obtained in interviews was not transcribed in its entirety, but was synthesised from notes made by the interviewers. The data obtained from the business plans, together with information garnered in the interviews, enabled us to complete an analytical grid. The grid analysis is a construction of the researchers, based on our understanding of the facts, and our previous knowledge of the field. The process of description may, of course, be seen as subjective, resulting from an interpretation; nevertheless, it is based on an analysis wherein each item has been subjected to an intermediate qualifying stage carried out separately by the researchers, and then assessed before being included in the final description.

Enterprises Analysed

The enterprises studied had to fall under the definition of 'high-tech start-up' which is a company less than eight years old, initiated originally by individuals, developing in an incremental or radical way an innovation which is primarily technical, but also commercial or organisational in terms of products, services or processes. In order to obtain the relevant information we had to ensure that the current CEO was one of the founders. For practical reasons the selected enterprises were located in the Sophia Antipolis area of France. The following factors were not taken into consideration: the 'growth phase' of the business: its sector, its precise age, or any specific problems. The characteristics of the enterprises studied are described below.

Alpha, created in 1996 by four former experts from a major electronics company, is a business specialising in system-on-chips. Alpha has created a unit for the development of system-on-chips using ARM technology that has the dual benefit of being cost efficient and offering considerable timesaving in the design process. The first formal business plan was drafted two and a half years after its creation, since the management team had already decided on the global strategy for the business, but had not, until that time, needed to formalise it as they were not looking for financing.

Beta is a software editor for the creation and transformation of images. Created in 1998, following technology transfer from a research institute, the business experienced significant personnel growth, reaching almost 100 employees in June 2001. The business plan was drafted six months after its creation.

Gamma is a service business specialising in restoring damaged film and making digital copies of film negatives. The business was established in 1997 as an extension of a European Union funded research project. The project had brought together several laboratories with the objective of defining and constructing a system for the digital rerecording of films. The business plan was created a few months before the business was started.

RESULTS

As mentioned earlier, the purpose of this research was to understand the evolution of the project, looking in particular at the differences between the initial and the current situations. The evolution of each project was analysed by looking at differences between the two states observed. Table 8.2 presents the results of the research on the description and, above all, the main factual differences exhibited by the different enterprises. We then present the principal conclusions relating to the development of each business.

Alpha

In the case of Alpha, there are few differences between the business plan and the realisation, in either its ambitions or the strategic implementation. Moreover, any 'hesitation in implementation', as expressed by the founding team must be assessed relative to the objectives. The different options projected ('supplementary' activity, financing by business angels, partnership with clients, and so on) were followed in large measure. Above all, the managers remained faithful to their principles, that is to say 'the most important thing was the research and development capacity and the microstructure developed within the enterprise'.

The distinguishing features of Alpha are that it constantly acted in the interests of developing the technological base and that it stressed the need for auto-financing or financing by client-partners with considerable interest in the success of the project.

The durability of their competitive advantage relies as much on the research and development carried out as on the experience accumulated. The formalisation of the experience was accumulated in a library of items that added to the potential of applications and the configurability of the developmental base.

In summary, in spite of the delay incurred in the development of the technological base, weaknesses in terms of both research skills and public finance, and a constant need for major investment in R&D, Alpha succeeded in mastering its development. Its progress, evident from growth both in revenue and in staff, seems to be the result of a near perfect understanding and management of the complex positive dynamic which evolved between the three major

Table 8.2 Case studies: principal differences noted

Accuracy of the characteristics	Factors	Scale of difference between forecast and realisation **Alpha**
High precision in strategic orientation	– segmentation – value chain – the offer – type of innovation	**None** Adequate in terms of professionalism, offer, value chain, and competitive advantage. Differences in the area of market strategy.
High level of ambition	– explanation of the vision – evolution of the capital – hoped-for leadership – speed of achievement of fixed objectives	**None** Global position and stock market launch.
High anticipation of implementation	– managerial resources and skills – organisational resources and skills – technological resources and skills	**Minor** Development options mainly followed in spite of some hesitation. Pertinent technological choices. Effective use of partners. One-year delay in technological development.
High accuracy in quantitative indicators	– staff – turnover	**Significant** Higher than projections.

183

Table 8.2   continued

Accuracy of the characteristics	Factors	Scale of difference between forecast and realisation
		Beta
High precision in strategic orientation	– segmentation – value chain – the offer – type of innovation	**Major** Business offer redefined (by the market). Product/market couplings reworked in depth (in accordance with expressed needs). Precise technological choices (abandonment of development options). Competitive advantage and value chain conform to the forecast.
High level of ambition	– explanation of the vision – evolution of the capital – hoped-for leadership – speed of achievement of fixed objectives	**None** Nature and date of exit remain undecided but the ambition was reaffirmed to emphasise value creation.
High anticipation of implementation	– managerial resources and skills: – organisational resources and skills – technological resources and skills	**Significant** Departure of one founder following disagreement on strategy. Organisational structure not anticipated in the medium term. Difficulties in raising funds. Partial geographical expansion. Technological resources and role of networks in accordance with forecast.
High accuracy in quantitative indicators	– staff – turnover	**Minor** Staffing: same, then higher than anticipated. Turnover: lower than anticipated.

		Gamma
High precision in strategic orientation	– segmentation – value chain – the offer – type of innovation	**Major** Change in activity due to a still uninterested market and to the to the aggressive reaction of the principal actors. Technological choice confirmed, but the advantage anticipated due to the level of industrialisation of the process did not materialise. Competitive analysis correct, but inadequate management responses.
Limited level of ambition	– explanation of the vision – evolution of the capital – hoped-for leadership – speed of achievement of fixed objectives.	**None** Remains weak after undergoing the risk of going out of business.
High anticipation of implementation	– managerial resources and skills – organisational resources and skills – technological resources and skills	**Major** Major risks not overcome: access to emerging markets and competitive strategy. Development not up to standard in the time. Early departure of a founder-manager due to the risk of failure.
High accuracy in quantitative indicators	– staff – turnover	**Major** Staff: same as projections. Turnover: lower than projections.

processes of the business development: financing, technological development, and market entry.

Alpha now appears ready for a second phase in its development that should see the launch of several new products, and its emergence on the international scene.

Beta

Beta has had to face different problems in the course of its development. The project evolved and activities emerged in directions that the business was not prepared for. Nonetheless, it experienced rapid growth with the attendant need to move from being a 'techno-driven' to a 'market-driven' business, and it proved capable of reacting correctly and making satisfactory organisational adjustments.

The enterprise seems to have experienced the greatest difficulties in the market launch. However, it avoided suffering negative consequences, thanks to the commercial alternatives found. Faced with various market-related incidents and technological barriers, the management team were able to reinvent their 'models' of reference, taking inspiration, for example, from 'Photoshop' whose products are identical and are used both by professionals and the public at large, but are accessed through different distribution channels.

It should be noted that, in spite of the expertise of its managerial team, the business underestimated the time needed to penetrate the markets. The synchronisation of the product offering with that of the market need was slow. Therefore, the business did not capitalise on the opportunities posed by selling under OEM licence as early as it could have, in spite of the obvious advantages such as market coverage, financial visibility, and so on.

Finally, the managerial team succeeded in redefining and re-igniting the project, abandoning their initial ambition in the light of another value-added alternative.

Gamma

Gamma went through a difficult development phase. Although the pertinence of its technological choices was not in doubt, the business did not succeed in developing the level of activity initially forecast. The analyses of the dynamics of the sector and of the competitive conditions were essentially correct, but the enterprise was not able to overcome the difficulties in reaching the market. As a result, the project did not possess, and has not succeeded in acquiring, sufficient negotiation power to penetrate the market and thereby accelerate the company's growth. However, it should have more success as soon as it finds its true market.

The project has maintained its level of ambition, which was, in any case, limited. The difficulties encountered in reaching the market have not impinged on the technological advantage possessed by the business.

The business has, moreover, been able to profit from its technological skills, recognised by professionals, in the development of complementary activities. However, such activities have not brought in sufficient auto-financing to cover development costs, let alone to consolidate the project. The differences observed between the anticipated and realised implementation of the project are both a cause and an effect of the new developmental axes.

General Observations

Based on a transversal analysis of the strategic choices, the ambitions and the anticipation of organisation of the start-ups studied, we can draw a number of general observations.

With regard to strategic choices, the founding teams were equipped with real commercial and technological expertise. Their a priori analysis of the markets, the dynamics of the sectors, and the technology, were appropriate. However, it must be noted that in achieving market access the enterprises did not follow their preconceived plans for a variety of reasons:

- market entry was made extremely difficult by major players, competitors, and third parties (for example Gamma);
- the applications planned did not systematically answer the demands of the clients targeted (for example Beta);
- the speed of access to the market was over-estimated (for example Gamma).

This difficulty in reaching the market led the managerial teams to diverge from their real aspirations and needs. It is noteworthy that the difficulties experienced in accessing the markets produced the effect, not only of redefining the offer, but moreover of modifying the initial business project in terms of activities and of models.

The real global ambition of each project was difficult to deduce, either from the business plan or from the interviews carried out. 'Modesty' or 'Conservatism' often meant that the ambition of the project was implicit, and thus ambiguous, needing an a posteriori confirmation by the founding team. Moreover, while the intention of achieving a viable project is often quite clear, the idea of an evolution of capital, from an opportunist perspective, is generally vague. This shows that both the vision and the hoped-for results are uncertain at the outset. Nevertheless, the final outcomes of the projects did not show a great degree of divergence from the initial ambitions. The major variation, whether in terms of a real success, either ongoing or in the future, has to do with the temporal horizon of the expected introduction on a stock market, which is always much further away than originally imagined.

ANALYSIS AND CONCLUSIONS

From the results of the analyses of the three high-tech start-ups, some interesting management issues they faced in their development are emerging.

There was considerable discrepancy noted between a clear *technological* ambition, which was well defined and emphasised, and a *commercial* ambition, which was much less defined and emphasised. The ambiguity noted earlier arises from this discrepancy. It would be interesting to understand the origins and the mechanism of this discrepancy, as well as its effect on the development of the project.

The original projects relied heavily on a high degree of anticipation of start-up success. However, the organisational choices (structure, organisation, decision, systems of communication, and so on) which needed to be implemented as the project developed, were always unanticipated, or merely formalised. Hence, in general, a much more problematic start-up phase than anticipated was observed.

Furthermore, the real-time technological development, independent of the period of R&D before the project, dedicated to the creation of concrete applications was greater than estimated.

The process of financing also proved to be more delicate and time-consuming than anticipated. This called for special attention from the managerial team in terms of communication, negotiation and organising contracts when preparing for fundraising and seeking public subsidies. The energy thus consecrated was lost to the technological and commercial development efforts.

Lastly, the implementation of a start-up depends inextricably upon the strategic choices made. The opportunity, or the need, to develop new activities affects the organisational decisions taken.

These case studies have highlighted two different configurations. The first is a project defined around precise, 'determined' strategic choices and a well-planned start-up. The second is a project defined around a precise strategic orientation that is nevertheless evolving. As a result, the start-up is equally dynamic and conceived in terms of different options to be acted upon depending on the circumstances. To attempt to demonstrate the *superiority* of one configuration over another would have neither meaning nor justification. However, the first configuration would seem to call the model into question in a more fundamental way than a configuration envisaging the need for permanent strategic and organisational adjustments from the outset. It would be interesting to carry out a further study of these configurations, both qualitatively by taking into account the dimension of ambition, and quantitatively, through new case studies and statistical research.

The objective was to deepen our understanding of the reality of the evolution of high-tech start-ups from a systemic and dynamic perspective. To analyse the enterprise evolution, we chose to define the business as the *implementation of a project*. The results indicate that this definition is appropriate as the enterprises observed did in fact experience significant evolutions. The analysis of the differences at two distinct points in the company's life has allowed us to identify the factors of evolution specifically, and to understand their effects on other factors of the enterprise and on the strategy of the whole enterprise. In particular, the research provides evidence for the importance of the triptych composed of the three processes of financing, technological development, and market launch. The sales process appears to be the most difficult to anticipate. The observations show, above all, that a variation in any one process has an overall impact and often requires a reconfiguration of the project. The capacity of the entrepreneurs to articulate successfully these three processes both during the planning process and during the reconfiguration process, emerges clearly as the principal factor in the success of a business.

While the research model proved to be effective and fruitful, the results did not bring any real new knowledge of the topic itself. The difficulties of market entry, the time required raising financing, and the delays in technology development have long been recognised in the literature. However, our approach reaches these conclusions using a new methodology, and emphasises the interrelationship between the factors. Therefore, the systemic approach fits perfectly with the objective of the research.

The methodological choice is also worth a review. The case study approach and the iterative interpretation proved to be suited to the task. The case studies allowed the researchers to become more immersed in the reality of the business operations than would have been possible with empirical studies based on questionnaires. The information provided by the enterprises and the background knowledge of the researchers allowed for the construction of an acceptable and communicable representation of the process being studied. The fact that the results cannot be generalised does not diminish the fact that a study of this nature contributes to a greater understanding of the way in which high-tech start-ups develop.

The purpose of this research was to use the systemic approach to complement the processual approach, more commonly used to observe the development process of high-tech start-ups. From that perspective, the results are fruitful. The results show that each company was unique in the manner that it exploited opportunities, articulating the three major processes in its own way.

The evolution process and the differences between forecast and realisation were specific to each one, as highlighted by Table 8.2. The systemic approach emphasised those specificities, rather than attempting to identify similarities in the sequentiality of the phases, or pointing out common best practices to succeed. There were, nevertheless, similarities among the three cases observed. As noted earlier, the difficulty to enter the first market was a common problem to solve for two companies, as is generally the case according to the literature. However, different paradigms produce different results. That research confirms that the systemic approach is relevant in the explanation of 'what is airily described as implementation problems in the literature' (Bhalla et al., Chapter 7, this volume) and therefore that this approach favours the creation of action-oriented knowledge directed at practitioners.

IMPLICATIONS

Our contribution to the field of entrepreneurship is reliant upon paradigmatic and methodological choices for the observation of high-tech start-ups. This approach appears to be complementary to other descriptive and processual approaches, and displays a particular pertinence to an exploration of actual life of high-tech start-ups. The concept of an enterprise as the implementation of a project is far from having been fully explored.

The results of this research show that the quality of the management in achieving product delivery, market launch, and finance availability is at the very centre of the evolution and survival of the project. Further research needs to be conducted in order to explore this critical issue further. This type of approach shows considerable promise for the understanding of such complex phenomena.

Other complementary research areas could be explored using the same approach. A resource-based approach, for example, allows an understanding of how new enterprises manage resources during the evolution of the project and would be of great interest. The literature shows that the 'habitat', or milieu, where the new high-tech venture is located, is important in its development. The approach could be relevant to understanding the way in which entrepreneurs take advantage of their milieu during the evolution of the project. Finally, both the complexity of the evolution of high-tech start-ups and the continuous change in the economic, technological and financial conditions, make this research field very interesting and attractive for the future.

REFERENCES

Adizes, I. (1999), *Managing Corporate Lifecycles*, Paramus, NJ: Prentice Hall.

Albert, P., A. Fayolle and S. Marion (1994), 'L'évolution des systèmes d'appui à la création d'entreprise', *Revue Française de Gestion*, no. 101, 100–112.

Basso, O. and P. Bieliczky (2001), *Guide Pratique du nouveau Créateur de Start-up*, Paris: Editions d'Organisation.

Bernasconi, M. and M. Monsted (2000), 'Les modèles de développement des entreprises high-tech' in M. Bernasconi, M. Monsted et al. (eds), *Les Start-up High-tech*, Paris: Dunod, pp. 59–75.

Bhidé, A. (2000), *The Origin and Evolution of New Businesses*, New York: Oxford University Press.

Blais, R. and J.-M. Toulouse (1992), *Entrepreneurship technologique: 21 cas de PME à succès*, Montreal: Les Editions Transcontinentales.

Bréchet, J.-P. (1994), 'Du projet d'entreprendre au projet d'entreprise', *Revue Française de Gestion*, June–August, 5–13.

Carter, N., W. Gartner and P. Reynolds (1996), 'Exploring start-up event sequences', *Journal of Business Venturing*, **11**, 151–66.

Chandler, A. (1962), *Strategy and Structure*, Cambridge, MA: MIT Press.

Chell, E. (2001), *Entrepreneurship: Globalization, Innovation and Development*, London: Thomson Learning.

Churchill, N. and V. Lewis (1983), 'The five stages of small business growth', *Harvard Business Review*, **61**, May–June, 30–50.

Davidsson, P. (2001), 'Toward a paradigm for entrepreneurship research', paper presented at the RENT XV Conference, Turku, Finland.

Davier, M. (2001), *Réussir sa Start-up après la Start-up Mania*, Paris: Dunod.

Delmar, F. and P. Davidsson (1998), 'A taxonomy of high-growth firms', *Frontiers of Entrepreneurship Research*, Babson College, pp. 399–413.

During, W., R. Oakey and S. Kauser (2001), *New Technology-based Firms in the New Millennium*, London: Pergamon.

Flamholtz, E. (1986), *How to Make the Transition from an Entrepreneurship to a Professionally Managed Firm*, San Francisco and London: Jossey-Bass.

Galbraith, J. (1982), 'The Stages of Growth', *Journal of Business Strategy*, Summer, pp. 70–79.

Garnsey, E. (1998), 'A theory of the early growth of the firm', *Industrial and Corporate Change*, **7**(3), 523–56.

Garnsey, E. and P. Heffernan (2001), 'Growth setbacks in new firms', *ESRC Priority Network on Complex Dynamic Processes*, proceedings of the conference on 'Limits to Knowledge', Budapest.

Gordon Bell, C. and J. McNamara (1991), *High-tech Ventures*, Reading, MA: Addison-Wesley.

Greiner, L. (1998), 'Evolution and revolution as organizations grow', *Harvard Business Review*, **76**(3), 55–64.

Hanks, S., C. Watson, E. Jansen and G. Chandler (1993), 'Tightening the life-cycle construct: a taxonomic study of growth stage configurations in high-technology organizations', *Entrepreneurship: Theory and Practice*, Winter, pp. 5–29.

Hansen, E. and B. Bird (1997), 'The stages model of high-tech venture founding: tried but true?', *Entrepreneurship: Theory and Practice*, **22**(2), 111–23.

Hlady-Rispal, M. (2000), 'Une stratégie de recherche en gestion: l'étude de cas', *Revue Française de Gestion*, January–February pp. 61–70.

Julien, P.-A., P. Mustar and M.-F. Estimé (2001), Dossier: 'Les PME à forte croissance: une comparaison internationale', *Revue internationale PME*, **14** (3–4).

Kazanjian, R. (1988), 'Relation of dominant problems to stages of growth in technology-based new ventures', *Academy of Management Journal*, **31**(2), 257–79.

Levie, J. and M. Hay (1998), 'Progress or just proliferation? A historical review of stages models of early corporate growth', London Business School Working Paper – FEM, no. 98.5.

McCann, J. (1991), 'Patterns of growth, competitive technology and financial strategies in young ventures', *Journal of Business Venturing*, **6**, 189–208.

Miller, D. and P. Friesen (1984), *Organizations: A Quantum View*, Englewood Cliffs, NJ and London: Prentice-Hall.

Mintzberg, H., B. Ahlstrand and J. Lampel (1998), *Strategic Safari,* New York: The Free Press.

Nesheim, J. (1992), *High Tech Start Up*, Saratoga, CA: Electronic Trends Publications.

O'Farrell, P. and D. Hitchens (1988), 'Alternative theories of small-firm growth: a critical review', *Environment and Planning*, **20**, 1365–83.

Quinn, R. and K. Cameron (1983), 'Organizational life cycles and shifting criteria of effectiveness: some preliminary evidence', *Management Science*, **29**(1), 31–51.

Reynolds, P. and B. Miller (1992), 'New firm gestation: conception, birth and implications for research', *Journal of Business Venturing*, **7**, 405–17.

Roberts, E. (1991), *Entrepreneurs in High Technology*, New York: Oxford University Press.

Sammut, S. (1998), *Jeune Entreprise, la Phase Cruciale du Démarrage*, Paris: L'harmattan.

Saporta, B. (1994), 'La création d'entreprise: enjeux et perspectives', *Revue Française de Gestion*, no. 101, 74–86.

Slevin, D. and J. Covin (1995), 'New ventures and total competitiveness; a conceptual model, empirical results, and case study examples', *Frontiers of Entrepreneur Research*, Wellesley, MA: Babson College.

Stanworth, M. and J. Curran (1976), 'Growth and the small firm – an alternative view', *Journal of Management Studies*, May, 95–110.

Steinmetz, L. (1969), 'Critical stages of small business growth: when they occur and how to survive them', *Business Horizons*, **7**(1), 29–36.

Storey, D. (1994), *Understanding the Small Firm Sector*, London: Routledge.

Thiétart, R.-A. et al. (1999), *Méthodes de Recherche en Management*, Paris: Dunod.

Verstraete, T. (2003). 'A French perspective on the singularity of entrepreneurship as a research domain', *Annual Review of Progress in Entrepreneurship, 2000–2001*, Brussels: European Foundation for Management Development.

Vesper, K. (1990), *New Venture Strategies*, Englewood Cliffs, NJ: Prentice Hall

Wittington, R. (1993), *What is Strategy and Does it Matter?*, London: Routledge.

Yin, R.K. (1990), *Case Study Research: Design and Method*, vol. 5, Beverley Hills: Sage.

9. A chaordic lens for understanding entrepreneurship and intrapreneurship

Frans M. van Eijnatten

INTRODUCTION

In the last twenty years, scientific thinking about entrepreneurship has slowly but steadily migrated from an entrepreneur-focused approach into an entrepreneurial-process-based endeavour (Bygrave and Hofer, 1991). Nowadays entrepreneurship may be best defined in a discontinuous, holistic and dynamic way: changing the competitive structure of the industry or service, incorporating both the system and its unique context, and understanding a venture as being an integral part of the total industry system (Bygrave and Hofer, 1991). Paula Kyrö distinguishes three forms of entrepreneurship (Kyrö, 2000, 43): '1) Entrepreneurship, referring to the individual entrepreneur and his firm; 2) Intrapreneurship, referring to an organization's collective behaviour; and 3) Individual, self-oriented entrepreneurship, referring to an individual's self-oriented behaviour.' In this chapter we will use these types of entrepreneurship rather loosely and interchangeably.

Reflecting on the 4th McGill Conference on International Entrepreneurship Marian Jones and Pavlos Dimitratos (2003, 159–60) state in an introduction to a special issue of the *Journal of International Entrepreneurship* that: 'entrepreneurial creativity, entrepreneurial culture, and the notion of time are three key elements contributing to the internationalisation process of firms'. These authors define entrepreneurial creativity as the recognition – by the entrepreneur – of opportunities for development, and the exploitation of resources to enable international market entry. In the special issue Pavlos Dimitratos and Emmanuella Plakoyiannaki define entrepreneurial culture as 'that organizational culture which facilitates and accommodates the entrepreneurial activities of the firm in the international marketplace' (Dimitratos and Plakoyiannaki, 2003, 193). The definition of time has proved problematic. According to Marian Jones and Pavlos Dimitratos 'time has seldom featured as the main construct, element or dimension in empirical research' (Jones and Dimitratos, 2003, 161). Leila Hurmerinta-Peltomäki (2003, 220) argues that researchers implicitly treat the concept of time in a static and linear way; time is predominantly forward directed and gradual (past–present–future). According to her, the resulting stage models, which are predominant in the literature, are lacking both descriptive and explanatory powers. In practice, time reversals, cycles and 'rapid progress with leap-frogging' may occur, resulting in situations which are far more complex than the stage models want us to believe.

This study presents a Chaordic Systems Thinking (CST) lens for understanding entrepreneurship/intrapreneurship that builds on Michael Hannan and John Freeman's Population-Ecology model about how organizations get born, survive and die (Bygrave and Hofer, 1991; Hannan and Freeman, 1977). However, Chaordic Systems Thinking (CST) tries to avoid at least one major downside of that approach, namely the neglect of the volition of an entre-/intrapreneur, by seeing the entre-/intrapreneur as a holon: an entity that is both dependent and autonomous at the same time.

We will use entrepreneurial creativity, entrepreneurial culture and the time factor as three basic themes in order to inquire how Chaordic Systems Thinking (CST) may enable researchers to understand entrepreneurship in a more profound way. Needless to say that CST is just one of many potential lenses which can be used to understand entrepreneurship.

THE FRAMEWORK

In order to understand CST better we will start with explaining the meaning of the term 'chaordic'. After that we will continue with some essentials of CST. Next, we will look at some main characteristics of CST, and explore in some detail its connection with entrepreneurial culture. In order to illustrate the CST framework, we will use the life cycle of a 'High-tech start-up' (Nesheim, 2000) as an example.

The Meaning of Chaordic

We start the explanation of the framework by stating that the Chaos metaphor understands systems as predominantly complex, dynamical and non-linear, in which chaos and order may co-exist. Chaos, originally formulated as the theory of complex, dynamical, non-linear systems (Gleick, 1987), essentially is the science of all simultaneously chaotic and orderly, that is 'chaordic' entities (Fitzgerald, 1996a). Although chaos theory assumes the co-existence of both chaos and order, we favour the term 'chaordic' to stress the concurrency of chaos and order even more. Originally Dee Hock – founder and former CEO of Visa Card International – coined the term 'chaord' being an amalgamation of *chao*s and *ord*er (Hock, 1996a; 1999). A chaord is any chaotically-ordered complex. Applied to social organizations it would mean 'the harmoniously blending of intellectual and experiential learning' (Hock, 1996b). According to the Chaordic Commons, a global network founded by Dee Hock as the Chaordic Alliance back in 1997, the term chaordic means: '1) Anything simultaneously orderly and chaotic; 2) Patterned in a way dominated neither by order nor chaos; 3) Existing in the phase between order and chaos' (The Chaordic Commons, 2003). Chaordic systems are complex systems that are able to thrive in Far-From-Equilibrium (FFE) conditions.

A chaordic system might be described as: 'a complex and dynamical arrangement of connections between elements forming a unified whole the behaviour of which is both unpredictable (chaotic) and patterned (orderly) . . . simultaneously. Chaos then is the science of such chaotic and orderly that is 'chaordic' entities' (Fitzgerald, 1997a, 1; Fitzgerald, 2002).

Chaordic Systems Thinking (CST) is a way of thinking and subsequently an approach to designing a complex organizational system that recognizes the enterprise not as a fixed structure, but as flow (Fitzgerald and Van Eijnatten, 1998; Van Eijnatten and Hoogerwerf, 2000; Van Eijnatten, 2001). CST offers new concepts in order to deal with uncontrollability, uncertainty and complexity in a business context.

CST: Some Essentials

Now we will turn to the chaordic lens as a change metaphor, and will explain the notions of discontinuous growth and time.

Chaordic thinking as a lens and a metaphor for change
In a special issue of the *Journal of Organizational Change Management* chaos is delineated as a lens, not as a theory (Fitzgerald and Van Eijnatten, 2002). Chaos is primarily seen as a particular way of looking at reality (Fitzgerald, 2002, 340–41):

> Chaos can be regarded as the science of 21st century management. . . . Rather, this newly emerging organizational cosmology is a specific way to look at and comprehend a specific reality – for our purposes, the increasingly complex organizations we find ourselves barely able to sustain in the turbulence and flux of the hyper-competitive global marketplace. . . . Given its common connotation, Chaos is a rather unfortunate moniker for the new science. Microsoft's thesaurus offers several synonyms for the term including 'confusion, bedlam, anarchy, pandemonium, disarray and madness'. Furthermore, more than one English-language dictionary has defined it as the 'complete absence of order'. In order to mediate the likelihood of misunderstanding, the convention of employing an uppercase 'C' when referring to the meta-view of reality . . . has been adopted.

Also in that *JOCM* journal issue, complexity is circumscribed neither as a theory nor as a lens, but rather as one – of many – characteristics of whole systems (Fitzgerald and Van Eijnatten, 2002, 405):

> The theory of chaos that eventually served as the catalytic agent for the metapraxis we now refer to as Chaos (note uppercase), was intended for use in predicting stochastic patterns in Nature's most intractable systems, the weather for instance. In contrast, what is often called 'complexity theory' cannot be attributed to the research of any individual or scientific institution nor can the date of its formulation be confirmed. . . . Consequently, due to its failure to meet these basic criteria for acknowledgement as a scientific theory, we are compelled to consider what is claimed under the complexity banner as an eclectic collection of concepts, premises and notions many of which have been borrowed from various branches of science including the chaos theory. . . . Although complexity may indeed help explain the rules governing our reality, Chaos is the lens through which we see that reality.

We take this position as a conceptual base for this study. So, we will not concentrate on chaos theory – which is a mathematical construction – instead we will use Chaos as a systemic way of looking at reality, as a worldview, as a metaphor for change which recognizes that systems are complex, dynamical, and non-linear. To escape any bedlam we will speak of 'chaos thinking' instead of chaos theory. So Chaordic Systems Thinking (CST) is the name of the framework that uses Chaos both as a lens and as a metaphor for change.

The notion of discontinuous growth
One of the key precepts of CST is discontinuous growth. Enterprises engage in cycles of both creation and destruction. Chaordic systems are supposed to grow in a leapfrog way. Ideas for a new product or service may be the starting point of such a qualitative leap. A High-Tech Start-Up – seen as a chaordic system – jumps into a higher level of complexity and coherence suddenly instead of gradually, see Figure 9.1. The life cycle of a chaordic enterprise may be described as a (r)evolutionary process: A High-Tech Start-Up is born or initiated, starts to develop and grows into maturity until it eventually hits its limits to growth after which it may die or leap to a next level of complexity, to start a novel cycle of development. In the period of growth into maturity a chaordic system finds itself in a state of relative stability (see the shaded rectangular areas in Figure 9.1). When it approaches its limits a chaordic system starts to bifurcate, and enters a period of relative instability.

During its development, a chaordic system may be in one of the following equilibrium states: Equilibrium; Near To Equilibrium; Far From Equilibrium; and Fatal Chaos, see Figure 9.1. Just following the birth of a High-Tech Start-Up the system is in an equilibrium state. That means that it does not grow. The founder CEO has built his or her Small or Medium-sized Enterprise and starts to 'pioneer the radical innovation' (Preston, 2003, 16). Considerable amounts of money have been invested, the innovative product or service is bound to be produced and sold to customers, but there is no cash flow, yet. When the new product or service is successful in the market, the High-Tech Start-Up starts to

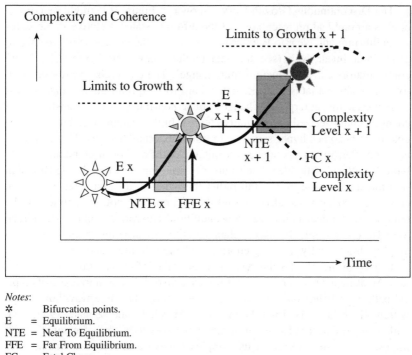

Notes:
❋   Bifurcation points.
E   = Equilibrium.
NTE = Near To Equilibrium.
FFE = Far From Equilibrium.
FC = Fatal Chaos.
▮   'Linear' development, see Figure 9.3.

Figure 9.1   Discontinuous growth curve of a chaordic enterprise

grow. The pace of growth may be slower or faster, dependent on the market, resulting in some return of investments. The High-Tech Start-Up evolves into a high-tech business, until it hits the limits of its growth, for instance because the market gets satiated, the lease of facilities are becoming a bottleneck, or because the competition introduces similar or more advanced products or services. Entering the Far-From-Equilibrium state means that the former High-Tech Start-Up – now an established high-tech medium-sized company – faces a number of unanticipated events which are impossible to control, such as a low stock market or endured highly aggressive price pressures from the competition. Under these turbulent circumstances the high-tech enterprise may die – entering the Fatal Chaos state – or may jump into a next level of complexity with a new product or service, which transcends and includes the functionality of the previous one, which gives the high-tech company a new competitive advantage. Walking the different states might be a fast or a slow process, resulting in shorter or longer life cycles of the original High-Tech Start-Up.

The Discontinuous Growth Curve, shown in Figure 9.1, might be considered as a graphical representation of the different states: Relative stable states – Equilibrium and Near to Equilbrium – in which the enterprise is expected to grow in a linear way (see the rectangular shapes in Figure 9.1). Some commentators call this 'incremental change'. The curve also represents relative non-stable – that is, chaotic, states: Far From Equilibrium and Fatal Chaos – in which the enterprise 'changes' in a non-linear way ('transformative change', characterized by qualitative leaps). In the chaotic unstable states the enterprise becomes hyper-sensitive to minor external changes. This condition is called 'Sensitive Dependence on Initial Conditions' or more popularly 'the butterfly effect' – the idea that a butterfly flapping its wings in the Brazilian rain forest can cause rain to fall rather than the sun to shine later in London (Lorentz, 1963a/b), see also (below) the section 'The notion of time'. In the complex dynamical non-linear non-equilibrial enterprise – like a High-Tech Start-Up is – a single minuscule change, a tiny perturbation in the system can amplify dramatically, yielding enormous changes in the outcome.

In each of these states the system is under the influence of different attractors. An attractor is a condition that forces a chaordic system to repeat its typical pattern of behaviour, not each time in exactly the same way, but always within clear and specified boundaries (Marchall and Zohar, 1997, 58). Although no external force, an attractor behaves as a sort of magnet which imposes the system to repeat its complex behavioural pattern over and over again. Douglas Polley defines an attractor basin as the region in which the attractor is successfully able to execute its magnet function in which any level of performance will be drawn to follow the attractor (Polley, 1997, 446–7; Çambel, 1993, 60). Chaordic development may be described as: 'A dynamical process passing from one attractor basin to the next in an incessant journey toward the 'edge' of chaos' (Van Eijnatten and Fitzgerald, 1998). An established enterprise is, so to speak, solidly 'imprisoned' in its attractor basin (Dilts, 1998) (see Figure 9.2).

Richard Priesmeyer (1992, 22) states: 'the outer limit of a basin of attraction defines the threshold between a return to established patterns and an escape to uncharted territory'. Put in other words, a (new) basin of attraction represents a (new) order. The founding of a High-Tech Start-Up may be seen as an entrepreneurial process of successfully escaping the known valley ('business as usual'), climbing the mountain ('exploring the radical innovation'), and gliding into a new unknown valley ('the new business process'). A Fitness Landscape is a constitution of multiple attractors (and their respective basins) to which a High-Tech Start-Up may become attracted during its travel: the product of service prototype may change, or the business focus may change.

Bifurcation is defined as a qualitative change in an attractor's structure. The

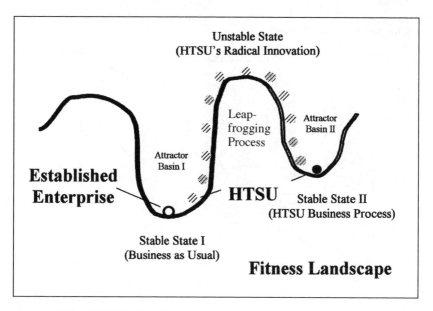

Note: HTSU = A High-Tech Start-Up.

Figure 9.2   Business as usual and the birth process of a High-Tech Start-Up

bifurcation point or window of opportunities marks the moment in time at a certain level of complexity at which an enterprise would come under the influence of different attractor basins: coming from a relative stable state the enterprise is entering a relative unstable one. It will experience all kinds of dilemmas and contradictions, and literally 'feels' the turbulence. At the end of the day either it may jump without any external help to a higher level of complexity, or alternatively it may dissipate altogether. These are extreme cases: parts of the enterprise may jump; parts of it may dissipate into Fatal Chaos.

Even in relatively stable periods a chaordic enterprise is thought to show small qualitative leaps instead of gradual changes (see Figure 9.3). We call this the fractal dimension of growth. The chaordic lens implies that incremental change on a macro level might be understood as a whole series of small qualitative leaps on a micro level.

These small leaps may occur in one or more individuals (that is a subsystem's transformation), while the chaordic enterprise as a whole is still gradually developing in a linear way (that is a whole system's re-formation). For instance, during the linear growth period of a High-Tech Start-Up, seen as a

Complexity and Coherence

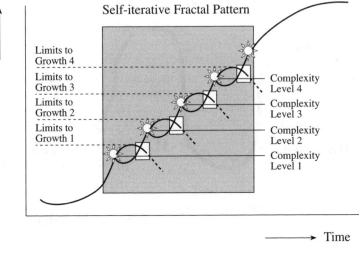

Self-iterative Fractal Pattern

Limits to Growth 4

Limits to Growth 3 — Complexity Level 4

Limits to Growth 2 — Complexity Level 3

Limits to Growth 1 — Complexity Level 2

— Complexity Level 1

→ Time

Notes:
✳   Bifurcation point.
▮ ▯   Scale invariance: the same pattern occurs at each level of aggregation (enterprise level, workgroup level, individual level).

Figure 9.3   The fractal dimension of growth: group and individual transformations in a High-Tech Start-Up

whole, individual employees may experience qualitative leaps in their thinking and working together, due to significant crises in their personal functioning.

During the period of non-linear change a chaordic (sub) system shows different modes of behaviours which compete with each other for existence. The system starts to oscillate between these modes: chaos and order co-exist in this unstable state. Let us look more closely at the transformative change from old into new behaviour patterns (see Figure 9.4).

Consider the two-by-two table which is enclosed by the two curves in Figure 9.4. Jaap Peters and Rob Wetzels call this region the 'Cross in the Chaos' (Peters and Wetzels, 1998 [2003]). The upper two cells I and II represent the dominant pattern embedded in the current context; the lower two cells represent the emerging pattern embedded in the new context. A typical successful transformative change or qualitative leap is defined as a transitional trajectory from cell I ('old thinking, old doing') into cell IV ('new thinking, new doing'). The transitional trajectories from cell I ('old thinking, old doing')

Complexity and Coherence

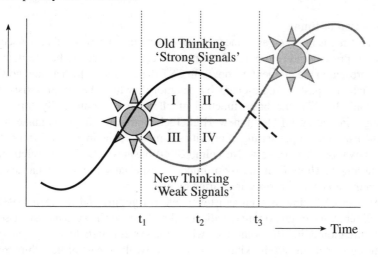

Notes:

*	Bifurcation point.
I	= Old thinking, old doing.
II	= Old thinking, new doing.
III	= New thinking, old doing.
IV	= New thinking, new doing.
$t_1 - t_3$	= Three crucial moments in the transformation process.

Source: Peters and Wetzels (1998).

Figure 9.4   Alternative trajectories for non-linear development

into cell II ('old thinking, new doing') and cell I ('old thinking, old doing') into cell III ('new thinking, old doing') are defined as unsuccessful or pathological changes which are not sustainable, and might be considered as temporary transitional states only. The birth process of High-Tech Start-Ups may show signs of unsuccessful, non-sustainable changes, since any leap-frogging attempt is seldom successful, the very first time.

Cell I is characterized by 'old thinking, old doing'. This cell represents the old context based dominant behaviour pattern that an established enterprise has been showing during the relative stable growth period ('business as usual'). Cell IV is characterized by 'new thinking, new doing'. This cell represents the new context based dominant behaviour pattern that a new High-Tech Start-Up shows immediately following the transformation. Cells II and III are intermediate stages – 'old thinking, new doing', and 'new thinking, old doing' – which are typified by serious confusions, dilemmas, tautologies and contradictions, showing a basic lack of clarity. In this unstable state the system oscillates between these modes, frequently and irregularly.

The notion of time

In CST, time is not seen as a linear cause–effect chain of events that connects the past, present and future. All three periods are considered to be simultaneously present in the moment of 'now'. In CST there is only 'the here and now', in which the past is represented by 'memory', while the future exists as 'mission'. In CST, the basic function of planning is momentarily 'priority setting'. Founding CEOs of new High-Tech Start-Ups may recognize this mechanism: the proper setting of priorities is most crucial in pioneering a radical innovation. According to Nesheim (2000) business planning is relatively absent among High-Tech Start-Up founders, especially in those instances in which these new enterprises are started by engineers.

Also in CST, time is seen as irreversible (Prigogine and Stengers, 1984) (see Figure 9.4). In this figure t_1 indicates that the chaordic system just passed the bifurcation point, the point from where the system starts to show – on top of strong signals of old thinking – all kinds of weak signals of new thinking. At t_2 the system oscillates heavily between the old and the new thinking. At t_3 the new behaviour has become the dominant pattern and the chaordic system starts a next development cycle at a higher level of complexity. A radical innovation often starts as a dream, and may develop into a booming business endeavour.

In the unstable state chaordic systems become hypersensitive: minor changes in initial conditions may have dramatic effects on the system's outcome (the butterfly effect). In a complex dynamical, non-linear, non-equilibrial system a tiny perturbation may amplify, yielding enormous changes in the outcome. High-Tech Start-Ups may experience butterfly effects more than once during their birth processes.

CST: Some Characteristics

To deepen our understanding of CST for both entrepreneurship and intrapreneurship, we now turn to some chaordic properties, and their associated processes of 'orienteering' and 'path finding'.

Chaordic properties

Enterprises seen as chaordic systems are characterized by the following five core chaordic properties (Fitzgerald, 1996a; 1996b; 1997b; 1999): 1) consciousness; 2) connectivity; 3) indeterminacy; 4) dissipation; and 5) emergence.

1. *Consciousness*. Mind more than matter is the essential motor of an enterprise seen as a chaordic system. Therefore the re-design of a chaordic enterprise should be initiated outward from the organizational mind. As long as the organizational mind fails to hold profound systemic change as both possible and desirable, any effort to affect a change strategy will be futile. In CST ideas are primary: the internal potential of a chaordic enterprise is the key.

2. *Connectivity*. CST certifies that the enterprise is both whole and part. No part can exist apart from the whole nor can any whole be sustained isolated from its parts. Each part is by itself a whole and this whole is part of a bigger whole. We can call this a 'holon'. Therefore the re-design of a chaordic enterprise should minimize boundaries and divisions. An enterprise is changed as a whole or it is not changed.

3. *Indeterminacy*. CST points out that in the dynamical complexity of an enterprise every event is both cause and effect. Because of this complexity the future is principally unknowable in advance. Therefore the re-design of a chaordic enterprise should maximize fluidity and resilience in all aspects of structure. The focus should be on preparing. The answer to the how of change must be made up as one goes.

4. *Dissipation*. Enterprises are dissipative systems engaging in cycles of creation and destruction. They eventually fall apart and then grow back together again, each time in a novel new form ungoverned by the past. They therefore fashion a permeable boundary to hold the system's essential assets loosely: that is people, knowledge, core competencies and so on, allowing the whole to fall apart (by intention) well before it is apparently time to do so. Even if a system receives clear and timely signals that it is approaching its limits it still can't change overnight. So entrepreneurs should stimulate change long before it is time. They may design in the chaordic enterprise a self-triggering mechanism – a way to shake things up that enables the system to automatically and continuously transform itself.

5. *Emergence*. Enterprises strive toward ascending levels of coherence and complexity, made possible by capacities for self-organization, self-reference and self-transcendence. They therefore foster in the core of the organizational mind a compelling and evolving collective vision that is created and shared by all and that feeds all thought and actions.

Emergents can develop within a chaordic enterprise under the influence of the organizational consciousness, the organizational mind or 'orgmind' for short (Fitzgerald, 1997b). These emergents can help the enterprise not to dissipate in a period of instability – the state of Far-From-Equilibrium – but to leapfrog to a more advanced level of complexity and coherence instead.

However, dissipation is always an alternative which would also make new forms possible (see section on 'Creativity' below).

In designing enterprises such as High-Tech Start-Ups in a chaordic way, both entrepreneurs and intrapreneurs may boost consciousness (developing the organizational mind), connectivity (minimizing boundaries), indeterminacy (maximizing fluidity of structure), dissipation ('changing before it is time') and emergence (letting go of control and accepting initiatives coordinated by a collective vision which guides all thinking).

Orienteering and path finding

The five chaordic properties can be distinguished but not separated. Together they form a single indivisible conceptual whole and enable an enterprise to jump to a higher level of complexity and coherence.

Unpredictability and uncertainty are basic characteristics of a chaordic enterprise and of a High-Tech Start-Up in particular. Therefore one should be careful with the detailed mapping of interference in the local environment for the benefit of some future governance. Both entrepreneurs and intrapreneurs as chaordic thinkers appreciate the fundamental unknowability and unpredictability of future occurrences in concordance with the CST characteristic of indeterminacy. They try to grasp patterns and probabilities in the midst of complexity. Paul Hannon and Andrew Atherton have called this process 'orienteering' (Hannon and Atherton, 1997a, 2): 'The successful orienteer needs no directional signs pointing in a specific direction or to a clear endpoint.' A very much related concept is 'path finding'. According to Wendy Freebourne 'path finding can help us to regain purpose, both for ourselves and the collective. . . . We each have a unique role in the collective vision, a larger whole of which we are part' (Freebourne, 2003). Lauren Holmes describes path finding in unknown territory as 'creating desired realities'. That is exactly what a founding CEO of a High-Tech Start-Up is trying to do. Lauren ascertains that 'path finding is the means to be at the right place at the right time for the information coincidences which will accelerate progress' (Holmes, 2001).

Managers are encouraged to elicit change by primarily letting go of control (Fitzgerald and Van Eijnatten, 1998). This implies re-directing the basic organizational renewal strategy from reacting – or active adaptation – to changes in the environment, to initiating or deliberately changing the system long before it is time. Crossan et al. (1996) call it the 'improvising organization'; an art learned through continuous practice. It is the striving for self-renewal – breaking up the status quo – that is the most important thing for both entrepreneurs and intrapreneurs. Costas Markides states that successful innovators should be: 'not afraid to destabilize a smooth-running machine and to do so periodically but continuously' (Markides, 1998, 39), in accordance with the CST characteristic of dissipation.

CST and Entrepreneurial/Intrapreneurial Culture

The relationship between CST and entrepreneurial/intrapreneurial culture is the subject of the next paragraph. I will discuss the notion of a holon, and will describe Wilber's quadrants in which human transformation is seen as the result of simultaneous development of the behavioural, social, intentional and cultural dimensions. We conclude that using a chaordic lens implicates more explicit attention for the interior aspects of an enterprise. Following Wilber we assume that culture essentially is a collective interior aspect ('thinking'), not a collective exterior attribute ('behaviour').

The notion of holons

As already mentioned before, another central feature of CST is the concept of holons. Holons are entities that are both wholes and parts of a greater whole, at the same time (Koestler, 1967 [1978]) (see Figure 9.5). High-Tech Start-Ups – seen as holons – are autonomous and dependent structures, at the same time.

In recent publications the Colorado-based American philosopher Ken Wilber has written a lot about holons (Wilber, 1995; 1996a; 1996b; 1998). Holons are structures that are simultaneously autonomous and dependent. Holons emerge, that is they evolve to higher orders of whole/partness by virtue of four fundamental capacities possessed by each (Wilber, 1996a): 1) Agency or identity; 2) Communion or membership; 3) Self-transcendence or to go beyond what went before; 4) Self-dissolution or decomposing into sub-holons.

Holons are able to generate emergents – novel qualities of the whole which are not present in the parts – because they are inherently self-organizing, self-referencing, self-iterating and self-adapting.

Holons emerge holarchically (they develop greater depth), transcend and include their predecessors (they preserve its component parts while going beyond the limitations of each) and holons know their worlds according to the terms and limitations of their core identity.

Holons dissipate: they are always subject to falling apart because they fail to leap or when they become unbalanced (the wholeness dominates and represses its partness or the part refuses responsibility for other than itself). Damaging or destroying any holarchical level will result in damage or destruction of all higher levels. Although the higher level is more significant, the lower holon is more fundamental (see Figure 9.5). Holons and holarchies are characterized by differentiation (generation of variety) and integration (generation of coherence). There is no such thing as a fully autonomous whole holon (all autonomy is autonomy-in-relationship). The adjective 'holonic' is used to indicate the 'both . . . and' character of entities: a holon is both whole and part of a bigger whole, at the same time.

Not all holons are equal: one whole/part is distinguished from another by

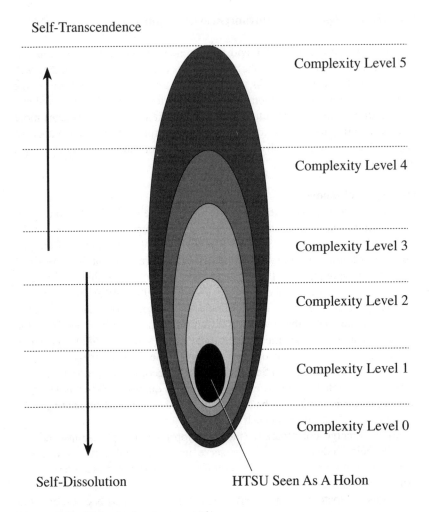

Self-Transcendence

Complexity Level 5

Complexity Level 4

Complexity Level 3

Complexity Level 2

Complexity Level 1

Complexity Level 0

Self-Dissolution   HTSU Seen As A Holon

Figure 9.5   Holonic development (1)

the relative degree to which it taps its internal or holonic capacity (Fitzgerald and Van Eijnatten, 1998). The higher a holon climbs the ladder of knowing or consciousness, the greater its ability to apprehend reality. Holonic capacity is the holons' ability to operate with greater mindfulness, expanded awareness, control- and response-ability (Fitzgerald and Van Eijnatten, 1998). Control-ability is the degree to which a holon is able to influence future events, and response-ability is the ability to respond to Far From Equilibrium conditions. The 'organizational mind' – the sum total of beliefs, assumptions, premises, values and conclusions that mostly tacit members of an organizational system hold commonly as truth – is the container of the holonic capacity of a chaordic enterprise.

CST suggests that by developing holonic capacity both entrepreneurs and intrapreneurs are able to see the window of opportunity on their way towards the edge of chaos. Only then is an enterprise able to leap to a higher order of coherence – a new stable dynamic that is, however, more complex and more effective – and therefore escaping dissipation. When the organizational mind is developed in such a way an established enterprise is able to transform itself from within into a totally new form which can grasp the pace of our changing world.

Exterior and interior aspects

An enterprise seen as a holon possesses both an exterior surface as well as an interior essence (Wilber, 1996a). In normal science our attention is focused on the exterior, exclusively. By exterior we mean any objectifiable entity or process that can be described by empirical observations, making use of our five senses or their extensions. Both the interior and exterior have individual and collective dimensions. A holon consists therefore of four quadrants (see Figure 9.6).

The exterior of the individual (YOU) can be described by, for instance, tasks and forms of behaviour. The exterior of the collective (THEY) can be seen as the noticeable patterns of social behaviour of groups. In these two right-hand quadrants the observer is not part of the observed.

The interior of the individual (ME) is characterized by emotions, thoughts and feelings, which could be called 'individual mind'. This quadrant is about consciousness. When individual thoughts are exchanged and shared with other individuals the result may be a collective worldview or commonly shared meaning (US). This is the interior of the collective that could be called entre-preneurial/intrapreneurial culture or entrepreneurial/intrapreneurial mind. This quadrant is about mutual understanding, cultural fit and justness. In these two left-hand quadrants the observer is part of the observed.

According to Wilber in each quadrant a different type of holarchy (holonic hierarchy) is operating and also a different type of validity test is appropriate: Truthfulness for the intentional domain (ME), Truth for the behavioural domain (YOU), Justness for the cultural domain (US), and Functional Fit for the social domain (THEY). Wilber states that a truly holistic approach should cover all four facets equally well (Wilber, 1996a). CST takes Wilber's Quadrants as its reference framework. Basically it combines both interior and exterior aspects, at the individual as well as at the collective levels. CST is advocating to re-unite the interior with the exterior, on both the individual and collective levels.

Applied to the field at stake, we hypothesize that both entrepreneurship and

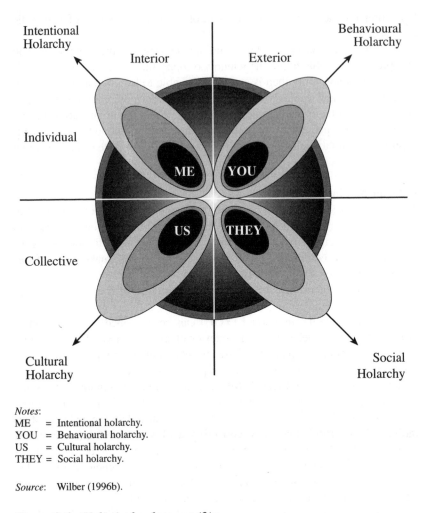

Notes:
ME   = Intentional holarchy.
YOU = Behavioural holarchy.
US   = Cultural holarchy.
THEY = Social holarchy.

Source: Wilber (1996b).

Figure 9.6   Holonic development (2)

intrapreneurship seen as processes might become more powerful and creative when executed by a self-managed team of professionals acting as a complex and coherent whole.

Holonic potential

The organizational mind – the sum total of beliefs, assumptions, premises, values and conclusions that mostly tacit members of an organizational system hold commonly as truth – is the container of the holonic capacity of an enterprise. CST suggests that by developing holonic capacity, entrepreneurs and intrapreneurs are able to see the window of opportunity more clearly when arriving at the edge of chaos. Only then is an enterprise able to leapfrog to a higher order of coherence – a new stable dynamic that is, however, more complex and more effective – and therefore escaping dissipation. When the organizational mind is developed in such a way, an enterprise is able to transform itself – from within – into a totally new form which can grasp the pace of our changing world. CST can facilitate 'learning from within' by means of deep dialogue, on top of mere surface learning, in accordance with the CST characteristic of consciousness. A way to survive is by tapping the interior potential that gives established enterprises the ability to transform themselves to a higher level of coherence. In this new state of order the enterprise is able to see through its complexity more effectively. It is assumed that in periods of instability enterprises should rely on the innovative character and creativity of their employees. Old control paradigms – for example cost reduction – are of less use under these circumstances and an enterprise may seek smarter ways of dealing with instability. The value added is the system's interior, the collective development of the organizational mind, the vision that is continuously created and shared by all.

Story telling and narratives can be used as a means of transferring codified experiences and learning to others (Hannon and Atherton, 1997b; Tsoukas, 1997). Also the inclusion of so-called soft issues is mandatory here (Ashford and Humphrey, 1995). Dorothy Marcic distinguishes between five dimensions of work: 1) Physical (work design and work conditions, financial issues); 2) Intellectual (challenging work, training, drive for further development and learning, freedom to fail); 3) Emotional (interpersonal work environment: Personal support, respect and appreciation); 4) Volitional (desire for change, willingness instead of resistance to make sacrifices at all levels); and 5) Spiritual (moral issues: integrity; capacity to love; justice and respect at all levels; nobility and dignity, wisdom of love) (Marcic, 1997, 28, 39). In order to boost human performance, she is suggesting a better balance between those dimensions, paying explicit attention to both the emotional and the spiritual dimensions (Marcic, 1997, 29):

> Trust, personal responsibility, dignity, and respect – all these issues reside in the organization's soul. To address the soul of an enterprise, we must look particularly at the third and fifth dimensions of work. . . . Until we do so, we will continue to find that many of the resources we are pouring into organizational change are indeed wasted.

Any disproportionality between those respective dimensions should be avoided. It is the balance that is essential.

Dialogue

Where structural approaches like Socio-Technical Systems Design may be quite helpful to develop the exterior of established enterprises, in CST the interaction process of dialogue may be helpful in developing the interiors of both the individual and the collective. One might think of dialogue as a stream of meaning, flowing among and through a group of people out of which might emerge some shared meaning (Bohm, 1987; Fitzgerald, 1996a; Ellinor and Gerard, 1998; Gerard and Ellinor, 1999). Dialogue moves beyond any one individual's understanding to make explicit and build collective meaning and vision. Dialogue slows down the pace of thought of the following mental activities so that we can become aware of them: reception of data, interpretations (perceptions), assumptions and conclusions. These four stages are usually carried out in an instant. Dialogue explores the four different stages explicitly with the aim to identify our assumptions, those things that are assumed or thought to be. By learning how to identify or recognize our assumptions we are able to identify inconsistencies. Persons who apply the chaos lens and use dialogue as their main mode of communication speak the truth, are present, pay attention, and let go. For a comparison between dialogue and discussion, see Table 9.1.

Individual roles in a chaordic enterprise are highly flexible rather than fixed. The CST concept of emergent leadership is illustrative in that respect: leadership is not allocated to a single person but will be taken up by different persons in a group of entrepreneurs or intrapreneurs, initiated at their own discretion. Individual role models of the carp, shark and dolphin can help

Table 9.1   Dialogue versus discussion

Dialogue	Discussion
Seeing the whole among the parts,	Breaking issues or problems into parts,
Seeing the connections,	Making distinctions,
Further inquiring into one's own assumptions,	Justifying/defending one's own assumptions,
Creating shared meaning among many,	Gaining agreement on one single meaning,
Listening deeply together without resistance,	Preparing to post better arguments,
Release of the need for specific outcomes,	Aiming at conclusions or decisions,
A slower pace with silences in between,	Continuous flashing battle of arguments,
Learning through inquiry and disclosure	Persuading, selling, telling,
Divergent.	Converging.

Source: Fitzgerald (1997b); Ellinor and Gerard (1998).

founding CEOs and engineers of High-Tech Start-Ups to understand emergent leadership. A carp's role stands for submissive behaviour, a shark's role for aggressive behaviour. A dolphin's role stands for a mixed role in which there is a choice between submissive and aggressive behaviours. The story of the dolphin illustrates the way one may adapt one's role in a particular situation. A dolphin is a metaphor for a personal way of life in which one consciously chooses either to change or accept the situation. A dolphin never chooses to suffer from a situation. The dolphin attractor can be described as a complex responsive process or pattern in which both entrepreneurs and intrapreneurs take up responsibility in their group to lead or be led, dependant on the circumstances, at their own discretion (Van Eijnatten and Van Galen, 2002a; 2000b; Van Eijnatten et al., 2003).

SUSTAINABLE WORK SYSTEMS

Holonic development might be considered as sustainable development (Van Eijnatten, 2000; Kira, 2003). According to Backström et al. (2002) a sustainable work system can be described as a work system that consciously strives towards simultaneous development at different levels: individual, group/firm and region/society. For instance, at the lowest level, an individual wants to stay healthy and enjoys continuous learning, at the group/firm level economic growth may be considered important to keep or raise shares in the market, and at the societal level the maintenance of employment opportunities may be most crucial. All these different aspects interact and materialize concurrently. They make the system both dynamic and very complex. Entrepreneurs and intrapreneurs might gain from adopting such a holistic view, if more balance is strived for.

Only a system that is in a continuous state of development can be called sustainable. Sustainability cannot be defined as a static characteristic of a structure or a process, because everything in the system is constantly on the move. A definition of sustainability should take into account time as an important factor, and should focus on the dynamic qualities of the system.

According to Backström et al. (2002, 67) there are three central features characteristic of sustainable work systems as seen through a CST lens:

1) Spontaneous and mutual alignment of individuals; 2) Successfully coping with rapidly changing external conditions; and 3) Fitness development for competitiveness.

1. A first key feature of a sustainable work system is the tendency of their members for spontaneous and mutual alignment; to pull in the same direction. This is a matter of the internal interaction and dialogue that promote collective learning

and self-organization, of creating a common culture, a flow of information, a frame for interpretation and a common vision. This situation makes it also possible for an individual to create and reconstruct meaning and understanding and, consequently, to handle worry, psychological wear and tear, that continuous change might cause, and to foster personal and professional development.

2. A second key feature of a sustainable work system is the ability of the organization to cope with unpredictable changes in the environment. This is a matter of relating to the surrounding world so as to control resources and markets and to adapt to external changes. There are numerous examples of companies that have suffered a bankruptcy because they failed to adapt to this change.

3. A third key feature of a sustainable work system is fitness development for competitiveness. Most organizations are facing strong competition in a global market. There is a continuous striving towards increased development in complex systems, in both the legitimate and shadow systems in order to be able to survive in this fast changing fitness landscape.

Systems designed for Far-From-Equilibrium are more sustainable than those caught up in the quest for stability. This seeming paradox makes us suspect another fundamental assumption: the notion that an enterprise is intrinsically equilibrium-seeking (Stacey, 1995). More than once, this seems not to be the case any more, for a chaordic enterprise is able to tap its inherent capacity to self-organize and to leapfrog to ever-higher orders of complexity and coherence. The enterprise's ability to self-transcend is virtually impossible in Equilibrium, improbable when Near-To-Equilibrium, but altogether ripe with potential in Far-From-Equilibrium (Fitzgerald, 1996a, 56). So, intrapreneurs might develop a more focused sensitivity to recognize the 'weak signals' which characterize an enterprise's infiltration into the Far-From-Equilibrium state.

As already said in the introduction to this chapter, CST is just one example among several others which explains the new contours of a chaos/complexity paradigm for both entrepreneurship and intrapreneurship, in some smaller or greater detail. For some other similar approaches, see The Chaordic Commons (2003); Lissack and Roos, (1999) or Gharajedaghi (1999).

CREATION, DESTRUCTION AND NOVELTY

CST delivers a framework for understanding both entrepreneurship and intrapreneurship. Central in this are the notions of creativity and its strong relationship with innovation, chaos and complexity, and organizational novelty. We will explore these issues next.

Creativity

Creativity is another basic notion in CST that is based on the chaordic property of emergence. According to Yiu and Briggs (2000, 2–3):

> Non-linear systems consist of multiple coupled 'positive' and 'negative' feedback loops, hence both stable and dynamic. Creativity is a process containing both 'positive' and 'negative' feedback loops, allowing a living system to constantly recreate itself. . . . Creativity is defined as an art of renewal and recreation. Chaos theory allows one to see the additional dimension that is the constant process of creation.

Intrapreneurs may note that deliberate destruction of an organization's structure may be an alternative to leapfrogging in order to unleash creativity. Creativity is strongly related with innovation, the corner stone of entrepreneurship/intrapreneurship (Drucker, 1954).

Creativity, chaos and complexity are interrelated concepts. As said in the beginning of this chapter, we use CST not as a theory but as a lens, a particular way of looking at reality. We see complexity as one among many specific characteristics of whole systems. Individual creativity is defined as the ability to react to weak signals and to change contexts quickly and easily. This is one of the basic competencies of both entrepreneurs and intrapreneurs.

Chaos and Complexity

In our view complexity is a characteristic of chaos as a world view. Our position does not necessarily deviate from other important contributions to the literature (Lissack and Roos, 1999; Kauffman, 1995; Cilliers, 1999; 2000). They argue that complexity stands for a field of study that penetrates many different disciplines: biology, mathematics, physics, cognition, computation, philosophy, medicine, psychology and human organization. According to Michael Lissack and Johan Roos complexity refers to 'the collection of scientific disciplines all of which are concerned with finding patterns among collections of behaviours or phenomena. The field looks at patterns across a multitude of scales in an effort to detect their 'laws' of pattern generation or 'rules' that explain the patterns observed' (Lissack and Roos, 1999, 10).

We think that other complexity research endeavours may fit CST because they build on the same new set of assumptions. From that particular point of view we cannot second Paul Cilliers in his assertion that chaos and complexity 'ha[ve] little to do with each other' (Cilliers, 2000, 26). This statement might be true for chaos and complexity viewed as separate theories or fields but not for CST as a lens (Fitzgerald and Van Eijnatten, 2002, 406):

> Nevertheless, there is no argument that the great majority of managers and practitioners are more readily conversant with its content than they would be with the highly technical esoterica comprising the chaos theory, not to mention more comfortable with the term itself. For many, the very mention of 'chaos' brings to mind discomfiting images of anarchy, mayhem and confusion.
> Our purpose in pointing out these distinctions is to disparage neither complexity nor the chaos theory. Rather . . . the term complexity has been used herein in the

more general sense of an attribute of a phenomenon, specifically that of the chaordic system. We recognize that this position deviates significantly from that of a number of organizational theorists who argue that complexity should be accorded the status of a science in its own right.

Looking at CST more broadly as a paradigm, not as a theory but as a meta-theory, makes it possible to create a common arena for dialogue and enables us to develop all kinds of models and theories based on the same set of new assumptions. Consequently we put into question the suggestion by Jeffrey Goldberg and Lívia Markóczy that 'chaos/complexity is not a challenge to traditional science, but instead constitutes analytical tools allowing traditional science and modelling to be extended to domains that were previously too difficult' (Goldberg and Markóczy, 2000, 94). We don't claim that traditional science is useless, rather that it is incomplete. We think that using the CST lens will produce quite a different kind of knowledge for a different purpose: that is it produces integrated knowledge about intact wholes – instead of frag-mented knowledge about isolated parts – not for predicting the future but for better understanding the present. Further we feel that managers and practi-tioners interested in CST can gain enormously from stories about transforma-tional change – for instance the creation of the first chaordic enterprise VISA, the credit card organization (Hock, 1999).

This brings us to the controversy about the use of metaphors versus scientific models (Lissack et al., 2000). We feel that CST definitely needs a metaphor in the first place, to make it easier for managers and academics to leap towards a totally different kind of thinking. However, we agree with Lissack et al. (2000) that one should not make it a habit to use a mere metaphor or analogy as a substi-tute for more formal models and theory. The development of scientific models is important to further explore the conditions in which emergence takes place. But we feel at the same time risk\that those models do not take into account the richness of the whole situation. We like the idea of using models not as predic-tors but as mediators (Lissack et al., 2000). To summarize, we think that the use of a metaphor is important to let people play with the new way of thinking. From the standpoint of action research we do not second the absolute premise that CST or complexity should go beyond metaphor.

Entrepreneurial/Intrapreneurial Novelty

CST may prevent any split between different frameworks of causality. By the identification of the five chaordic properties, consciousness, connectivity, inde-terminacy, dissipation and emergence, we propagate in line with Stacey et al. (2000) the exclusive use of a transformative teleology. In that sense we speak of entrepreneurial/intrapreneurial renewal or entrepreneurial/intrapreneurial

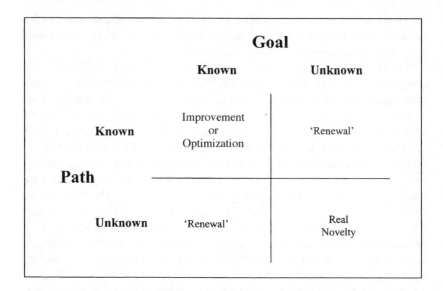

Figure 9.7   Entrepreneurial/intrapreneurial novelty as contrasted with entrepreneurial/intrapreneurial improvement

novelty as transformation instead of re-formation, the latter of which we will call improvement (see Figure 9.7).

By actually stressing the importance of the interior aspects of individuals and groups we enable the development of dialogical relations between all human agents in order to develop the orgmind. This process comes close to what Ralph Stacey and his group have called 'Complex Responsive Processes of Relating' (Stacey et al., 2000; Stacey, 2001).

ADDED VALUE OF CST FOR UNDERSTANDING ENTREPRENEURSHIP/ INTRAPRENEURSHIP

Especially because entrepreneurship is a young field of study, the methodology of which is still developing (Kyrö and Kansikas, 2002), we think that the CST lens may have some added value. Like Howard Stevensen and Susan Harmeling, we think that entrepreneurial management needs a more chaotic theory: 'Chaos is real, both in physics and in management, and it is time to recognize the fact that in order to lead efficient, competitive organizations, we have to join the fray' (Stevensen and Harmeling, 1990, 13). We would like to elaborate this statement by stressing the principal Far-From-Equilibrium nature of both entrepreneurship and intrapreneurship.

As announced in the introduction, we will evaluate the added value of CST on the basis of three themes: entrepreneurial/intrapreneurial creativity, entrepreneurial/ intrapreneurial culture, and the time factor.

The first theme is entrepreneurial/intrapreneurial creativity. CST may overcome a major pitfall of the population ecology approach because it fundamentally accepts the volition of an entre-/intrapreneur: in CST, initiatives are seen as part of the autonomous functioning of a holon. At the same time, CST acknowledges the entrepreneur's dependency on the business context: in CST adapting to this relevant environment is seen as part of the dependent functioning of a holon. CST sees dilemmas, tautologies, and contradictions – which may be the outcome of the process of entrepreneurship – as normal phenomena that occur in Far-From-Equilibrium situations. The only way an entrepreneur can solve these 'chicken-and-egg' problems, is to act as impulsively and naively as possible (Vos, 2002). If an engineer rationalized his or her decisions all the time, no single High-Tech Start-Up would ever happen. Successful entre/intrapreneurs might be particularly competent in anticipating and recognizing potential bifurcation points. They could be trained to listen to the weak signals. They might create new enterprises or change existing enterprises long before it is actually time to do so, or before competitors intend to do so. This might be the case with respect to both product/service and process improvements, renewals and inventions (creation of real novelty), dependent on the relative position of the enterprise on the growth curve.

For entre-/intrapreneurial research the focus may be on novelty and reciprocal causality instead of on improvement and unidirectional causality. That means that in the analysis minute triggers, non-linear relationships and idiosyncratic phenomena are more important than common denominators, linear relationships and repetitive events (Stevensen and Harmeling, 1990). The birth of a High-Tech Start-Up more often than not is the result of a triggering event. By using a chaordic lens the attention of the researcher is focused on the unique outcomes of the entre-/intrapreneurial process embedded in a highly specific context.

The second theme is entrepreneurial/intrapreneurial culture. Because culture is defined by Wilber (1996a) as 'collective thinking', entrepreneurial/intrapreneurial culture is closely related to (entrepreneurial/intrapreneurial) consciousness. This CST property puts great emphasis on non-observable phenomena (intentions and thoughts). Especially for members of normal science in Kuhn's sense, this is the most controversial part of CST. As Wilber (1996a) has explained, holons possess both an exterior and an interior domain. Wilber (1998) spent a whole book closing the gap between sense and soul using the scientific method. Based on the CST property of consciousness it is hypothesized that founding CEOs of High-Tech Start-Ups will materialize already available potentials of the system by the very act of thinking. This may be the essence of self-organization. According to Juarrero (1999), time and context are of crucial importance here. The process of self-organization, defined by Cilliers (1999, 90–91) as 'an emergent property of complex systems which enables them to develop or change internal structure spontaneously and adaptively in order to cope with, or manipulate, their environment' will only become feasible from within the system originating from its interior. Based on the CST property of consciousness any attempt to deepen the mindfulness of an enterprise by the development of both the individual and organizational minds might be an appropriate preparation for transformational change as an emergent.

Further deepening of the organizational mind can be stimulated by means of dialogue (Bohm, 1987; Ellinor and Gerard, 1998). Unlike the conventional means of conversing in modern life the objective of dialogue is to discover flaws and faulty assumptions in one's own thinking so they might be corrected. In a typical dialogue process people are exploring their own thinking to discover flaws in it and to discover the assumptions behind it. Being aware of these assumptions may trigger entrepreneurs to change them in order to unleash the enterprise's potentials for transformation.

For entre-/intrapreneurial research using the CST lens the inclusion of the interior aspects is most challenging. It means that a researcher can't stay a distant observer, but has to engage in deep dialogue with all stakeholders in the entre-/intrapreneurial process to better understand their thinking, and to evaluate their respective levels of development.

The third theme is time. Unlike Hurmerinta-Peltomäki (2003) we think that systems can't go back to previous developmental stages. We second the late Ilya Prigogine and Isabelle Strengers in their assertion that time is fundamentally irreversible. That means that High-Tech Start-Ups do change all the time, sometimes in a more predictable way, sometimes in a rather unpredictable way. Also the pace of change may differ: High-Tech Start-Ups may show both evolutionary and revolutionary developments. Our main argument is that they never fall back into previous stages. Remember the saying: 'You cannot step twice in the same river.' In both entrepreneurship and intrapreneurship the time factor is of vital importance. We think CST is well suited to explain the complex cycles entre-/intrapreneurial processes go through, because the attractor concept honours the irreversibility of time. When a new behaviour pattern is developed, it usually will be repeated over time, but never in exactly the same way. On the other hand, all behaviour patterns (habits) are bounded: they always stay within specific limits. Founding CEOs of High-Tech Start-Ups might want to be extremely competent in leading the system away from its known dominant attractor basin into a new unknown and uncharted attractor basin. This role asks for visionary leadership. Also the CST idea to use planning primarily as a priority setting instrument for acting in the present is a powerful concept which may help to explain entrepreneurial behaviours in High-Tech Start-Ups.

With respect to decision-making under conditions of uncertainty, Young Back Choi states that individuals 'must have an understanding about any given situation, and holds this idea with sufficient confidence to follow the course of action it suggests'. . . under uncertainty, individuals seek ideas that enable them to deal with given situations, terminating this search only when such understandings have been obtained' (Choi, 1993, 31). Related to this is the concept of Holographic Decision-Making (Van Eijnatten and Keizer, 2002; Keizer and Van Eijnatten, 2003). In Holographic Decision-Making the sequential character of design phases is purposely abolished. Basically, it is a concurrent process of reflecting on all different phases of a High-Tech Start-Up (preparation, realization, evaluation) simultaneously, as if time has approached zero. Certainly, in actual practice only one single activity is executed at a time, but all other activities are 'co-executed' simultaneously as thought experiments, as Jimme Keizer and Frans van Eijnatten state (2003, 10):

> So, together with the focal activity the whole cycle of decision-making activities is executed, quickly. This offers a first glance of the resulting system or process. Of course, this decision-making is not final. It is used as a quick approximation. Typically, during the course of a project, actual decision-making shifts from one to other activities, which are actually executed, one at a time, while the other activities are evaluated simultaneously but more lightly. . . . The principle of Holographic Decision-making . . . is an iterative process in which all activities are evaluated simultaneously, time and time again, but with different degrees of depth.

Holographic decision-making is consistent with the CST idea that planning is primarily used for priority setting in the present, and parallels Choi's suggestions for entrepreneurial decision-making under uncertainty.

A proper consideration of time is vital in entre-/intrapreneurial research. We second Howard Stevensen and Susan Harmeling that a prerequisite in entrepreneurial research will be a longitudinal approach: 'By understanding time and sequence, we can better understand the shape of the future, shape the way in which events unfold, and influence the analysis of value at all levels' (Stevensen and Harmeling, 1990, 7). CST may successfully add value to entre-/intrapreneurial creativity, entre-/intrapreneurial culture and the entre-/intrapeneurial use of the time factor.

Our final comment is about Paula Kyrö's three forms of entrepreneurship (Kyrö, 2000, 43): '1) Entrepreneurship, referring to the individual entrepreneur and his firm; 2) Intrapreneurship, referring to an organization's collective behaviour; and 3) Individual, self-oriented entrepreneurship, referring to an individual's self-oriented behaviour.' Based on the notions of both a holon and a fractal we think that CST as a framework might be of use for each of these three forms of entrepreneurship. But more research will be needed to explore the particularities of each respective form of entrepreneurship.

REFERENCES

Ashford, B.E. and R.H. Humphrey (1995), 'Emotion in the workplace: a re-appraisal', *Human Relations*, **48**(2), 97–125.

Backström, Tomas, Frans van Eijnatten and Mari Kira (2002), 'A complexity perspective on sustainable work systems', in Peter Docherty, Jan Forslin and Rami Shani (eds), *Creating Sustainable Work Systems: Emerging Perspectives and Practice*, London: Routledge, pp. 65–75.

Bohm, David (1987), *Unfolding Meaning: A Weekend of Dialogue with David Bohm*, London: Ark Paperbacks.

Bygrave, W.D. and C.W. Hofer (1991), 'Theorizing about entrepreneurship', *Entrepreneurship Theory and Practice*, **16**(1), 13–22.

Çambel, Ali B. (1993), *Applied Chaos Theory: A Paradigm for Complexity*, Boston: Academic Press/Harcourt Brace Jovanovich.

Chaordic Commons, The (2003), World Wide Web: http://www.chaordic.com/learn/res_def.html.

Choi, Young Back (1993), *Paradigms and Conventions: Uncertainty, Decision-Making and Entrepreneurship*, Ann Arbor, MI: The University of Michigan Press.

Cilliers, Paul (1999), *Complexity and Postmodernism: Understanding Complex Systems*, London: Routledge.

Cilliers, Paul (2000), 'What can we learn from a theory of complexity?', *Emergence*, **2**(1), 23–33.

Crossan, M.M., H.W. Lane, L. Klus and R.E. White (1996), 'The improvising organization: where planning meets opportunity', *Organizational Dynamics*, **24**(4) Spring, 20–34.

Dilts, Robert (1998), *NLP and Self-Organization Theory*, Santa Cruz, CA: World Wide Web: http://www.nlpu.com/Articles/artic23.htm.

Dimitratos, P. and E. Plakoyiannaki (2003), 'Theoretical foundations of an international entrepreneurial culture', *Journal of International Entrepreneurship*, **1**(2), 187–215.

Drucker, Peter F. (1954), *The Practice of Management*, New York: Harper.

Eijnatten, Frans M. van (2000), *From Intensive to Sustainable Work Systems: The Quest for a New Paradigm of Work*, Keynote speech at the TUTB/SALTSA conference 'Working Without Limits: Re-Organizing Work and Reconsidering Workers' Health', Brussels: 25 September, World Wide Web: http://www.etuc.org/tutb/uk/conference200062.html.

Eijnatten, F.M. van (2001), 'Chaordic systems for holonic organizational renewal', in William A. Pasmore and Richard W. Woodman (eds), *Research in Organizational Change and Development*, Vol. 13, San Francisco, CA: JAI Press/ Elsevier, pp. 213–51, World Wide Web: http://www.elsevier.nl/inca/publications/store/6/2/2/4/3/4/index.htt.

Eijnatten, Frans M. van and Laurie A. Fitzgerald (1998), *Designing the Chaordic Enterprise: 21st Century Organizational Architectures That Drive Systemic Self-Transcendence*, paper presented at the 14th EGOS Colloquium, Maastricht, Netherlands, 9–11 July.

Eijnatten, F.M. van and M.C. van Galen (2002a). 'The dolphin attractor: dialogue for emergent new order in a Dutch manufacturing firm', *International Scientific Journal of Methods for and Models of Complexity*, 5(1) June, Special Issue on Chaos Theory, Cor J. van Dijkum and Dorien J. DeTombe, (guest eds), World Wide Web: http://www.fss.uu.nl/ms/cvd/isj/.

Eijnatten, F.M. van and M.C. van Galen (2002b), 'Chaos, dialogue and the dolphin's strategy', *Journal of Organizational Change Management*, 15(4), 391–401, special issue: 'Chaos, applications in organizational change', Laurie A. Fitzgerald and Frans M. van Eijnatten (guest eds), World Wide Web: http://www.emeraldinsight.com/vl=1/cl=2 /nw=1/rpsv/cw/www/mcb/09534814/v15n4/contp1-1.htm.

Eijnatten, Frans M. van and Lieke E.C. Hoogerwerf (2000), 'Searching for new grounds: beyond open systems thinking', in Elayne Coakes, Raymond Lloyd-Jones and Dianne Willis (eds), *The New Sociotech: Graffiti on the Long Wall*, London: Springer-Verlag, Series Computer Supported Co-operative Work (CSCW), pp. 39–50.

Eijnatten, F.M. van and J.A. Keizer (2002), 'An inductive model for holographic decision making in industrial workspace design', *International Journal of Management and Decision Making*, 3(3/ 4), 211–28.

Eijnatten, Frans M. van and Jan-Peter Vos (2002), *Tautologies of Work Life Balance*, paper presented at the Annual Meeting of the SUSTAIN Network, Madrid, Escuela Tecnica Superior de Ingenieros Industriales, Universidad Politécnica de Madrid, Spain, 13 September, World Wide Web: http://www.chaosforum.com/nieuws/ index_eng.html.

Eijnatten, F.M. van M.C. van Galen and L.A. Fitzgerald (2003), 'Learning dialogically: the art of chaos-informed transformation', *The Learning Organization*, 10(6), 361–7, Special Issue 'The implications of complexity and chaos theories for organizations that learn', Peter Smit (guest ed.).

Ellinor, Linda and Glenna Gerard (1998), *Creating and Sustaining Collaborative Partnerships at Work: Dialogue, Rediscover the Transforming Power of Conversation*, New York: John Wiley.

Fitzgerald, Laurie A. (1996a), *Organizations and Other Things Fractal. A Primer on Chaos for Agents of Change*, Denver, CO: The Consultancy.

Fitzgerald, Laurie A. (1996b), *Chaordic System Properties, Classical Assumptions and the Chaos Principle*, Denver, CO: The Consultancy.

Fitzgerald, Laurie A. (1997a), '*What is Chaos?*', World Wide Web: http://www.orgmind.com/chaos/whatis.html.

Fitzgerald, Laurie A. (1997b), 'What in the world is the matter with systems thinking? a critique of modern systems theory and the practice of systems thinking it informs', in Tom Chase (ed.), *Readings of the STS Roundtable, Seattle, Washington, Oct. 21–24*, Northwood, NH: STS Roundtable, pp. 41–8.

Fitzgerald, Laurie A. (1999), *Chaordic System Properties Chart*, Denver, CO: The Consultancy, World Wide Web: http://www.orgmind.com/chaos/propchart.html.

Fitzgerald, L.A. (2002), 'Chaos, the lens that transcends', *Journal of Organizational Change Management*, 15(4), 339–58.

Fitzgerald, L.A. and F.M. van Eijnatten (1998), 'Letting go for control: the art of managing in the chaordic enterprise', *International Journal of Business Transformation*, 1(4), 261–70.

Fitzgerald, L.A. and F.M. van Eijnatten (2002), 'Reflections: chaos in organizational change', *Journal of Organizational Change Management*, 15(4), 402–11.

Fitzgerald, L.A. and F.M. van Eijnatten (guest eds) (2002), 'Chaos: applications in organizational change', *Journal of Organizational Change Management*, **15**(4), 339–423.
Freebourne, Wendy (2003), 'Pathfinder Workbook', World Wide Web: http://www.relationshipscentral.com/.
Gerard, Glenna and Linda Ellinor (1999), 'Dialogue: something old, something new; dialogue contrasted with discussion', World Wide Web: http://www.thedialogue-grouponline.com/whatsdialogue.html.
Gharajedaghi, Jamshid (1999), *Systems Thinking: Managing Chaos and Complexity. A Platform for Designing Business Architecture*, Boston: Butterworth-Heinemann.
Gleick, James (1987), *Chaos: The Making of a New Science*, New York: Wiley/ London: Heinemann.
Goldberg, J. and L. Markóczy (2000), 'Complex rhetoric and simple games', *Emergence*, **2**(1), 72–100.
Hannan, M.T. and J. Freeman (1977), 'The population ecology of organizations', *American Journal of Sociology*, **85**(5), 929–64.
Hannon, Paul D. and Andrew M. Atherton (1997a), 'Small firm success and the art of orienteering: the value of plans, planning, and strategic awareness in the competitive small firm', in Eric Lefebvre and Robert Cooper (eds), *Proceedings Hasselt Conference on Uncertainty, Knowledge and Skill*, Diepenbeek: Limburg University/ Keele University, 7–8 November, no pagination available.
Hannon, Paul D. and Andrew M. Atherton (1997b), 'The practice of building strategic awareness capability in entrepreneurial small firms', in Eric Lefebvre and Robert Cooper (eds), *Proceedings Hasselt Conference on Uncertainty, Knowledge and Skill*, Diepenbeek, Belgium: Limburg University/ Keele University, 7–8 November, no pagination available.
Hock, Dee W. (1996a), 'The chaordic organization: out of control and into order, 21st Century Learning Initiative, World Wide Web: http://www.cyberspace.com/~building/ofc_21clidhock.html.
Hock, Dee W. (1996b), 'The birth of the chaordic century: out of control and into order (extension as chaordic organization), paper presented to the Extension National Leadership conference, Washington, DC, 11 March.
Hock, Dee W. (1999), *Birth of the Chaordic Age*, San Francisco, CA: Berrett-Koehler.
Holmes, Lauren L. (2001), *Peak Evolution: Beyond Peak Performance and Peak Experience*, Toronto, Ontario, Canada: Naturality.Net LLC, Distributor: Bridgewater, NJ: Baker and Taylor.
Hurmerinta-Peltomäki, L. (2003), 'Time and internalisation: theoretical challenges set by rapid internationalisation', *Journal of International Entrepreneurship*, **1**(2), 217–36.
Jones, M.V. and P. Dimitratos (2003), 'Editorial introduction: creativity, process, and time: the antithesis of "instant international"', *Journal of International Entrepreneurship*, **1**(2), 159–62.
Juarrero, Alicia (1999), *Dynamics in Action: Intentional Behaviour as a Complex System*, Cambridge, Massachusetts: The MIT Press.
Kauffman, Stuart A. (1995), *At Home in the Universe: The Search for the Laws of Self-Organization and Complexity*, New York: Oxford University Press.
Keizer, Jimme A. and Frans M. van Eijnatten (2003), 'Holographic decision-making: A holistic way to enhance organizational participation', paper presented at the 19th EGOS Colloquium, 'Organization analysis informing social and global development, Copenhagen, Denmark, 3–5 July, Subtheme 26: 'New roads in organizational participation'.

Kira, Mari (2003), *From Good Work to Sustainable Development: Human Resources Consumption and Regeneration in the Post-Bureaucratic Working Life*, Stockholm: Royal Institute of Technology, Ph.D. thesis.

Koestler, Arthur (1967), *The Ghost in the Machine*, London: Hutchinson.

Koestler, Arthur (1978), *Janus: A Summing Up*, London: Hutchinson.

Kyrö, P. (2000), 'Entrepreneurship in the postmodern society', *Wirtschafts Politische Blätter*, **47**, 37–45, Vienna: Wirtschaftskammer Österreich.

Kyrö, Paula and Kansikas Juha (2002), 'Current state of methodology in entrepreneurial research and some expectations for the future', paper presented at the European Summer University, Valence, France.

Lissack, Michael and Johan Roos (1999), *The Next Common Sense: Mastering Corporate Complexity Through Coherence*, London: Nicholas Brealey.

Lissack, Michael, Max Boisot, Bill McKelvey, Jan Rivkin, Kevin Dooley and Michael Cohen (2000), 'Past/future, research/practice, science/metaphor: does research add value to management practice? The complexity perspective', Panel Presentation, Academy of Management, 2000, Toronto, 8 August.

Lorenz, E.N. (1963a), 'Deterministic non-periodic flow', *Journal of the Atmospheric Sciences*, **20**(2), 130–41.

Lorenz, E.N. (1963b), 'The mechanics of vacillation', *Journal of the Atmospheric Sciences*, **20**(2), 448–64.

Marchall, Ian and Danah Zohar (1997), *Who's Afraid of Schrödinger's Cat? The New Science Revealed: Quantum Theory, Relativity, Chaos and the New Cosmology*, London: Bloomsbury.

Marcic, Dorothy (1997), *Managing with the Wisdom of Love: Uncovering Virtue in People and Organizations*, San Francisco, CA: Jossey-Bass.

Markides, C. (1998), 'Strategic innovation in established companies', *Sloan Management Review*, **39**(3), Spring, 31–42.

Nesheim, John L. (2000), *High Tech Start Up: The Complete Handbook for Creating Successful New High Tech Companies*, Riverside, New Jersey: Simon and Schuster.

Peters, Jaap and Rob Wetzels (1998), *Niets Nieuws Onder de Zon en Andere Toevalligheden. Strategie uit chaos (Nothing New Under the Sun and Other Coincidences: Strategy out of Chaos)*, Amsterdam: Business Contact, in Dutch, fully reworked 5th edn 2003.

Polley, D. (1997), 'Turbulence in organizations: new metaphors for organizational research', *Organization Science*, **8**(5), 445–57.

Preston, J.T. (2003), 'Building success into a high-tech start-up', *The Industrial Physicist*, June/ July, pp. 16–18.

Priesmeyer, H. Richard (1992), *Organizations and Chaos: Defining the Methods of Non-Linear Management*, Westport, Connecticut: Quorum.

Prigogine, Ilya and Isabelle Stengers (1984), *Order out of Chaos: Man's new Dialogue with Nature*, New York: Bantam.

Stacey, Ralph D. (1995), 'The science of complexity: an alternative perspective for strategic change processes', *Strategic Management Journal*, **16**, 477–95.

Stacey, Ralph D. (2001), *Complex Responsive Processes in Organizations: Learning and Knowledge Creation*, London: Routledge.

Stacey, Ralph, Douglas Griffin and Patricia Shaw (2000), *Complexity and Management: Fad or Radical Challenge to Systems Thinking?*, London: Routledge.

Stevensen, H. and S. Harmeling (1990), 'Entrepreneurial management's need for a more "chaotic" theory', *Journal of Business Venturing*, **5**, 1–14.

Tsoukas, Haridimos (1997), 'Reading organizations: uncertainty, complexity, narrativity', in Eric Lefebvre and Robert Cooper (eds), *Proceedings Hasselt Conference on Uncertainty, Knowledge and Skill*, Diepenbeek, Belgium: Limburg University/ Keele University, 7–8 November, no pagination available.

Vos, Jan-Peter (2002), *The Making of Strategic Realities: An Application of the Social Systems Theory of Niklas Luhmann*, Eindhoven University of Technology, The Netherlands: Center for Innovation Studies, Ph.D. thesis.

Wilber, Ken (1995), *Sex, Ecology, Spirituality: The Spirit of Evolution*, Boston: Shambhala.

Wilber, Ken (1996a), *A Brief History of Everything*, Dublin: Newleaf.

Wilber, Ken (1996b), *Eye to Eye: The Quest for a New Paradigm*, Boston, MA: Shambala.

Wilber, Ken (1998), *The Marriage of Sense and Soul: Integrating Science and Religion*, New York: Broadway.

Yiu, Lichia and John Briggs (2000), Conference on 'Chaos Theory and the Arts in the Context of Social, Economic and Organizational Development', Geneva: Centre for Socio-Eco-Nomic Development, 7/doc/chaos-Summary2A.doc.

PART III

Enterpreneurship, Innovation and Culture as a
Set of Interrelated Fields: Why the European
Context is of Importance

10. The entrepreneurial and innovative orientation of French, German and Dutch engineers: the proposal of a European context based upon some empirical evidence from two studies[1]

Alain Fayolle, Jan Ulijn and Jean-Michel Degeorge

INTRODUCTION

Economic history has shown us the innovating and entrepreneurial tendencies of many engineers in France, The Netherlands, Germany and also in other countries. Gustave Eiffel, André Citroën, Francis Bouygues, and Conrad Schlumberger are some of the most famous French entrepreneur engineers; Gerard Philips, Hubert van Doorne (founder of DAF Trucks), Cornelis Lely (hydraulic works) and Anthony Fokker (see Heerkens and Ulijn, 2000) are Dutch examples; Werner von Siemens, Gottlieb Daimler and Rudolf Diesel are German ones. In other countries, James Watt, Richard Trevithick, Robert Fulton and John Fleming fall into the same category.

The international literature on these subjects, surprisingly enough, has little on the entrepreneurial behaviour of engineers, much more on their propensity to innovate. The interest of an international study focusing on the entrepreneurial and innovating behaviours of engineers seems to us obvious. Entrepreneurial engineers seem to be innovators and creators of economic wealth: they contribute heavily to the renewal of social and industrial structure. A yearly study carried out by 'l'Usine Nouvelle' in France on the 'Champions of Innovation' gives us an overview of innovating young start-up companies. The results show that, very often, engineers are at the origin of the innovating companies selected for the study.

It seems that, worldwide, the engineer is a key element in technological innovation. The economic future of an industrialised country lies essentially in its ability to innovate in the technological field.

Entrepreneurial and innovating behaviours depend on cultural factors, and looking at this phenomenon certain authors have pointed out the importance of cultural differences between countries (see for example McGrath and MacMillan, 1992). So, our approach will take into account national characteristics of engineers and entrepreneurial engineers (or innovators).

The first part of our chapter will concern the notion of cultures of the engineer. National culture certainly plays an important role, but we cannot neglect other levels of culture, such as corporate culture and, in particular, professional culture.

We will focus, in the second part, on the specificities of French engineers and we will talk about the entrepreneurial behaviour of French engineers through the results of a field study made in France in the 1990.

The third part of the chapter will develop a European perspective built around the behaviour of French, Dutch and German engineers and using the results of a case comparison of 12 innovative German and Dutch firms.

CULTURES OF THE ENGINEER

One aim of this chapter is to examine whether the engineer in France (F), The Netherlands (NL) and Germany (G) shifted from the traditional technological orientation towards a more market oriented view, and whether this change would occur differently in the three countries compared. For NL and G, we analysed possible intercultural differences, researching the transition in both countries by interviewing chief engineers and personnel managers who hire them. For F, we have to be speculative, since empirical evidence has still to be gathered. As Ulijn and Weggeman (2001) point out, people are affected by four different cultures: the national culture (NC), the branch culture (BC), the professional culture (PC) and the company or corporate culture (CC). Since this work deals with engineers and their companies, we exclude branch culture from this study.

National Culture (NC)

The most obvious differences in human behaviour and mutual conception can be found in national cultures. In the modern, globally oriented business world the confrontation with foreign cultures is constitutional, and the reports on the importance of culture awareness in communication are numerous. National cultures can be investigated under many different aspects but they are frequently determined by the five dimensions used by Hofstede (1980a; 1980b; 1989; 1991; 2001). The first four (Power Distance, Individualism, Masculinity and Uncertainty Avoidance) are widely known. The fifth, being the Confucian Dynamism Index (CDI), outlines, for example, if the engineers are willing to accept only one truth or many, if they are traditional, with a short-term orientation or pragmatic, with a long-term orientation and if they accept changes easily or prefer stability (low CDI vs. high CDI). The human behaviour in companies is obviously influenced by the national culture of the countries they are based in. Those variables also have an effect on, for example, the innovation strategies of companies. German companies, for instance, are influenced by bureaucracy and seem to be rather convention-ally slow. Criteria such as flexibility and mobility are becoming more and more important compared to professional experience. But what about the global players? They have strong reasons to have a unified culture, so they must create a culture of their own which is the same everywhere around the world.

Corporate Culture (CC)

As Ulijn and Weggeman (2001) define it,

> corporate culture is the fundamental totality of all common value and norm concep-tions and shared models of thinking and behaving which influence decisions and behaviour of the employees in the company. The group considers these values and norms to be proven to be helpful and successful, so they are presented as the proper way to think and to do things to new members.

Corporate culture is the way the employee in the company thinks, talks and works. One should keep in mind that the company culture is very impor-tant for the realization of strategic goals. While the strategy determines what should be done to achieve certain goals, the corporate culture influences intensively how the strategy will be implemented into detailed plans and finally realized. Corporate culture and strategy are interdependent. A strong culture in line with the strategy can have a very strong positive effect on the company's success, but when it is time for a necessary value change, culture might impede flexibility. The influence of culture, however, should not be imposed on the employees by, for instance, asking them to sing the firm's hymn every morning. On the other hand flexibility could be made an essen-tial part of the company's culture. Consequently businesses should use corpo-rate culture. It shows a certain message to the outside world and it has positive effects on the corporate identity of the employees. After all, commu-nication is led by emotions. One could say that culture is the social putty that holds the company together. And secondly it can be said that culture can give a strong competitive advantage to a company, because competitors cannot copy it so easily.

Professional Culture (PC)

Wever (1990) notices that many employees do not feel loyal to the company any more but to their profession, their own outline of their profession and their professional code of ethics. Those different types of professional cultures could be examined for the same variables that Hofstede (1980a; 1980b; 1989; 1991 and 2001) used for countries. For example Wiebecke (1987) and Ulich (1990) carried out research in the 1980s on the differences of environment-orientations and time-perspectives (aspects of Hofstede's Confucian dynamism) of researchers on one hand and marketers on the other hand. According to this research, R&D (Research and Development) and Marketing have different views about the relationship of the whole organization to the environment. R&D considers the technological and scientific relationship to the environment to be crucial: the scientific and technical quality of the products justifies the existence of the whole firm, and the provision of technically useful products to the environment as the fundamental task of the organization. Marketing, however, regards the firm's role in the economic environment as most important: by supplying products that suit the market demand the financial input is obtained, and the organization survives through its commercial activities. Marketing also has a shorter time perspective than R&D; it is today-oriented and focuses on the rapidly changing markets. R&D, on the other hand, have a long-term perspective and has to carry out long-term projections into the future. These research results do not lead to a concrete CDI value, because each profession might have both a short and a long-term perspective. PC can probably not be researched with the same parameters as NC or CC. In our chapter, the professional culture of the German and Dutch engineer will be described using studies by Ogilvie (1992), Trompenaars and Hampden-Turner (1999 and 2000), and Kympers (1992) which depart from non-NC or CC parameters. The second part of this chapter deals only with the specificities of Dutch and German engineers, since the study of the French engineers focuses rather on their entrepreneurial behaviour and less on their Technological or Market orientation (TO vs. MO). The first study summarised below has to be replicated for the Dutch and the German engineer, the second for the French one.

THE FRENCH ENGINEER: SPECIFICITIES AND ENTREPRENEURIAL BEHAVIOUR

Firstly we will talk about the cultural specificities of the French engineers. Secondly, through the results of research, we will address some questions and issues related to their entrepreneurial behaviour.

The Specificities of the French Engineer

To understand French engineers and their behaviour we have to take into consideration three kinds of elements. The first is the historical evolution of the engineer's social status in France. The second is the nature and the functioning of the French engineer's educational system. Finally the third element is the particular relationship between the professional career of French engineers and their educational system.

The historical evolution of the French engineer's social status

As a French sociologist (Lasserre, 1989) highlights, the notion of engineer in France is ambiguous and unclear. It designates a diploma, a function, and a professional status. These three aspects do not coincide. Not every graduate of an engineering school carries out the functions of an engineer. The common denominator of the engineer is the training, which is principally scientific and technological. The social status of the engineer has evolved strongly through time, and this evolution has led to a transformation of the place and the role of the engineer within companies and within the social and economic system.

During the second half of the eighteenth century and the first half of the nineteenth one, engineers were civil servants, working for the state. According to Shinn (1978), around 1850 a new type of civil engineer came into being whose function was to apply theoretical and empirical knowledge to the concrete problems of industrial production. The industrial revolution, and other factors such as the intellectual climate, which affirmed the prevalence of industry amidst human activity as a whole, favoured the rise of civil engineers as a professional group.

At the beginning of the twentieth century, engineers were at the forefront of industrial leadership. They fulfilled an essential role particularly linked to their ability to innovate techniques and organise work scientifically, to improve industrial output, and to reduce costs. These organisational qualities allowed engineers to envisage a historical alliance with business people, which could transform them into social agents of production and, from there, to partners of heads of companies. The social power of engineers remained strong until the crisis in the 1930s when engineers realised that they were merely executives and they became conscious that they belonged to the middle class.

In the 1960s, the traditional concept of the engineer as one who combined and associated the technical and executive roles evolved and these roles became dissociated. More and more, engineers were defined by their technical–scientific function. Emphasis was placed on the purely intellectual aspect of their profession: the engineer was someone who applied scientific knowledge to production. His or her managerial function disappeared. This change was seen in the curriculum of the French 'Grandes Ecoles', where the necessity for scientific and theoretical studies became more evident and opened the way to the creation of more theoretical courses, and allowed the addition of research projects.

During the same period, new links between science and industry were established, revealed in a dependence of technological and industrial progress on the development of basic technological knowledge. Thus we saw the arrival of applied science, or research and development, which acquired the status of a productive factor in economic activity. This gave innovation great importance as a factor in the maintenance of steady growth in the productivity of work. An even greater division of these factors contributed to the reduction of the engineers' autonomy and to the delimitation of their work.

The collective result of this evolution was to bring about erosion in the traditional allegiance of executives, as highlighted by the French sociologist Crozier (1975). Considerable uneasiness within the executive population set in. This can explain on the one hand the appearance of the first great social conflicts in which many engineers and managers actively participated, and on the other hand, in certain sectors, the adherence of managers to workers' unions. The traditional attitude towards managers as the sole reference of authority, along with faithfulness and loyalty to them, was eroded and replaced progressively by a very different attitude: that of 'professionalism'. 'Professionalism' is an attitude that constitutes the possession of authority and the judgement of one's peers. Thus, the authority of a manager is only accepted if it is based upon manifest competence and not merely on the principles of hierarchy.

Finally, for Lasserre (1989), there are two main models of professional identity for engineers. One of them is based upon the ability to manage people, the other upon technical expertise.

The cultural dimension of the French engineer educational system
The family of French engineers is not homogeneous. There are those engineers who come from the classical model of French 'Grandes Ecoles', and others who are more oriented towards technical aspects, application and production. The latter are trained in different systems: schools, universities and other institutes. One of the most remarkable elements of the training of French engineers is the extraordinary diversity of paths of access to the title of engineer and the many possibilities for specialisation, which contribute to the reinforcement of the engineers' world heterogeneity. In this abundance of situations, the title of qualified engineer is protected by the 'Commission des Titres d'Ingénieur' and so it constitutes a discriminatory element. The fact that the engineers, and therefore the engineering profession, are not regulated in France, gives the title of engineer an extreme importance.

Coming back to the French 'Grandes Ecoles', their appearance in the French higher education system goes back to the sixteenth and seventeenth centuries, coinciding with a great and lasting decline of universities. In the eighteenth century, the 'Grandes Ecoles' saw a truly significant expansion. The 'Ecole des Ponts et Chaussées' was created in 1715, the 'Ecole de l'Artillerie' in 1720, the 'Ecole des Mines' in 1783. From then on engineering 'Grandes Ecoles' multiplied and the system was consolidated. The apotheosis of engineering 'Grandes Ecoles', the 'Ecole Polytechnique', came into being in 1794. Before 1816 there were six schools. After a pause during the first half of the nineteenth century, this figure rose to 56 in 1914, then to 82 in 1945, 151 in 1978 and now more than 200.

Even if 'Grandes Ecoles' have characteristics in common: strong selectivity, a small number of students, close links with professional circles, high quality of training programmes and professors, it is nevertheless clear that some are more important than others. The system is very hierarchical and is based on the reputation of the schools. A peculiarity of the French system is that engineering 'Grandes Ecoles' fulfil a social function. Thus, for the most important schools, the academic title carries a double function of social reproduction. On the one hand, it legitimises the transmission of economic capital among families from the 'owner' section of the ruling class. On the other hand, it constitutes a substitute for economic capital absent in other sections of the ruling class. The 'Grandes Ecoles' undeniably allow the ruling class to reproduce itself, firstly by allowing the transmission of privileges, and, secondly, by organising a whole series of barriers into the social group. The dominating class, the 'Noblesse d'Etat', as the French sociologist Bourdieu (1989) refers to it, legitimises its reproduction through an academic meritocracy. And, to further ensure the reproduction of its privileges, the ruling class has conferred upon 'Grandes Ecoles' a very efficient function: the creation and development for its graduates, of a social capital in the form of networks of relations and protection. The aim is to give more value to the academic capital that each student possesses by creating and developing a group spirit, and a feeling of belonging to a social elite.

The links between the professional career and the educational system
The training for engineers, based on mathematics and physical sciences, is conceived as if the technical and managerial branches were fundamentally different. The overriding importance given to logico-deductive sciences compared with experimental sciences and the technical emphasis of the training give the qualified engineer a strong technical culture. This creates specific behaviour patterns and ways of thinking which make it difficult for engineers to take into account what is not measurable.

So, many authorities underline the need to train engineers in economics and management as quickly as possible in order to prepare them to carry out the executive functions that they will face sooner or later, and to acquire a certain professionalism in their area of activity. Management training and the openings that it offers, allow engineers to move out of their profession and head towards other careers. Management training could be seen, from this viewpoint, as a 'career accelerator' for engineers.

Thus the role of the company and of continuing education is essential. It can make up for the effects of the initial training and allow the engineer to move into new fields. In this way engineers can change the direction of their professional path, influenced initially by the school they attended and the specialisation it proposed, and later by their accumulated experiences and complementary training, particularly in management and social sciences. From this point, access to top managerial functions is possible for an engineer along three prevailing paths:

- The first is linked with the school, the 'Grande Ecole' status being connected with its prestige, its reputation, and its interconnections with the ruling class.
- The second is linked with complementary training in management acquired either on leaving the engineering school or after several years of professional experience in a prestigious management-training establishment.
- Finally, there is the entrepreneurship position, which allows the engineer to leave his or her employee status by creating, or taking over a company.

The French educational system plays an important role in strongly influencing the engineers in their career and specially in discouraging them from obtaining an entrepreneurial position. In effect, this very hierarchical and stratified system (Maurice et al., 1982; Silvestre, 1990) guarantees superior positions to the graduates of the best engineering 'Grandes Ecoles': exclusive and high-status functions in large companies and administrations. This particular way of functioning does not encourage graduates of these schools to follow an entrepreneurial path which is, by definition, less prestigious and presents more risks. For the French engineer, entrepreneurial tendencies occur in inverse proportion to the rank of the school attended. This is even more marked in that the entrepreneur is a nomadic figure who is not easy to classify within the French social hierarchy. The immediate social profits of the diploma are worth more than the real aptitudes that it sanctions. A higher diploma can satisfy the search for a social identity whereas the lack of a diploma or a lower diploma leads to a search for this identity.

Some Aspects of the Entrepreneurial Behaviour of the French Engineers

To develop this section we use some results of research that was carried out in France in 1993.[2] Our objective here is to give a first characterisation of the French entrepreneur engineer. We will first describe our methodological approach and then we will develop our results. Finally, we will discuss two main models of entrepreneur engineers.

The methodological approach
Our methodological approach is based on a qualitative field study using semi-structured interviews lasting, on average, three hours (see Appendix A for the questionnaire used). The sample was made up of 20 engineers who have either set up or are setting up their own companies. It was constituted in such a way as to cover the different modes of engineering training in France, to give a sufficiently wide sample in terms of age of entrepreneuring, and to present a large diversity of sectors of activity. An interview guide was prepared and used. It was constructed around the following themes:

- personal and family background
- initial and complementary training
- social origin
- career path
- personal and professional processes
- characteristics of the company created

The guide was used in semi-directive interviews which served as a basis for a thematic content analysis.

Some results
We will see here the role of three kinds of factors: school of origin, initial training and specialisation, previous experience, and the nature of the repre-sentations of the entrepreneur engineers.

The role of the school of origin   The school plays an important role at two levels: the status of the school and the structure of the studies. Both these factors divided schools into those more or less favourable to entrepreneurial attitudes and behaviour. The status of the school was often mentioned during our interviews. The entrepreneur engineers who were interviewed all empha-sised the opportunities represented by entrepreneurship, as a privileged path leading to the position of managing director. Here, there seems to be a clear opposition between engineering 'Grandes Ecoles', which prepare future managers of public and private companies, and other engineering schools. In fact, engineering 'Grandes Ecoles' train a ready-made group, which permanently supply the system. For engineers who are unable to follow this model, access to a top managerial function is considerably reduced. In this case entrepreneurial behaviour, even if it includes difficulties and risks which cannot be neglected, remains a preferred, if not unique means to the managerial goal.

Some entrepreneur engineers (ten out of 20) highlighted the importance of the structure of their studies. The structure of the curriculum in certain schools may predispose students to future entrepreneurial behaviour by encouraging them very early to develop behaviour close to that which will later allow them to set up or take over a company. Thus all courses of action that allow the student engineers to interact with their training and to set up their own programme by choosing options, electives, and other similar possibilities, were seen by the engineers as an element contributing to the development of entrepreneurial behaviour. Naturally, such courses of action should allow the student to make a personal investment, make choices adapted to his or her project and his or her own situation, and above all to be capable of execution. For the last point, the role of the institution is of utmost importance.

The role of training and specialisation   Ten of the 20 engineers interviewed had acquired high levels of specialisation in various fields. Eight of these ten engineers had created or taken over a company strongly related to their original specialisation. The question of specialisation is not very easy to deal with. Engineering schools offer specialities and majors, but students also have the opportunity to specialise, independently of these majors, by taking options and other electives. To understand this situation, it is thus necessary to look beyond what is indicated on the diploma. A few examples describing the career paths of entrepreneur engineers will illustrate the importance of this factor.

The first concerns an engineer from a school generally considered to be generalist. This person specialised in electronics and then obtained a doctorate in his speciality. After working for fifteen years in this field he created a company for which the accumulated expertise in his specialisation proved crucial.

The second example concerns a computer engineer who set up a service company in seven years after leaving school, a service company in the field of computer engineering.

A generalist training can open up greater opportunities and can lead to executive and managerial functions. A specialist training can endow the engineer with technical expertise, which can be extremely useful in the creation or acquisition of a company. The attitudes towards the entrepreneurial opportunities and the nature of innovation are quite different in these cases.

The role of previous experience All the start-ups in our study show a link with the previous activity of the entrepreneur engineer. This finding corresponds with the conclusions of Vesper (1980), Hoad and Rosko (1964), and Ronstadt (1984). Certainly, the technical expertise of the engineer is partly acquired during specialised training. But, more important, it is nourished by knowledge developed throughout professional history. The accumulation of experience differentiates engineers from each other. Thus the creation of a company must necessarily be seen within the context of a professional trajectory.

Our interviews show that engineers do not move too far away from the activities and professions that they are familiar with. Moreover, their professional history has allowed them to build up a dense network of relations. The close links between pre- and post-creation activities will allow them to take advantage of this network, particularly during the launching phase of the new activity. The entrepreneur engineers we met very often highlighted the importance of this point. The influence of networks has also been noted in the entrepreneurial literature (see, for example, Birley, 1985).

To sum up, previous professional experience seems to bring to the engineers technical knowledge, skills, relation networks, and the necessary access to their environment which can allow them to spot the best opportunities for creating or taking over a company. So, it can strongly influence their initial behaviour and attitudes as an entrepreneur.

Some representations of the entrepreneur engineer The majority of engineers interviewed wished to create 'human-sized' companies. This is probably meant as opposition to the large companies with very structured organisations they worked previously for. This point was frequently reiterated. The entrepreneur engineers of our sample seemed attached to human management, and anxious to build their employer–employee relationship on a different basis from the one they experienced. The majority of engineers interviewed spoke of the 'social dimension' or the 'social project', of 'human participation', even 'company citizen', without, however, elaborating these notions.

The engineers in our sample claimed to have a sense of rigour, of method, of professional work, and they try to spread these values throughout the companies they have created or taken over. What comes out of our interviews is that the engineers use levers such as innovation or creativity. The project which they perform constitutes a powerful engine to reach their goals. It is of such great importance that they will not hesitate to question their own ability if this can contribute to the project's continuation, to comfort themselves or to put themselves back on the right track. What guides them is the will to concretise. For this they are ready to 'give up some of the capital' or 'all of it' or even 'to take very important decisions'. The engineer can also 'separate from his best friend', who is carelessly promoted to the position of wage-earning partner.

The functions carried out by the entrepreneur engineers in our sample are linked to the application of technical skills: design, research and development, production. Very quickly, at the same time, the engineer takes on functions linked to management, which become more and more important as the company develops. In our sample we have noticed a cultural opposition to the commercial function which is usually delegated and which he carries out only when he has to. This he does with much reticence, prudence and clumsiness.

These types of behaviour and attitudes towards the commercial function create strong psychological impediments for entrepreneur engineers. Yet it also appears that the engineers interviewed meet no major difficulties in the setting up of accounting and financial functions. The last element, which we would like to highlight, is the tendency of engineers to work by building teams. This occurs when the sharing of essential common values and the search for complementary characteristics are unifying and fundamental elements.

To sum up, it seems to us that the entrepreneur engineers of our sample have a model of professional identity focusing on expertise and favourable toward collective action. The social legitimacy and power of this model are mainly based on the technical skills of the engineer.

Two models of entrepreneur engineers
Looking at studies that we carried out throughout this research on the French entrepreneur engineers, it appears to us that, at the beginning of their professional life, the scientific and technical training of engineers leads them to concentrate on technical aspects. During this stage, in fact, the approach is that of the apprentice who diversifies his or her knowledge and skills. Following on from this, engineers can, with more or less rapidity, look to concentrating on other aspects and develop other dimensions in accordance with professional changes and promotions.

Rapidly[3] or progressively engineers have the choice of:

- Moving towards activities and functions where the technical aspect becomes relatively less important as compared to other aspects (for example, management).
- Following their scientific path in order to acquire a real and strong technical expertise in their specific fields.

We find here two main models, which could characterise the engineer and the entrepreneur engineer.

The first model is this one of the engineer who leaves his or her technical context before setting up (or acquiring) a business. We call this kind of entrepreneur engineer, the 'manager' entrepreneur engineer.

In the second model, the engineer does not leave his or her technical context before setting up (or acquiring) a business. He/she remains strongly focused on the technical dimension of his/her job. We call this type of entrepreneur engineer, the 'technician' entrepreneur engineer.[4]

We will now develop each of these models and illustrate with examples.

The model of the 'manager' entrepreneur engineer   This path takes engineers, focused on the technical dimension at the beginning, to a growing involvement with wider functions, allowing them to acquire new non-technical skills. Pushed by diverse motivations and having identified a good business opportunity, they take the entrepreneurial path. The main functions for this type of entrepreneur engineer are as innovator and as resource co-ordinator. They innovate in service activities and have a propensity to take calculated risks. They create companies mainly in services activities and in consulting domains. The 'manager' entrepreneur engineer does not hesitate to create companies in areas that are not linked to his/her previous experience and to his/her initial specialisation.

In this model are included entrepreneurial engineers who, from the beginning of their career paths, have chosen non-technical professions.

The most telling example of this in our sample is offered by the history of a 38-year-old engineer who graduated in 1975. The main stages in the development of his career are given below. During the first period (year one) of his career, he finished the first part of his training with a period of applied research in a scientific and technical centre in the branch of a construction company. Then, he joined a national company working in water planning. There, he worked as public works engineer in charge of design and compilation of technical dossiers (plans, descriptions, and so on). In this company he was offered the opportunity of partially giving up his 'concentration on the technical aspect' by taking on a project concerning the creation of a technical data-processing department. For the first time, having just turned 30, this engineer was allotted a mission that concerned the general management of a project. With this experience as a basis, and with newly acquired skills, this engineer continued his career and joined a computer consultancy company where he stayed for five years as head of project. During this period, his own perception was that he managed to move out of the 'technical bubble', where only the technical dimension was taken into consideration, towards managerial functions, helped by the acquisition of new skills. This change was accompanied by short training periods intended to help him put his ideas into practice. Following this, he joined another computer service consultancy, which was larger than the first and where he was appointed head of department. He spent three successful years in this company but had some dissatisfaction, and spotting a unique opportunity, he decided to create his own company.

The 'technician' entrepreneur engineer   In this model the engineers, very often, go into business pushed by a technical project, which they can no longer develop within their present company, although they are still concentrated on the technical dimension. This type of entrepreneur engineers conceive their entrepreneurial role as technicians. At the beginning of this activity they have a tendency to see themselves as inventors. Following on from this they can either continue this behaviour, in which case they must delegate managerial functions to others, or they can progressively evolve towards combining several dimensions, both technical and non-technical. The 'technician' entrepreneur engineer innovates in technologies and also in products. They create industrial and/or technological companies in fields that are very close to their scientific and technical background and knowledge.

The most representative example in our sample is offered by an engineer, 44 years old, who graduated in 1970 and who was interested very early in technical matters. This was shown at a young age by an evident willingness in this direction within the engineering profession. Very quickly, this engineer specialised in electronics and successfully prepared a doctorate at the Ecole Centrale de Lyon where he successively climbed all the levels within the electronics laboratory between 1970 and 1980. While following his pedagogical and scientific activities in 1988, this engineer, pushed by 'the desire to carry out technical projects which I was unable to do at the CNRS[5]', created a company. The opportunity for creating depends on the discovery of a product which does not exist and which can be made concrete in an industrial context. This engineer has the skills and the knowledge to design and produce it. Furthermore, a quick analysis of the situation led him to think that any attempt to transfer this product towards industry would certainly lead to failure. During the first years of this young company, this engineer immersed himself firmly in the technical functions where the research and development and production aspects dominated. At present, because of external pressure, he seems to have accepted other tasks even though there has been no significant evolution towards a different status.

To sum up, the path which leads engineers to setting up a business is strongly influenced by their initial training, by the status of the school from which they graduated, by the professional experience which they have acquired, by the technical skills which they have developed, and by some personal factors. This path leads to two very contrasting entrepreneurial profiles. The first gives a significant place to the managerial dimension. The second does not recognise this aspect, or only slightly so, and emphasises the technical dimension.

The making of a French engineer is strongly influenced by the NC. The

French national culture highlights the social role of higher education and mainly of the 'Grandes Ecoles'. Around 200 'Grandes Ecoles' are dispensing education specifically geared to technical, administrative and business needs in the civil service, state and private industry. Engineering schools are especially preponderant both in number and in terms of historical influence. Their curriculum involves sciences and engineering of a fairly theoretical kind.

National culture orientates the French engineers, through the higher educational system, to professional positions, which appears to be not in line with entrepreneurial and innovative behaviour.

During the career development phase of the French engineers the PC seems to play a significant role because it contributes to the construction of a professional identity: technical identity or more management-orientated identity. The CC is less important in the French context.

In a perspective of comparison between engineer samples from different countries it could be very interesting to look at the respective influences of these layers of culture (NC and PC) on entrepreneurial and innovative behaviours. Is the French model of making and developing engineers unique or not? Does the technical dimension play the same role in other countries?

COMPARING ENTREPRENEURIAL AND INNOVATION CULTURES: THE EUROPEAN PERSPECTIVE OF GERMAN AND DUTCH ENGINEERS

In the second part of this chapter we were focusing on the entrepreneurial behaviour of French engineers in their national context. In this third part we will adopt a European perspective to evaluate the role of national culture on engineers behaviour towards entrepreneurship and innovation. At this level of our research programme the main objective is to identify some similarities and differences among behaviour and also to suggest some first hypotheses or research questions for further research.

We will firstly talk about the specificities of German and Dutch engineers. We will discuss the results of a study (see Ulijn et al., 2001, for more details) showing us the behavioural differences and similarities towards innovation between Dutch and German engineers. Finally we will develop a European perspective including French (as we have presented before), German and Dutch engineers.

The Specificities of German Engineers

When questioned about a change in the innovation strategy of their companies, 11 out of 12 interviewees report on a re-orientation towards more Market

Orientation (MO). This indicates a significant transition in engineering culture. A close survey of the individual argumentation reveals that the judgement is mainly based on organizational changes in the companies. These changes were initiated within the last eight years; three companies were re-organizing their structure at the time of our interviews. There is an obvious trend away from a divisional set-up with separate marketing, engineering and central research departments to a structure organized with respect to customer groups: a branch-oriented structure has replaced the product-oriented divisions. These branch departments have their own sales, design and marketing staff. Nevertheless, the marketing component is not dominant. The interviewed persons were mostly using a strict definition of marketing as an instrument of sales promotion – as opposed to a wider definition used in marketing science (Specht, 1996). One manager reports: 'Marketing is a problem. It does not exist in investment-goods industry, not so distinct as for consumer goods, so you cannot call it marketing'.

More intense transitions towards a stronger Market-Orientation component can be found in the large firms, especially in the automotive industry. One company initiated a simultaneous engineering process that implies an intense marketing component about six years ago. Another car manufacturer is just in the process of re-organizing towards a project team oriented development procedure. It started about one and a half years ago when six so-called 'projectivity-teams' began to work. These examples refer to companies that manufacture consumer products, but there are also examples in the investment product industry: a manufacturing company that has called itself a service company for more than 60 years has nevertheless restructured its set-up at the beginning of this year and formed the position of a so-called 'Solution-manager'. This engineer looks after their customers and his brief is to find out all their specific needs, no matter which products could fulfil them. It is then his job to find a solution for the customer in his company, either with a combination of existing products or the order for a new design. Another manager describes an analogous procedure in his firm, where no more undirected basic research is allowed. All research has to be ordered and paid for by some sales-unit. In all cases the interviewees neither justified the organizational changes by some proactive management conceptions nor did they report explicit wishes from R&D for such reorganization. Instead, they described the changes as a reaction to the deteriorating economic situation of their company. When asked about the reasons for the change towards more Market Orientation, one interviewee replies: 'I believe it is purely economical. The recession can be distinctly experienced. You have to orient yourself much more to the customer's wishes and produce concepts than can be put into action immediately.'

We have the impression that there is a significant transition towards Market

Orientation in the corporate culture, however, it is a transition forced by top management. It did not evolve as a natural process, initiated at a working level. The variety of problems that developed with the organizational change indicates an intense acceptance barrier at a personal level. People were afraid to lose their influence or even their job, but also problems with work overload and stress were reported. Teamwork and simultaneous engineering require an intense and steady communication demanding excellent discussion and negotiation skills and the ability to see things from a different perspective. The companies questioned used varying training programmes to inform their staff about the changed aspects of their corporate culture and to train the people to become more customer oriented. However, there were still remaining problems with engineers not being able to adapt. These people either had to be given a new job within the firm where not so much customer contact was necessary or had to retire. The interviewees backed up this observation of personal inflexibility when they were questioned about possible changes in professional culture. It became clear that the expectations towards engineers are changing; expectations proclaimed by management, consultants and education. Those who face these expectations, have difficulties when their rigid set of values and habits as engineers – their professional culture – is endangered. This is a very much generalized observation. A few opposing statements were also made, for example, by older engineers who had to painfully experience the failure of their Technology-Oriented (TO) strategy and are now requiring market input even more than young engineers were. But the majority believe that the personal orientation towards innovation strategy is part of 'individual human nature'. People might judge themselves to be MP (Market Pull) oriented and agree when the benefits of this strategy are mentioned, but their actions might still indicate a strong TP (Technology Pull) orientation.

The Specificities of Dutch Engineers

Here we summarize the basic answers of the Dutch respondents from the same study.

In The Netherlands, there is a consistent pattern of business-related practices built around a 'consensus' principle. It is important that decisions are made after everyone has been listened to and if there are disagreements, then a solution will be searched for that is agreed on by everyone. In connection with this, Dutch managers also want freedom to adopt their own approach to the job and to create their own ideas. Dutch managers take their tasks seriously. 'Business is business' and 'Business before pleasure' are two Dutch expressions. The orientation of Dutch managers is short-term planning. They want to see results quickly. On the other hand, when the results do not come quickly, they have perseverance; you almost might call it stubbornness. Dutch engineers are less specialized in a technical area than their German colleagues. To acquire technical knowledge Dutch engineers think that this has to be bought or that they should develop it themselves rather than getting it from internal education programmes. Still a Dutch manager's authority is also based on knowledge. The Dutch are more impressed by actions than by words. Another positive point mentioned by Kympers (1992) is the efficient and economic way of managing. The negative side of this way of managing is an urge towards perfection. This leads to rigidness.

In sum: five interviewees claimed there has been a change towards MP/MO as similar notions, whereas four said that there had been no change. Causes of the change in orientation are: market demand, performance improvement, profile in the market and need for more commitment from the different participants in projects. One interviewee even stated the transition as: 'We cannot do business in any other way any more!' The next question was if the interviewee was satisfied with the current situation. Some of the respondents stated 'no' at first, but after more questions it turned out that all of the respondents were more satisfied with the situation of more MP or a mixed orientation of the company. Forty per cent of them did think that improvement was necessary. Improvement could either be found in even more co-operations between disciplines or in better introduction of new concepts in the company through more education and participation of the involved people. Five of the participating companies were influenced by a major change during the last five to ten years. In two of those companies the increase in importance of information technology influenced their way of doing business. One other company was integrated into another bigger organization. In another company the importance of projects in the organization increased. In the fifth company there had been a reconsideration of the core business in the last five to ten years. This indicates that a lot of companies are adapting to the dynamics of the market in which they operate. There is no relation found between the branch and the need for major changes. Apparently in many different industries there was a need for a major change during this decade. When asked what the positive and negative effects of the changes were, the respondents answered the following. As positive effects there are:

- more pressure to achieve so that new projects are seen as challenges;
- better product quality;
- more responsibility at the shop floor, which accounts for more challenging tasks and more involvement;
- new products which create more value;
- more flexibility;
- better control of the time and money aspects of projects.

As negative effects were mentioned:

- resistance against change;
- more stress for the individual employee because of the broader responsibility.

It is our impression that the Dutch companies from the bottom up consider market orientation more as a natural prerequisite for the success of a firm, whereas in the German firms a reorientation from TP to MP might be more imposed by and accepted from the top management. Is this a matter of conflict between CC and PC? If the PC of the German engineer has a stronger technological orientation, an increasingly market-oriented CC has to come to grips with this.

In Germany, there is a consistent pattern of business-related practices built around 'competence first'. The professional culture of the German engineer is based on this principle. The German apprentice system leads to an exceptionally well-trained work force. About two thirds of German supervisors hold a Master's certificate. German managers are chosen for their positions on the basis of their expert knowledge, and they consider this knowledge to be the most important basis of their authority. The people on the shop floor respect their managers and this respect leads to a satisfying working relationship. The German engineer finds it self-evident that he teaches his subordinates his knowledge and experience. When a supervisor leaves the firm or makes a promotion, it is usual that a subordinate of his preference would take over his job.

If personnel are highly qualified and they respect their supervisors, there will be little guidance needed. Therefore in Germany the average proportion of staff personnel to the total personnel is less than 30 per cent. This leads to a comparatively flat organization, because fewer levels in the hierarchy require fewer (indirect, supporting, controlling) staff to assist the supervisors and managers of fewer different levels. A flat organization has as an advantage that new technologies can be introduced more easily (also because the personnel have a high level of education). Considering innovation, the German engineers are technology oriented. Marketing is seen as a distraction from the primary goal. To maintain knowledge for innovation German managers think that it is necessary to invest in R&D instead of buying knowledge through acquisitions, joint ventures and so on. German managers consider unions and work councils as stabilizing factors. This leads to less time spent on labour disputes. German managers think and act in a business-like manner. They try to reduce uncertainties.

To evaluate the role of the Dutch and German engineers in their respective societies more research needs to be done, but it is clear that the engineering professionalism of the German engineers has a higher status in their society than their Dutch colleagues have in theirs. For the role of innovation in entrepreneurship we refer to a comparison between French, Dutch and German engineers in Ulijn and Fayolle (2004) and in the broader context of other national cultures in which engineers are embedded as well: Ulijn and Brown (2004).

Different Culture-bound Ways to Reach Innovation in The Netherlands and in Germany

The traditional place of The Netherlands as a market place for the large surrounding nations, such as Germany, Great Britain and France, might explain why this country has kept its independence, since its foundation in 1648. Where scientists and philosophers, such as Erasmus, Descartes and Spinoza found the social tolerance to do their work in the 17th century, since the middle of the 20th century Rotterdam has become the first port in the world to serve a European market. In comparison then with their German colleagues, Dutch engineers might become market-oriented earlier in their career. The Ulijn et al. study (2001) allowed two hypotheses to be verified in this context:

- Dutch engineers are more market-oriented than their German colleagues in 12 comparable firms for each country.
- The transition from TO (Technology Orientation) towards MO occurred earlier for engineers in 12 Dutch than in 12 comparable German firms.

This is not the place to give all the details of this empirical study which are published elsewhere (see the above source); a summary is provided here (as for the French study) to characterize engineers in three countries with respect to their entrepreneurial and innovative capabilities. As a statistical analysis of the results, a sign test was used for the first and a Θ-test for the second to evaluate the German–Dutch differences (see Ulijn et al., 2001, for more details about the statistical analyses used). On the basis of the above tests, both hypotheses were confirmed by interviews on the basis of the questionnaire of Appendix B with engineers and personnel recruiters of 12 Dutch and 12 German firms comparable in size (both SMEs and MNCs). Both samples included a percentage of women working there of around 8 per cent, industry sectors, such as automotive, machinery, chemical and semiconductor/IT, both low tech and high tech. The Dutch engineer appeared to be more MO than the German one and his transition from TO to MO took place earlier. Is there a possible culture explanation for this? Are there different culture-bound ways to reach innovation?

A good way to consider possible NC-bound ways to innovation would be to use Hofstede's data (1980a; 1980b; 1989; 1991 and 2001) on both countries. Ulijn and Weggeman (2001) argue that a low Power Distance and Uncertainty Avoidance foster innovation. Both NL and G do not show very much difference, so the first cultural dimension might not be a barrier (38 vs. 35); the second, however, should be lower in both countries than 53 vs. 65 to reach innovation at least at the initiation stage of a new product development process. On one dimension, however, the two countries diverge: G has a rather high masculinity score (66), which means, for instance, a high assertiveness; NL has a low one (14), which means a high femininity index, that is, a high affiliation with others, the family, showing empathy etc. (see Hofstede, 2001, for more details). Nakata and Sivakumar (1996) found that a high femininity, such as in the NL case, would have a positive effect on the initiation stage of an innovation, whereas a high masculinity, such as in a German firm, would help in the implementation stage. In this respect both countries might work in a complementary way. Dutch engineers might be better at initiating and German engineers are better at finishing an innovation process.

Do CC and/or PC-differences matter? There seems to be a suggestion from our results that the engineer in both countries is still more TO than his/her company or colleagues (being marketers as well!) The top management might impose a MO/CC in the German case, but the PC of the engineers might protest! It is our impression that the Dutch companies from the bottom up consider MO more as a natural prerequisite for the success of a firm, whereas in the German firms a reorientation from TO to MO might be more imposed by and accepted from the top management in line with the earlier mentioned need of German technical managers for leadership. This conflict between CC and PC seems to be more obvious in German than in Dutch firms where the transition from TO to MO both occurred earlier and more smoothly. Both initiation and implementation of a new product development is served by reconciling PC and CC differences. The interviews suggested a few non-cultural explanations as well for the differences of MO of Dutch and German engineers due to a different social, industrial and educational context:

- In The Netherlands shareholder value is more important than in Germany.
- In Germany the level of technical education is higher.
- In Germany the investments in R&D are higher.

How would those results for The Netherlands and Germany relate to the level of the French firm and the position of the French entrepreneurial and innovative engineer in it?

The professional positions of French engineers show a great diversity at the technology and market orientation levels. These positions could be explained by interactions between NC and PC. The French national culture shapes the engineer's professional positions in terms of social status and does not consider the technological ones strongly. The French system selects the best individuals by offering them the opportunity to enter a 'Grande Ecole'. The well ranked French engineering 'Grandes Ecoles' then prepare their students for general management and not for specialised engineering studies. These engineering schools are called 'généralistes'. People who do not have the opportunity in this very selective system to enter a 'généraliste' engineering school are oriented to more specialised engineering schools. The former have a managerial orientation including a market orientation but do not only have this dimension. The latter have a strong technological orientation and sometimes only a technological one. This initial position can then move depending on the state of their PC. If the professional identity is strongly rooted in the technological dimension, any position change will be difficult. If it is not, everything is possible, including in particular a change to a more market orientated position.

Comparing these different positions to those of the Dutch and German engineers, it is probably easiest to consider the French engineers coming from the specialised engineering schools. Those who have a technological orientation are quite similar to the German engineers but they are probably more influenced by the intellectual dimension in relation to their education in the French system. Those who have moved towards a market orientation show some similarities with the Dutch engineers. The French engineers coming from the generalist 'Grandes Ecoles' do not easily come into the analysis because their focus is on specific professional situations for which management as an intellectual activity plays an essential role. These engineers very often work with the French administration and the large public and private companies.

A European Perspective including the Above Orientations of French, Dutch and German Engineers

First of all even if the two parts of our research are quite different, they both show the discriminating character of the technological dimension for the engineers. This key dimension strongly shapes the career of engineers in France, Germany and the Netherlands. The main notions that were used in our chapter, are those of invention, innovation and entrepreneurship. All of them are essential for our economies and societies. We also show the importance of market orientation in the innovation process and the fact that cultural variables affect the transition from a technological orientation to a market orientation. The transition processes are not similar for German and Dutch engineers. Our study on the French engineers highlights two different profiles, two different types of entrepreneur engineers. The 'technician' entrepreneur engineer profile is very close to the one of the inventor. This type of entrepreneur engineer invents new technologies, new products or new manufacturing processes. He/she very often needs other competencies (related mainly to marketing, finances, human resource management) to carry out these inventions and to bring them onto the markets. One way could be to acquire these competencies. The other could be to build an entrepreneurial team. The latter is generally the one that is chosen for a lot of reasons, such as time constraint and efficiency or requirements from the financial environment. The 'manager' entrepreneur engineer profile is very close to that of the innovator. This type of entrepreneur engineer innovates more or less in the service activities, business to business and business to consumer. He or she has a good ability to manage all the aspects of the innovation process and he/she is particularly interested in and oriented to the market dimension. The 'manager' entrepreneur engineer is, therefore, an engineer who succeeds in the transition process from the technological orientation to the market orientation.

Hence, the results of our study show that both 'technician' and 'manager' entrepreneur engineers are involved in the innovation phenomenon. The nature and the processes of innovation are not similar, but both kinds of innovation are useful for our economies. Under these conditions one main question is how to improve our knowledge about the different forms of using the scientific, technological and managerial knowledge of European engineers in our European societies.

CONCLUSION FOR FUTURE RESEARCH

Should French engineers design the technical innovation, their German colleagues implement it into a well-controlled manufacturing process and the Dutch, for instance, sell to the market, as they are often positively stereotyped? Our research suggests that diversity might already be built in systematically in a cross-border innovation team as a competitive asset and not as something which happens to us as a handicap on the European and global scene. The French might focus their innovation on creativity, imagination and design (Jules Verne was French!), the Germans on operational efficiency, the technical perfection and quality of the innovation and the Dutch (as well as the English?) on the customer needs of the innovation, as a base to sell it. To reach those different culture-bound ways of innovation, however, the European development of technology management education serving technical entrepreneurship and innovation is beneficial to start-ups and mature companies of any size. We are happy that some initiatives are unfolding in this direction, such as the activities of the Roundtable on Entrepreneurship Education for Engineers (REEE

Europe) and CLUSTER. It goes without saying that sound comparative research on entrepreneurship and innovation across NC/CC/PC borders is an essential part of this.

On the basis of the two above approaches, we would like to suggest a set of possible research questions. The entrepreneurship, innovation and market triangle for the ideal European entrepreneur engineer could be investigated in the three countries using research questions, such as:

- What is the historical evolution of the Dutch and German engineer's social status?
- What is the cultural dimension of the Dutch and German engineer educational system?
- Do the two French models of entrepreneur engineer exist also for the Netherlands and Germany?
- Where is the French entrepreneur engineer located in the TO–MO continuum? The Ulijn et al. study (2001) could be replicated for 12 comparable French firms as suggested above. The interesting NC and CC comparative case work done by d'Iribarne (1993) for French, Dutch and American management might offer some interpretation of, at least the French–Dutch differences to be found.
- Is it possible to delineate a universally valid ideal entrepreneurship and innovation profile for the European engineer? The HAIRL-model of Trompenaars and Hampden-Turner (1999) (Helicopter view, Analysis, Imagination, Reality sense and Leadership) could be further verified for the above-mentioned representative samples including the opinions of future engineers as well (see also Ulijn and Fayolle (2004) for French/German/Dutch engineer differences).
- What would be the ideal mix of NC/CC and PC in a European innovation culture and technical entrepreneurship, as a possible explanation for findings on the above research questions?

As we can see, scientific knowledge has to be produced in order to improve our understanding of European engineer orientations and behaviour towards innovation and entrepreneurship in a period of the socio-economic life where these types of orientations and behaviour are perceived as being of prime importance. A perfect innovation culture seems to merge not only out of national, but also out of corporate and professional cultures of the European engineers and their firms researched. Needless to say that in the development of our French–Dutch research initiative, an expansion to entrepreneurial and innovation cultures other than the French, Dutch or German would be required to increase validity of its outcomes for Europe as a whole.

NOTES

1. This chapter is based upon an extension of an original paper contributed to the ECIS Conference, *The Future of Innovation Studies*, 20–23 September 2001, Eindhoven University of Technology.
2. The main characteristics of the sample are the following:
   - Average age: 35 (standard deviation: 6.8)
   - 20 per cent of entrepreneur engineers come from French engineering 'Grandes Ecoles'
   - 50 per cent of engineers are very highly specialized:
     - chemistry: one person
     - computing, electronic, electricity: six people
     - mechanics: three people
   - In all, the 20 entrepreneur engineers interviewed have created 17 companies (three companies were created by teams composed of two engineers who we met separately). These companies are in different businesses:
     - Three consulting companies
     - Nine dealing with services and the development of computer products
     - Five industrial companies.
3. Sometimes young engineers without experience move quickly to consulting or management activities. Very often they graduated from generalist engineering schools.
4. In our sample 12 engineers belong to the first model. The remaining eight belong to the second model.
5. CNRS (Centre National de la Recherche Scientifique) is the French centre for scientific research.

REFERENCES

Birley, S. (1985), 'The role of networks in the entrepreneurial process', *Journal of Business Venturing*, **1**(1), 107–17.

Bourdieu, P. (1989), *La Noblesse d'Etat: Grandes Écoles et Esprit de Corps*, Paris: *Les Editions de Minuit*.

Crozier, M. (1975), *Les Cadres et l'organisation*, Paris: ADSHA.

Fayolle, A. (1994), 'La trajectoire de l'ingénieur entrepreneur', *Revue Française de Gestion*, no. 101, 113–25.

Fayolle, A. (2000), 'Exploratory study to assess the effects of entrepreneurship programmes on French student entrepreneurial behaviors', *Journal of Enterprising Culture*, **8**(2), 169–84.

Fayolle, A. and Y.F. Livian (1995), 'Entrepreneurial behaviour of French engineers. An exploratory study', in S. Birley and I. MacMillan (eds), *International Entrepreneurship*, London: Routledge, pp. 202–228.

Heerkens, H. and J. Ulijn (2000), 'Fokker: a clash of cultures?', *Journal of Enterprising Culture* (JOKE) (Singapore: World Scientific), **8**(3), 291–320.

Hoad, W.M. and P. Rosko (1964), 'Management factors contributing to the success and failure of new small manufacturers', Ann Arbor, MI: Bureau of Business Research, University of Michigan.

Hofstede, G. (1980a), 'Motivation, leadership and organization: do American theories apply abroad?', *Organisational Dynamics*, no. 9, 42–64.

Hofstede, G. (1980b), *Culture's Consequences: International Differences in Work Related Values*, Beverly Hills, CA: Sage.

Hofstede, G. (1989), 'Cultural predictors of national negotiation styles', in Maurner-Markhoff, F. (ed.), *Processes of International Negotiations*, CO: Westview Press, pp. 193–201.

Hofstede, G. (1991), *Culture and Organizations: Software of the Mind*, London: McGraw Hill.

Hofstede, G. (2001), *Culture's Consequences: Comparing Values, Behaviors, Institutions, and Organizations across Nations*, 2nd edn, London: Sage.

d'Iribarne, P. (1993), 'La logique de l'honneur: gestion des entreprises et traditions nationales', Paris: Editions du Seuil.

Kympers, L. (1992), 'Een Belgisch-Vlaamse kijk op Nederlands zakendoen', *Holland Management Review*, **33**, 59–69.

Lasserre, H. (1989), *Le Pouvoir de l'ingénieur*, Paris: Editions l'Harmattan.

Maurice, M., F. Sellier and J.J. Silvestre (1982), *Politique d'éducation et Organisation Industrielle en France et en Allemagne*, Paris: PUF.

McGrath, R.G. and I.C. MacMillan (1992), 'More like each other than anyone else? A cross cultural study of entrepreneurial perceptions', *Journal of Business Venturing*, **7**(5), 419–29.

Nakata, Ch. and K. Sivakumar (1996), 'National culture and new product development: an integrative review', *Journal of Marketing*, **60**(1), 61–72.

Ogilvie, R. (1992), 'Management: made in Germany', *Holland Management Review*, **33**, 50–58.

Paffen, P. (1998), 'Careers of engineers in general management', Ph.D. thesis, Twente University, the Netherlands.

Ronstadt, R. (1984), *Entrepreneurship: Text, Cases and Notes*, Dover, MA: Lord.

Shinn, T. (1978), 'Des corps de l'Etat au secteur industriel: génèse de la profession d'ingénieur, 1750–1920', *Revue Française de Sociologie*, **19**(1), 39–71.

Silvestre, J.J. (1990), 'Systèmes hiérarchiques et analyse sociétale', *Revue Française de Gestion*, no. 77, 107–15.

Specht, G. (1996), *F&E-Management*, Stuttgart: Schäffer-Poeschel.

Trompenaars, F. and C. Hampden-Turner (1999), *Riding the Waves of Culture: Understanding Cultural Diversity in Business*, London: The Economist Books.

Trompenaars, F. and C. Hampden-Turner (2000), *Building Intercultural Competence*, London: Sage.

Ulich, E. (1990), 'Technik und Unternchmenskultur Zehn Anmerkungen', in C. Lattmann (ed.), *Die Unternehmenskultur*, Heidelberg: Physica, pp. 81–105.

Ulijn, J.M. and T. Brown (2004), 'Innovation, entrepreneurship and culture: the interaction between technology, progress and economic growth', in J.M. Ulijn and T. Brown (eds), *Innovation, Entrepreneurship and Culture*, Cheltenham, UK and Northampton, MA, USA: Edward Elgar, pp. 1–38.

Ulijn, J.M. and A. Fayolle (2004), 'Comparing entrepreneurial and innovation cultures: the European perspective of French, German, and Dutch engineers, some empirical evidence about their technology vs. market orientation', in T. Brown and J.M. Ulijn (eds), *Entrepreneurship, Innovation and Culture*, Cheltenham, UK and Northampton, MA, USA: Edward Elgar, pp. 204–32.

Ulijn, J.M. and W. Weggeman (2001), 'Towards an innovation culture: what are its national, corporate, marketing and engineering aspects, some experimental evidence', in C. Cooper, S. Cartwright and C. Early (London School of Economics and UMIST Business School, Manchester, eds), *Handbook of Organisational Culture and Climate*, London: Wiley, pp. 487–517.

Ulijn, J.M., A.P. Nagel and W-L. Tan (2001), 'The impact of national, corporate and professional cultures on innovation: German and Dutch firms compared', contribution to a special issue of the *Journal of Enterprising Culture*, **9**(1), 21–52, on 'Innovation in an international context' (edited by A. Nagel, J. Ulijn and W-L. Tan).

Vesper, K. (1980), *New Venture Strategies, Englewood Cliffs*, NJ: Prentice-Hall.

Wever, U.A. (1990), *Unternehmenskulture in der Praxis: Erfahrungen eins Insiders bei 2 Spitzenunternehmen (Corporate Culture in Practice: Experience of an Insider with Two Top Enterprises)* 2nd edn, Frankfurt am Main: Campus.

Wheelwright, S.C. and K.B. Clark (1992), *Revolutionizing Product Development: Quantum Leaps in Speed, Efficiency, and Quality*, New York: The Free Press.

Wiebecke, G. (1987), *Lehrbuch der Organisationsphilosophie*, 2nd edn, Psychologie Verlags Union.

APPENDICES

A   Exploratory Study of the Entrepreneurial Behaviours of French Engineers: Questionnaire used by Fayolle, 1994 and Fayolle and Livian, 1995

1.   Is one of your parents an engineer?
2.   Is one of your parents an entrepreneur or an independent worker?
3.   What is the profession of your father?
4.   What is the profession of your mother?
5.   At what time of your life did you envisage an entrepreneurial career?
6.   Could you describe your entrepreneurial process step by step?
7.   Did you spend any time abroad? Where and why?
8.   Did you create associations or are you strongly involved in association life during your studies?
9.   Do you think your engineering education and your engineering school play a role in your entrepreneurial decision?
10. Where did you initially graduate? (In what engineering school?)
11. Could you describe your educational path up to the engineering school?
12. Did you get additional degrees? Which ones? In what kind of institutions?
13. Could you talk about your complementary training: areas, periods, and objectives?
14. What are the main steps of your professional career?
15. How many companies did you work with?
16. What are the different functions you have practised?
17. What is your current professional orientation?
18. Why did you decide to start a company? What were your main motivations?
19. How much time did you need to set up your company?
20. What are the characteristics of your own company? Activities? Technologies used? Number of employees? Sales? Profits?
21. What are the main functions you are dealing with daily?
22. Did you employ other engineers? What are, eventually, their functions?
23. Were you alone in the starting phase or did you work with an entrepreneurial team? Who were those people?
24. From your point of view, could you talk about the characteristics of the entrepreneur engineer?
25. How do you imagine being an entrepreneur? How do you imagine being an engineer? How both?

B   Culture-bound Ways to Reach Innovation: Questionnaire used by Ulijn, Nagel and Tan, 2001

1.   In which commercial branch is your company operating?
2.   What is your actual position in the company?
3.   Which education did you choose?
4.   Please state the size of your company; how many employees does your company have in Germany?
5.   Please characterize your personal view of a technology-driven innovation and a rather market-oriented innovation strategy.
6.   Which of the two strategies do you prefer?
7.   Does the theoretical discussion matter in practice?
8.   Do you consider innovation to be a question of market-pull or technology-push?
9.   Did the different orientations in the self-assessment of the engineer always exist or did they evolve over the past five–ten years?
10. What are the reasons for this development?
11. What do your colleagues think about this? Do you judge them rather to be product- or market-oriented?
12. How do you judge the present orientation of your company?
13. Is there a strict division between Research & Development and Marketing or do you co-operate in project teams?
14. Are you satisfied with this situation?
15. Were there any changes in this regard in the past five–ten years?
16. What were the reasons for the change?
17. Which positive effects and problems occurred due to this change?
18. How would you personally influence the orientation of your company?
19. In the future, do you see any changes in the co-operation of R&D and marketing?
20. What is the influence of company size in the selection of the innovation strategy?
21. Do you see differences in the orientation of experienced and younger engineers?
22. Do you see any differences between men and women?
23. · How many women are working in your technical departments?
24. What are your requirements for the engineer whom you would hire today?
25. Have these requirements changed over the past five–ten years?
26. What is the role of education? Do the universities initiate positive developments in the companies or must the universities adapt to evolving requirements of industry?

11. The strategic spin-off project: an opportunity for organizational learning and change

Allen Vernier

INTRODUCTION

The spin-off process, created at the beginning of the 1980s, soared considerably during the 1980s and the 1990s by bringing alternatives to crisis and its unpopular social plans. This practice, today clearly bound to the field of 'entrepreneurship' of which it represents one of the possible modes, has won acclaim little by little as the general press and scientific publications testify. For many years, it has been used in a very economic and liberal way. But now the spin-off practice has integrated a societal level contributing to creating employment, developing the local companies network, and so on. At the same time, as the Human Relations school and works on Motivation have made their way into mainstream Western thought, Personal Development also became of real value. This is why, even if there is no point in claiming that companies have discovered themselves as humanists, we can assert that the spin-off process is now one of the major tools in developing these practices and engraving some values in people's minds.

But, beyond this updating bound to the evolution of the context and possibly to the development of a social conscience in firms, spin-offs have sometimes changed their form rather radically. At the end of the 1990s, corporate spin-offs became strategic (Descamps, 2000). This practice participates in some cases in the creation of competitive advantages for firms and also enriches the strategic reflection while questioning it at the same time. Built around such notions as innovation, development of the know-how technique and creation of growth options, such policies are not necessarily the product of structured actions and are not planned straightaway. Until today, this option was often spontaneous. Consequently the studies in this field should progressively turn to reflect upon on the use of the spin-off practice.

Our work appears in this logic. We are going to be interested mainly in the link that can exist between spin-offs, the dynamics of change and organizational learning. Change is hence deeply registered in the genes of our firms and the desire for adaptability and opening up to what is outside the firm have become very important. To our knowledge, there are very few inductive materials about strategic spin-offs and still fewer on the existence of this triple link. That is why this chapter is going to deal with a precise corporate case. We will see that the spin-off can be a source of organizational learning and can go as far as looking like a successful management of change. We will also try to identify the key factors of success of such a dynamic and to look at wider implications.

THE SPIN-OFF PROCESS

In this section we will give to the reader a few general reference marks on the spin-off process, which will lead us to clarify the distinction, which is important for the rest of our study, between the classical spin-off and the strategic spin-off.

Definition and Typology

The single spin-off phenomenon is much more complex than it appears, so we can find almost as many definitions. As a European author I will state European definitions and realities.

Each country has its statistical definition according to the criteria of the national statistics agencies. Moncada and his Spanish research team used, in their generic European study, the following definition: 'a corporate spin-off is the division of an existing company into two, usually a bigger one (the parent company) and a smaller one (the spin-off)' (Moncada et al., 2000). For our work and because it fits with the sense of the practice of our sponsor, the spin-off process is defined as 'a practice which, for an employee, consists of creating their own firm or rescuing an existing one which is independent from the parent company and which derives all sorts of supportive measures and benefits from the company that has been left' (Daval, 2000).

In this last definition, the part of the entrepreneur (the ex-employee) is underlined and the role of the parent company is specified. In most common cases, the new firm is economically and legally independent. In fact, this statement remains theoretical since variants do exist.

The reader may note that the chapter focuses on the corporate spin-off, one of the two most studied forms.[1] We can distinguish two types of spin-offs (Moncada et al., 2000 and Tübke, 2003):

- 'restructuring driven spin-offs'. In this case, 'activities that are not within the company's core-competencies and that do not meet minimum

performance requirements are either closed down or spun-off.'
(Moncada et al., 2000). This type is linked to strategic or externalization
logics, or to social plans.

- 'entrepreneurial spin-offs' in which it is essential that the entrepreneur
  is proactive. The new firm exploits critical know-how acquired during a
  previous professional experience or assets (namely intangible assets) it
  intends to develop with the parent company's approval. As for the latter,
  new entrepreneurial potential is used to advantage.

According to the economic conjuncture and to geographic specificities, one of
the two types is more commonly used in each of the European countries. For
instance, restructuring driven spin-offs are mainly practised in France and
Germany, whereas in Spain and Denmark many entrepreneurs are involved in
entrepreneurial spin-offs.

Classical Spin-off and Strategic Spin-off

The previous typology is helpful but does not fit perfectly with our needs. This
chapter is focused on a corporate case and the former distinction is not sufficient to explain the phenomenon we studied. Moreover we intend to spare the
reader the impoverishment of over-simplifications. Indeed, many words are
used in order to describe the spin-off process, which are no longer used without qualification.[2] We suggest the following typology:

- The classical spin-off or project spin-off: This first form is about
  projects which are not linked to the strategy of the parent company. It
  can lead, for example, to the creation of beauty shops, bars or crafts
  workshops. In this case, the parent company is interested in allowing the
  staff to leave voluntarily instead of dismissing them. These spin-offs
  mainly occur at the time of staffing assessments or restructuring.
- The strategic spin-off: the second form of spin-off concerns projects
  which have a strategic dimension for the parent company. The latter is
  interested in boosting and channelling them. A strategic spin-off is characterized by an activity which is complementary to the business of the
  parent company. This complementarity does not need to be effective, a
  simple potential is enough to qualify a project. A large number of start-
  ups (hi-tech or dot-coms) have thus been created but less innovating
  projects can occur. For instance, national electricity providers which
  were often not involved in the house fittings market can start a spin-off
  policy in order to penetrate this segment. The purpose is mainly to set
  up a network of craftsmen. The strategic spin-off can be compared with
  the logic of externalization[3] or of extrapreneurship,[4] namely, when it is

about spinning-off a whole project (personnel, patents, know-how, and so on).

The link with Moncada and Tübke's typology should be stressed here. Indeed, a restructuring driven spin-off and an entrepreneurial spin-off can both be the source of a strategic spinning-off process.

Generally the adoption of the spin-off process is realized without real scheduling, without clear strategic intention, but rather in an opportunist way. The classical spin-off ('project spin-off') has spread widely over the last fifteen years, among other things for very societal reasons which are understandable, as a partial palliative to the staff plans or as a smoke-screen, we won't argue over this. The strategic version of spin-offs then sometimes developed without being expected. These sorts of projects – and their creators – appeared among the classical spin-offs, and the parent companies discovered their specificities progressively and tried to control them. The firms quickly realized how helpful a structured spin-off policy could be. While encouraging the exit of projects close to the core business, the spin-off becomes:

- an alternative to the classic externalization, offering prospects of big reactivity like the mythical start-ups.
- a means to valorize the technologies and know-how or even to share them with the competitors.
- a solution in the case of budgetary restriction allowing projects to be completed

As we will see, the spin-off is also a very efficient means to develop innovation and entrepreneurship, and to be more competitive.

The experimentation achieved by other groups has enabled some companies to dedicate themselves only to the strategic spin-off. We will also grant that some structures practised this type of spin-off without sticking definitely to this concept, generally because there were no supportive measures. Among them, we will mention the major national laboratories, the consulting audit and legal firms. Anyway, the word 'strategic' only appeared quite recently with the launch of the New Economy companies, like the start-ups.

The Reality of the Phenomenon in Europe

According to the European JRC–IPTS's study (Moncada et al., 2000), the spin-off phenomenon is 'an important source for industrial reinvigoration and competitive advantage'. Its shares in entrepreneurship phenomena are significant.

- In terms of new firm formation, 'the expert estimations in Europe suggest that [spin-offs] make up for an average of 12.9 per cent of new firms created'
- The rate of success seems to be higher than the average for new firms. Indeed, between 70 and 90 per cent of the spin-offs are still economically alive after five years whereas the average amounts to only 50 per cent.[5]

The authors of this study stress some other benefits for employment, innovation, regional competitiveness, and new market creation. They also underline that 'corporate spin-offs are important in unleashing entrepreneurial potential' (cf. our results).

If we focus on the strategic spin-off form, Swedish and French firms have good results (and not only in the sector we studied, that is the Telecom sector). In Sweden the Stockholm School of Economics' researchers are working on start-ups and spin-offs in their department called 'entrepreneurship and business creation'. In France some large firms are associated and are thinking about strategic spin-off. It is probably not a coincidence that these countries are also those in which restructuring driven spin-offs are very common.

For a comprehensive understanding of our point, two other pieces of information should be added. On the one hand, Moncada et al.'s study (2000) asserts that corporate spin-offs experience a transition period during which they have to finance the separation with the parent company and during which the growth can be high, but the profitability is weak or negative. This period lasts from three to five years and explains why these spin-offs are often highly leveraged. On the other hand some sectors, high purveyors of spin-off, were hit by deregulation. In European energy and telecommunications markets these measures caused extensive and radical modification of the R&D and business structures.

ORGANIZATIONAL LEARNING

In light of the case studied, we will see that the spin-off process requires organizational learning. In this part, we will define what learning means for an organization and then we will describe the learning process.

Definition and Analysis

Organizational learning can be defined as follows: 'a collective phenomenon of acquisition and development of expertises that, by varying amounts, and for varying periods of time, modifies the management of the situations and the situations themselves' (Kœnig, 1994; 1995).

As Argyris and Schön (1996) have underlined, learning refers to a content, to a process and to the learner. The two authors were among others at the root of the concept of organizational learning.[6]

Concerning the learner, the organization learns by and for itself but it also learns through the individuals (who compose it or pass through it) in the context of human action. If we try to synthesize all the authors' contributions, we can claim that organizational learning is related to:

- cognitive elements with creation and transformation of knowledge and the mental diagrams,
- behaviour elements, that is the evolution of rationality and the different ways of decision making, the expansion of the possible options field,
- cultural elements, with changes of meaning, of routines, of myths and so on.

Concerning the process, we wish to focus on two elements. Firstly, Kœnig (1995) explains that it is based on the management of 'the accumulated experience' and on 'the intelligence of the experimentation' (the action or the insights of Argyris and Schön). Secondly, the collective dimension can be activated by:

- the circulation of ideas and the diffusion of practices which depends directly on the value granted to them, on a community of understanding and, at the same time, on the variety or the depth of the interpretations;
- the creation of relations between pre-existing expertise, through the cognitive or relational mix (Kœnig, 1994; 1995).

Organizational learning requires collective and individual processes. It is illustrated, at the individual level, by a knowledge storage through cognition or behaviour and, at the organizational level, by all sorts of other 'stocks', that we can associate with the notion of culture.

For the rest of our work we need a precise definition of an organizational culture. Schein (1991, 373) gave us the following one:

> a pattern of shared basic assumptions that the group learned as it solved its problems of external adaptation, and internal integration, that has worked well enough to be considered valid and, therefore, to be taught to new members as the correct way to perceive, think, and feel in relation to those problems.

In our results we will also consider the cultural pattern (Johnson and Scholes, 1999) and its seven components: paradigm, symbols, myths, rites and routines, systems of control, structures of power, and finally organizational structures.

The Learning Process

In this part, we will try to detail the learning process we rapidly defined previously. Organizational learning is a collective process of diagnosis (Argyris and Schön, 1996) and a change of beliefs, postulates, paradigm, knowledge, routines (March, 1999) and structures. In a way, it modifies the map but, also, the territory.[7] Indeed, as Senge (1990), then Argyris and Schön (1996) have underlined, the evolution of the postulates and the capacity to understand the reasons of dysfunction enable the interactions between actors to be more productive.

According to Argyris and Schön (1996), two forms of learning exist:

- 'Single loop learning' is the most common one. It draws from an index of possible actions without questioning either the values or the norms of the theories in use. This type is also called 'type I'.
- 'Double loop learning' (type II) implies a double recursive movement in which actors unlearn[8] before learning new values and norms again, which allows them to adapt the strategies of action. The authors underline that the theories and the indexes of action both change in this case.

Of course organizations only implement learning of the second type when the first is insufficient to adapt itself to a new situation.

Senge (1990), and then Nonaka and Takeuchi (1995; 2002), have highlighted two crucial elements necessary for a learning organization to be built: firstly that 'it is the development of knowledge that constitutes the learning' and secondly that it must be possible to join the two types of learning in a dynamic model (a spiral for Nonaka and Takeuchi). Learning has a direct impact on the processes of organizational change and on innovation.

A SPIN-OFF CASE STUDIED IN THE TELECOM SECTOR

The present work stems from an 'action research'[9] and thus deals with corporate cases. Our sponsor called us in to give an outsider's view of the spin-off process (solely in its strategic version) and to help to find synergies between the group and the small firms thus created. The I.M. group[10] is a European company established in the telecommunications sector. In order to give a comprehensive description we must add that it was partially privatized in the 1990s and the European Union enforced deregulation on this market. The group experienced a modification of its competitive environment, which plunged it into a necessary and rather important change. It also had to cope with a culture unsuitable for its requirements and with policies introducing a necessary break or change. One of these has had radical effects on the whole firm since the State demanded fundamental research to be stopped immediately and a reorientation of a strong applied R&D. Our work highlights and is based on this change.

The Stakes of the Spin-off Process for our Sponsor

When we intervened, this group had already implemented about twenty strategic spin-offs since 1998. Most of them stemmed from its research laboratories and therefore implied asset exits. This policy is relatively expensive with, for instance, sums invested in various forms of supportive measures and equity financing, free work time during the upstream phase of the process for the entrepreneur(s), costs associated with structures and management.

A firm does not spend money and time without good reasons. Table 11.1 lists the stakes we identified and some of them are apparently contradictory. The reader's attention must be drawn to the fact that learning is not an end in itself, but that it can also underlie the logic of some objectives.

Another explanation of the success of the spin-off practice has to be listed here: networking, entrepreneurship and start-ups were booming concepts and to some extent had begun to be considered as one of the best forms of business practice. Our sponsor was probably attracted by the idea of applying methods used extensively in the technological sectors. We must not forget that the Silicon Valley forged a sort of myth of innovative and business superiority and of a good way of life.

Description of our Sample and the Method of our Study

The results we will present are derived from seven cases, chosen among 20 start-ups. The cases and the criteria chosen are detailed in Appendix 1. Our selection was also led by qualitative indications supplied by the spin-off cell. We tried to find the most interesting projects in term of period, impact on the group, difficulties met during the process and some other criteria. The last criterion was the success or the potential success of the spin-offs. We dismissed project failure or spin-offs that had no relationships with the group since our initial purpose was to analyse business or innovation opportunities and the relevance of the concept of networking with them.

Then we met the spin-off entrepreneurs (of course), the R&D laboratories they left, the internal structures in charge of the spin-off process and of its financing, and the established or potential customers inside the group. Finally to complete our picture, we got in touch with peripheral experts and with some external start-ups (or innovating SMEs) that had entered in

Table 11.1   Identified stakes

Initial stake	• Create value, valorize some technologies *The idea was to valorize the heritage of the I.M. group. Moreover the concept of Eva (Economic Value Added) led to this choice.*
Secondary or posterior stakes	• Contribute to pilot innovation (as much technological as managerial) *We will deal with this again in the part dedicated to the organizational learning that ensues from this experimentation.* • Manage the mobility of the wage-earners *Manage the evolution of human resources efficiently, encourage turnover, leave some room for manoeuvre in case of downsizing, or allow strong experiences and therefore learning (even a failure could be seen as a major learning experience and to be valuable).* • Contribute to the emergence of new markets *The sector in which I.M. is now evolving has entered a permanently turbulent phase, bound to a chain of very powerful technological innovation. The large integrated firms, characterized by classic institutional resistance, are used to moving and industrializing a process slowly. Resorting to small and light structures does allow them to adjust more quickly.* • Increase the societal conscience *The spin-off process can contribute to an opening up into the local environment.*[11]

'synergies' with the group. The relationships could be of a commercial nature or in terms of innovation and co-development. To have an exhaustive explanation of our method and of the questionnaire used, see Appendix 2.

All in all, we talked to more than thirty people and we extracted seven cases with a complete analysis. This work enabled us to gather rather exhaustive data on the nature of the relationships between spin-offs and the I.M. group in order to highlight the learning dynamics and to identify some intervening organizational changes resulting from this experience. These transformations are about cultural as well as organizational aspects. Furthermore, they do not concern only actors and systems directly connected to the spin-off process, but the whole firm. Seen in some lights, an entrepreneurial and innovative virus seemed to spread in the group and even the hostile bastions seemed to fall one by one.

What virus are we talking about? This is what we are going to see now.

THE RESULTS: WHEN A SPIN-OFF PROCESS CONSTITUTES A CONCLUSIVE EXAMPLE OF ORGANIZATIONAL LEARNING AND CHANGE

In this part, we will try to outline the learning generated by the spin-off process in the I.M. group, as shown by Ingham (1994) who worked on the cooperations.

During our work, we identified six elements of learning. The first concerns the process itself (which it is an endogenous element), the others concern the exogenous elements or the products of the spin-off policy. We will also try to reveal the organizational changes which occurred at the same time.

The Formalization of the Process

The first learning generated by the spin-off policy lies in the progressive formalization of the process. After a period when vagueness was voluntarily allowed in order to initiate the dynamics and to reinforce it, our sponsor must have wondered about the degree of formalism. The latter can be divided into three levels:

- *The procedure itself*: From the beginning of the process the procedure was progressively improved. Case B (cf. Appendix 1) was the first spin-off that was not a result of reorganization and the first led by an entrepreneur (as this person liked to described themselves). This case set the question of minority shareholding since the I.M. group could benefit from such an operation. The industrial investment amounted to 10 per cent of the total capital for reasons that are too numerous to describe here. But, to some extent, this case contributed to define an inviolable rule for all the other spin-offs. We called it the '10 per cent rule' and, in fact, no rational reasoning can support it.

  The reflection was then about the projects' formalism, the supportive measures and training system, and finally the orientation of the spin-off process and follow-up. This evolution is partially demanded by the importance of success and by internal auditing procedures. This continuous improvement began on a trial and error basis and still uses this method a great deal. Gradually pilot procedures and structures were implemented. We can conclude that the group is learning, but the learning remains relatively poor (it concerns mainly cognitive elements) and remains at a type I level ('single loop learning').

We must also underline that in a very few cases, the procedure failed to manage the spinning-off. Two reasons could be put forward. Firstly, the cumbersome and complicated nature of the process was criticized by some entrepreneurs or their hierarchy (in this case, entrepreneurs preferred to pull out of the project). Secondly, the spin-off practice was led by a mainstream, that is, start-ups. When a project did not match up to this paradigm, the entrepreneurs did not want to enter into the process. We cannot find out why. There are two possible explanations: on the one hand a disheartening projection of this paradigm by the spin-off on the project leader and on the other hand a feeling of inferiority experienced by entrepreneurs. Case F was significant and showed that a project that does not enter into the spinning-off procedure, is not identified and so is not managed in the downstream phase.

- The downstream phase of the spin-off process, that is to say, the research of synergies through commercial cooperation or through co-innovation.[12] The entrepreneur of Case B confirmed to us that commercial relations are normalized after an 18-month period of latency. In two cases (A and D) the length of time was even shorter. R&D and innovation cooperations take more time, but these trial periods remain very short in comparison with the average quoted by Moncada et al. (2000), that is five years. All in all it is not surprising that an adaptation period is necessary, mainly for the laboratories impacted by the spin-off. As for the Business Units, confidence must be restored. The I.M. group showed extraordinary skill in adaptation, not only on cognitive levels but also on behavioural and cultural ones. An implicit and underlying change of type II ('double loop learning') has taken place.

With regard to the downstream management of the process, the I.M. group is tempted to acquire a minimum level of commercial cooperations and innovative relationships, even though this has not been agreed about, mainly for the first spin-offs. The possibility of combining these start-ups in a network was also considered. However, we identified important deficiencies in the management of this step. Indeed it is not structured around a unique actor. The different entities concerned in this downstream phase have different stakes and their relationships with the spin-off entrepreneurs are different. And finally none is truly in charge of the instigation and amination of this network. The dysfunction is not explicitly identified by the management of our sponsor and remains ignored. No learning has taken place because it has to be of type II. To define a unique pilot would demand an upheaval in the structures of power.

- And finally 'the spin-off indication' that we contributed to define as a topic of analysis and study. It is a process made up of analysis, negotiation and formalization actions, and which works towards the final spin-off decision.

If Case B, already described, posed the question 'why do the I.M. group gain by losing competencies and technologies by spinning-off?', another case we studied is more revealing. The firm C showed the risk taken by a spinning-off corporation, when it did not explore all the components of the project, and mainly used a medium and long-term analysis. The I.M. group wanted to keep internal competencies and business in the networks' engineering field. They authorized the spin-off although its business model was clearly competitive with I.M.'s activities. The reasons for this choice were not sufficiently discussed or formalized. The decision was made on apparently objective grounds but, in fact, the motivations were subjective (people affinities, false belief, power and sociological games, and so on). In August 2001, that is to say almost 18 months after the spinning-off, relationships were jammed whereas they could have been objectively promising in the field of innovation.

So, the notion of 'spin-off indication' deserves particular attention because its mastery constitutes one of the key factors of success for the spin-off technique and for future relationships. It is also a key to understanding the feedback on the process. In the end, it can promote significant learning, maybe of type II ('double loop learning'). To highlight the relevance of the concept, it is necessary for us to proceed in two stages, in a sort of forward–backward process. Firstly, every new indication questions the strategy of the group since every spin-off decision integrates the definition of what is, or is not, a core business. Therefore each spin-off could constitute an opportunity for redefinition or enrichment of the strategy. Secondly, and here is the returning part of our reflection, let us raise the issue of 'strategic intention' (Johnson and Scholes, 1999). We have questioned the strategy, and we now plead for the intention to be subordinated to it. Rather than managing a flux of spin-off projects and wondering about their strategic consistency, we suggest creating this flux according to the 'indication' that becomes prescriptive – the word is given in all its meaning. This vision requires a type II learning ('double loop learning') in which the values and the theories in use are questioned again and readapted. The work of definition and explanation we led with our sponsor prepared this huge transformation. It had to cope with individual resistance but we recommended it to the management (in order to maintain performance and ethic).

The Integration of the Process

The spin-off process was gradually but firmly integrated: some laboratories and some business units became the heralds of this policy. We identified a direction of R&D (those of Case D) which realized four spin-offs, and which seemed willing to let some other projects go. The director explained nevertheless that the first spin-off was a tremendous challenge since 20 per cent of its staff spun-off while he had to maintain its research activity. Many other laboratories also experienced successful spinning-off and we can assert that the spin-off policy also benefited the recruitment process.

The process even seemed so anchored in some units that some drifting could be feared. Two fears seemed to us to be likely to come true. On the one hand, it might be possible to initiate R&D projects out of the core business with a very good chance of being spun off. (We should remind the reader that it is not relevant according to the purpose of the I.M. group.) On the other hand, we suspected the spin-off cell would urge people to spin off with the intention of maintaining the dynamics and so prolonging its existence.

But, if we reflect in a different way, these forms of behaviour may not be so unusual. Why does the group manage without some R&D projects out of the core business? They could trigger innovation or market exploration. They may also question strategy, question the definition of what is a core business, open the field of possibilities and attract expertise and knowledge. Let us remind ourselves that the latter (expertise and knowledge) are the source of competitive advantage. Company management has to find a delicate balance between uncertainty and risk-taking on the one hand, and security and respect of established norms on the other.

If we cannot answer these questions definitely, their great merit is that they highlight the necessity for 'smart' and relevant modes of control on a protean and complex subject.

Acquisition of New Research Skills and Development of New Internal Relations

In 1998, the year when the first spin-offs emerged, the R&D division of the I.M. group had no operational image. Until that time the researchers had focused on fundamental research and the business units had the feeling that the technical solutions proposed by the laboratories were disconnected from the reality of the market and from their needs. Researchers were often considered as 'children in their cradle'. There was a missing link between research and technical solutions. The latter were generally bought outside.

The spin-off policy showed that researchers were capable of industrializing projects and of giving concrete expression to some opportunities. Let us give two illustrations of this:

- on the one hand, some researchers using the spin-off process became fully-fledged manufacturers (certainly more or less successfully and often with the help of partners who had complementary abilities), as Cases B, C, D and E show. Firm B is, for instance, operational in European countries as well as in the USA and has a double Stock Exchange quotation (one on the Nasdaq).
- on the other hand, the laboratories started some collaborations with the spin-offs and then with other start-ups in order to develop a competitive and technological monitoring, to innovate together but especially to co-develop technical solutions. This very simple and very flexible structure of alliance, and the choice to spin-off at the right moment thus enabled the I.M. group to launch some services to the customers at the same time as its competitors, and sometimes to take a competitive advantage (mainly in services). Indeed, the I.M. group would have had some diffi-culties in launching its WAP services at the same time as its competitor if it had had no start-ups around it. The spin-off called 'Case A' was one of them. The group was also looking for innovative 3D mapping (Case G) and geolocalization which can be linked with its directories and mobile services. We may underline that this speed in the adaptation was not the strong point of this group which had a dominant position in the past and consequently was not used to being very reactive.

This demonstration required a 'double loop learning' mainly about values, representations and routines (the theories in use). This learning concerned researchers as well as their 'internal customers'. R&D is now respected more in the group. New, more frequent and fuller cooperation was created between these two worlds. What is also interesting is that we did not find any formal announcement from the I.M. group concerning this change, but the new situation seemed positively obvious to those we interviewed.

The Opening up of the I.M. Group to Foreign Firms

In its previous configuration our sponsor used to get supplies from huge French groups whose history was often the same, that is to say public. In its core business this supply mode was quasi obligatory. The company also dealt with foreign firms or with competitors on condition that they were assessed as worthy of interest according to I.M.'s criteria.

Through this description, the reader can understand that the group was not really open to foreign firms and even less to small businesses. Buyers, technicians and engineers of the business units as well as of the laboratories reacted in a condescending way to small firms. To our knowledge, the situation seemed critical in the R&D field in 1998. The supply of small firms has no credibility and in some cases inspires real fear. In the past, the I.M. group had indeed purchased technical solutions that appeared hardly maintainable or non-durable. Moreover, the core of the business is above all the business of a colossus, since it must offer a wide geographic cover and develop economies of scale.

Our work indicates that the 'spin-off experimentation' modifies this cultural resistance in a very short time. The first spin-off experienced some difficulties in entering into business connection with the group during the first 18 months. It seems as if the I.M. group's buyers were adopting a pertinent and cautious approach. Then the situation improved quickly following the success of some spin-offs. The first IPO (Initial Public Offer) and the business development work also had a terrific and clearly identifiable effect on attitudes.

Most of the R&D laboratories and the business units developed partnerships and signed supply contracts with small firms, and not only with spin-offs. Skilled workers inside the I.M. group learned to work with external organizations and foreign workers. Tripartite agreements associating internal or external labs, business units and start-ups were settled, which brought about this change dynamics. This movement created value and new competences. To sum up, values, routines and maybe paradigms are altered. The possibilities for action are also wider. We are facing a type II ('double loop learning') organizational learning.

The Development of New Skills and New Processes of Entrepreneurship Development

Other learning brought about by this practice involves entrepreneurship and its specific skills. The I.M. group has settled a portfolio of competences for the establishment of companies: among them, we can find funding, valuation, creation of business plans, control of contractual and conventional elements (for example the shareholder pact), and so on. Moreover the company has discovered other entrepreneuship experiences like 'intrapreneurship,[13] and what we can call 'SMIsation by capture'.[14] These experiments have been started nearly at the same time as the spin-off practice. For example, an intrapreneurship experiment has been started at the end of the 1990s. We firmly believe that without successful spin-off tests, the group would definitely have given up other entrepreneurship modes.

These first experimentations, apart from spin-off, came up against difficulties in the coordination of activities, strategies and people (namely in the areas of motivation and rewarding or remuneration). They had to cope with cultural problems and inability to adjust. Intrapreneurship, like 'SMIsation by capture' often results in semi-failures. But, the spin-off examples gave a reference of success and contributed to reflections and new experiments on business creation. We noted that the I.M. group has never tested options like pure extrapreneurship or 'SMIsation by repulsion'.[15] Our work also consisted in demonstrating the interest of these options.

To sum up, the spin-off technique enriched and threw light on the reflection and the processes of business creation. It has guided and formalized the integration/acquisition of new skills concerning entrepreneurship, all the supportive measures and the funding. The spin-off also contributed to the development of a better understanding of the phenomena linked to coordination, motivation, organization flexibility or corporate culture. Some of these abilities have been maintained in-house (in laboratories, in business units, in in-house financiers and in the 'spin-off cell'), while others have left the group. Even in this case, they left an indelible mark: business plans, spin-off indications, a formalization of the process, pinpointing of in-house and external networks of experts who can be easily mobilized, and so on. We tried also to promote the idea that the spin-off process can be reversible, that is to say all or part of the spin-off, especially the abilities, could be brought back into the I.M. group.

A Fresh Look on the Valuation of the Spin-off Process

This learning, which is still a potentiality, could be a decisive discovery because it could fundamentally change the culture of the firm. Firstly, we should accept the fact that the present valuation mode is not satisfactory, and then understand why before extending the research to many projects in the company.

When we started working on the subject, the start-up phenomenon was becoming what we can call the 'start-down' effect. Until this date, the success of the spin-off policy was mainly based on financial valuation. At the start of 2001, the industrial share holdings of the I.M. group bound to spin-offs come to more then 150 million euros and several Stock Exchange quotations. With the deflation of the speculative bubble, this financial godsend has decreased significantly. The other assessment the group used was based on how many jobs have been created. With the strategic spin-offs, 1500 jobs have been created. This indicator is useful in checking the company's health and the impact of spin-offs on the I.M. group's environment. On these two aspects, the positive conclusions have also been challenged and criticized. In concrete terms, some spin-offs met serious trouble, while others kept on growing, but the damage has been done.

Did these disappointments have to lead to the whole spin-off process being questioned or was it the establishment of the failure of the evaluation process based on quantitative and financial criteria? Both conclusions have been made inside the I.M. group. Some thought the experience has shown its limitations and wanted to preserve the benefits of the process. Others thought that the spin-off technique was not the cause of the failure (one of the best pieces of evidence could be that the group's Stock Exchange valuation also decreased deeply). What we can say is that the assessment system needed to be questioned because it was clearly inadequate. We proposed to use the real options[16] (Jacquet, 1998) to get together experts in financing and managers of the spin-off policy. We also proposed a debate about qualitative and quantitative indicators which took into account the impact on R&D, turnover, margin, environment and image of the I.M. group, recruitment, and so on. We mainly encouraged the group to identify a major positive factor: the learning and the change created. Thus, we were proposing to replace the quantitative and financial assessment process by social and qualitative measures which gave a place to tests and errors, to risk taking, to the creation and the management of knowledge, to the learning. . . . To sum up, we are not very far from the learning organization concept (Senge, 1990).

CONCLUSION

This chapter is integrated in a part dedicated to entrepreneurship, culture and innovation. We saw that spin-off in its strategic form can lead to learning that is able to:

- inspire a whole group with entrepreneurial spirit, desire and abilities where they were completely missing previously.
- significantly modify cultural evidence namely in terms of opening up to foreign firms, valuation and control methods, formalization requirements, and so on. It also enables sub-cultures to be changed, in the case in point R&D and Strategic Business Unit sub-cultures.
- boost innovation through new skills, new R&D projects, exploration of new markets, launching of new products or services and so on.

Our purposes were to stress the link created between the learning and the spin-off concept. In the case of the I.M. group we hope that the reader found a real richness of learning. Some are activated and some are still potential.

The two concepts are both bound by a strong interaction and their combination helps to create a competitive advantage.[17] This new potential subject could interest the strategic discipline. In any case, strategists of the firms should take it into account.

But, the most important surprising element in this research is elsewhere: in the case we studied we are witnessing a non-scheduled but very effective change. . . . The spin-off process was started without any reflection on its underlying sense and its impact on the cultural system (all in all, the structure precedes the culture). We do believe that culture and values should be the core of the firm's management and that structure, process, and management tools should come from it.

But anyway, we should also be pragmatic. Would it be possible to rely on inductive work and intentionally to launch a spin-off policy in order to reach a goal of change management? The answer seems to be yes. The case we have studied (the I.M. group) is probably not unique. Of course it has its own specificities. It is a big multidivisional firm compelled to make a major and rapid change and the group is established in a high-tech market. But, we do believe that this result does not depend on these factors of size, history, structure or market. We think that the relevant key factor is the ability to create a high complementarity with the strategy of the parent company.

In the introduction we announced our intention to list the key factors of success. We still owe them to our reader. Our proposal relies on the data we collected and on an inductive reasoning whose limitations we acknowledge. We have identified four main recommendations:

- define the modes of the spin-off process and probably split strategic spin-offs and classical spin-offs. This division would allow energy to be concentrated in the right way and for an accurate operational model to be designed.
- position the structure in charge of the spin-off process in a transversal function and ensure consistency from the upstream phase to the downstream period, probably with a single actor.
- reflect on the 'spin-off indication' and in this way maintain a real link between strategy and the process.
- design a process evaluation which would allow learning to be identified among other purposes. This assessment model has to give people the opportunity to make mistakes and has even to valorize them.

We are convinced of the relevance of our approach and of the importance that a strategic spin-off process can have for firms. The areas of benefit are numerous: innovation, business, strategy, general management, recruitment, competences, and knowledge. . . . Here is a relatively new field in Western countries. It is waiting for theoretical and deductive as well as inductive works. In order to operationalize the concept of the strategic spin-off process and of more specific ones, we hope that other researchers will join us. A lot of points still need to be enlightened: the outlines of the subject, the assessment and management tools, the key factors of success and also the relevance of the phenomenon in the functioning of economic sectors and cycles needs to be qualified.

NOTES

1. The other form is usually called 'university spin-off'.
2. The list is too long to be enumerated here, but we can quote a few of them, such as financed spin off, competitive spin-off or neutral spin-off.
3. Externalization is the process by which a firm splits off from an activity. The latter is assessed as being outsourced with more efficiency and success or as belonging no more to the firm's core business. The concept is linked with principles of sharing resources (financial and human resources, know-how as so on).
4. Extrapreneurship is a venturing strategy implying that an employee encouraged by her/his employer creates a concerted spin-off replacing the employment contract with a business agreement (Johnsson and Hägg, 1987). It is a particular mode of externalization.
5. These figures are supplied by APCE (Agence Pour la Création d'Entreprises i.e. the French Business Start-Up Agency as they call themselves) (www.apce.com).
6. Argyris and Schön promoted this concept during the 1970s. Merton in the 1940s and March and Simon in the 1950s initiated this fertile trend but their approach was focused on the individual action and not on an organizational specificity. We should also stress the fact that an organization learns permanently.
7. Cf. the work of Korzybski and his general semantic (Korzybski, 2002).
8. 'Unlearning' is more specifically brought to the fore by Hedberg (1981).
9. This type of research is based on earlier works of K. Lewin (1951), Dewey (in the 1930s and 1940s, for example, Dewey, 1938) and then Argyris et al. (1985). For European references, see Moisdon (1984), Roy (1992) and Hatchuel (1994).
10. This name is of course fictitious.
11. Some companies use the spin-off process either to minimize the impact of a downsizing on a local economic network or to be in favour with local councillors concerning projects that public opinion does not accept.
12. The spin-off process is often limited to the active period from the emergence of the project to its realization. In practice, some firms extend it by a few extra months in order to finalize the supportive logic. The new structure is supposed to acquire its independence quickly, and therefore the spin-off process stops when the new company is ready to soar without any help. But the strategic spin-off technique changes this deal completely. Indeed, the companies have progressively surrounded themselves with small firms and have tried to get synergies out of them. The product of the spin-off process must be supervised. In order to make the most of it, it can even be oriented towards a network (either through a social or relational network with some business development, or through a real network organization). Firms and specialists must therefore deal with the downstream phase.
13. An intrapreneur is a person within a large corporation who takes direct responsibility for turning an idea into a profitable finished product through assertive risk-taking and innovation.
14. Nunes (1991) developed the concept of '*PMIsation par captation*' which can be literally translated by 'SMIsation by capture'. It consists in overtaking an SMI (Small and Medium Industry) whose activity is very close to the one of the buying firm. The two entities or their action systems can be more or less merged. Nunes suggests another option: the '*PMIsation par répulsion*' (or 'SMIsation by repulsion') activated for business reorientation purposes. That last mode is very close to the externalization form.
15. See the previous footnote.
16. A real option is an investment that provides the right, but not the obligation, to obtain the

cash flows produced by some real world asset. A real option is a derivative of the classic financial option. Its major interest is to delay the decision and to wait for a more comprehensive report. It reduces uncertainty and allows only good news to be retained. The price of an option is among other things a function of uncertainty. This is why every risked activity gets a high valuation with this approach.
17. Organizational learning constitutes the only durable competitive advantage according to some authors (de Geus, 1988; Edmondson and Moingeon, 1996).

REFERENCES

Argyris, C. (1976), 'Single-loop and double-loop models in research on decision making', *Administrative Science Quarterly*, no. 21, 363–75.

Argyris, C. and D.A. Schön (1996), *Organizational Learning II: Theory, Method, Practice*, New York: Addison Wesley.

Argyris, C., R. Putman and D. MacLain Smith (1985), *Action Science: Concepts, Methods, and Skills for Research and Intervention*, San Francisco: Jossey-Bass.

Daval, H. (2000), 'Le processus entrepreneurial d'essaimage', Ph.D. thesis, Pierre Mendès-France University, Grenoble II, Ecole Supérieure des Affaires.

De Geus, A. P. (1988), 'Planning as learning', *Harvard Business Review*, March–April, pp. 70–74.

Descamps, M. (2000), *L'essaimage Stratégique, Guide Opérationnel*, Paris: Ed. d'Organisation.

Dewey, J. (1938), *Logic: the Theory of Inquiry*, New York: Henry Holt and Co.

Edmondson, A. and B. Moingeon (1997), 'Apprentissage organisationnel et avantage concurrentiel', in Village Mondial (ed.), *'L'art de l'entreprise globale'*, Paris: Les Echos.

Edmondson, A. and B. Moingeon (1996), *Organizational Learning and Competitive Advantage*, London: Sage.

Hatchuel, A. (1994), 'Les savoirs de l'intervention en entreprise', *Entreprise et Histoire*, no. 7, pp. 59–75.

Hedberg, B. (1981), 'How organizations learn and unlearn', in C. Nystrom and W.H. Starbuck (eds), *Handbook of Organizational Design*, (Adapting organizations to their environments), Vol. 1, Oxford: Oxford University Press.

Ingham, D. (1994), 'L'apprentissage organisationnel dans les coopérations', *Revue Française de Gestion*, no. 97, January–February.

Jacquet, D. (1998), 'La R&D: un portefeuille d'options financières?', *Séminaire Ressources Technologiques, Les Annales de l'Ecole de Paris*, Vol. 5.

Johnson, G. and H. Scholes (1999), *Exploring Corporate Strategy*, 5th edn, Edinbourgh: Prentice Hall Europe.

Johnsson, T. and I. Hägg (1987), 'Extrapreneurs between markets and hierarchies', *Intrenational Studies of Management & Organization*, **XVII**(1), 64–74.

Koenig, G. (1994), 'L'apprentissage organisationnel: repérage des lieux', *Revue Française de Gestion*, no. 97, January–February.

Koenig, G. (1995), *Management Stratégique, Paradoxes, Interactions et Apprentissages*, Paris: Nathan.

Korzybski, A. (2002), *General Semantics Seminar 1937: Transcription of Notes from Lectures in General Semantics given at Olivet College*, edited by Homer J. Moore Jr, Brooklyn, NY: Institute of General Semantics.

Lewin, K. (1951), *Field Theory in Social Science*, Chicago: University of Chicago Press.

276

March, J. (1999), *The Pursuit of Organizational Intelligence*, Malden, MA and Oxford, UK: Blackwell Publishers.

Merton, T. (1949), *Seeds of Contemplation*, Westport, CN: Greenwood Press.

Moisdon, J.-C., (1984), 'Recherche en gestion et intervention', *Revue Française de Gestion*, no. 39, May–June.

Moncada, P., A. Tübke, J. Howells and M. Carbone (2000), *The Impact of Corporate Spin-Offs on Competitiveness and Employment in the EU*, IPTS-Report 44/technical report, Seville, May, http://www.jrc.es/home/report/report_main.html; http://www.jrc.es/pages/projects/corporate/CSO.EUR-19040-EN.pdf.

Nonaka, I. and H. Takeuchi (1995), *The Knowledge-creating Company*, New York: Oxford Unversity Press.

Nonaka, I. and H. Takeuchi (2002), *Apprentissage Organisationnel, Théorie, Méthode, Pratique*, Paris: De Boeck University,

Nunes, P. (1991), 'Les opérations de PMIsations: pratique ou stratégie?', Ph.D. thesis, Université Pierre Mendès-France, Grenoble II, Ecole Supérieure des Affaires.

Roy, B., (1992), 'Science de la décision ou science de l'aide à la décision', *Revue Internationale de Systémique*, **6**(5), 497–529.

Schein, E.H. (1991), 'What is culture', in P. J. Frost et al. (ed), *Reframing organizational Culture*, Newbury Park, CA: Sage Publications, pp. 243–53.

Senge, P.M. (1990), *The Fifth Discipline: The Arts and Practice of the Learning Organization*, New York: Currency Doubleday.

Tübke, A. (2003), *Success Factors of Corporate Spin-offs*, Dordrecht: Kluwer Academic Publishers.

Tübke, A. and T. Empson (2002), 'Companies as incubators', *International Journal of Entrepreneurship and Innovation*, **3**(4), 257–64.

Tübke's Internet site on corporate spin-offs, http://www.corporate-spin-offs.com/.

APPENDIX 1:   TABLE OF CASES

	Case A	Case B	Case C	Case D	Case E	Case F	Case G
Date of creation	Aug. 1999	Dec. 1998	Mar. 2000	June 2000	Jan. 2000	Dec. 2000	[c]
Business	WAP services (chat, games, diary . . .)	IP technology (telephony and voice)	Consulting in network engineering and optimization	Streaming technologies (based on MPEG4 standard)	Software for commercial offers on internet	Services	'3D worlds', simulation, geolocalization
Number of entrepreneurs (entrepreneurs from I.M. Group)	4(1)	1(1)	6(6)	7(6)	8(8)	2(2)	2(N/A)
The entrepreneurs' leader: function in I.M. Group/gender	Marketing (Mbile division)/male	R&D/male	R&D (lab. director)/male	R&D (researcher)/Male	R&D (R&D orientation)/males	Commercial dpt. (Mobile division)/male	N/A
Nature of the interest taking; industrial or financial[a]	Financial	Both	Both	Industrial	Both	N/A[d]	Industrial
Technology transfer	Yes	Yes	Yes	Yes	Yes	No	N/A
In business with the I.M. group[b]	Yes	Yes	Lightly	Not intending	Negotiations in progress	Yes (increasing)	Partnership agreement signed
Co-development with I.M. group[b]	Exchanges at a technical level	Lightly	Contract signed	Contract signed	Not intending	Not intending	Agreement signed

Notes:

N/A: not applicable.

[a] The I.M. group has two independent financing structures. The first one is dedicated to industrial interest-taking and is located in the R&D division. The other one is a capital risk fund operating on a large and European scale. In the last fund the I.M. group interest was about 15%.

[b] Situation at the end of the first semester 2001.

[c] This start-up would have to be merged in the start-ups network. The I.M. group took interest in it because of its technological lead on a nascent sector: this operation opened an option for growth in what could be a decisive market in the near future.

[d] This start-up is not a spin-off because the entrepreneurs and their managers did not want to enter in the I.M. group's procedure of spinning-off. We studied this case in order to understand the impact of such a situation on the spinning-off firm and if the further relationships between the start-up and the I.M. Group could be modified. The reader will note that our sample did not include any women. There were actually a few. The only one we got in touch with rejected our interview proposal for reasons she did not want to explain.

APPENDIX 2:   QUESTIONING AND INTERVIEWING

People interviewed:

- For each case, three people were met: the entrepreneur (if there were several of them, the leader of the spin-off project), the manager of the service from which they had spun-off and a responsible member of the main Strategic Business Unit, interested in or impacted by the spinning-off. We also consulted the spin-off cell manager to get his appreciation and interpretation of the spinning-off.
- People in charge of the spin-off policy: the spin-off cell's people, two members of the orientation committee.
- People of the industrial interest-taking service and of the capital risk fund (namely its responsible for business development).
- Several members of internal and external committees.
- Experts in spin-off or firm creation consulting, in financing and in training programmes.

Entrepreneurs	Other interviewed people
Characteristics of the spinning-off (date, nature of supportive measures, length of the process, spinning-off indication, nature of the financing operation, contracts signed or negotiations in progress)	
Quantitative and qualitative data on the relationships between the spin-off and the I.M. group (innovation and business ones)	
Quantitative and qualitative data on the entrepreneur	Impact of the spin-off on commercial and R&D structures in terms of organisation, competencies, learning, affects
Gestation of the project	Development potentialities of the relationships with the start-up
Perception on the spin-off process	

During our work of interviewing and data collecting, we took pieces of information into account at various periods: at the spinning-off time, then 18 months later and at the time of our study.

12. Cultural change from entrepreneurship to intrapreneurship

Iiris Aaltio

INTRODUCTION

Management of innovation and change is an area that creates attention widely: in addition to practitioners and educators it is a central focus in plenty of academic research. As Tushman and Nadler (1996, 135) state: 'there is no executive task more vital and demanding than the sustained management of innovation and change. . . . Companies must adopt innovation as a way of corporate life.' Edgar Schein (1990; 1983; and 1985b) has pointed the central role of founders and owner-managers in creation of innovative organizational culture of enterprises. Galbraight (1996, 161) has compared the operating and innovating organizations and, especially, shows the impact of components like organizational structure, organizational processes, reward systems and Human Resource Practices on innovative organizational culture. Kanter (1988, 172) notes that the innovation process is uncertain and unpredictable, knowledge intensive, controversial, and that it crosses boundaries. She also states that although innovation stems from individual talent and creativity, the organizational context mediates this individual potential and channels it into production. Williams and Yang (1999, 373–91) also discuss theories of creativity and their applications to organizations, pointing to the multiple theoretical debates behind entrepreneurial organizations and innovations.

Even if we have knowledge about entrepreneurial organizations and organizational cultures in general, there is still a lack of knowledge about how entrepreneurial organization cultures develop. There is only limited understanding on managerial issues related to creation and change of entrepreneurial organization cultures. Lack of empirical insights and, more specifically, empirical studies based on longitudinal data are scarce (Davidsson and Wiklund, 2002, 27–28). In this chapter we deal with questions on entrepreneurship and intrapreneurship, and study the cultural change of a business firm that is merged to a bigger company. How to remain entrepreneurial over time and how to fill the cultural gap that the founding entrepreneur leaves in the company are some specific questions addressed in the study.

ENTREPRENEURIAL ORGANIZATION CULTURES

Cultural Debate

Organizational educators and practitioners raised the notion of organizations as 'mini-cultures'. This debate encouraged research that explored the complex factors influencing behaviour within organizations. In particular, the relationships between non-rational factors and multiple-level organizational outcomes were explored, and the focus was on the symbolism of organizational life in general. The first approaches of organizational culture emphasized its invisibility, whereas nowadays multiple methodologies and methods of analysis and interpretations are accepted. Exploring organizational cultures and their gendered nature means making them visible (Aaltio and Mills, 2002). Culture debate opened a way to study organizations as cultures: this means, to profoundly enlighten them, their financial basis, their organizational structures, and their management in terms of culture. Often entrepreneurship and organizing are seen as opposite terms, entrepreneurship emphasizing creativity, enthusiasm and even chaos, and organization suggesting bureaucratic working style, inertia and rationality. However, the terms are interrelated in many ways. Entrepreneurship needs organizing, and organizations need entrepreneurial spirit. In this chapter we explore a cultural transformation process of a business enterprise, especially from the angle of how entrepreneurship remains in the culture over time.

The cultural approach to organizations became popular in the 1980s. Reasons for the emergence of organizational culture studies are manifold. As suggested, there was a need to seek new methods to study organizations and to find 'subjective' concepts to replace the old 'objective' concepts in order to understand organizational essence (Alvesson and Berg, 1988). Culture became a theoretical tool to bridge the traditional micro- and macro-level organizational analysis (Morey and Luthans, 1985, 227–8). In general, internationalization of corporations gave impulses to study cultural aspects of business communication. Nowadays the cultural approach has broadened itself into multiple theoretical discourses; among those is identity and the many approaches that argue for the specificity of cultural concept in differing business firm contexts, like small firms (Trice and Beyer, 1984; Parker, 2000, Alvesson, 2001, Gerzen et al., 1999). In some recent approaches correlations between organizational culture and identity approach are also made (see Uljin, 2001; Parker, 2000).

Organizational culture as a concept derives from anthropology. It is closely linked to particular anthropological approaches and schools. Depending on the approach, the focus on organizational culture phenomena becomes different and each theoretical justification of organizations as cultures acquires a tone of its own. Culture in organizations is created in the same way as culture in general. Working communities are groups of people, unique social formations of a permanent nature, and groupings of individuals (adults), which aim to fulfil an external operational function by means of work. These communities may create a culture of their own, expressed by specific language, values, norms, attitudes, customs, beliefs, and so on. When a shared conception of reality is born within the community, a set of self-evident facts begins to have effect on the behaviour of the members of the organization beyond their individual background. The common history of the working community and the experiences shared by its members form the basis for social adjustment.

The events that take place within the community are controlled by rules, principles or norms, being organizational by nature. The goals of the organization and the system created to achieve those goals are features which make them working communities with an identity of their own, in relation to other communities such as village or family communities.

Business enterprises are financially autonomous and their existence is based on their capability to meet certain social obligations such as payment of taxes. Their existence becomes justified only if they fulfil this social condition legitimately. External institutions have a certain right of disposal regarding such organizations – for example, creditors may declare a private enterprise bankrupt. Their existence itself is contractual and culture-bound. The existence of public administrative organizations, on the other hand, is not in the same way tied to self-financing, but is controlled by a particular system of norms and their legitimization. The working communities of private enterprises and public administration may also differ in relation to their cultures (see Whorton and Whortley, 1981, 357–61). Cultures of private organizations differ from non-profit ones.

In organizations people get together in an 'organized' form for the purpose of doing something together. As Berg (1985, 291–2) notes, they therefore have to reach a mutual understanding about what to do and how to do it. 'Organizing' is the means by which the working communities attempt to achieve their goals, and it may, in this sense, be regarded as a method or tool for the production of work. Leaders in the community interpret reality for the other members and also define the manner of organizing. The organization is bound together by 'organizing' principles (Hosking and Morley, 1991).

Strength of Organizational Cultures: Ideals and Financial Performance

In our attempt to understand more about the uniqueness of organizational cultures, we may now turn to the question of cultural strength. Geertz (1973, 144) shows how stability serves as a basis for a strong culture:

culture and social structure will . . . be seen to be capable of a wide range of modes of integration with one another . . . a case common only in societies which have been stable over such an extended time as to make possible a close adjustment between social and cultural aspects. In most societies, where change is characteristic rather than an abnormal occurrence, we shall expect to find more or less radical discontinuities between the two.

Clans are particularly strong cultures. They emerge if there is a strong social memory. A long history, stable membership, and locality of circumstances encourage their development (Alvesson and Lindqvist, 1990, 3).

From an ethnographic standpoint, a community may create a strong culture if it has been in existence for a sufficiently long time to develop a unique culture, and if its members have lived in the community for a long period of time (Conklin, 1968, 172; Redfield, 1952). The people of the community begin to share a complex understanding of the world, which becomes taken for granted and is labelled by a language of its own. A strong culture is one in which the actions and speech of the people in the community are highly influenced by its values and norms. In order to be able to understand such a culture, its language and its typical activities, an outsider must find his way into its specific, strong world of meanings (Wilkins and Ouchi, 1983, 469). Organizations may also act as clans. The uniqueness of an organizational culture derives from the possibility of organizations to learn and to utilize a collective social memory. Individuals learn to understand the special system of symbols used by the organization and apply it themselves to predict the actions of other members of the culture.

There are certain differences between organizations on one hand, and communities, such as villages, on the other. Formerly, local communities such as factory neighbourhoods also had a type of intense, homogeneous culture, which resembled village culture. Crafts were handed down from parents to children and the factory environment also had a profound influence on all other experiences besides work. The social status became permanent. Villages are static communities, whereas organizations may change, emerge, or die in unpredictable ways. Organizations may be set up, closed down, cut up, and transferred from one place to another. They may be bought and sold. Such actions will change their culture and diminish the possibility that the culture could grow strong. Several studies (for example Napier, 1986; Navahandi and Malenkzadeh, 1988) have dealt with the cultural integration of two organizations in a merger, called 'acculturation'. This may result in the weaker organizational culture being assimilated by the stronger culture in the merger.

As a whole, social structures in organizations tend to be more liable to change than those in villages or other stable communities. This might lead to the possibility that organizational cultures are likely to be weaker than the cultures of more stable communities. The role of a strong culture in the financial profitability of a firm has aroused interest in organizational culture. It is assumed that there is a particular correlation between a strong organizational culture and good financial performance. A strong culture is related to a high commitment by the organizational members. The commitment to one's work has to do with a sense of uniqueness, the feeling that one's own working community has specific, desirable characteristics which other communities lack (for example Kanter, 1972). She argues that an individual who feels commitment, feels a correspondence between his/her own set of values and those of his/her working community. A strong, unique organizational culture creates commitment.

Soeters (1986, 299–312) argues that there is a correspondence between successful companies and social movements, which are based on a strong culture and high commitment of the members. He refers to the implicit sociological theory underlying the work by Peters and Watermann (1982) entitled *In Search of Excellence*, which identifies successful business enterprises with social movements. The creation of culture within a working community can also be illustrated by giving explanatory force to the role of the organizational system. It exerts control over social relationships, for example, by the division of duties or by physical nearness or distance (Parker, 2000, 9–29). Based on this type of organizational 'map', the organization forms a frame of reference for its members.

Leadership has specific importance in the creation of organizational culture. Smircich and Morgan (1982, 257–73) examine leadership and the role of the leader in the development of the meaning world of an organization. Leaders structure the world of collectively gained experience by providing it with meanings. When an enterprise is set up, it is the founder especially who influences the culture being created in the community through his or her personality and operating principles (Schein, 1985a and b). The role of values in the development of organizational strategies is considered important and has been a focus of study in a number of cases (Aaltio-Marjosola and Takala, 2000). Culture, the special world of meanings shared by a community, evolves as a dialectic process through interaction between leaders and their subordinates. In a sense, reality is created in these contexts. The opportunity for leadership arises only if there are people who are prepared to give up the possibility of defining their own reality themselves. Legitimacy has a central role in this act of submission; it is important that the right of the leaders to define reality is regarded as legitimate and justified (Smircich and Morgan, 1982, 257–73).

Intrapreneurship and the Meaning of Work

Intrapreneurship is an issue raised in organization theory especially in the 1980s (Kanter, 1972; 1983; 1989), and Pinchot (1985). Intrapreneurs are defined as entrepreneurs working within an existing organization. In addition to the new ideas that intrapreneurship presents, its disciplines are in many ways related to the previously written literature about organizational behaviour, motivation theories and leadership. Intrapreneurial literature deals with themes such as how individuals and groups become intrapreneurial in a company. Another central theme is how the organizational culture is able to support evolving intrapreneurship.

Motivation and the meaning of work are at the heart of organizational behaviour research. However, not much explicit work is done on relating entrepreneurial organization culture on topics that arise there. Entrepreneurial people are those who establish enterprises, carry on innovations, being a crucial part of any economic system. Furthermore, the motivation for high achievement and the pursuit of opportunity are considered essential in entrepreneurial actions (seen in the classical studies of McClelland, 1961). Intrapreneurship emphasizes innovativeness, initiative, risk-taking and diligence in the same way as entrepreneurship (Hisrich, 1990), but without ownership of the company. Maybe the most crucial idea in intrapreneurship is the claim that the employees of large enterprises are able and willing to act with the same kind of enthusiasm as entrepreneurs in their own companies. The terms 'intrapreneurship' and 'individual initiative', therefore are close to each other. Similarities between entrepreneurs and intrapreneurs exist also in terms of innovativeness.

In addition to the theories of work motivation, the meaning of work may serve as an important framework for understanding intrapreneurship. Although being a psychological concept that serves as a tool to understand individual work orientation, its origins are in the philosophy of science. According to Heidegger, the creation of meaning is crucial to the ways in which a person orientates himself for the future (Heidegger, 1972). The debate on whether a happy life and a meaningful life are synonyms reached the conclusion that they are not, but that meaning has something to do with sorrow, suffering and disarray and, in the end, with death itself (Sievers, 1994). If a person loses the meaning of life outside himself – as may happen in the case of mental diseases – he will note that his thoughts and wishes become completely disconnected from society and the surrounding world. A person's subjective world then becomes socially unmeaning, because it is not reflected back from the outer world.

It is often argued that strong organizational cultures create circumstances in which the organizational members experience their work as especially meaningful (for example Peters and Watermann, 1982). Such cultures are based on a high rate of achievement among the personnel and a high commitment towards work – both of which are elements of intrapreneurship. Strong organizational cultures have been criticized especially because of their inability to change (for critiques about strong organizational cultures, see Kunda, 1992, and Soeters, 1986). They may also act as hegemonistic communities, which repress their members' initiatives in the long run.

If what we mean by intrapreneurship in general is highly motivated behaviour in an organization, we should note that motivation theory itself has been criticized as having become a functionalistic instrument for an enterprise, used as a surrogate for meaning in work. As Sievers (1994) argues, motivation theory was developed at a time when work itself was losing its meaning. Motivation thus may become only a means to trigger achievement and efficiency in companies, without questioning the meaning of work for the individual. Research on motivation also gives only partial answers to our understanding about work motivation at the individual level, because it is often based on assumptions about standard or average people. This is true especially if the studies are based on quantitative analysis: we find answers to questions about how motivation is generally formed, but no answers concerning the individuality of the person or the organization studied.

There is also criticism of the emphasis on the individual instead of social issues when defining entrepreneurship and intrapreneurship. The social dimensions of entrepreneurship may become neglected, and entrepreneurship is not studied in relation to its social context. Merger processes and the reasons for their failure have often been studied, with the main emphasis on the difficulties that are caused by the cognitive processes of individual people in the enterprise. Schemata do not change at once, and there are many emotional obstacles as well. In general, this separation of 'people' as soft facts and 'organizational effectiveness' as hard facts does not offer a very helpful framework for understanding these processes (Cartwright and Cooper, 1992; Gerzen et al., 1998). We need an approach that combines the micro-level – the individuals – and the macro-level – individuals in the organizational culture context.

HOW THE CULTURE WAS TRANSFORMED: ILLUSTRATIONS FROM THE FENIX CASE

Ethnographic Study Design

Empirical data for this study is based on an analysis made in three phases: between 1966 and 1989 (Aaltio-Marjosola, 1991), 1993 (Aaltio-Marjosola, 1996) and in 2000. The object of the study is the FENIX organization, a business firm founded by an entrepreneur, merged to a bigger company and later faced with several other changes in ownership. The first part of the company's life cycle is defined and characterized by the personality, skills and authority of one person – the entrepreneur. In its second state of development, FENIX was sold to a large enterprise, and the earlier working patterns and habits, which were closely related to the personality and style of the entrepreneur, now had to change. This second stage of development called for intrapreneurial – no longer entrepreneurial – skills.

The first part of the data was gathered in 1987–89, three years after the acquisition. Later on the company was sold to an investment company in 1997. Ethnographically oriented fieldwork methods were employed, focused on collecting material on which to base the analysis of the corporate culture and its change in the company. The data consists mainly of material collected in interviews with 52 persons. In addition to the interview material, stories and anecdotes were obtained by means of a questionnaire. Other sources of data include minutes of meetings as well as observations made by the author in a number of meetings and on informal occasions such as during coffee breaks. The second part of the data was gathered in 1993 by interviewing 25 persons employed at FENIX, who now worked in two factories. The aim was to examine how the cultural change in the company had progressed so far, and to compare the findings of the first part of the study to this new material. The third part of the data was gathered in 2000, by interviewing 38 organization members in the firm. The data also consists of other sources of material like minutes of meetings, organizational charts, advertisement material and visible cultural artefacts in the company, like buildings, architecture and so on.

Interview questions presented were:

- What has happened in this firm since the mereger? Describe any possible changes in the enterprise as a whole and in your own job.
- What is your present job? With whom do you have contacts? How often do you take part in meetings or get-togethers?
- Describe the year preceding the change in ownership.
- What is it like to work in this firm? What kind of expectations did you have when you joined the firm?
- What kind of contacts do you have with the current management and owners?
- What was the owner-manager like? How much did you personally have to do with him and in what connections?
- Tell about the formal meetings held in the firm and about the informal events outside working hours.
- Do you remember any anecdotes or stories about the 'old times' or the present?
- Have you often thought of changing your job? Why you have not? Are you planning to change your job?
- What would you like to change here? How do you view the future?

The interviewed people were also asked if there are any stories about success, anecdotes or jokes that they think are important at the present time. Some of those were collected and used in the cultural analysis as well.

Findings of the Study

The creation of the earlier culture of FENIX had been closely connected to the owner-manager (here referred to as VB) and his ways of operating. FENIX had been a very entrepreneurial company in terms of structural arrangements and the cultural patterns of work. Strong emphasis was placed on initiative, spontaneity and innovativeness. After two years of implementation of the organizational change programme, the principles of the programme had taken over a central position in the 'self-evidences' guiding daily work. The new self-evidences regarding 'correct' practices were now concerned with the ways in which a normal, modern, productive firm operates and with 'how we should operate to be normal'. There were, however, some complaints that the new culture was bureaucratic, even if the legitimacy of the new principles was not questioned. Although, with certain feelings of cynicism and depression, the entrepreneurial culture had started to turn towards a formal 'culture of rules'.

At the same time, the previously unique and distinctive organizational culture began to lose its intensity. The unique traits of the former culture had created a specific character for the firm as a workplace, by which it could be clearly distinguished from other firms. A change in these traits simultaneously meant a weakening of the organizational culture with its specific working habits. The original culture contained a strong social memory and well-established social networks and norms that guided the activities. In the new situation there was general agreement about the new principles which were to be followed as well as about the new cultural set of values on which they were based, but these did not have similar importance in the experience world of the organizational members as the old culture used to have. The new principles were followed, they did not form a part of a strong culture specific to FENIX; their legitimacy relied on the idea that 'this is how everyone operates'. The antagonistic, nonconformist corporate culture had largely collapsed. This process of change in the organizational culture of FENIX can be simplified by calling it a change from a strong entrepreneurial culture to a weak culture of rules.

The main organizational change that was made at FENIX was the discontinuation of the R&D department and company headquarters in Helsinki. All related activities were moved into the firm's two manufacturing plants (referred to here as Factory A and Factory B). Both factories had to begin to search for new identities based on their special products: Factory A was now to concentrate on ski poles and other leisure products (surfing masts, golf clubs, and so on) and Factory B on products made of hard plastic composite (ladders, shelves, army products, garages, knitting machines, and so on). For Factory A this meant focusing on products which were very central to the general image of FENIX and thus formed an easy starting point, whereas for Factory B it meant starting with products that were not as well-known or meaningful as a basis for the identity of the factory. In terms of profits, 1993 was expected to be the first year of positive result after the merger.

Feedback and incentive systems also were found to need development at both factories. This was very well expressed in one of the interviews, where a female worker in the packing department reported that she could not understand how a few workers at the department could actually remain in their job without doing anything during the day – 'running at minimum capacity'. This woman longed for even a small extra bonus for the intense effort she made for the company. According to the product manager at Factory A,

> there are many kinds of people here, a great many of them work enthusiastically, but a small minority not so enthusiastically. The ones who are not motivated to work think that the big owner company will take care of them anyway. Usually you will not get feedback and encouragement from your manager, but when you succeed you know it yourself, and sometimes the customers give you encouragement, and good or bad feedback.

In summary, it was possible to see signs of a new, team-oriented work pattern in the company, especially at Factory A. The gap that had appeared after the owner-manager left the company in 1986 had gradually been compensated for by new practices.

The preliminary data analysis from 2000 still shows a shift from the bureaucracy towards a more intrapreneurial organization culture. Technological innovation, however, as a guiding principle, has lost its attractiveness and impact, and marketing, as well as quality aspects of innovations are emphasized today. Instead of the early history ideals of 'innovativeness', 'spontaneous working-style', 'sense of togetherness' and 'risk-taking', ideals such as 'thorough work', 'independency', 'flexible', 'professional', 'communicative', 'committed' and 'willing to learn' have taken root in the company values. There is a shift towards individuals who are team-work oriented, but who are managers of their own professional capacity; and the clan-culture time, when people were very dependent on the owner-manager, and later, felt the gap after his disappearance, is gone. The CIO of the company is called 'a big Boss', and he is appreciated as a professional, whose background is principally in marketing and sales.

The umbrella kind of guiding principles of organizational culture in the 35 years have slowly transformed. It contains features from the earlier phases, but, in addition, it has changed over time. The morality, the rules, the principles have undergone change, when teamwork has gained an important role in the company culture instead of an individual technical innovation orientation. How people interpret the right of existence to themselves and to each other outlines the relations between the subordinates and the managers, clients and the organizational members, the nature and the work in the organization. The firm has grown from a very technically oriented company, producing leisure-time products like ski poles and highly specialized sports goods, towards even more everyday sport products. Walking-poles, for instance, are produced on a large scale nowadays, and they were shown in one of the latest James Bond movies. There are success stories again in the company.

As the case illustration shows, technical innovations are needed through the life-cycle of the firm. How these technical innovations are promoted, stems partly from the cultural practices present at the company. The organizational culture of the company becomes vulnerable at times when the entrepreneurship orientated phase ends, such as when the entrepreneur retires as in the case study, and new innovative practices and leadership are required instead. Evidently the cultural transformation needs time to be successful, as seen in this case. The area where major changes are needed are 1) the new team-work orientated style is needed instead of the entrepreneur-centred style; 2) new intrapreneurial practices are needed and team-members should also take individual responsibility and initiative without entrepreneurial authority behind them.

FINAL REMARKS

The study findings show that entrepreneurship can evolve into intrapreneurship over time in a business firm. This needs profound cultural transformations in the way people are used to working together at the company and in the way they use their initiative. This does not happen without managerial efforts; it takes time, and it is a complicated, iterative process where success in new product development, innovative teamwork spirit, and marketing efforts are all important components. Based on the study findings, we may even ask, does the existence of the entrepreneur sometimes exclude the existence of the intrapreneurs. In family enterprises this is especially important as well, because the close relations between the family members might encourage or discourage entrepreneurship. The effects of an entrepreneurial management style are not only encouraging but, paradoxically, they also might create a dependence on authority. Entrepreneurial spirit in the company culture is worth saving, but it often needs transformation. If the manager-owned enterprise is able to educate good intrapreneurs, this transformation is easier to handle.

REFERENCES

Aaltio, Iiris and Albert J. Mills (2002), *Gender, Identity and the Culture of Organizations*, Routledge (forthcoming).

Aaltio-Marjosola, I. (1991), *Cultural Change in a Business Enterprise. Studying a Major Organizational Change and Its Impact on Culture*, Acta Academiae Oeceonomicae Helsingiensis, Series A, no. 80.

Aaltio-Marjosola, I. (1994), 'From a "grand story" to multiple narratives? Studying an organizational change project', *Journal of Organizational Change Management*, **7**(5), 56–67.

Aaltio-Marjosola, I. (1996), '*From Entrepreneurship to Intrapreneurship*', in M. Koiranen and M. Koskela (eds), Conference Proceedings RISE'96, *Research on Innovative Strategies and Entrepreneurship*, Publications of the University of Jyväskylä, Department of Economics, pp. 25–35.

Aaltio-Marjosola, Iiris and Tuomo Takala (2000), 'Charismatic leadership, manipulation and the complexity of organizational life', *Journal of Workplace Learning*, **12**(4), 146–58.

Alvesson, Mats (2001), *Understanding Organizational Culture,* London: SAGE.

Alvesson Mats and Per Olof Berg (1988), *Företagskultur och organisationssymbolism, Utveckling, teoretiska perspektiv och aktuell debatt*, Lund: Studentlitteratur.

Alvesson, Mats and Lars Lindqvist (1990), 'Transaction costs, clans and corporate culture', paper presented at the conference in Vaasa, 22–24 August.

Berg, Per-Olof (1985), 'Organization change as a symbolic transformation process', in Peter J. Frost, Larry F. Moore, Meryl Reis Louis, Craig C. Lundberg and Joanne Martin (eds), *Organizational Culture*, Beverly Hills: Sage, pp. 181–99.

Cartwright S. and C.L. Cooper (1992), *Mergers and Acquisitions: The Human Factor*, Oxford: Butterworth-Heinemann.

Conklin, H. (1968), 'Ethnography', in D.L. Sills (ed.), *International Encyclopedia of the Social Sciences*, Vol. 5, New York: Free Press.

Davidsson, P. and J. Wiklund (2002), 'Conceptual and empirical challenges in the study of firm growth' in Donald L. Sexton and Hans Landström (eds), *Handbook of Entrepreneurship*, Oxford: Blackwell Publishing Ltd, pp. 26–44.

Galbraight, Jay R. (1996), 'Designing the innovating organization', in Ken Starkey (ed.), *How Organizations Learn*, London: International Thomson Business Press, pp. 156–82.

Geertz, Clifford (1973), *The Interpretation of Cultures*, New York: Basic Books Inc.

Gerzen, Martine C., Anne-Marie Soderberg and Jens Erik Torp (eds) (1998), *Cultural Dimensions of International Mergers and Acquisitions*, Berlin: De Gruyter.

Heidegger, M. (1972), *Sein und Seit*, Tubingen: Max Niemeyer Verlag.

Hisrich, R.D. (1990), 'Entrepreneurship/Intrapreneurship', *American Psychologist*, **45**(2), 209–22.

Hosking, D.M. and I. Morley (1991), *A Social Psychology of Organizing. People, Processes and Contexts*, UK: Harvester Wheatsheaf.

Kanter, Rosabeth Moss (1972), *Commitment and Community: Communes and Utopias in Sociological Perspective*, Cambridge, MA: Harvard University Press.

Kanter, Rosabeth Moss (1983), *The Change Masters. Corporate Entrepreneurs at Work*, New York: Unwin Paperbacks.

Kanter, Rosabeth Moss (1988), 'When a thousand flowers bloom: structural, collective, and social conditions for innovation in organizations', in B.M. Staw and L.L.

Cummings (eds), *Research in Organizational Behaviour*, Vol 10, London: JAI, pp. 123–67.

Kanter, R.M. (1989), *When Giants Learn to Dance. Mastering the Challenge for Strategy, Management and Careers in the 1990s*, New York: Simon and Schuster.

Kunda, Gideon (1992), *Engineering Culture: Control and Commitment in a High-tech Organization*, Philadelphia: Temple University Press.

McClelland, D. (1961), *The Achieving Society*, New York: Free Press.

Morey, Nancy C. and Fred Luthans (1985), 'Refining the displacement of culture and the use of scenes and themes in organizational studies', *Academy of Management Review*, **10**(2), 219–29.

Napier, Nancy K. (1986), 'Mergers and acquisitions, human resource issues and outcomes: a review and suggested typology', *Journal of Management Studies*, **26**(3), May, 271–89.

Navahandi, Afsaneh and Ali R. Malenkzadeh (1988), 'Acculturation in mergers and acquisitions', *Academy of Management Review*, **13**(1), 79–90.

Parker, Martin (2000), *Organizational Culture and Identity*, London: Sage.

Peters, T.J. and R.H. Watermann (1982), *In Search of Excellence: Lessons from America's Best Run Companies*, New York: Harper.

Pinchot, Gifford (1985), *Intrapreneurship*, New York: Harper & Row.

Redfield, Robert (1952), *The Little Community*, Chicago: University of Chicago Press.

Schein, Edgar (1983), 'The role of founder in creating organizational culture', *Organizational Dynamics*, Summer, pp. 13–28.

Schein, Edgar (1985a), *Organizational Culture and Leadership*, San Francisco: Jossey-Bass.

Schein, Edgar H. (1985b), 'How culture forms, develops and changes', in Ralph H. Kilmann, Mary J. Saxton, Roy Serpa et al. (eds), *Gaining Control of the Corporate Culture*, San-Francisco: Jossey-Bass.

Schein, Edgar H. (1990), 'Organizational culture', *American Psychologist*, **45**(2), 109–19.

Sievers, Burkhard (1994), 'Work, death and life itself', *Essays on Management and Organization*, Berlin: Walter de Gryiter.

Smircich, Linda and Gareth Morgan (1982), 'Leadership: the management of meaning', *The Journal of Applied Behavioral Science*, **18**(3), 257–73.

Soeters, Joseph (1986), 'Excellent companies as social movements', *Journal of Management Studies*, **23**(3), May, 299–312.

Trice, Harrison M. and Janice M. Beyer (1984), 'Studying organizational cultures through rites and ceremonials', *Academy of Management Review*, **9**(4), 653–69.

Tushman, Michael and David Nadler (1996), 'Organizing and innovation', in Ken Starkey (ed.), *How Organizations Learn*, London: International Thomson Business Press, pp. 135–56.

Ulijn, J. and Martin Parker (2001), 'Organizational culture and identity', *Organization Studies*, **22**(6), 107–22.

Whorton, Joseph W. and John A. Whorley (1981), 'A perspective on the challenge of public management: environmental parcedox and organizational culture', *Academy of Management Review*, **6**(3), 357–61.

Wilkins, Alan and William G. Ouchi (1983), 'Efficient cultures: exploring the relationship between culture and organizational performance', *Administrative Science Quarterly*, **28**, 468–81.

Williams, Wendy M. and Lana T. Yang (1999), 'Organizational creativity', in Robert J. Sternberg (ed.), *Handbook of Creativity*, USA: Cambridge University Press, pp. 373–92.

13. Gender and sector effects on Finnish rural entrepreneurs' culture: some educational implications

Seija Mahlamäki-Kultanen

INTRODUCTION

Rural municipalities and villages all over the world, including Finland, are losing their younger inhabitants and enterprises at the same time as bigger centres (towns and cities) keep growing (Cecora, 2000). Sustaining the population of rural areas by increasing the number of rural enterprises is a big challenge for vocational education and entrepreneurs. According to Finnish Law, each Finnish vocational curriculum includes entrepreneurship education, and a vocational degree should guarantee the competence for independent business ownership. The restructuring of the Finnish vocational education system meant that at least 20 credit units of work-based learning and everyday contact with entrepreneurs are included in the 120 credit units of the vocational study programme. This study sets out to see what the entrepreneurial culture in Finnish rural areas is like and whether it gives cultural room for the young students from vocational institutes to become entrepreneurs. Basically, vocational education is culture-bound and the cooperation between educational institutes and entrepreneurs depends largely on mutual understanding of each other. The methodology used is qualitative triangulation; cultural narratives, metaphor analysis and theory-based rating of the sectoral business cultures according to the theory of cultural differences by Hofstede (2001) are used.

CULTURE AND CULTURAL DIMENSIONS

According to Hofstede (2001), culture is the collective programming of the mind. Still, not everyone in a given culture adheres to the same dominant thought pattern. Hofstede found four cultural dimensions originally from an international questionnaire study of IBM employees, which asked people about an imaginary ideal job. The dimensions are called power distance, individualism/collectivism, masculinity/feminity and uncertainty avoidance.

Power distance refers to the degree of inequality within a society and the way the society's members have accepted or reconciled this inequality. On an individual level, power distance is the measure for interpersonal power between two people as perceived and accepted by the subordinate. Individualism/collectivism refers to the relationship between the individual and the collectivity in a given society. It also expresses the culture's tolerance for and approval of individual thought. Individuals in countries with low individualism are often extremely concerned with security and, by extension, doing the 'right' things and not taking risks. The masculinity/feminity refers to the society's determination of how much polarisation there should be between men and women in their socialised roles. The predominant socialisation pattern is for men to be more assertive and women more nurturing. Moreover, masculinity/feminity refers to the value a culture places on assertiveness and material success versus relationship maintenance and high quality of life. Uncertainty avoidance refers to the collective level of tolerance for uncertainty or ambiguity. Societies have ways of reducing the anxiety by avoiding it and creating pseudo-certainty through rules, rituals and religions (Hofstede, 2001). Hofstede's cultural dimensions and respective indexes from one to one hundred have been used successfully in numerous studies on the national, corporate and also individual level on different populations and work organisations, but not on rural entrepreneurs, who mostly do not employ many other people but instead work alone. Hofstede's (2001) results for Finland are presented in Table 13.1.

According to Hill (2000), the common belief about the Finns' lack of personal confidence might seem to be related to the national reasonably high uncertainty avoidance index. The Finns compensate for this lack of personal confidence through thorough data gathering and processing and trusting 'the system' learned through age and experience. Hofstede's work is sometimes criticised for making the assumption that geographical and cultural boundaries coincide. However, the Finnish population is dominated by one cultural group with a small Swedish-speaking minority.

Table 13.1   Hofstede's cultural dimensions of Finland

Dimension scale 0–100	Power distance	Individualism	Masculinity	Uncertainty avoidance
Index for the Finnish national culture	35	63	26	59
Rank order among 50 nations and 3 areas	46	17	47	31

Finnish Entrepreneurial Culture

Peltomäki (2002) recently analysed Finnish literature, books, poems and journals from the 16th century. He searched for the historical roots and the soul and essence of Finnish entrepreneurship. He concludes that Finnish business owners are allowed to try, but not to succeed. They can earn their living well and be business owners but not succeed better than their neighbour. They should be humble and 'not move ahead too visibly, because other people might get worried'. Hyrsky (1999) describes entrepreneurship in Finland as being not too highly appreciated until the early 1990s. He continues by saying that it was not a mainstream activity and entrepreneurs were often regarded as rather exceptional and somewhat obsessive individuals who persevered against the odds. Entrepreneurial venturing was not deemed to be a very prestigious or popular pursuit, and neither financially nor socially rewarding. A successful venture might even have invited a begrudging attitude, one's peers resenting one's success. Moreover, an unsuccessful endeavour may have caused embarrassment or ridicule (Hyrsky, 1999).

After the economic depression of the early 1990s, the Finnish economy began to change rather rapidly. The year 1990 marked the start of the worst recession in Finland in the last 50 years. The traditional large-scale trade with the former Soviet Union collapsed at a time when an international recession further weakened Western exports. The growth figures of the late 1980s turned down sharply and signalled the start of a steep economic decline which left in its wake very high levels of unemployment (from 3.5 per cent in 1990 to 20 per cent in July 1995) and a financial crisis for the state. Against this background, drastic changes in society and the economy were needed to stimulate business growth and create employment. The ensuing major downsizing of the public sector and the restructuring of the industrial sector led to the re-discovery of the importance of small-scale economic activities. This was expected to result in a widespread industriousness, regeneration and national recovery. In the midst of the emerging importance of small business activity, the terms 'entrepreneurship' and 'entrepreneur' have started to thrive as catchwords in the political and social arena (Hyrsky, 1999). Still, according to the latest Global Entrepreneurship Monitor, the Finns have almost the least motivation to become entrepreneurs even though there is the potential and competence for it (Arenius et al., 2001). Finland is a country with low masculinity index as shown in Table 13.1, which certainly has a lot to do with its generally low entrepreneurial activity.

Metaphors and Culture

A metaphor is a figure of speech, a contrasting concept used instead of the literal expression (Soskice, 1985). Metaphors are used in speech as well as in formal written texts. Metaphors are deeply rooted in the basic assumptions of the culture and value system of its people. Metaphors are also effective, economical and deep in nature (Lakoff and Johnson, 1980; Ogborn and Martins, 1996). Metaphors are ways for an individual to show that he or she belongs to a certain group of people with the same cultural meanings and beliefs. These cultures and subcultures can be, for example, vocational sectors. Of course, all the people in the same field do not share absolutely the same values and beliefs, and they are constantly both maintained and changed (Lakoff and Johnson, 1980). The significance of metaphors in the description, analysis and realisation of cultural change is great (Marshak, 1993; Luechauer and Shulman, 1998). Metaphors are used unconsciously, and their influence on thoughts and actions is equally imperceptible.

Culture and metaphors are both holistic in nature. It is difficult for a member of any culture consciously to analyse their own culture, and comparison makes the differences between cultures and also one's own culture more visible. Typically cultural metaphors used by people living in the same culture form a logical system. For example spatial metaphors, which express physical positions, are very important in the language of leadership. The leaders can be described as being above their staff and the staff under their leader (Lakoff and Johnson, 1980). Metaphors affect our language and thought, but also our behaviour. Typically, however, people do not realise it, which is one of the explanations for the efficiency of metaphors. Metaphors can express ideas in a meaningful way. They not only express something, they also maintain it (for example, organisations) and help people to understand a culture and the functions in it. Education is basically communication. People tend to arrange their life and thought into meaningful wholes and systems. By using metaphors people can make their own identity understandable and somehow stable. This is the way that people learn who they are and also teach their identity to others. 'This is the way people like us tend to speak about things' (Beavis and Thomas, 1996). Metaphors are a logical frame of reference for people to realise and understand culture. At the same time, however, metaphors effectively hide some aspects of it. Some scientists argue about whether metaphors are real science. At the same time, all scientific paradigms develop their own concepts, which very often are purely metaphorical in nature (Clegg and Gray, 1996). Study of entrepreneurial metaphors, both international and Finnish, has been carried out in Finland by Professor Koiranen (1995) from the University of Jyväskylä and his colleague Hyrsky (1999). By taking into account their studies in entrepreneurial research with metaphors, I have developed the methodology for this study with an emphasis on qualitative interpretation and the entrepreneurship educational implications of metaphors. Metaphors and their critical reflection are strongly recommended for career counselling by Amundson (1997), Vance (1996) and Chen (1998) and for entrepreneurship education by Gundry and Kickull (1996).

RESEARCH METHODOLOGY AND DATA

The study methodology is based on method-triangulation; the analysis of metaphors and narratives is used as well as the rating of business sectoral culture according to Hofstede's cultural dimensions on the basis of open qualitative interview data. The level of cultural analysis is the sector. Metaphors are an ontologically and epistemologically grounded research methodology because they are an inevitable part of being a human, communicating and giving meaning to life in general (Lakoff and Johnson, 1980). The metaphors used by entrepreneurs about themselves and their work show how they view themselves. Metaphors refer to the innermost layer of the cultural onion of Hofstede (2001), but they also refer to the outer layers of it, like myths and norms.

The research questions of this study are:

1.   What is the rural entrepreneurial culture like in Finland?
2.   How does it differ according to entrepreneurial sector and gender?
3.   Are the general findings of Hofstede about Finnish national culture valid and equal across rural entrepreneurial sectors and gender?
4.   What kind of entrepreneurship educational implications does the Finnish rural entrepreneurial culture have?

The open qualitative data for the hermeneutic analysis was collected in two separate development projects. In the first, nine business owners from the field of private nursing homes were interviewed with an open qualitative approach in 1999. This pilot study is covered in more detail in Mahlamäki-Kultanen et al. (2001). The rest of the interviews were carried out in cooperation with six rural vocational institutes in 2000–2001. The process is also reported in separate articles (Mahlamäki-Kultanen, 2001a; 2001b; 2002). A total of 146 Finnish business owners were carefully selected from ten business sectors, which later proved to have cultural subsectors. The criteria for selecting the sample were that the chosen fields of business ownership were regarded as important areas for the future in each college, and the business owners were active and potentially cooperative with the vocational institutes. This is why the sample size varies somewhat. The saturation point of the results affected the sample size. The entrepreneurs were typically middle-aged although the exact age was not asked. The 10 vocational teachers from related professional fields informed the entrepreneurs thoroughly about the interview themes and vocational curricula and carried out the interviews just after that. The themes in the interviews covered very broadly the being, and the upbringing of, an entrepreneur from a typical sixteen-year-old student entering initial vocational secondary level studies in cooperation with the entrepreneurs and the local vocational institutes. The interview themes were:

1. Background history, moments of success, difficulties encountered and current situation of the business owner and the business;
2. Future vision and competence needs in the future;
3. Expectations of students while in vocational education and after graduating;
4. Evaluation of the vocational curriculum of the field in question;
5. Attitudes towards, experiences from and wishes concerning work-based learning of the young students in vocational education;
6. The image and experiences of the local vocational institute.

All the interviews were carried out at the sites of the enterprises to get as authentic an atmosphere and as open data as possible. The interviews typically lasted about one to two hours. It was not especially suggested that the entrepreneurs should produce any metaphors but they rather used them in their original discourse. All the interviews were transcribed verbatim. The transcribed data was then analysed and reflected on in cooperation with the teachers who carried out the interviews. The purpose was to validate the interpretations from both professional and cultural viewpoints. The emerging ideas and assumptions about each field of business ownership were member-checked by the teachers. The analysis of metaphors was then carried out. That was preceded by a phase of careful factual and referential coding for cultural meanings, including the metaphors naturally appearing in the data, utilising Nvivo 1.3 qualitative data analysis software (Kelle, 1998). The interpretations were checked and validated by another researcher. The cultural meanings were interpreted holistically, also taking into account the literal expressions of the people interviewed and knowledge of their background. This study concentrates on the culture carried by the metaphorical expressions, although the facts provide understanding and scientific accuracy to the interpretation. The facts and literal expressions were quite consistent with the metaphorical data although often slightly more positive. The metaphors were retrieved from the data according to different background variables and each context, to find a culturally meaningful way for analysis. That proved to be the rural entrepreneurship sector. The next phase of the analysis, as well as the first way to present the results, was the construction of narratives from each business sector to reduce the large amount of data, to find the core cultural thinking and root metaphors. A collection of original metaphors from entrepreneurs' natural speech is embedded in the text. On the basis of the rich data it was also possible for the author to rate the sectoral cultures according to Hofstede's cultural dimensions to apply and test the theory with qualitative data. A rough scale ranging from 1 (= very low) to 5 (= very high) was used. The power distance index was rated separately 1) in general and 2) for the relationship between the young vocational student and the rural entrepreneur, because there was a striking difference between these scores in most entre-preneurial sectors. This kind of a difference was not present for the other dimensions of Hofstede. The ratings were multiplied by 20 to make them comparable with the original Hofstedian scale. The original quantitative scale from 1 to 100 would have been too detailed for the qualititative data.

The entrepreneurs in the study were those with whom cooperation is going to continue in other ways and this long-lasting relationship between people partly guarantees the quality and trustworthiness of the qualitative data. More than three years was spent in collecting, analysing, reflecting on and making use of the interview data and results. Practice and careful reflection enhance the credibility and reliability of the results. Most of the interviewing teachers in this study, and also the author, have a rural family entrepreneur background themselves. This subjective stance should be taken into account when consid-ering the results and interpretations. Subjectivity is inevitable, necessary and it enhances understanding, but it can also narrow perceptions. A theory is not the formulation of some discovered aspect of a pre-existing reality 'out there'. Theories are interpretations made from given perspectives as adopted or researched by the researchers. One way to enhance the credibility of the inter-pretation is to describe the method of analysis as exactly as possible and to use *in-vivo* expressions of the people (Strauss and Corbin, 1995).

RESULTS

To start the presentation, cultural narratives are first displayed to call to the readers' minds some of the nuanced cultural features of entrepreneurial sectors.

Agriculture

There were two differing and competing cultures among the farmers inter-viewed, a 'success culture' and a 'hopeless culture'.

Success Culture

Finland has always been a bird's nest, but it is not that any more. Being a farmer means total commitment to the job. Each entrepreneur is the architect of one's own fortune. You have to cut the unproductive branches of the trees. Vocational teachers should not need to ride with stones in their sleigh, because really reluctant students will never manage in the profession. We have to be prepared for the day when 50 million people from Central Europe start to want fresh and unpolluted food from our country. Then we will go up with the speed of a rapid elevator like the ICT people.

Hopeless Culture

> Most of us have just been driven to this field of entrepreneurship. We work by
> ourselves, with the family and sometimes the neighbours and other slaves helping
> us. In the last few years I have felt hopeless. This EU time is quite controversial
> from the viewpoint of an entrepreneur. It gives you no benefit from trying anything.
> It is like pretending to be an entrepreneur. It is somehow bitter to answer my son's
> questions. He questions whether there is any possibility in this, whether it is worth
> trying to take cattle. The cattle have already left all the farms nearby and so will
> ours also do.

Service Sector

There has been an astonishing number and variety of entrepreneurial cultures
in the different service sectors and, in particular, home economics. For many
people they all mean the same thing, and have their roots somehow in the rural
peasant culture, our welfare state and, later on, the restructuring and partially
privatizing of the public services. In the Finnish countryside family festivals
like anniversaries and funerals have typically been quite large parties with
many guests served with traditional home-made food and bread from a
common serving table. Earlier, each village had a local cook. Nowadays, the
habit to have traditional parties still exists and 'the local cooks' should find
their markets, expand to rural tourism and restructure their business culture.
There have been two competing cultures since the first years of the new
emerging business of rural tourism and catering, the dominant 'demanding,
but profitable business' culture, and the minority 'evil others' culture. In the
modern welfare state of Finland home and elderly care have been provided
until the last few years as a public service, funded and organised by the state
or municipalities. Private services are fairly recent and they have increased
from the 1990s. In 2000, there were 2664 private social service units in
Finland (Stakes, 2001). The cleaning service seems to reflect more of a
marketing culture and searching for customers, with the business idea of serving busy people.

Cooking and Festival Service

> This is still not real business, only a housewife's hobby that has increased in size.
> The future in our business will be the same toiling up the hill. Old people will
> always save enough for the children so that they can afford a coffin and a funeral.
> Only when I have a real rush do I buy something small from another entrepreneur.
> I have always been running out of ideas. Anyhow, many entrepreneurs have fallen
> because they have bought big cars and driven around showing them to others.
> That will not cause a happy end. Watchful students should be searched for this
> sector. If you don't watch carefully, young people are lazy and do not do their
> duties.

Rural Tourism and Catering: Demanding but Profitable Business

You have to be well above average to have the competence for service and for business. The task of the teacher is to provide good instructions for life and resources
for learning so that they are not educating casual labourers who are good for nothing. All too often young students have a short attention span, but there are also
competent persons for our field. You can't mix business with other things, because
if you do not ask a reasonable price for your service, you will not survive. We in
rural tourism have managed to network reasonably well, which has meant the emergence of new services and products. That is what we want – to fly with our own
wings and see our own ideas flourishing. Only the bureaucracy is always there. First
they cry everywhere for new initiative and enterprises and then you get stuck in
their bureaucracy and nets.

Rural Tourism and Catering: Evil Others

We were the first to start and go through all the difficult phases, to make the
mistakes which the following ones can avoid, if they just listen. Starting rural
tourism business meant a total change in our social networks. All the neighbours
were against our initiatives; even the officials from the municipality tried their best
to prevent our business from succeeding. Still, we would not leave this job and
never take a job in a factory. We do not need students who believe themselves to be
ready and capable for everything. Education makes a young person believe she/he
is the one who decides. I know for sure that if the student is good in mathematics
he/she will never become a good worker.

Confectionery and Bakery: Baking as a Hobby

This is not a real gold mine. It is difficult to sell, to make phone calls and present
your products. Most of our products have just disappeared somewhere. It is important to keep this from growing too big, so that we manage to produce everything
ourselves. Our children hesitate choosing this job; at their age this kind of job is not
so attractive. Young students are not capable of being entrepreneurs. They have to
be self-supportive and able to do physical labour. Education alienates young people
from practical work.

Confectionery and Bakery: Baking as a Profitable Small-scale Business

Everybody believes that if she/he is able to bake, she/he can also have a bakery.
It is totally another thing to make it succeed. It is real business, and you have to
compete with the big bakeries and open the doors to chains. I like the freedom and
decision making. This is not a way of life for us. Workers and their competence
is our resource. We cannot behave like owners of old iron factories because we
want to keep our staff. All too often young students are helpless. You notice it
immediately by looking at the way she takes the wiper and starts to clean the
tables.

Grocery Shop and Selling Domestic Articles

The idea is to get rid of the things, to see the customer walk away with the bread you just sold in her bag. The best type of success is teasing a difficult customer to buy. My soul feels relaxed when working with living people. By time, my appetite for bigger markets has grown. Two groups of young students are not suitable for this job: lazy ones waiting for the first coffee break; and girls with all too short dresses, perfume and red, long nails. If the student really wants to work and learn, she/he will be recruited. The right ones are people with the ability to speak when necessary and stand for days in the crowded grocery store with their nose in the refrigerator and their back in the icebox. Still, selling high quality food and products means that you are not a Cheap Jack. You are not working, you are an entrepreneur.

Private Nursing and Elderly Care

This is like a big family in their own home and I am the mother of it. Taking care of everyone, his or her every need, each moment the day around. There have been so many young students who have called and asked for a job but then suddenly just disappeared. It is out of the question to recruit young people with black nails, rings in fingers and nose and rainbow-coloured hair. I am not going to recruit so many anyhow. Less trouble from others if I get fewer customers. The moments of success have been so sudden, small pieces of luck. I just get my daily bread.

Cleaning Service

We have found our markets even in a country of mainly public services. I have always liked to take risks and be an entrepreneur, and I also like this cleaning work. I have had all the possible problems, the typical case of an entrepreneur. Still, the wheels keep turning and money moving. All the time we search for new customer segments, families with children, busy people, old people, to give an example. You have to listen to the customer, guess the needs for service and make him/her a little bit more satisfied than he/she was expecting. Every time I have a feeling of being free and having something of my own, when I open the door and go into the dark and rainy weather finding my way to the customer. I also raise my own children and trainees in the same atmosphere.

Breeding and Taking Care of Pet Animals

In our field you have to be really fond of animals. Then, you can live in a hotel for cats or understand how it feels when the customer has to give up keeping an old dog. Entrepreneurs are born with different genes, just like people who like animals. Being an entrepreneur is like a stony path, on which you toil year after year. Still, I would never trade my freedom and work in a factory. If you want to earn more, you work more and that's it. Still, I want to keep this fairly small to be sure about the quality of the care of the animals and to avoid too high costs. The students must understand that this is not a delicacy, just being gentle to rabbits. This is for the most part faeces, dirt, bad odour, blood and nervous customers. The trainer has to compel the students to do also the unpleasant things like counting.

Arts and Handicraft

I knew what entrepreneurship was: endless working days without holidays. Still, I wanted to try my own wings and lead the daily life of an entrepreneur. Somehow I get strength from the customer. The most difficult thing for me was to start to beg for work: to bend down on your knees to ask for an order. I like students, who know at least something about quite many things. Still, the most important thing is to be able to work with your hands and realise the need for efficiency. The student must look like he/ she is willing to be where he/she is.

Timberman

You have to know how the money moves. An entrepreneur must always have many customers, doors and possibilities to change strategies. This is not a delicacy, this is hard struggle, but I would not like to trade my freedom. This has gone extremely well: given my family and me our daily bread. I do not value a bit any projects and networks built by bureaucrats. Carried water does not keep in a well. The historical tradition in our field is to hide the best tricks from competitors and students and it is still a good piece of advice. I always recruit new students according to their practical skills. I never even look at their records. The teachers should at least teach the students to look at their watch better than nowadays. They do not mention the word efficiency and economical surplus at schools.

Construction

We managed the recession of the early 90s by being flexible, working by ourselves and learning many new things. Most of us have been here ten to twenty years and seen quite a lot. This field is quite hard somehow; a young student can sometimes be teased heavily if he starts to teach the older people and present his brilliant ideas. Teachers in the vocational colleges do not understand us. They give value to reading. We want to educate mainly students with low marks in theory and give our support to them instead of the students who are good in theory. The best students will not stay in our enterprise; they just go to polytechnics.

Electronics

I never sell too cheaply just to get the job. Surviving under recession during the beginning of the 90s made me realise my own value. I have always wanted to lead my own life and be an entrepreneur. Although now I take even bigger risks, the quality of my life is higher. Tomorrow it can be totally different than today. Young students should be humble and ready to learn from an older person. They should be educated first quite well in the college, because work in an enterprise is like being in a jungle. No one will help you. I never take students who have too high marks in theory. The very next day they are in polytechnics or work in some big city as an entrepreneur. Most of us work so hard that the meetings organised for trainers by the colleges are just skipped. We entrepreneurs do not want to gather together to give a name to a kitten.

Car Repair Shop

I knew what entrepreneurship would be: few holidays and hard toiling in daily duties. By trying hard I will succeed. The most important thing in entrepreneurship is the freedom. Young students must tolerate the realities of work life; they should not be treated too softly during work-based learning periods in enterprises. All too often practical skills are lost and attitudes towards work are spoiled in schools and polytechnics, because the students do not even see other people working. In rural areas it is still different to be an entrepreneur compared to cities. The customer should trust you like he/she trusts in God. When the farmers have to hurry, they have it all at the same time. This is not a goldmine, but I am quite happy to have earned a living for my family by doing the most of the work myself with my brother.

Transport

Somehow I was born at the wheel. The gummy wheels of my lorries are still rolling fairly well. We will always need new staff; cars are not going anywhere without a human being. My business started from my own idea. The work has changed and it is nowadays quite modern with ICT. It is not enough to be strong like it used to be. Now you have to be smart, too. I am always a little bit afraid of recession. Being an entrepreneur in rural areas is different and you can't set the prices like you would like to do even though the costs for you are the same as in the cities.

The telephone answering and selling service is a new rural business sector and we do not even have any vocational degree for it. The new business seemed to reflect the new business culture.

Telephone Answering and Selling Service

This business is dependent on technique and efficiency. You have to be smart, react quickly and have accurate psychological skills. Every now and then you have to check the level of your own service quality. When you notice it from the decreasing sales, it is too late. The only reason can be your voice, which just does not appeal to the customer. It is chemistry. It is the customer, not the staff, who chooses. People nowadays believe that this is a goldmine and competitors are emerging like mushrooms after the rain.

In Table 13.2 the results are presented as root metaphors of each sectoral culture and as ratings according to Hofstede's cultural dimensions. All the metaphors are from the entrepreneurs' original discourse.

The findings in Table 13.2 show a general similarity with the earlier findings of the Finnish national culture according to Hofstede's cultural dimensions, but with a target-dependent power-distance index, more masculinity and with detailed cultural nuances in each rural entrepreneurial sector and male/female field. Although there were many cultural differences, the entrepreneurs also demonstrated common cultural beliefs about entrepreneurship. These are presented in Box 13.1.

Table 13.2   *Finnish rural entrepreneurial sectors and cultural subsectors, their root metaphors and cultural dimensions rated according to Hofstede (2001)*

Business sector	Amount of men and women	Subculture when existing and root metaphors of the culture/subculture	Sectoral cultural dimensions rated with a roughly estimated scale from 1 = very low to 5 = very high. Ratings are multiplied by 20 to be comparable with Hofstede's scale			
			Power distance in general/against a vocational student	Individualism	Masculinity	Uncertainty avoidance
1. Agriculture	11 men 7 women	Success culture 'Architect of ones own fortune'	40/60	60	60	40
	2 men	Hopeless culture 'People driven to the field of agriculture'	40/60	60	40	80
2. Service sector	2 women	Cooking and festival service 'A housewife's hobby'	20/60	60	20	80
	13 men 17 women	Rural tourism and catering 'People well above the average make a success in this business'	40/60	80	80	40
	1 man	Rural tourism and catering 'Evil others'	60/80	80	80	60
	1 woman 3 women	Confectionery and bakery 'Baking as a hobby'	20/60	60	20	80
	4 men 2 women	Confectionery and bakery 'Baking as a profitable small-scale business'	20/60	80	80	40
	3 men 5 women	Grocery shop and selling domestic articles 'The idea is to get rid of the product you are selling'	20/60	60	60	40

Sector	Respondents				
Private nursing and elderly care 'A mother in a home for patients'	1 man 11 women	20/60	60	20	80
Cleaning service 'Fair job for fair people'	3 women	20/60	60	40	60
3. Breeding and taking care of pet animals 'Living in a dog hotel'	3 men 5 women	20/40	60	40	60
4. Arts and handicraft 'You feel like begging for work and an order'	2 men 2 women	40/60	60	40	80
5. Timberman 'The entrepreneur is like a square and the school is like a circle, they do not fit' 'You have to have many doors open and keep many customers hot'	15 men	40/80	80	80	60
6. Construction 'Tough survivors after the recession of the early 90s'	15 men	40/60	60	80	60
7. Electronics 'The young should honour the older entrepreneurs who have suffered but survived by working hard and not selling for free'	5 men 1 woman	40/80	80	80	60
8. Car repair shop 'Hard toiling according to farmers' timetable'	3 men	40/60	60	60	60
9. Transport 'You have to be born at the wheel, but also be smart'	3 men	40/60	60	80	60
10. Telephone answering and selling service 'Efficient quality voice'	2 men 4 women	60/60	100	100	40
The mean of all sectors	83 men 63 women	30/60	70	60	60
Finnish culture in general according to Hofstede (2001)		35	63	26	59

305

BOX 13.1   FINNISH RURAL ENTREPRENEURS' COMMON BASIC ASSUMPTIONS REGARDING ENTREPRENEURSHIP

1. Entrepreneurship is demanding. It means hard work and total commitment.

    'An entrepreneur in elderly care is like a mother taking care of everybody's needs around the days.' Business owner in private nursing and elderly care

    'We are not dancing this kind of a rumba forever.' Business owner in rural tourism

    'The students must understand that this is not a delicacy. This is for the most part faeces, dirt, bad odour, blood and nervous customers.' Breeding of pet animals

2. Entrepreneurs earn their living if they do unpaid labour or are exceptionally competent, but they never make a big profit.

    'We work by ourselves, with the family and sometimes the neighbours and other slaves helping us.' Farmer

    'I just get my daily bread.' Business owner in private nursing

    'This is not a gold mine.' Business owners in confectionery and bakery, electronics and car repair shop

3. Entrepreneurship is insecure.

    'Agriculture is not anymore a bird's nest.' Farmer

4. Entrepreneurship means doing always about the same jobs but entrepreneurs have an inner feeling of subjective freedom.

    'Being an entrepreneur is like a stony path on which you toil year after year. Still, I would never trade my freedom and work in a factory.' Breeding of pet animals

    'I knew what entrepreneurship was: endless working days without holidays. Still I wanted to try my own wings and lead the daily life of an entrepreneur.' Business owner in arts and handicraft

5. Entrepreneurs should be humble.

    'This has gone extremely well: given my family and me our daily bread.' Timberman

    'You have to start from the floor and be humble.' Catering and festival service

    'The most difficult thing for me is to bend down on my knees to ask for an order.' Business owner in arts and handicraft

THEORETICAL IMPLICATIONS

The findings in Table 13.2 show a general similarity with the earlier findings of the Finnish national culture according to Hofstede's cultural dimensions, with the exception of target-dependent power distance and higher masculinity. The original dimensions of Hofstede/the mean result of this study compared, are 33/30 for power distance in general and 33/60 against a vocational student, 63/70 for individualism/collectivism, 26/60 for masculinity/femininity and 59/60 for uncertainty avoidance. The reasonably high masculinity index refers to the necessities of entrepreneurship. It seems that rural entrepreneurs differ from the general Finnish population by being more masculine, but still their masculinity is fairly low compared to other national cultures. There certainly has to be more achievement orientation if one wants to succeed in business, whether it is a question of a male or female entrepreneur. Quite striking and somehow an exception from the Finnish popularly-held belief was the quite high power distance index in Finland, when speaking about the expectations from the behaviour of young students compared to rural middle-aged entrepreneurs. This cultural expectation and the consequences of it should be treated consciously in vocational and entrepreneurial education of the young students. It would also be relevant to analyse the cultural expectations of teachers and vocational students.

There were both sectoral and gender differences in culture. The men, in general, demonstrated higher Hofstedian masculinity, as they emphasised efficiency and economical facts, but that was also the case with some female fields. Still, most of the primarily or totally female fields showed an emphasis on the customer or the subject area of business, to be making food, baking on a small scale or care of the elderly. The women demonstrated lower uncertainty acceptance and were quite cautious and not highly business minded, except for the entrepreneurs in more recent businesses of rural tourism and catering, in grocery stores and selling of domestic articles. The gender-based, peasant-like division of entrepreneurial sectors and the traditional culture of women and men in rural business seemed to be changing only slowly. It seems more difficult to depart from the old culture in traditional business sectors than to create something totally new in new business sectors like a telephone answering and selling service. The new business areas such as telephone answering services seem to differ from the traditional national Finnish culture with a greater emphasis on masculine thinking. Perhaps they also have greater potential to change the national rural culture than the traditional rural entrepreneurial sectors. It must also be remembered that the difference between the life and culture of cities and rural areas in Finland is not as great as in many other European countries (Paunikallio, 2002).

Differences between the sexes seem to have their roots in historical thinking. Hyrsky (1999) found that female entrepreneurial metaphors often contained more controversial and negative imagery compared to male observations. He concluded that many women perceived entrepreneurship as perhaps requiring too full a commitment to business, thereby reducing the time and energy available to pursue other important avenues of their lives. 'To be a woman is to be a mother in the deepest meaning of the word' was told to the readers of one of the first Finnish journals for women in the year 1898 (Sulkunen, 1988). It was interesting to notice quite the same kind of metaphors, responsibilities and the ethos of true love for a living human being, in the fields of private elderly care and in the care of pet animals where mostly women, but some men work. On the other hand, men in the study of Hyrsky (1999), just like most male entrepreneurs in this study, saw entrepreneurship in a more favourable light than women. Business owners in the field of home economics, private nursing and elderly care are mainly women in Finland and also in this study. Their narratives describe general motherhood for society. The concept is rooted in a gendered concept of a human being and his/her private and public life during the industrialisation of society (Sulkunen, 1988). The social policy of Finland has also partly sustained the gendered society. The early social policy of Finnish society in particular sustained the gendered division of labour; men worked as paid labour and women as mothers and care workers (Anttonen, 1989). Women have been building the Finnish welfare state since the 1950s to be a country with quite comprehensive public care and other services. Women have been the basis for the system, whether it is as paid labour or unpaid labour at home and in the so-called third sector, various voluntary organizations (Kosonen, 1987; Anttonen, 1988). It seems difficult to integrate historical motherhood and modern business metaphors. It was astonishing to find still so many survival narratives from the times of the economic recession told by male entrepreneurs in technical sectors. The traditional view that every man has to fend for himself and make due sacrifices in order to manage, surfaced time and time again in the narratives just as in the study of Hyrsky (1999). The important thing for men was to be able to earn a living for one's family. Perhaps they partly reflect the masculinity aspect of the men in a quite feminine Finnish society.

In agriculture, the two contrasting cultures – success culture and hopeless culture – certainly have their roots in the deepening polarisation of farmers and agriculture. According to Bläuer (2001), the number of active farmers will decrease dramatically before the year 2010. At the same time, about one third of the existing farmers are planning to increase their production and make rather big investments, and one fifth of farmers believe that the benefits in farming will increase. The region where the data was gathered is one with the largest number of organic farmers in Finland. Results are based on a statistical survey carried out in the same area as this qualitative study during the years 1997–2000. About one third of the active farmers in the region were interviewed in that study. The common cultural beliefs held by entrepreneurs presented in Box 13.1 seem to be mostly international but the need to be humble and to hide the fortune is something typically Finnish. In the Scandinavian countries money is viewed with respect, but it would be considered bad taste and greediness to flash it in public (Altman, 1992).

It was very fruitful to explore qualitative methodology with the theory of Hofstede (2001) and find it to fit very well for the purpose of analysing entrepreneurial culture.

EDUCATIONAL IMPLICATIONS

One may question whether the male survival stories and commitment-demanding female metaphors attract youth into entrepreneurship. Career counsellors and we vocational educators should listen to the narratives carefully and appreciate their negative messages to the students entering the work-based learning environment. We know that the attitudes of young people towards rural areas have become even more positive since the 1960s (Paunikallio, 2002). When these cultural beliefs of rural middle-aged entrepreneurs are inevitably encountered by young people during work-based learning periods, it is very important also to help other kinds of images to emerge. They should be critically analysed, and quite a lot of encouragement is needed if we want young people to choose entrepreneurship. Beliefs and metaphors should be openly discussed and even questioned by both business owners and vocational teachers. As reported, the beliefs described may prevent them from rather than encourage them to enter entrepreneurship. Just as Amundson (1997), Vance (1996) and Chen (1998) use metaphors in career counselling, they also suggest there should be critical reflection on them.

The expectations of the entrepreneurs about the vocational students emphasise the willingness and motivation to work, not that they should demonstrate their theoretical knowledge. They expect culturally proper behaviour. The students are not regarded as a resource for new innovations or people whom the entrepreneurs should encourage to become entrepreneurs themselves. Rather they see them as a possible future workforce. There are big challenges for future cooperation if entrepreneurs want to educate people to continue their business in rural areas: to teach vocational and entrepreneurial skills to students, and especially to present the values and give a positive, but realistic image of the culture and life of an entrepreneur to young people entering the field, entrepreneurs and teachers should realise the importance of their choice of words and the seriousness of their linguistic imagery. They really do reveal something about their own thinking and therefore need to consider what type of an image they wish to convey to their audience (Marshak, 1993). In order to change the gendered thinking about rural entrepreneurship we have to offer the gendered metaphors and narratives of the mainly middle-aged business owners for overt and critical reflection by modern girls and boys in our vocational colleges in order to search for more innovative and entrepreneurial thinking. The values of young people are diversifying at a growing rate (Kuure, 2002). There are still many young people who would see rural areas as an ideal place to live, if only work possibilities were available.

REFERENCES

Altman, Y. (1992), 'Towards a cultural typology of European work values and work organisation', *The European Journal of Social Sciences*, **5**(1), 35–45.

Amundson, N. (1997), 'Myths, metaphors, and moxie: the 3ms of career counselling', *Journal of Employment Counselling*, **34**(2), 76–84.

Anttonen, Anneli (1988), 'Hyvinvointivaltion feministinen kritiikki – lähtökohta uusille sosiaalipolitiikkatulkinnoille' ('The feminist critique of the welfare state – a starting point for new interpretations of social policy'), in Leena Simonen (ed.), *Naistutkimuksen ajankohtaisia ongelmia (Current Issues of the research on Gender)*, Series C 30/1988, Yhteiskuntatieteiden tutkimuslaitos. Tampereen yliopisto (Research Institute for Social Sciences. University of Tampere), Tampere, pp. 39–64.

Anttonen, A. (1989), 'Hyvinvointivaltion feministinen ymmärtäminen' ('A feminist approach to the welfare state'), *Sosiaalipolitiikka 1989 (Social Policy 1989)*, Sosiaalipoliittisen yhdistyksen vuosikirja (Annals of the Social Policy Society), pp. 23–35.

Arenius, P., E. Autio, A. Kovalainen and P.D. Reynolds (2001), 'Global Entrepreneurship Monitor. 2001 Finnish Executive Report', internet reference read 3 October 2003, http://www.tuta.hut.fi/research/gem..htm.

Beavis, A.K. and A.R. Thomas (1996), 'Metaphors as storehouses of expectation. Stabilizing the structures of organizational life in independent schools', *Educational Management & Administration*, **24**(1), 107–14.

Bläuer, M. (2001), 'Maatilatalous Pirkanmaalla vuonna 2010', PMK-verkosto ja

Pirkanmaan TE-keskus, internet reference 3 October 2003, http://www.pmkv.sci.fi/03-julkaisut.html.

Cecora, J. (2000), 'Entrepreneurs and SMEs in regional economies: policy issues for sustainable development in a globalizing economy', *International Review of Sociology*, **10**(1), 83–102.

Chen, C.P. (1998), 'Ethnography and counselling: comparative ways of meaning-making', *Guidance & Couselling*, **13**(2), 12–17.

Clegg, Stewart R. and John.T. Gray (1996), 'Metaphors in organizational research: of embedded embryos, paradigms and powerful people', in David Grant and Cliff Oswick (eds), *Metaphor and Organizations*, London: Sage, pp. 74–93.

Gundry, L.K. and J.R. Kickull (1996), 'Flights of imagination: fostering creativity through experiential learning', *Simulation & Gaming*, **27**(3), 334–50.

Hill, J. (2000), 'Cognitive style and socialisation: an exploration of learned sources of style in Finland, Poland and the UK', *Educational Psychology*, **20**(2), 285–306.

Hofstede, Geert (2001), *Culture's consequences. Comparing Values, Behaviors, Institutions, and Organizations Across Nations*, 2nd edn. Thousand Oaks and London: Sage Publications.

Hyrsky, K. (1999). 'Entrepreneurial metaphors and concepts: An exploratory study'. *International Small Business Journal*, **18**(1), 13–34.

Kelle, U. (ed.) (1998), *Computer-aided Qualitative Data Analyis: Theory Methods and Practice*, London: Sage Publications.

Koiranen, M. (1995), 'North-European metaphors of "Entrepreneurship" and "Entrepreneur"', *Frontiers of Entrepreneurship Research*, Babson College, Wellesley, MA, pp. 203–216.

Kosonen, P. (1987), 'Hyvinvointivaltion haasteet ja pohjoismaiset mallit' ('The challenges of the welfare state and Nordic models'), *Sosinalipoliittisen yhdistyksen tutkimuksia* (*Research Publications of the Social Policy Society*), Tampere: Vastapaino.

Kuure, Timo (2002), Oral communication, 17 April, (Nuorisoasiain keskus, Researcher in The Centre for Youth Affairs).

Lakoff, George and Mark Johnson (1980), *Metaphors We Live By*, Chicago: The University of Chicago Press.

Luechauer, D.L. and G.M. Shulman (1998), 'Using a metaphor exercise to explore the principles of organizational culture', *Journal of Management Education*, **22**(6), 736–44.

Mahlamäki-Kultanen, S. (2001a), 'Making vocational education strategy as a collective process', paper presented at IVETA Conference 29 July–4 August, Montego Bay, Jamaica.

Mahlamäki-Kultanen, Seija (2001b), 'The use of information technology (IT) of small business entrepreneurs', in Nor Aisham Buang, Lilia Halim, Ruhizan Mohd Yassin, Ramlee Mustapha, Abdullah Mohd Noor and Faridah Serajul Haq (eds), *Technology and Vocational Technical Education. Globalisation and Future Trends*, Vol. I, Proceedings of the International conference on technology and vocational-technical education, 12–13 November. Faculty of Education, Universiti Kebangsaan Malaysia, pp. 24–30.

Mahlamäki-Kultanen, Seija (2002), 'Typifying rural family entrepreneurship in Finland: cultural and educational perspective', in Matti Koiranen and Nina Karlsson (eds), *The Future of Family Business. Values and Social Responsibility. Research Forum Proceedings*, University of Jyväskylä, pp. 469–84.

Mahlamäki-Kultanen, S., I. Virta and T. Lylynperä (2001), 'Students as co-researchers

– case high tech and entrepreneurship in nurse education', Annual Meeting of American Educational Research Association, Seattle 9–14 April.

Marshak, R.J. (1993), 'Managing the metaphors of change', *Organizational Dynamics*, **22**(1), 44–56.

Ogborn, J. and I. Martins (1996), 'Metaphorical understandings and scientific ideas', *International Journal of Science Education*, **18**(6), 631–52.

Paunikallio, Marja (2002), *Nuoret Maaseudun ja Kaupungin Vuorovaikutuksessa Tutkimus Arvoista, Asenteista ja Odotuksista* (*The Youth and the Co-operation between Rural and Urban Areas. A Study on Values, Attitudes and Expectations*), Series B:23, Helsingin yliopiston maaseudun tutkimus- ja koulutuskeskus (University of Helsinki. Institute for Rural Research and Training).

Peltomäki, Mikko (2002), *Maan keskellä mammon vuori. Suomalaisen yrittämisen henki* (*In the Middle of the Earth there is a Treasure. The Spirit of the Finish Enterpreneurship*), Report 58, Koulutussosiologian tutkimuskeskuksen. Turun yliopisto. (Research Unit for the Sociology of Education. University of Turkey), Turkey.

Soskice, J.M. (1985), *Metaphor and Religious Language*, Oxford: Clarendon Press.

Stakes (2001), 'Yksityiset sosiaalipalvelut 2001 – tiedonantajapalaute 11/2001. Sosiaali- ja terveystilastot' ('Private social services 2001 – information 11/2001') Internet reference 15 June 2004, http://www.stakes.info/files/pdf/tiedonanta-japalautteet/tp11.pdf.

Strauss, Anselm and Juliet Corbin (1995), 'Grounded theory methodology: an overview', in Norman Denzin and Yvonna Lincoln (eds), *Handbook of Qualitative Research*, London: Sage Publications, pp. 273–86.

Sulkunen, Irma (1988), 'Naishistorian kysymyksenasetteluja ja tutkimusteemoja' ('Themes and issues of female history'), in Leena Simonen (ed.), *Naistutkimuksen ajankohtaisia ongelmia* (*Current Topics in feminist Research*), Series C30/1988, Yhteiskuntatieteiden tutkimuslaitos. Tampereen yliopisto (Research Institute for Social Sciences. University of Tampere), Tampere, pp. 27–38.

Vance, P.R. (1996), 'Constructivist career counselling and assessment', *Guidance & Counselling*, **11**(3), 8–15.

14. Factors associated with the performance of UK SMEs: are they country specific?

Graham Hall and Ana Paula Silva

There is not as yet a strong tradition within research into businesses of attempting to establish the strength of possible influences on their performance. Writers and consultants on business matters have far less scope for drawing on the results of large-scale empirical studies than has the medical profession, though arguably there are close parallels between improving the health of companies and of people. An alibi for not conducting such studies of those aberrant companies with over 100 employees is provided by their limited number (in the UK they represent only one per cent of the total population of businesses), by their complexity and by their diversity. The great majority of firms, however, are not so complex or diverse that their amenability to large-scale statistical studies should be rejected out of hand.

It might be asking for too much of such a young discipline as business studies that consensuses should have emerged. There are no unambiguous 'give up smoking' lessons to be drawn from the body of empirical research. It might have been hoped that at least the battle-lines would be clear. Sometimes this is the case with respect to the importance of a specific possible influence on performance, for example formal planning (Robinson and Pearce, 1983; Ackelsberg and Arlow, 1985; Orpen, 1985; Shuman et al., 1985; Bracker and Pearson, 1986; Bracker et al., 1988; Cragg and King, 1988; Pelham and Clayson, 1988; Carland et al., 1989; and Shrader et al., 1989) and, even more so, on the relationships of company age and size to performance (Ganguly, 1985; Evans 1987a and 1987b; Hudson, 1987; Dunne et al., 1988; 1989; with Jovanovic, 1982, providing the seminal theoretical underpinning).

There is far less clarity about the areas of disagreement between studies that have attempted to establish the relative importance of a range of possible influences on performance. This is the subtext of Berryman (1983, on the factors leading to corporate failure), Cragg and King (1988, profitability), Storey (1994, growth in employment levels), Bates (1990, survival/failure),

Hall (1995, failure/survival, profitability and change in sales), Westhead (1995, change in employment), Lussier (1995 and 1996, survival/failure), Low and Abrahamson (1997, survival), Mascarenhas (1997, market share and survival), Sapienza and Grimm (1997, growth in sales and in employment), Brush and Chaganti (1998, net cash flow and log of growth in employment levels), Gadenne (1998, return on investment), Kotey (1999, business growth, increased productivity, improved technology, revenue generation, job creation and community development), Kangasharju (2000, turnover growth), Lussier and Pfeifer (2000, survival/failure), McMahon (2001, business growth, annual sales turnover, profitability, and experience of liquidity crises), Zinger et al., (2001, sales and profits), Watson et al., (2003, profit and growth) and Zahra et al., (2002, subjective performance). Setting aside any reservations about the value of research based on samples drawn from populations narrowly defined in terms of activity and geographical location and then analysing the resulting data with fairly unsophisticated methodologies – both features not uncommon within this area – the breadth of the range of possible influences that in total have been encompassed by the various studies, and the variability between writers in their specification of variables intended to measure the same influences, render ready comparison rather difficult.

Even if variables are identically specified, consensus will be hampered by the effects of national culture. The question is, when allowance is made for differences in sectoral composition, will there still be variation between countries in either the factors that influence performance, or the strength of their influence? The evidence from the well-known STRATOS project (Hall and Adams, 1993, with a description of the project in Bamberger, 1983) is that across European countries there certainly is a 'country effect' on the growth of SMEs but its nature was left unexplored. This chapter is based on a sample drawn from only one country but it will centre much of its discussion on how national culture could have affected its results.

This discussion should be read in conjunction with the analysis contained in the following chapter (Chapter 15) which considers the factors associated with the growth of Portuguese SMEs. If national culture may be said to have any bearing on the factors influencing performance, or, at least, the strength of that influence, the SME sectors in the UK and Portugal make obvious candidates for comparison. According to Hofstede (2001) their location on the four dimensions on which he measured national culture would be as seen in Table 14.1.

If any truth lies in Hofstede's classification, the cultures of the UK and Portugal are clearly very different.

Table 14.1   Index scores of Portugal and UK on Hofstede's dimensions of national culture

	Power distance	Uncertainty avoidance	Individualism	Masculinity
UK	35	35	89	66
Portugal	63	104	27	31

Source: Hofstede (2001), p. 500.

OBJECTIVES

The theme of this book is entrepreneurship in all its many aspects. A stream of literature extols its virtues (for example Gartner, 1989) whilst another considers the characteristics of entrepreneurs (for example Wennekers and Thurik, 1999 and Gundry and Welsch, 2001). Commonly these characteristics include a preference for risk, innovation and growth.

This chapter will consider the factors associated with the last of these objectives, growth, during the start-up phase of SMEs and the factors associated with their profitability once they are established. It will also briefly report those factors associated with a failure not only to grow or to achieve profitability, but even to survive at all. For entrepreneurs, whether attempting to launch a new company or to manage an established one, the fatal pitfalls they might encounter cannot be without interest.

Given that our methodology is statistically based, the causation of relationships may not be unambiguous, albeit that common sense will often dictate interpretation. However, the limitation of statistical methodology will induce a certain modesty as to the objectives of the study which are to establish the factors most strongly *associated* with the performance of small firms, and then to speculate as to the extent that relationships are embedded in the UK culture.

METHODOLOGY

The sample consisted of 285 firms in which 3i, Europe's largest venture capitalist, made investments during the 1990s. Their average employment level was 33, though with about a dozen with over 100 employees, launching them into the medium-sized bracket. They were drawn from throughout England and Scotland and operated in manufacturing (59 per cent), distribution/services (35 per cent) and retailing (6 per cent); 121 were start-ups defined by age of less than two years, with survival defined as being in a position to make a repayment (see Table 14.2).

Table 14.2   Description of sample

Total sample size	285
Number of start-ups (less than 2 years)	121 (42%)
Number of established firms	164 (58%)
Average employment level	33
Sectors in the sample:	
Manufacturing	59%
Distribution/services	35%
Retailing	6%

3i files contained a comprehensive range of information, allowing 51 variables to be generated (see Appendix for full list). These encompassed the personal characteristics of owners, for instance, their ages and educational qualifications, aspects of their marketing, such as the number of markets in which they operated and channels of sales, financial data that would normally be displayed in published accounts and their approach to strategy. The last factor was subjectively determined by the MBA student who acted as a research assistant on this project.[1] On the basis of the plans that owners submitted to 3i, he was able to categorise them as being 'strategically aware' and, if so, whether their strategies were of focus, differentiation or cost minimalisation. This categorisation was conducted without knowledge of financial performance as a safeguard against bias that might otherwise result.

An additional variable that was included in the study was the change in sales nationally within the relevant Minimum List Heading. Data on this were collected from national statistics.

Stepwise logit regression was employed to establish the factors most strongly related to survival and OLS stepwise, those most strongly associated with growth and profitability. As a safeguard against multicollinearity, regressions were re-run with various variables and cases omitted. Additionally 't' tests were applied to the means of all variables with respect to survivors/failures, high growth/low growth and high profitability/low profitability, defined in relation to mean values.

It should be noted that our stepwise procedure precluded hypothesis testing of specific variables. However, whilst we discuss *ex post* the possible reasons for our results, the state of knowledge, whether derived empirically or theoretically, especially the latter, does not allow the most important factors to be identified *ex ante*. For instance two of the seminal papers in this area (Evans and Jovanovic, 1989 and Cressy, 1996) assume the benefits of the volume of human capital with hardly any theoretical justification.

FACTORS ASSOCIATED WITH THE GROWTH OF START-UPS

Table 14.3 shows the factors associated with growth among start-ups.

1. Focus

Owners of start-ups with a clear view of their intended customers achieved higher growth rates than those who appeared to be expecting to sell across a range of customers. Being focused can prove dangerous if the object of focus does not display the level of demand that is hoped. On the other hand a shot-gun approach risks spreading marketing effort too thinly.

The results would suggest the latter is dominant and are consistent with Hall (1995) on instrumentation. The importance of focus is underlined by the lower rates of growth enjoyed by start-ups intending to sell in more than one sector, rather than to concentrate on only one, albeit that the level of significance on this coefficient is not particularly high.

It would appear that focus is important to the growth of UK start-ups but whether this is mirrored in the small firm sectors of other countries will partially depend upon the degree of segmentation within their markets and the need to supply products with characteristics that exactly meet the preferences of the various segments. In the UK, customers, whether consumers or businesses, are increasingly demanding and it is not at all surprising that focus facilitates growth. Other cultures may not have achieved this degree of sophistication and small businesses will be less concerned with focusing on the needs of particular types of customers and more on securing as wide a customer base as possible.

2. Product (Service) Differentiation

Firms that distinguished their products in a marked fashion from those supplied by competitors were far more likely to grow than those that attempted to imitate them with the statistical significance of this variable, dramatically increasing when the collinear 'focus' is omitted from the model. Such collinearity is to be expected given the difficulty of achieving focus without differentiation. All businesses face the strategic choice between including in their products characteristics that are distinctly different from those embodied in other products serving the same targeted market, or supplying essentially the same products as competitors. Differentiation represents a gamble. Potential customers may be attracted or repelled about whatever is different about their product or, if attracted, may not be prepared to pay the extra price that it would imply. A follower strategy at least facilitates exploitation of a

Table 14.3 *Factors associated with growth amongst start-ups*

Dependent Variable = proportionate change in sales over three years post-3i investment

$80.1\,X_1$	$-$	$338.6\,X_2$	$-$	$538.87\,X_3$	$+$	$208.5\,X_4$	$+$	$110.59\,X_5$	$-$	$1.94\,X_6$	$+$	$121.17\,X_7$	$+$	$133.64\,X_8$	$-$	$9.66\,X_9$
(66.2)		(227.3)		(117.3)		(171)		(76.4)		(0.17)		(95.2)		(88.1)		(5.5)
0.24		0.14		0.004**		0.009**		0.16		00.00**		0.21		0.14		0.09

Notes:
$R^2 = 0.84$.
$F = 22.0$ (significance = 0).
X_1 = Constant.
X_2 = selling in many sectors.
X_3 = whether the firm exports.
X_4 = adopting a focus strategy.
X_5 = whether second owner had a degree or equivalent.
X_6 = profitability pre-investment.
X_7 = whether pursuing a policy of product differentiation.
X_8 = whether investment was intended for fixed capital.
X_9 = profits three years post-investment.
Numbers in brackets refer to standard error. Third line gives level of significance, where * indicates significant ($p < 0.05$) and ** indicates highly significant ($p < 0.01$).

level of demand that has already been created, a variation on the economics of clustering (Swann et al., 1998). However, if differentiation proves a success it allows monopoly profits to be earned.

The evidence would suggest that for the start-up firms in which 3i made an investment, the gamble has generally proved worthwhile. Whether this would be replicated in samples drawn from populations of businesses operating in other countries can only be established empirically.

3. Profitability

Owners who made the greatest personal investments before their application to 3i, who injected more into their business than they received in profits, enjoyed the highest growth rates post-investment.

A willingness to incur losses provides a message of commitment to the capital market, in this case as represented by a venture capitalist but for small firms normally by a bank. The importance of such commitment will reflect the nature of the principal–agent relationship between the suppliers of finance to small firms and their recipients (Hutchinson et al., 1993). This relationship will, in turn, differ between economies and will be culturally determined. The validity of pecking order theories for predicting the capital structure across countries will crucially depend upon international differences in the ease with which finance can be raised from the various sources and the conditions that are concomitantly attached. Consequently, models based on pecking order theories, which emphasize the importance of the signals provided by agents (the owners of small firms) to their principals (the suppliers of capital), are far better predictors of the ratios of long-term and of short-term debt to assets in an Anglo Saxon culture such as the UK's than in a southern European culture such as Portugal's (Hall et al., 2004).

4. Export Orientation

Start-ups that intended to sell overseas were likely to achieve lower growth rates than those intending to concentrate on the domestic market.

This is consistent with the ROIs of UK exporters on average being lower than non-exporters (Hall and Tu, 2003). The reasons for this are the high level of fixed costs associated with seeking and securing business overseas and the psychological hurdles to entering markets that are in more than one sense 'foreign'. Both costs and psychological hurdles will be partially determined by the psychic distance between countries, reflecting their differences in culture (Johanson and Wiedersheim-Paul, 1975; Johanson and Vahlne, 1977; Bilkey and Tesar, 1977 and Cavusgil, 1980).

It is commonly argued, for instance, that the psychic distance between the

UK and Australia is shorter than between the UK and France. Though this case can be overstated, Europe being the UK's principal market, there would seem little doubt that the British display a low degree of sensitivity to the nuances of other cultures as evidenced, not least, by their notorious unwillingness to learn other languages. In countries whose populations do not share similar inhibitions, the difficulties of exporting may be smaller and the damaging effect of exporting reported here may be absent.

5. Human Capital

The only measure of human capital that might make any difference to the growth of start-ups was whether second owners had a degree or similar qualification, but the level of significance hardly merits very much optimism about the strength of the relationship.

6. Purpose of the Investment

Firms that intended the 3i investment to fund the purchase of fixed capital achieved the highest rates of growth.

FACTORS ASSOCIATED WITH THE PROFITABILITY OF ESTABLISHED FIRMS

Table 14.4 details the factors associated with profitability in established firms.

1. Product Differentiation

The most significant result, both statistically and for its implications for strategy, is the strong contribution made to profitability by product differentiation.

2. Number of Employees

Size of workforce was correlated with profitability. This may reflect economies of scale or that success not only provides higher returns but also facilitates expansion of workforce.

3. Age

In this study the energy of youth would appear to have outweighed the experience of age but whether this is likely to be replicated in other cultures is clearly an open question.

Table 14.4 *Factors associated with profitability amongst established firms*

$12.54\,X_1$	$-$	$0.26\,X_2$	$-$	$3.14\,X_3$	$+$	$0.2586\,X_4$	$+$	$6.45\,X_5$	$+$	$0.0299\,X_6$	$+$	$0.224\,X_7$	$+$	$3.476\,X_8$
(6.6)		(0.15)		(2.1)		(0.17)		(2.2)		(0.15)		(0.02)		(2.28)
0.07		0.10		0.15		0.14		0.009**		0.07		0.15		0.14

Notes:
$R^2 = 0.47$.
$F = 3.9$ (significance = 0.005).
$X_1 =$ Constant.
$X_2 =$ age of managing director.
$X_3 =$ whether second director has a degree.
$X_4 =$ years of experience of second director in same sector.
$X_5 =$ pursuing product differentiation.
$X_6 =$ number of employees.
Numbers in brackets refer to standard error. Third line gives level of significance, where * indicates significant ($p < 0.05$) and ** indicates highly significant ($p < 0.01$).

4. Human Capital

There is some hint that the educational attainment and previous experience of second directors had some impact on profitability but the low level of statistical significance on the relevant coefficients does not suggest the relationship to be strong.

FACTORS ASSOCIATED WITH THE SURVIVAL OF START-UPS

The low likelihood ratio index of 0.07 and pay-off matrix of 71 per cent reflects the difficulties faced by all venture capitalists in their attempts to spot the winners. However, two factors would appear to be strongly related to the probability of survival, albeit that their effects are swamped by the influence of variables not apparently included in our data set.

1. Commitment

This is reflected in the difference between the amount injected into their companies by owners and the profits they make in the last audited accounts before the year of investment. The coefficient is significant at 4 per cent but perhaps more telling is a simple comparison of averages: for survivors their 'profitability' was –69.2 per cent and for failures –18 per cent.

The losses initially incurred are actually positively correlated with the average profitability earned in the third year after the investment (or year of failure if earlier). For survivors the average was 9.4 per cent, for failures –133.6 per cent.

2. Export Orientation

Not only did survivors that looked for business overseas achieve lower growth rates than those concentrating on domestic markets but within the full sample of start-ups those expressing an export orientation were not even as likely to survive; evidence again of the inadvisability of SMEs leaving their domestic markets.

FACTORS ASSOCIATED WITH THE SURVIVAL OF ESTABLISHED FIRMS

The likelihood ratio index of 0.012 was marginally improved on the start-ups, survival model but its pay-off matrix marginally worse at 67 per cent. Factors that appear related to survival amongst established firms are:

1. Creditor Days

Survivors paid their creditors more quickly than did failures. This is identical to a result from Hall (1995) with respect to UK construction and is consistent with Hall, ibid., on the factors associated with the profitability of small firms in the instrumentation sector. Slow payment of creditors allows interest to be earned in the interim but can create ill-will amongst suppliers. The extent that either this will occur, or that it will matter if it does, will to some extent be culturally determined.

Cultures vary in the extent that attitudes are relaxed towards late payment of bills or, indeed, the observance of formal contracts. Moreover, even if suppliers are not content with late payment, the extent that this can be translated into retaliatory action will be largely determined by conditions within their own markets; supplier power will be weaker in markets in decline or with low concentrations.

2. Product Differentiation

Firms that distinguished their products in a marked fashion from those supplied by competitors were far more likely to survive than those that attempted to imitate them, for reasons discussed above.

3. Industrial Production

Firms that sold to other firms were more likely to survive than those that sold to final consumers or to retailers. Business-to-business marketing is usually quite different from business-to-consumer, not least because in the former the level of technical expertise of purchasers is probably higher, requiring more emphasis on the actual characteristics of what is being marketed and less on image.

This may be the reason why selling to other firms is less hazardous than selling direct to consumers or retailers. Alternatively it may have more to do with the nature of the small firm sector in the UK. On the whole, UK small firms do not supply chains of retail outlets, except possibly with fruit and vegetables. The retailers they do supply are usually locally based. Moreover, if small UK firms sell direct to consumers it will either be because they are retailers or that they are the sort of businesses that typically are locally based, for instance, professionals, restaurants and hotels. It may be that in the UK the ebbs and flows of local market conditions are more difficult to manage than those confronted in the business-to-business sector. It may also be that these differences may be of a different order in other cultures.

4. Overdraft Facilities

Survivors had higher overdraft facilities. This might be interpreted in two ways. Failure might have resulted from cash starvation, indicating an unnecessarily cautious attitude from banks, which would be a common argument from small firm pressure groups and, indeed, is the reason most cited for their failure by the owners of British firms that have been rendered involuntarily insolvent (Hall, 1995). Alternatively, it may represent the good judgement of banks, though this would beg the question of why any overdraft facility would be made available to a firm deemed likely to fail.

5. Purpose of Investment

Companies that used their investment from 3i primarily to fund working capital suffered a significantly greater probability of failure than those intending to fund fixed capital or a mix of working and fixed capital. However, as only a few cases devoted the money they raised to working capital alone, the conclusions that can be drawn from this result should not be regarded as particularly strong.

DISCUSSION

This chapter should be regarded as a first attempt at exploring the factors affecting the performance of UK SMEs based on the 3i database. Some interesting issues arise:

1. Adopting a focus strategy, or its close cousin, differentiation, would appear a key to the growth of start-ups and to their subsequent profitability, once established. Theory would suggest that either relationship could be culturally embedded and, indeed, the results presented in the subsequent chapter would lead us to believe focus to be counterproductive to growth in Portugal, arguably characterized by less sophisticated consumer behaviour than is commonly exhibited in the UK.
2. A strong degree of commitment from owners, as reflected by their willingness to incur losses in the early life of their companies, would appear associated with the rate of growth that they subsequently enjoy.
3. Seeking business overseas would not appear a route to the growth of start-ups, indeed such a strategy is actually more likely to end in their failure.
4. In spite of the employment of a data set with such a comprehensive coverage it was not possible to produce models with strong predictive power of survival/failure amongst either start-ups or established firms. Even if the

variables introduced were not well specified, one would nevertheless have expected some degree of predictive power to have been achieved. Clearly some other factors are determining success within the SMEs sector, if this is not purely a matter of luck. These are open to conjecture but the personality of owners may well play a part. This is clearly a vital issue, as is whether the lack of importance of prima facie important factors is replicable in other cultures.

5. Of the variables not important in any of the models, the most surprising are any measures of human capital and the trends in sales of the sectors in which firms operate. Both are counter-intuitive. Perhaps they reflect misspecification. The level of formal education, even years of business experience, may be regarded as crude measures of human capital. As for the apparent irrelevance of growth within sectors, the latter may be defined too broadly to capture the impact of sector performance.

NOTE

1. Kuljit Rhana, to whom grateful thanks are extended.

REFERENCES

Ackelsberg, R. and P. Arlow (1985), 'Small business do plan and it pays off', *Long Range Planning*, **18**(5), 61–7.

Bamberger, I. (1983), 'Value systems, strategies and the performance of small and medium sized firms', *European Small Business Journal*, **1**(4), 25–39.

Barringer, B.R. and A.C. Bluedorn (1999), 'The relationship between corporate entrepreneurship and strategic management', *Strategic Management Journal*, **20**, 421–44.

Bates, T. (1990), 'Entrepreneur human capital inputs and small business longevity', *Review of Economics and Statistics*, **72**(4), 551–59.

Berryman, J. (1983), 'Small business failure and bankruptcy: a survey of the literature', *European Small Business Journal*, **1**(4), 47–59.

Bilkey, W.J. and G. Tesar (1977), 'The export behaviour of smaller sized Winsconsin manufacturing firms', *Journal of International Business Studies*, **8**(1), 93–8.

Bracker, J.S. and J.N. Pearson (1986), 'The impact of consultants on small firm strategic planning', *Journal of Small Business Management*, **23**(3), 23–30.

Bracker, J.S., B.W. Keats and J.N. Pearson (1988), 'Planning and financial performance among small firms in a growth industry', *Strategic Management Journal*, **9**, 591–603.

Brush, C.G. and R. Chaganti (1998), 'Business without glamour? An analysis of resources on performance by size and age in small service and retail firms', *Journal of Business Venturing*, **14**, 233–57.

Carland, J.W., J.C. Carland and D.A. Carroll, Jnr (1989), 'An assessment of the psychological determinants of planning in small businesses', *International Small Business Journal*, **7**(4), 23–34.

Cavusgil, S.T. (1980), 'On the internationalization process of firms', *European Research*, **8**, 273–81.

Cragg, P.B. and M. King (1988), 'Organisational characteristics and small firms' performance revisited', *Entrepreneurship: Theory and Practice*, **13**(2), 49–64.

Cressy, R. (1996), 'Are business start-ups debt-rationed', *Economic Journal*, **106** (September), 1253–70.

Dunne, T., M.J. Roberts and L. Samuelson (1988), 'Patterns of firm entry and exit in US manufacturing industries', *Rand Journal of Economics*, **19**(4), 495–515.

Dunne, T., M.J. Roberts and L. Samuelson (1989), 'The growth and failure of US manufacturing plans', *Quarterly Journal of Economics*, **104**(4), 671–98.

Evans, D.S. (1987a), 'The relationship between firm growth, size and age: estimates for 100 manufacturing industries', *Journal of Industrial Economics*, **35**(4), 567–82.

Evans, D.S. (1987b), 'Tests of alternative theories of firm growth', *Journal of Political Economy*, **45**(4), 657–74.

Gadenne, D. (1998), 'Critical success factors for small business: an inter-industry comparison', *International Small Business Journal*, **17**(1), 36–56.

Ganguly, P. (1985), *UK Small Business Statistics and International Comparisons*, London: Harper & Row.

Gartner, W.B. (1989), '"Who is an entrepreneur?" is the wrong question', *Entrepreneurship: Theory & Practice*, **13**(4), 47–69.

Gibrat, R. (1931), *Les Inegalités Economiques*, Paris: Sirey.

Gundry, L.K. and H.P. Welsch (2001), 'The ambitious entrepreneur – high growth strategies of women-owned enterprises', *Journal of Business Venturing*, **16**(5), 453–70.

Hall, G. (1995), *Surviving and Prospering in the Small Firm Sector*, London and New York: Routledge.

Hall, G. and G. Adams (1993), 'Influences on the growth of SMEs – an international comparison', *Entrepreneurship and Regional Development*, **5**(1), 73–84.

Hall, G. and C. Tu (2003), 'Internationalisation and size, age and profitability in the UK', in L.P. Dana (ed.), *The Handbook of Research in International Entrepreneurship*, Cheltenham, UK and Northampton, MA, USA: Edward Elgar.

Hall, G. and C. Tu, 'Stage theory: some myths exploded', (unpublished paper).

Hall, G.C., P.J. Hutchinson and N. Michaelas (2004), 'Determinants of capital structures of European SMEs', *Journal of Business Finance and Accounting*.

Hofstede, G. (2001), *Culture's Consequences: Comparing Values, Behaviours, Institutions, and Organizations Across Nations*, 2nd edn, London: Sage.

Huang, X. and A. Brown (1999), 'An analysis and classification of problems in small business', *International Small Business Journal*, **18**(1), 73–85.

Hudson, J. (1987), 'The age, regional and industrial structure of company liquidations', *Journal of Business Finance and Accounting*, **14**(2), 199–213.

Hutchinson, P.J., R.G.P. McMahon, S. Holmes and D.M. Forsaith (1993), *Small Enterprise Financial Management: Theory and Practice*, Australia: Harcourt Brace.

Johanson, J. and J.E. Vahlne (1977), 'The internationalisation process of the firm: a model of knowledge development and increasing commitments', *Journal of International Business Studies*, **8**, 23–32.

Johanson, J. and F. Wiedersheim-Paul (1975), 'The internationalisation of the firm: four Swedish cases', *Journal of Management Studies*, **12**(3), 305–22.

Jovanovic, B. (1982), 'Selection and the evolution of industry', *Econometrica*, **50**(3), 649–70.

Kangasharju, A. (2000), 'Growth of the smallest: determinants of small firm growth during strong macroeconomic fluctuations', *International Small Business Journal*, **19**(1), 28–43.

Kotey, B. (1999), 'Debt financing and factors internal to the business', *International Small Business Journal*, **17**(3), 11–29.

Low, M.B. and E. Abrahamson (1997), 'Movements, bandwagons, and clones: industry evolution and the entrepreneurial process', *Journal of Business Venturing*, **12**, 435–57.

Lussier, R.N. (1995), 'A non financial business success versus failure prediction model for young firms', *Journal of Small Business Management*, **33**(1), 8–20.

Lussier, R.N. (1996), 'A start-up business success versus failure prediction model for the retail industry', *The Mid-Atlantic Journal of Business*, **23**(2), 79–92.

Lussier, R.N. and S. Pfeifer (2000), 'A comparison of business success versus failure variables between US and Central Eastern Europe Croatian entrepreneurs', *Entrepreneurship Theory and Practice*, **24**(4), 59–67.

Mascarenhas, B. (1997), 'The order and size of entry into international markets', *Journal of Business Venturing*, **12**, 287–99.

McMahon, R.G.P. (2001), 'Growth and performance of manufacturing SMEs: the influence of financial management characteristics', *International Small Business Journal*, **19**(3), 10–28.

Orpen, C. (1985), 'The effects of long-range planning on small business performance: a further examination', *Journal of Small Business Management*, **23**(1), 16–23.

Pelham, A.M. and D.E. Clayson (1988), 'Receptivity to strategic planning tools in small manufacturing firms', *Journal of Small Business Management*, January, 43–50.

Robinson, R.B. Jnr and J.A. Pearce II (1983), 'The impact of formalized planning on financial performance in small organisations', *Strategic Management Journal*, **4**, 197–207.

Sapienza, H.J. and C.M. Grimm (1997), 'Founder characteristics, start-up process, and strategy/structure variables as predictors of shortline railroad performance', *Entrepreneurship Theory and Practice*, **22**(1), 5–24.

Shrader, C.B., C.L. Mulford and V.L. Blackburn (1989), 'Strategic and operational planning, uncertainty and performance in small firms', *Journal of Small Business Management*, **27**(4), 45–60.

Shuman, J.C., J.J. Shaw and G. Sussman (1985), 'Strategic planning in small rapid growth companies', *Long Range Planning*, **18**(6), 48–55.

Storey, D.J. (1994), *Understanding the Small Business Sector*, USA and Canada: Routledge.

Swann, G.M.P., M. Prevezer and D.K. Stout (eds) (1998), *The Dynamics of Industrial Clustering: International Comparisons in Computing and Biotechnology*, New York: Oxford University Press.

Watson, W., W.H. Stewart and A. BarNir (2003), 'The effects of human capital, organizational demography and interpersonal processes on venture partner perceptions of firm profit and growth', *Journal of Business Venturing*, **18**(2), 145–64.

Wennekers, S. and R. Thurik (1999), 'Linking entrepreneurship and economic growth', *Small Business Economics*, **13**, 27–55.

Westhead, P. (1995), 'Survival and employment growth contrasts between types of owner-managed high-technology firms', *Entrepreneurship Theory and Practice*, **20**(1), 5–27.

Zahra, S.A., D.O. Neubaum and G.M. El-Hagrassey (2002), 'Competitive analysis and new venture performance: understanding the impact of strategic uncertainty and venture origin', *Entrepreneurship Theory and Practice*, **27**(1), 1–28.

Zinger, J.T., R. Le Brasseur and L.R. Zanibbi (2001), 'Factors influencing early stage performance in Canadian microenterprises', *Journal of Development Entrepreneurship*, **6**(2), 129–51.

APPENDIX: DEFINITIONS OF VARIABLES

1. Age of principal owner
2. Average age of other directors
3. Whether the principal owner had a degree or equivalent (= 1, 0 otherwise)
4. Years of experience of principal owner in the same type of business
5. Total business experience of principal owner
6. Whether any secondary directors had a degree or equivalent (=1)
7. Average years of experience of other directors in the same type of business
8. Average total business experience of other directors
9. Company age in terms of years of trading
10. Whether the management team included a finance director (=1)
11. Whether the management team included a marketing director (=1)
12. Total amount of 3i investment
13. Ratio of 3i investment to total assets (fixed tangible assets and current assets in the last audited accounts before year of investment)
14. Total number of employees including management
15. Whether investment was to fund primarily working capital (=1)
16. Whether investment was to fund primarily fixed capital (=1)
    The alternative to 15 and 16 of a mix of purposes was omitted to avoid a dummy trap
17. Whether investee was purchasing equity in the company (=1)
18. Whether 3i exercised its right to appoint a non-executive director to the company (=1)
19. Whether 3i's controller of the case was changed during the life of the investment (=1)
20. Whether the company's customers were other companies rather than retailers or end-users (=1)
21. Whether sales were only made through agents (=1)
22. Whether sales were made directly to end-users (=1)
23. Whether sales were made through a mixture of channels (=1)
24. Whether the company exported or, for absolute start-ups, intended doing so (=1)
25. Whether the marketing effort was clearly to be focused on a particular type of customer (=1)
26. Whether the company was clearly introducing features into its products to differentiate them from those of other companies (=1)
27. Whether the company was clearly implementing a low price strategy
28. Whether the company had a clear idea about its goals, future plans and implementation techniques

29. The percentage growth in sales forecast by 3i for the three years following its investment
30. The percentage change in sales over the three years prior to the 3i investment
31. Profits before interest and tax as a percentage of sales in the year preceding the 3i investment
32. Quick ratio = current assets minus total stocks/creditors payable within one year
33. Current ratio = current assets/creditors payable within one year
34. Cash headroom = bank overdraft facilities available to the company
35. Income cover = profit before interest and tax/interest
36. Debtor days = trade debtors x 365/sales
37. Creditor days = trade creditors x 365/sales
38. Stock days = total stocks x 365/sales
39. Proportion of 3i investment that was unsecured
40. Proportionate change in sales three years after the 3i investment
41. Profit before interest and tax/sales in the last audited accounts before the year of 3i investment
42. Profits before interest and tax/sales in the third year after the investment
43. Whether the firm survived (=1)
44. Whether the company tailor-made its products to meet the individual needs of customers (=1)
45. Whether the company traded in more than four sectors at Standard Industrial Classification level
46. Whether firm was judged to offer a wide range of products for the sector in which it operated
47. Historic working assets ratio = Stocks + Trade Debtors – Trade Creditors/Sales, in last audited accounts before year of 3i investment
48. Future working assets ratio = stocks and trade debtors – trade creditors/sales, in the third year after the 3i investment
49. Profit before interest and tax in the year prior to 3i investment
50. Profit before interest and tax in the third year after the 3i investment
51. Proportionate change in sales of the sector at SIC level over the three years prior to the 3i investment.

15. Influences on the growth of Portuguese SMEs

Ana Paula Silva and Graham Hall

A formidable amount of literature has been devoted to the factors influencing the performance of small and/or medium sized enterprises. For the most part this dates from the 1980s though the most famous contribution was made 50 years earlier (Gibrat, 1931), albeit that it attempted to prove the lack of relationships, that is, between firm size and the mean and standard deviation of the distribution of proportionate rates of growth. Virtually all researchers in this area have drawn their samples from populations of SMEs located in Anglo Saxon economies. This chapter represents a tentative first step towards rectifying this imbalance by examining the influences on the performance of SMEs in the epitome of Southern European culture, Portugal.

There would seem little doubt that a nation's culture can potentially affect its level of entrepreneurial activity and the form it might take. Within Hofstede's (2001) seminal categorization, a country's location on his 'Uncertainty avoidance' axis, for instance, might be expected to be correlated with its entrepreneurs' willingness to take risks, whilst all four axes could arguably be related to the degree of innovativeness displayed.

Theoretical constructs underlying growth modelling have been mostly developed from an Anglo American point of view. Yet, Hofstede's (2001) seminal categorization illustrates how polar-opposite is the location of Portugal on the one hand, and those of Great Britain and USA on the other hand in terms of all the four primary dimensions on which he differentiates cultures. According to Hofstede's (2001) study, Portugal has high index scores for power distance and uncertainty avoidance (63 and 104, respectively), which are the two dimensions on which both Great Britain and the USA have the lowest index scores (35 on both for Great Britain, and 40 and 46 respectively for the USA). Furthermore, Portugal scores very low on individualism and masculinity (27 and 31 respectively), whereas both Great Britain and the USA were found to score strongly along these two dimensions (89 and 66 for Great Britain, and 91 and 62 for the USA, respectively).

It is possible that the factors influencing growth, and even more so, the strength of their influence, will be affected by Portugal's culture. Portugal is a country where inequalities of power and wealth may hinder the scope for opportunity that predominates in Anglo Saxon countries; it is further characterized by low tolerance of uncertainty and it is, consequently, a rule oriented country where bureaucracy and controls are very much instituted, a situation in clear contrast with the easiness to accept change and the readiness to take risks in Anglo Saxon countries; finally, the collectivist nature of the Portuguese culture and low degree of gender discrimination also sets this country very much apart from the Anglo Saxon countries in cultural terms. Despite the cultural gap, it need come as no surprise if many of our hypotheses based on Anglo Saxon studies are nevertheless confirmed, because often there is more than one cultural group within a country, so the value of stereotyping of countries according to culture should not be exaggerated.

Over the past two decades a number of efforts have been developed both to define the entrepreneur and to develop categories of entrepreneurs, not always in a consistent manner. Nevertheless, an essential consensual point is that entrepreneurship is not an occupation but rather a behavioural characteristic of persons that moves them towards change and growth (Wennekers and Thurik, 1999). Firm growth has been almost implicitly construed as a condition of entrepreneurship (Gundry and Welsch, 2001). For instance, a great deal of small business research has been devoted to showing that more entrepreneurship could mean more economic growth (for example, Schmitz, 1989). In one definition of the entrepreneur he can be singled out from the small business owner manager in that the latter is satisfied with the status quo whereas the entrepreneur exhibits a desire to grow the business more rapidly (Gundry and Welsch, 2001). Nevertheless, few attempts have been made to incorporate entrepreneurship in small firm growth models. Furthermore, research on entrepreneurial growth phenomena has mostly focused on rapidly growing new ventures, failing to compare high growth firms with low or no growth firms (Gundry and Welsch, 2001). This chapter attempts to uncover the differences between the two groups of firms by focusing on the dynamic role of entrepreneurship and exploring which aspects of management, broadly defined, have the greatest impact on growth, adopted as a measure of entrepreneurial success. We measure growth by assets as it has been strongly suggested in the bulk of literature that no substantial differences in results emerge from it being measured in terms of assets, turnover or employment.

We focus on the small and medium sized enterprises. Entrepreneurship and small (and medium) firms are not synonymous. But, as the small size lends itself to the firm being an extension of whoever is in charge, smaller firms are an outstanding vehicle for the entrepreneur to channel his expansionist ambitions (Wennekers and Thurik, 1999).

Section one of our chapter describes our sample and choice of variables, section two our methodology, section three our results and section four will provide concluding remarks.

CHOICE OF VARIABLES

Table 15.1 details the variables used in the research.

Dependent Variable

This is the growth of companies in relation to their sector average over three years (1997–99). Firms are divided categorically into those displaying growth in assets $\geq 10\%$ above sector average or $\leq 10\%$ below. Nineteen companies fell within the group of relative low growth and nine companies in the relative high growth group.

Independent Variables

Size
Gibrat's theory (which is sometimes elevated to the status of 'law') has been provided with very little empirical support. Instead researchers disagree about the direction of the relationship between size and rates of growth. Roper (1999) found it to be positive, explained by the financial constraints on small firms, whilst Storey et al. (1987) and McMahon (2001) found the opposite, perhaps reflecting the need to achieve a minimum efficient scale, especially in sectors that are cost driven.

Age of company
Consistent with the thrust of the literature (Jovanovic, 1982; Storey et al., 1987; Storey, 1994; Hall, 1995; Roper, 1999; Kangasharju, 2000; Robson and Bennett, 2000) our hypothesis is that younger firms will grow faster. The older a firm the more likely that it will have reached the relevant minimum efficient scale for its sector; young firms are therefore more likely to be expanding towards this level of output. It could be that the owners of younger firms are more ambitious for growth, but this view would contradict some writers, for instance, Heshmati (2001), who finds that only when growth is measured in terms of employment is age negatively associated with growth; when measured in either sales or assets, age was positively related to growth, which he ascribes to older companies' movement along their respective learning curves, consistent with Jovanovic (1982).

Table 15.1   *Variables in the research*

Dependent variable	Independent variables	Operationalization of independent variable	Hypothesis tested
Growth group: 1. Below sector average 2. Above sector average	Size	Average turnover over 1997–99, measured in Portuguese 'contos' or thousand escudos	1. Size and growth have some relationship of indeterminate sign
	Age of company	Age from the year of set-up until 2001	2. Age of company is negatively assocciated with growth
	Age of owner	Average age in 2001 of active owner-manager	3. Age of owner-managers is negatively associated with growth
	Commitment to business	Percentage of active owner-managers working full-time for the company	4. Commitment to business (% of owners working full-time) is positively associated with growth
	Regular training	Open question: 'How often has training been provided over the previous four years?' It was closed *a posteriori* as follows: 1 = (Quite) rarely 2 = Almost comintuously 3 = Continuously −9 Missing because no training has been provided over the previous four years	5. Training regularity is positively associated with growth
	Education level	Percentge of active owner-managers possessing a degree or above	6. Education is positively associated with growth
	Use of external advice . . . 1. from lawyers 2. from suppliers	Open questions: 'Over the last four years, which sources of external advice have you used?' (list provided); 'Out of those used, which do you consider to be the most important?' So, the three variables were coded *a posteriori* as follows:	

334

3. from business associations	1 = No 2 = Yes 3 = Yes – (one of) the most important sources of advice	7–9. All three sources of external advice are positively associated with growth
Adoption of a focus strategy	Open questions: 'Are there any particular customers to whom you sell?' Question was coded *a posteriori* as follows: 1 = No 2 = Yes 'On a 5-point scale (from "never have done" to "do it frequently") please rate the extent to which you make an explicit tracking of the policies and tactics of your competitors worldwide'. This question was then converted into a 4-point Likert scale by merging neighbour categories to account better for the assumption of a minimum expected count of five in each cell for the chi square test: 1 = Neglectable/Little 2 = Some 3 = Often 4 = Very Often	10. There is a relationship between a focus strategy and growth of indeterminate direction
Scanning competition		11. Following competition policies and tactics is positively associated with growth
Accurate cost accounting	Open questions: 'How is your cost accounting system? (Probings: software, procedures, . . .)?'; 'What is considered in the cost of each product?' This question was closed *a posteriori* as follows: 1 = Firm knows approximately the cost without specific software 2 = Firm knows approximately the cost with specific software 3 = Firm knows exactly the cost with spectific software	12. Accuracy of cost accounting is positively associated with growth

Age of owner
Whilst Southern European cultures display an instinctive respect for age, now largely absent in Anglo Saxon societies (consistently with the asymmetric power distance indexes of the two cultures), the evidence from studies based on Anglo Saxon economies does not provide much evidence for the wisdom from age outperforming the energy of youth (Hall, 1995; Kangasharju, 2000). At best the relationship may be 'U' shaped (Bates, 1990), implying the optimal time for starting a company is early middle age. Given that Portugal is, in some respects, an emerging economy, in the process of shaking off the intellectual shackles of its Fascist past, it may be the young entrepreneurs who are best equipped to meet the challenges and exploit the opportunities that this implies.

Commitment to business
The higher the percentage of owner-managers working full-time for the company the greater the assumed commitment and therefore emotional as well as intellectual capital. This hypothesis is given some credence by Clark et al. (2001) who, when categorizing owner-managers of SMEs in the clothing sector into 'stagnant satisficers', 'thwarted expanders' and 'capricious manufacturers', according to their attitudes towards growth, found the first category preferred stability to growth, partly because of parallel business interests.

Regular training
SMEs, unable to enjoy economies of scale, have limited portfolios of management skills which increases their vulnerability to failure in the face of traumas in their environment (Hall, 1995) and acts as a constraint on their growth. Training should increase the size of these portfolios but will only prove beneficial to their recipients' organizations if the skills provided are relevant. Human capital is in this regard, analogous to physical capital; investment in either form is not, in itself, any guarantee of improved performance. This may be the explanation for why, whilst writers may argue for the benefits of training (for example, Huang and Brown, 1999) the majority of studies based on samples drawn from Anglo Saxon economies have failed to find a link (Westhead and Storey, 1996, Patton et al., 2000). Management training in Portugal, which is currently in nascent form, may well provide even fewer benefits.

Education level
Whereas training is intended to provide a specific set of skills, the objective of education is to develop the recipient in a much more rounded manner. There is some evidence that a result may be greater success in running their businesses as measured by their rates of growth (Roper, 1999; Kangasharju, 2000).

Whether this holds in a Portuguese context will partly depend upon the quality of Portugal's education system and the attitude towards education of its populations.

Use of external advice

Seeking external advice represents an additional method of increasing the size of the portfolio of managerial skills but, as with training, irrelevant (or even wrong) advice can be provided. The evidence does not suggest that this is generally the case (Bracker and Pearson, 1985, Hall 1994). Robson and Bennett (2000) found the sources of external advice most likely to be associated with growth were lawyers, suppliers, business associations, customers, families and business friends. As Southern European culture tends to make interaction with the last three the norm attention was limited to the first three, which were treated as separate variables.

Focus strategy

SMEs usually have some scope for choosing between focusing on particular types of customer or selling to as wide a range of customers as possible. The choice is not easy. Focus will probably prove more cost effective in marketing and, by providing a product which meets targeted customers' preferred characteristics, offers the opportunity for higher mark-ups. On the other hand focus implies the disadvantages of portfolios with a low number of income earners.

Without the ability to spread risk, the penalty will clearly be higher if levels of demand are lower than expected or faulty judgements are made as to preferred characteristics.

Evidence from the UK would suggest focus strategy to be associated with higher levels of performance (Hall, 1995). Whether this is replicated in Portugal will partly depend upon the weight Portuguese customers attach to preferred characteristics in the products they are offered. As consumer behaviour is not yet quite as sophisticated as in Anglo Saxon cultures there is less strong reason for expecting focus to be important for performance.

Scanning competition

SMEs do not usually closely monitor the behaviour of their competitors. This, by no means, need reflect an ignorance on their part of the benefit of understanding the strategies of their competitors but, more likely, is an indication of the difficulty of collecting the relevant information, either because of the crudeness of the data with which they would be working or because of the sheer size of their potential competition, given that SMEs typically operate in markets conforming to monopolistic competition.

Whether Portuguese SMEs find scanning the behaviour of their competitors to be cost effective will partly depend upon the ease with which pertinent data can be collected. If their markets are characterized by high degrees of inter-competitor networking, as is often the case in less developed economies, the cost of collecting information will be less than in the more arm's length cultures of Anglo Saxon business communities.

Accurate cost accounting
It was expected that firms that have a well implemented cost accounting system will be in a better position to grow because they will be stronger at managing the increase in complexity accompanying growth.

METHODOLOGY

Data was collected through personal interviews with owner-managers of SMEs operating in the Braga district of Portugal. The full list of variables on the original working file is displayed in the Appendix, many of which were taken from our earlier study in Chapter 14 so as to replicate the study in a different culture. But the lists of variables in the UK and the Portuguese studies do not overlap entirely, which is due to the different data sources used: Chapter 14 is based on the relevant variables that could be generated from the 3i files, whereas data underlying this chapter comes from face-to-face interviews. Thus some variables analysed in this chapter were absent in the UK study and vice versa because it was our aim to focus on the factors that remain most unexplored and/or controversial in the Portuguese setting as to their impact on growth. This chapter addresses a small set of the variables present on the working file, namely those that appeared to be (nearly) significantly related to growth.

Despite 36 face-to-face interviews having been conducted, only 29 of the interviews yielded usable information as seven firms did not provide us with growth figures and these were unavailable from any secondary source. Furthermore, as one of the 29 firms exhibited an average growth rate over 1997–99 that was neither 10 per cent above nor below the corresponding sector average (recall our dependent variable definition), our analysis was carried out on a sample size of 28.

Firms are SMEs as defined by the EU Commission Recommendation 96/280/CE, dated 3 April 1996. Accordingly, 14 (48 per cent) of those firms employ less than 50 people and account for an annual trade volume less than 7 million euros, and so are small.

As depicted in Table 15.2, our sample covers mostly mature firms. So to the extent this chapter addresses the entrepreneurship theme, it is not subscribing to the view that entrepreneurship is simply the creation of organizations. Entrepreneurship extends to persons aiming to grow rapidly as established firms.

Table 15.2   Description of sample

Percentage of small firms	48%
Percentage of medium firms	52%
Average size of the labour force	79
Age range (all firms)	3–45
Median age (all firms)	19
Sectors in the sample:	
Textile industry	31%
Clothing industry	14%
Construction	14%
Trading	10%
Myriad industrial activities	31%

The sample composition approximately reflects the nature of the sector activity within the Braga district, with the textile industry together with clothing and construction representing nearly 60 per cent of the sample.

Differences in the characteristics of companies displaying above average growth from those displaying below average were identified through a comparison of means using the appropriate statistical test in SPSS. The small sample size hindered the usage of more advanced statistics.

For the hypotheses involving a continuous variable we used the t-test because in every case the Kolmogorov–Smirnov test suggested normality. Pooled t-tests were carried out when Levene's F-test statistic was not significant, indicating equal variances could be assumed; otherwise, separate variance t-tests were carried out. Finally, for the hypotheses involving non-continuous variables, we used the chi square test. Fisher's exact probability test was used instead of the chi-square for two by two contingency tables where any of the cells had expected frequency less than ten. Having followed these guidelines, the next section reports the significance levels from the suitable statistical test and some further descriptive data.

RESULTS

Table 15.3 details the different characteristics of companies displaying above-average growth and those displaying below-average growth.

In the few instances where the relevant statistical test indicates non-significance ($p > 0.05$) we believe this is the case only because of the small sample size. Thus, relying on theoretical grounds and supplemented with the descriptive statistics, we draw the following conclusions:

Table 15.3 *Differences in the characteristics of companies displaying above-average growth from those displaying below-average growth*

Hypothesis	Statistical test	Significance level	Descriptive statistics of variable in growth group 1 (below sector average)	Descriptive statistics of variable in growth group 2 (above sector average)
1. Size and growth have some relationship of indeterminate sign	Separate variance t-test	p = 0.239 (2-tailed)	Mean: 802 861.21 Median: 680 000 Std. Deviation: 775 564.3	Mean: 1 878 384 Median: 800 000 Std. Deviation: 2 496 197
2. Age of company is negatively associated with growth	Separate variance t-test	p = 0.026* (1-tailed)	Mean: 23.21 Median: 21 Std. Deviation: 12.35	Mean: 16.11 Median: 16 Std. Deviation: 6.05
3. Age of owner managers is negatively associated with growth	Pooled t-test	p = 0.055 (1-tailed)	Mean: 49 Median: 47 Std. Deviation 8.12	Mean: 44.18 Median: 43 Std. Deviation 4.66
4. Commitment to business is positively associated with growth	Pooled t-test	p = 0.065 (1-tailed)	Mean: 0.51 Median: 0.5 Std. Deviation: 0.43	Mean: 0.77 Median: 1 St. Deviation: 0.38
5. Training regularity is positively associated with growth	Pearson chi square	p = 0.0315* (1-tailed)	Valid % in the two high regularity categories (almost continuous or continuous training): 50%	Valid % in the two high regularity categories (almost continuous or continuous training): 71.34%
6. Education is positively associated with growth	Pooled t-test	p = 0.358 (1-tailed)	Mean: 0.30 Median: 0.33 Std. Deviation: 0.34	Mean: 0.35 Median: 0.33 Std. Deviation: 0.33

7.	External advice from lawyers is positively associated with growth	Pearson chi square	$p = 0.048$* (1-tailed)	Percentage that use this advice: 78.95%	Percentage that use this advice: 77.78%
8.	External advice from suppliers is positively associated with growth	Pearson chi square	$p = 0.053$ (1-tailed)	Percentage that use this advice: 63.16%	Percentage that use this advice: 100%
9.	External advice from business association is positively associated with growth	Pearson chi square	$p = 0.0025$** (1-tailed)	Percentage that use this advice: 31.58%	Percentage that use this advice: 77.78%
10.	There is a relationship between a focus strategy and growth of indeterminate direction	Fisher's exact probability test	$p = 0.042$* (2-tailed)	Percentage that pursue a focus 68.42%	Percentage that pursue a focus 22.23%
11.	Scanning devices: following competition policies and tactics is positively associated with growth	Pearson chi square	$p = 0.0375$* (1-tailed)	Percentage that follow competition either often or very often: 52.6%	Percentage that follow competition either often or very often: 44.45%
12.	Accuracy of cost accounting is positively associated with growth	Pearson chi square	$p = 0.035$* (1-tailed)	Percentage of companies that know exactly their cost with specific software: 36.8%	Percentage of companies that know exactly their cost with specific software: 66.67%

Note: * Indicates significant ($p<0.05$); ** Indicates highly significant ($p < 0.01$).

1. Bigger companies achieved the higher rates of growth. Possible explanations are: having achieved the minimum efficient scale for their sector, they were then in a better position to expand, or, alternatively, that SMEs in Portugal face a similar finance gap to that of SMEs in Anglo Saxon countries.

2. Younger companies exhibited the higher rates of growth, probably reflecting their expansion towards their respective minimum efficient scales.

3. The younger owners in our sample saw their companies experience the higher rates of growth. Whilst it is foolish to succumb overly much to ageist stereotypes, one conclusion is that younger owners are more frequently better equipped emotionally to free themselves from the cultural constraints imposed by Portugal's history: Portugal has consistently been a country with a low tolerance for uncertainty.

4. Owner-managers demonstrating the greatest commitment in terms of time achieved the higher growth rates. Running a Portuguese SME would not seem to be a part-time job, a rule which may well be observed across economies, regardless of culture.

5. Training its workforce would appear to lead to a company experiencing a higher rate of growth, probably as a result of enhanced human capabilities.

6. The alumni of an institute of higher education would appear to make better managers than non-graduates, obvious testimony to the impact that education can achieve in the Portuguese business world. But results from Chapter 14 based on the UK firms suggest that the positive contribution of educational attainment to growth can be largely culture-specific: possession of a degree by the principal owner was found to be negatively associated with growth, and possession of a degree by the second owner was found to make a positive, but non-significant, contribution to growth.

7. Taking external advice would appear to be clearly related to rates of growth, and this holds whether supplied by suppliers or business associations.

8. Adopting a focus strategy would appear to lead to lower rates of growth, a result that is in clear contrast to that of our earlier study (Chapter 14). This may reflect a major cultural difference in terms of the degree of sophistication of customers. As we discussed in Chapter 14, UK customers are increasingly demanding which makes it not at all surprising that focus facilitates growth (for both start-ups and established firms). Portuguese customers on the other hand have not yet achieved this degree of sophistication and if they do not possess particularly strong preferences then firms should be more concerned with securing as

wide a customer base as possible. The cost involved in focusing on the needs of particular types of customers does not seem to be compensated in a culture like Portugal's.

9. Scanning competitor behaviour would not appear to lead to higher rates of growth. Portuguese SMEs seem to face the same problems as their Anglo Saxon counterparts with gathering market intelligence.

10. Working with accurate internal data would appear to be beneficial to chances of success as measured by growth. This is probably a relationship that is found across cultures.

CONCLUSIONS

Nearly 99 per cent of companies in the European Union are small and account for 52 per cent of employment in European Union firms. Needless to say, there are important differences across the member states as to the percentages of jobs in small firms, evidence suggesting these are higher in Southern European countries such as Portugal (IAPMEI, 2000).

Creation of employment is a matter of priority throughout the European Union. Small (and medium) firms take an outstanding role in the achievement of this goal, particularly in countries like Portugal. Given that the starting point for policy making towards small (and medium) firms must be the identification of characteristics and needs of such firms, research is fundamental.

A paper that is based on a sample that is small must be regarded as exploratory. Despite the small sample size having hindered the usage of advanced statistics, we obtained consistent results. Future work must verify these. If they are confirmed, a number of further issues could fruitfully be addressed. Older companies appear to enjoy lower growth rates. Further research could explore whether this reflects economic factors such as movement towards minimum efficient scales or such behavioural factors as attitudes of owner-managers at different stages of Portuguese business' life cycle. Similarly the superior growth rates achieved by younger owners may result from differences in such areas as willingness to change, to accept new ideas or in their degree of energy. It could be that entrepreneurs happen to be younger than business owner-managers happy with their status quo. Alternatively it could reflect other aspects of Portuguese culture, such as ageism within the suppliers of capital.

The very high score of Portugal on power distance is reflected in the extremely high status of education. As nowadays more people graduate from university, training is becoming increasingly valued as a way of building further status. Entrepreneurs are by definition those who assume a more proactive behaviour so it comes as no surprise that those that lead high growth firms are also those who are more prone to studying and to training. We do not dismiss, however, the argument that firms grow more because they are better equipped in terms of the human capabilities set.

The reason for the relatively poor performance of companies pursuing a focus strategy is of interest because so little is known about small business strategic management. If there are indeed cultural contexts in which pursuing a focus strategy produces benefits, and contexts in which it does not, this must be the subject of further work and the resulting knowledge will surely be of great benefit to decision makers within SMEs.

Similarly, any lessons provided on whether competition can be fruitfully scanned will also be usefully received.

In short our chapter has raised far more questions than it has answered.

REFERENCES

Anscombe, F.J. (1973), 'Graphs in statistical analysis', *American Statistician*, **27**, 17–21.

Arksey, H. and P. Knight (1999), *Interviewing for Social Scientists*, London: Sage.

Barringer, B.R. and A.C. Bluedorn (1999), 'The relationship between corporate entrepreneurship and strategic management', *Strategic Management Journal*, **20**, 421–44.

Bates, T. (1990), 'Entrepreneur human capital inputs and small business longevity', *The Review of Economics and Statistics*, **72**(4), 551–9.

Belson, W. (1981), *The Design and Understanding of Survey Questions*, Aldershot: Gower.

Bergström, F. (2000), 'Capital subsidies and the performance of firms', *Small Business Economics*, **14**, 183–93.

Bracker, J. and J.N. Pearson (1985), 'The impact of consultants on small firm strategic planning', *Journal of Small Business Management*, **23**(3), 23–30.

Brush, C.G. and R. Chaganti (1998), 'Business without glamour? An analysis of resources on performance by size and age in small service and retail firms', *Journal of Business Venturing*, **14**, 233–57.

Churchill, G.A. (1991), *Marketing Research – Methodological Foundations*, 5th edn, Chicago: Dryden Press.

Clark, D., N. Berkeley and N. Steuer (2001), 'Research note: attitudes to growth among owners of small and medium-sized enterprizes and the implications for business advice: some evidence from the clothing industry in Coventry', *International Small Business Journal*, **19**(3), 72–7.

Converse, J.M. and S. Presser (1987), *Survey Questions: Handcrafting the Standardized Questionnaire*, Beverly Hills: Sage.

Foddy, W. (1993), *Constructing Questions for Interviews and Questionnaires: Theory and Practice in Social Research*, Cambridge: Cambridge University Press.

Gadenne, D. (1998), 'Critical success factors for small business: an inter-industry comparison', *International Small Business Journal*, **17**(1), 36–56.

Gibrat, R. (1931), *Les Inegalités Economiques*, Paris: Sirey.

Gill, J. and P. Johnson (1997), *Research Methods for Managers*, 2nd edn, London: Paul Chapman Publishing.
Gundry, L.K. and H.P. Welsch (2001), 'The ambitious entrepreneur – high growth strategies of women-owned enterprises', *Journal of Business Venturing*, **16**(5), 453–70.
Hakim, C. (1989), *Research Design: Strategies and Choices in the Design of Social Research*, London, USA and Canada: Unwin Hyman.
Hall, G. (1994), 'Factors distinguishing survivors from failures amongst small firms in the UK construction sector', *Journal of Management Studies*, **31**(5), 737–60.
Hall, G. (1995), *Surviving and Prospering in the Small Firm Sector*, London, USA and Canada: Routledge.
Heshmati, A. (2001), 'On the growth of micro and small firms: evidence from Sweden', *Small Business Economics*, **17**, 213–28.
Hofstede, G. (1991), *Cultures and Organizations*, London: HarperCollins.
Hofstede, G. (2001), *Culture's Consequences: Comparing Values, Behaviours, Institutions, and Organizations Across Nations*, 2nd edn, London: Sage.
Huang, X. and A. Brown (1999), 'An analysis and classification of problems in small business', *International Small Business Journal*, **18**(1), 73–85.
IAPMEI (2000), 'About SME in Portugal', Lisbon: Scarpa, Lda.
Jovanovic, B. (1982), 'Selection and the evolution of industry', *Econometrica*, **50**(3), 649–70.
Kangasharju, A. (2000), 'Growth of the smallest: determinants of small firm growth during strong macroeconomic fluctuations', *International Small Business Journal*, **19**(1), 28–43.
Khan, A.M. (1986), 'Entrepreneur characteristics and the prediction of new venture success', *Omega*, **14**(5), 365–72.
Kinnear, P.R. and C.D. Gray (2001), *SPSS for Windows Made Simple – Release 10*, East Sussex, UK: Psychology Press.
Kinnear, T.C. and J.R. Taylor (1983), *Marketing Research – An Applied Approach*, 2nd edn, New York: McGraw-Hill.
Kotey, B. (1999), 'Debt financing and factors internal to the business', *International Small Business Journal*, **17**(3), 11–29.
Lovell, M. (1983), 'Data mining', *The Review of Economics and Statistics*, **65**(1), 1–11.
Low, M.B. and E. Abrahamson (1997), 'Movements, bandwagons, and clones: industry evolution and the entrepreneurial process', *Journal of Business Venturing*, **12**, 435–57.
Mascarenhas, B. (1997), 'The order and size of entry into international markets', *Journal of Business Venturing*, **12**, 287–99.
McMahon, R.G.P. (2001), 'Growth and performance of manufacturing SMEs: the influence of financial management characteristics', *International Small Business Journal*, **19**(3), 10–28.
Miller, D. and J. Toulouse (1985), 'Chief executive personality and corporate strategy and structure in small firms', *Management Science*, **32**(11), 1389–409.
Opler, T.C. and S. Titman (1994), 'Financial distress and corporate performance', *The Journal of Finance*, **49**(3), 1015–40.
Pallant, J. (2001), *SPSS Survival Manual*, Australia and UK: Open University Press.
Patton, D., S. Marlow and P. Hannon (2000), 'The relationship between training and small firm performance; research frameworks and lost quests', *International Small Business Journal*, **19**(1), 11–27.
Payne, S.L. (1951), *The Art of Asking Questions*, Princeton, NJ: Princeton University Press.

Peel, M.J., N. Wilson and C. Howorth (2000), 'Late payment and credit management in the small firm sector: some empirical evidence', *International Small Business Journal*, **18**(2), 17–37.

Robson, P.J.A. and R.J. Bennett (2000), 'SME growth: the relationship with business advice and external collaboration', *Small Business Economics*, **15**, 193–208.

Roper, S. (1999), ' Modelling small business growth and profitability', *Small Business Economics*, **13**(3), 235–52.

Sadler-Smith, E., A. Sargeant and A. Dawson (1998), 'Higher level skills training and SMEs', *International Small Business Journal*, **16**(2), 84–94.

Schmitz, J. (1989), 'Imitation, entrepreneurship, and long-run growth', *Journal of Political Economy*, **97**(3), 721–39.

Storey, D.J. (1994), *Understanding the Small Business Sector*, 1st edn, USA and Canada: Routledge.

Storey, D., K. Keasey, R. Watson and P. Wynarczyk (1987), *The Performance of Small Firms*, Surry Hills: Croom Helm Ltd.

Voulgaris, F., M. Doumpos and C. Zopounidis (2000), 'On the evaluation of Greek industrial SMEs' performance via multicriteria analysis of financial ratios', *Small Business Economics*, **15**, 127–36.

Wennekers, S. and R. Thurik (1999), 'Linking entrepreneurship and economic growth', *Small Business Economics*, **13**, 27–55.

Westhead, P. and D. Storey (1996), 'Management training and small firm performance: why is the link so weak?', *International Small Business Journal*, **14**(4), 13–24.

Wonnacott, R.J. and T.H. Wonnacott (1970), *Econometrics*, USA: John Wiley and Sons, Inc.

Zahra, S.A. (1996), 'Technology strategy and financial performance: examining the moderating role of the firm's competitive environment', *Journal of Business Venturing*, **11**, 189–219.

APPENDIX: FULL LIST OF VARIABLES ON THE WORKING FILE

Dependent Variable

1. (Assets) growth group: 1 = lower than sector average; 2 = higher than sector average.

Independent Variables

Demographics of company
1. Size, defined by average turnover over 1997–99 (measured in Portuguese 'contos' or thousand escudos, as are all monetary units)
2. Age of company, measured from the year of set-up until 2001
3. Total ownership spread, defined by total number of owners
4. Active ownership spread, defined by number of active owners.

Human capital
1. Gender of active owner-managers (1 = exclusively/predominantly male; 2 = not exclusively/predominantly male)
2. Age of owner, defined as the average age in 2001 of active owner-managers
3. Commitment to business, defined as the percentage of active owner-managers working full-time for the company
4. Experience, defined as the average years of experience of active owner-managers in same sector
5. Extent to which business was family-owned at set-up (1 = 0%; 2 = <50%; 3 = 50–90%; 4 = 91–100%)
6. Extent to which business is family owned today (1 = 0%; 2 = <50%; 3 = 50–90%; 4 = 91–100%)
7. Succession stage, defined by the number of generations involved with the business to date (–9 = missing because it is not a family firm)
8. Whether training had been provided over the previous four years (1 = no; 2 = yes). If the answer to this question were 'yes', we would ask about the following training-specific variables reporting to the previous four years:
    a) Degree of external training (1 = exclusively/predominantly internal; 2 = equally internal and external; 3 = exclusively/predominantly external; –9 = no training over the past four years)
    b) Training selection criteria, defined by five variables: whether training had been provided out of (1) training needs analysis; (2) a company training plan; (3) a requirement imposed by the quality certification

process of the company; (4) employees/department director request; (5) training marketing materials (1 = no; 2 = yes; –9 = no training over the past four years)

c) Motivation role of training subsidies (1 = no role at all; 2 = some role; –9 = no training over the past four years)

d) Recipients of training, defined by three variables: whether training had been provided to (1) owners/top managers; (2) administrative staff; (3) production assembly line employees (1 = no; 2 = yes; –9 = no training over the past four years)

e) Areas of training, defined by nine variables: whether there had been any training on (1) computers; (2) production assembly line; (3) accounting/financial domain; (4) production/service quality; (5) marketing/commercial domain; (6) hygiene and security at work; (7) management; (8) languages; (9) human resources management (1 = no; 2 = yes; –9 = no training over the past four years)

f) Average duration of training programmes (1 = less or equal to 30 hours; 2 = more than 30 hours; –9 = no training over the past four years; –10 = too heterogeneous to estimate an average)

g) Regular training, defined by how often training had been provided (1 = (quite) rarely; 2 = almost continuously; 3 = continuously; –9 = no training over the past four years)

9. Education level, defined as the percentage of active owner-managers possessing a degree or above

10. External advice, defined by three variables: whether over the previous four years there had been any external advice from (1) lawyers, (2) suppliers and (3) business associations (1 = no; 2 = yes; 3 = yes, (one of) the most important source of business advice)

Strategy
1. Adoption of a focus strategy (1 = no; 2 = yes)
2. Use of scanning devices, defined by six variables: (1) regular gathering of customers opinions; (2) explicit tracking of the policies and tactics of competitors worldwide; (3) preferences and technology forecast; (4) formal market research; (5) professional magazines, government publications and news media; (6) regular gathering of information from suppliers or other channel members (1 = negligible; 2 = little; 3 = some; 4 = often; 5 = very often)
3. Risk readiness, assessed by the average of five-point ratings on 3 polar opposite sets of sentences (1 = none; 2 = little; 3 = some; 4 = quite; 5 = very much)
4. Product innovation, assessed by the average of five-point ratings on 3 polar opposite sets of sentences (1 = none; 2 = little; 3 = some; 4 = quite;

5 = very much; –9 = not applicable because the business only produces to order)

5. Proactiveness, assessed by the average of five-point ratings on 3 polar opposite sets of sentences (1 = none; 2 = little; 3 = some; 4 = quite; 5 = very much; –9 = not applicable because the business ignores competition)

6. Product differentiation, as assessed on a five-point scale from 'extremely similar' to 'extremely different' (–9 = not applicable given the nature of the product/service)

7. Type of pricing, assessed by the average five-point ratings on the importance of five items for the pricing of major product (1 = very aggressive (< = 2); 2 = aggressive (2–4); 3 = (very) prestige).

Financial management

1. Accuracy of cost accounting system (1 = firm knows approximately the cost without specific software; 2 = firm knows approximately the cost with specific software; 3 = firm knows exactly the cost with specific software)

2. Typical delay allowed in customer's payment (1 = less than 15 days; 2 = 15 days–1 month; 3 = more than 1 month; 4 = no pattern identifiable; –9 = not applicable because firm does not suffer from late payment problems)

3. Use of credit insurance or factoring services (1 = no; 2 = yes)

4. Number of debtor days

5. Number of creditor days.

Index